THE GLASS OF TIME

The Glass of Time

Cyril Bulley
63rd Bishop of Carlisle

Foreword by
Bishop Donald Coggan
Archbishop of Canterbury 1974–1980

THE
Alpha
PRESS

First published privately, Worthing, 1985

This edition published 1994

The Alpha Press
18 Chichester Place
Brighton BN2 1FF, United Kingdom

British Library Cataloguing in Publication Data
A CIP catalogue record for this book is available from the British Library.
ISBN 1 898595 06 2

Typeset in 11 on 12 Bembo
by Grahame & Grahame Editorial, Brighton, East Sussex
Printed and bound in Great Britain

To the young of the family – to Terry and Richard,
Tina and Tony – with an uncle's love and in an uncle's
confidence that they will remain ever within the
Church which is the Family of God.

Love took up the glass of Time, and turn'd it in his glowing hands;
Every moment, lightly shaken, ran itself in golden sands.

Tennyson, *Locksley Hall*

Contents

Foreword by Bishop Coggan

I am a great believer in the power of biography and autobiography. I use the word 'power' advisedly, because reading such books pricks the bubble of personal pride or pomposity, and lifts one's eyes to visions brighter and broader than one's own.

This book is a case in point. A leisurely journey by rail from Winchester to Lancaster and back gave me the opportunity to read *The Glass of Time* without hurry – and with much appreciation. It is the story of a man who believed profoundly in the truth of some words he quotes more than once: 'When the will is dedicated, the way is directed.' Cyril Bulley acted on that dictum through a long and fruitful life.

Here is the story of a man who never lost the sense of enormous privilege that was his in being a priest (and eventually a bishop) in the Church of God, and who devoted himself to that office and work with dedication and joy. He 'could no other', nor did he want to. To that God had called him; to that he would give all that he had and was.

He exercised his ministry in two main fields – parochial (that was to include thirteen years as a bishop, first suffragan and then diocesan) and educational. In both spheres his interests were in *people*, whether they might be in the schools of the dioceses where he worked, or in the parishes where he laboured as curate, vicar, rural dean, archdeacon and bishop. The sheer privilege of entering the homes of his people and of ministering to their needs, of celebrating the sacraments, of ordaining and instituting the clergy, of preaching the Gospel in all its fulness, upheld him in the rough times of his ministry and spurred him on to fresh ventures.

Cyril Bulley was a man of prayer and discipline – the daily Offices were at the heart of his devotional life; his nearness to God was the source of the freshness of his mind and activity. A sense of history helped him to appreciate the beauty of the churches where he served, and a delicious sense of humour and of the ridiculous found an outlet in verses which combine fun

ix

and shrewdness in one. Those who have read his *Faith, Fire and Fun* (1985) and his *Glimpses of the Divine* (1987, second edition 1994) will appreciate how easily the sublime and the ridiculous combine in his writings. All of them illustrate the character of a man who was supremely happy in the work God had given him.

I would like to give a copy of this book to anyone who is contemplating the possibility of ordination, and to anyone who has grown weary in the exercise of his/her ministry. They would find it to be at once a rebuke, a stimulus and an encouragement.

DONALD COGGAN

Preface

Though it was to the son of a country rector, Alfred Lord Tennyson, that I turned for my title, it was to a country rector himself, George Herbert, that I turned for my *modus operandi*. I picture Tennyson looking intently at an hour-glass and seeing in the movement of the grains of sand through its narrow channel a picture of the myriad incidents which make up a human life pressed into the brief passage of Time. I picture Herbert standing before a window, maybe in his parish church of Bemerton – looking through the glass and then at it and finding the inspiration which gave him his quaint lines

> *A man that looks on glass*
> *On it may stay his eye,*
> *Or if he pleaseth through it pass*
> *And then the heaven espy.*

I suspect that both poets were seeking to expound the same theme – that the quintessence of life resides in its Godward orientation. Certainly Herbert's poem, significantly entitled *The Elixir*, sustains the theme throughout – 'Teach me my God and King, in all things thee to see'. It has, of course, become one of our most popular hymns and I have taken the verse which I have quoted as the pattern for my story. Looking through the window of the present I see the panorama of my past and the scene, like some Lowry painting, is dotted with myriads of people – men and women, boys and girls, rich and poor – some receding into the background, some as large as life in the foreground, but each significant in identity and personality. I can put names to hundreds of them – my school and college friends, my colleagues in different fields of work, my pupils, my parishioners, my clergy, my fellow workers within the fellowship of Christ's Church.

Beyond the horizon I picture others to whom I have spoken through radio and television and the printed word and still others with whom I have corresponded. Then a memory, an experience, a circumstance, prompts me to stay my eye on the present, perhaps merely to note a contrast with the past or to venture a relevant comment on the twists and turns of the contemporary scenes in the light of past experience. If in a day of spiritual malnutrition such as it is ours to experience, when there is so much to disturb, so much to distress, so much to regret that life does not invariably run 'itself in golden sands' and that we cannot always 'the heaven espy', I hope that my Credo breaks through in what I have written.

I have had in mind all the time in my writing not the scholars or the critics but the host of my clerical friends, the parish priests of the Church of England ever in the front line of the Church Militant, the far bigger circle of ordinary folk 'high and low, rich and poor, one with another' whom it has been my privilege to serve through a long and varied ministry, and the people in the church pews on Sundays who, we are told, far outnumber the people in the football stands on Saturdays. These same people with whom a parish priest establishes a unique relationship cannot but be interested in him as a person – whence he came, how he came to be what he is, what he knows of success and failure, of sorrow and joy, of hope and despair, what doubts and fears assail him or have ever done and what confidence sustains.

Is he really 'one of us' or has he ever been providentially shielded from the doubts which disturb the mind, the sorrows and sufferings which break the heart and the fierce temptations which batter against the sanctuary of the soul? Some such questionings as these have directed this story of my life – through infancy and boyhood, through student days, as a teacher, as a parish priest, as a bishop. Thus this narrative does not shun the anecdote; it embraces the serious and the trivial, the personal and the professional; it carries pathos and humour, sorrows and joys, achievements and failures, struggles and triumphs; it mingles fun with hard work and moving from the past to the present offers comment and criticism. There is a progression of change all through but the end is constant and that, in all the aspects of ministry is nothing less than the leading of God's people to the knowledge and love of God through Christ.

Bishop Hensley Henson, who on any reckoning must be regarded as one of the outstanding bishops of this century, called his autobiography *Retrospect of an Unimportant Life*. It was an odd title but it deceived no one, least of all the author as those who have read the preface to that nine-hundred page volume might discern. Henson's contribution to the life of Church and State in his day was significant, if only for its critical assessment of current affairs in each, for its relish of controversy and for the impeccable English in which it was offered whether in utterance or in writing. The truth is, however, that no man's life is unimportant and a life such as that within the ministry of the Church, which touches in its course thousands of people in caring and concern, in informing and inspiring, in guiding and teaching, is a life which assumes immense significance however unimportant the person who lives it might count himself to be. It is never the person who is important, but the office he holds and the work which he does which together make his life important in the eyes of those whom he serves.

This is the story of one who at the age of twelve found within himself a burning desire to become a priest, who never thought for a moment that such a privilege could ever be his, who battled his way towards that high calling against scholastic and material difficulties, and who from the day of his Ordination as a deacon to the day of his retirement from one of England's ancient episcopal Sees, has found in the fulfilment of his vocation a deep satisfaction, a continuing exhilaration and an abounding joy. I have never been a VIP nor sought to be; I have been content indeed to be what Bishop Henry Wilson of Chelmsford called himself 'a Back Bench Bishop', but I still count my life important for what God has done with it and through it. To do otherwise would be a blasphemy.

*   *   *

Certainly the Church today has its weaknesses and must accept its share of the blame for the spiritual poverty of the hour, but neither in history nor in personal experience can I find any sanctions for an attitude of despair. We need to remind ourselves, and frequently, that dryness and darkness and dullness and defeat have beset the Christian Church time and time again in the two thousand years of its history, and time and time again new light has emerged from the darkness and new life has sprung up from the dry ground. Emperors and States, dictators, Marxists, secular humanists and, sadly but truly, unworthy Christians, clerical and lay, have in their turn dealt grievous blows either by open opposition from without or infidelity from within. Fierce unbelievers from Nero to Stalin have sought to kill the Church, and their ilk are still around today.

But every 'Good Friday' has been followed by an 'Easter Day' and Christ's declaration that the gates of hell would not prevail against his Church has been repeatedly and magnificently vindicated. The truth is that God speaks to man's condition, and that whether he climbs up into heaven or goes down into hell (see Psalm 139), his God is inescapable and to Him 'the darkness and the light are both alike'. So can God's people ever be what Matthew Arnold calls 'beacons of hope' and that in the darkest hour. But such hope is born only of a trust in the living God which comes not with wishful thinking nor is it so sustained. The hope which is sure and steadfast derives from a trust so strong that it persists even when we cannot trace God's presence in the circumstances of the hour. Rare is the man who would dare to claim, in this century of doubt and strife, that his trust has never faltered! Happy is the man who though he stumbles reaches ever and again for the outstretched hand of God! He can say with Robert Browning,

> '*There is but one way to browbeat this world,*
> *Dumb-founder doubt, and repay scorn in kind —*

> To go on trusting, namely, till faith move
> Mountains!

But how? I cannot answer for another, but for myself – by staying my eye on God, in meditation, in corporate worship, through ties of sacrament and prayer. I know no other way – but I know that for me and countless millions these ways suffice.

Acknowledgements

I express my thanks to Mr. R. Honeywill of Ipplepen, Devon, who kindly researched the Bulley family in the registers of the Parish Church there; the Reverend G. P. Jenkins, Vicar of Bulley, Glos.; Mr. Roger Jones, Librarian of Newton Abbot; the Reverend Dr. W. J. Bolt, a fellow Newtonian; Canon Donald Nicholson, a college friend who checked the Durham chapter; Mr. Oswald Allen, Librarian of Newark Parish Church and Mr. Norman Dowse, sometime verger of Newark; Mr. G. Yewdale of Bassetlaw District Council; Canon Peter Boulton, Vicar of Worksop; Mr. Arthur Butcher, chief clerk in the Carlisle Diocesan Registry; Mr. Jim Hiscox and officers of the Salvation Army in London and Carlisle; Fr. Laurence Wells, formerly of the Roman Catholic Church of St. Bede in Carlisle; the Venerable Walter Ewbank, Archdeacon of Carlisle; Canon John Norman, formerly Rector of Greystoke and Founder of the Greystoke Pre-Theological College; Miss Appleyard of the *Daily Telegraph* Information Bureau; the Rt. Hon. George Thomas, M.P. Speaker of the House of Commons; Mr. W. Saumarez Smith, sometime Archbishop's Appointments Secretary and the Venerable T. R. B. Hodgson, Archdeacon of West Cumberland and formerly my Domestic Chaplain who has with great patience checked the Carlisle chapters.

Publishing houses who have kindly permitted quotations from their books include: James Nisbet Co. in respect of quotations from Bishop Barry's *Vocation and Ministry*; Hodder & Stoughton in respect of quotations from Bishop Barry's *Period of My Life* and Bishop Hensley Henson's *Retrospect*; the Central Board of Finance of the Church of England for quotations from the *Paul Report*. I have drawn too from Dean Stanley's *Life and Correspondence of Thomas Arnold* (5th Edition published by B. Fellowes in 1845) and I have his permission to quote an extract from an article in *Theology* (February 1949) by Professor Thomas Wood, Head of the Department of Theology at St. David's College, Lampeter.

1

Childhood

I remember, I remember
The house where I was born,
The little window where the sun
Came peeping in at morn . . .

Frankly, I don't and I suspect that the poet was exercising to the full the licence which his art allows him as he fashioned this word picture of his childhood days. I do remember, however, standing up in class at the age of eleven and reciting Thomas Hood's poem to the satisfaction of an English master whose inability to control a class of small boys was matched only by his ineffectiveness as a teacher of them. In fairness it must be said that if the master failed to excite the interest of the small fry in the poets as artists it can be said, to his credit, that he compelled us to learn by heart a dozen or so lines of their works every week.

Thus was I introduced to Wordsworth, to Tennyson, to Longfellow, to Gray, to Arnold and many others, including Thomas Hood who so excited my interest. In his short life of 45 years Thomas Hood juggled with words in so masterly a fashion, moving rapidly from the pathetic to the humorous and back, that fun, fact and fiction are all happily blended in his works. He left behind him a delicious semantic fricassee served up with not a little sauce. And thus I open my own story with lines from his simple poem, the first I ever learnt by heart. I cannot resist the conviction that far from remembering the house where he was born, and the little window through which the morning sun peeped — not to mention the roses white and red, the violets and the lily cups, and the fir trees dark and tall — all these were figments of his imagination, the artist's picture of an idyllic childhood when all the days were sunny.

Childhood is not really like that. It has its problems, its frustrations and its disappointments, but mercifully as the years pass, Providence draws a veil over these, so that in later years the screen of memory is bright with the happiness

1

and excitements of childhood, with its discoveries and achievements, its frolics and fun. That, I am persuaded, is what Hood meant and so far I can go all the way with him save, that is, to his last three lines where he laments:

> *'Tis little joy*
> *To know I'm farther off from Heaven*
> *Than when I was a boy!*

That last is a judgement which I shall leave to Another. Suffice it at the beginning of this story to say that the faith in which I was nurtured as a child, though battered in the course of my life by doubts from within and opposition from without, has survived all its testings. I go further and say, in all humility but with conviction, that that faith has not for a single moment been within a thousand miles of repudiation. It is, after all, not the doubts which are challenged but the doubts which are cherished that dig the grave of faith.

But what was the basis of my boyhood faith? I think in fact that I was a little panentheist – as opposed to a pantheist. For me God was no more 'out there' than he was here, there and everywhere. He not only held 'the whole wide world in his hand', he created it, penetrated every part of it, was concerned with everyone and everything within it, and was bigger than all of it put together. How well I remember trying, as a child of twelve, to express all that in a poem. The transcendence and the immanence of the Living God in twenty-four rhyming lines! Yet a child frequently discerns things that are hidden from the wise. I recall, for example, a twelve-year-old choirboy of Carlisle Cathedral who expressed his belief as I might have expressed mine at his age. A service had just ended with John Mason Neale's hymn '*Come ye faithful, raise the anthem*'. The young choristers had thrown themselves with full voice and vigour into the closing words of that great hymn:

> *Consubstantial,*
> *Co-Eternal*
> *While unending ages run.*

The vestry prayer over, I planted a hand on the shoulder of the nearest choirboy and said, 'Consubstantial, Co-Eternal – that's what you sang just now. What does it mean?' A moment's silence, a shrug of the shoulders, an impish smile, and then the counter question, 'Does it mean, my Lord, that God's the Greatest and goes on being the Greatest for ever?' A theologian would have answered my question with talk of the Blessed Trinity, of the Arian controversy and much else. But here in a sentence, and with the homeliest of words, a little child spelled out his understanding of the Godhead. It was not the first time, nor will it be the last, that from the 'mouth of very babes and sucklings' simple words have wrapped up profound truths. For me too God was 'the Greatest' when I was twelve years old.

But what of Jesus? I never found it difficult to believe in the uniqueness of Jesus and I remember with what fervour I invariably entered into one of my favourite hymns, now banished – or perhaps should I say 'excommunicated' by 'radicals'? – from *Hymns Ancient and Modern*. Frederick Faber's hymn of the Incarnation, which in the standard edition of *Hymns A & M* has printed at its head the first verse of the Gospel According to St John, asserts at the beginning of each verse, and unequivocally at that, 'Jesus is God'. No Nicodemus question – 'How can these things be?' bothered me at that tender age. The Church Catechism, which I could recite faultlessly by the time I was twelve, reminded me that my first duty towards God 'is to believe in him', and that I did. I saw him and I knew him in the person of Jesus who for me, whatever the hymn said, was never 'above the clear blue sky' but near at hand as Lord and Saviour, Master and Friend. It was a faith which was all so clear yet so compelling, so simple yet so satisfying. No wonder Our Lord said 'Except ye become as little children . . . '. I cannot pretend that private prayers were as real or as regular as they ought to have been, but I recall two favourites which were offered frequently if not always on my knees. The first was the exuberant outburst of a carefree boy who loved life:

> *God who created me*
> *Nimble and light of limb*
> *In three elements free*
> *To run, to ride, to swim*
> *Not when the sense is dim*
> *But now, from a heart of joy,*
> *I will remember Him*
> *Take the thanks of a boy.*

The second, and this was among my night prayers – said by the bed in the summer and in the bed on cold winter nights in an unheated room – was the well-known and much used prayer of St Richard of Chichester, which expressed for me a relationship to Christ that was real and which I longed, but frequently failed, to reflect in my daily life.

Clearly through my infancy and early childhood there had been formative influences that had brought this boyhood faith to birth, and human agencies that had sustained and strengthened it. But believing, as I do, that the initiative lies ever with God, I ask myself where and when I first became conscious of what would be called the spiritual dimension of life, when, if you like, God became real for me as he became real for the boy Samuel. I do not find it difficult to answer that question and must confess at once that it was long past the 'God-bless-Daddy-and-Mummy-and-make-me-a-good-boy' stage.

Whenever I read stories of people who claim to recollect vividly experiences they allege to have happened to them at the age of two or three, my reaction oscillates between incredulity and envy. Whilst doubtless the things that happened to me in the first six years of my life lie buried in the subconscious, and could be brought to life by some prying psychoanalyst, my earliest memory takes me back no further than the spring of 1914 when I was a month or two under seven years of age. It could fairly be called a religious experience in that it awakened within me what Wordsworth might have called 'a sense sublime'. It was in the city of Exeter, where the family lived for a very short time, that I recall returning from a shopping expedition with my mother when I insisted on stopping to listen to a Salvation Army band playing on the steps of Holy Trinity Church which the family attended and in whose choir my father sang. The Vicar was there, too, conducting with the assistance of the band what I imagine might well have been an open-air Lenten service or act of witness – surely one of the earliest exercises in ecumenism, though the word was not then current in ecclesiastical jargon. I could not possibly have understood what it was all about, but the total experience – the crowd, the bared heads, the band playing 'Beneath the Cross', the hearty singing and, I doubt not, the Presence promised to those gathered in His name, all this must have moved me so deeply that the scene is printed indelibly on memory's slate. Never do I hear the words of Elizabeth Clephane's mission hymn 'Beneath the Cross of Jesus', sung to Sankey's famous tune, without re-living that moment.

Quite recently I paid another visit to that church intending to meditate within it upon an experience which I believe to have been significant in my pilgrimage. I discovered, alas, that it was no longer in use. The doors were bolted and barred; the notice boards were bare of announcements; the scene was one of dereliction. Scrawled across the main door was a very searching graffito – 'Why empty?' – a graffito that could be repeated on dozens of disused churches up and down the country. And the answer? Movement of population? Area over-churched? Development of site? But do those answers plumb the depths of the graffitist's penetrating question? Or does his question pose another? Is it that man, mesmerised by his vast material achievements, has come to believe that he can, after all, live by bread alone, that he has lost all sense of the spiritual dimension of life, the consequence being that God is redundant? Ever within the fellowship of the Church my faith in the living God has been nurtured by its ministry of Word and Sacrament. The Jesus Christ to whom I was introduced in my childhood became my Lord and Master and his teaching the touchstone of my life. I deplore the disfiguration of buildings with graffiti but I confess that I walked from Holy Trinity Church to the Cathedral that morning hoping that no one would rub that question out. Considered in depth there are few more important, and maybe passers-by might be challenged by it. On the steps of that church in the spring of 1914 the Salvation Army had been drawing the attention of passers-by to the truth that, as William Barclay translates the well-known text, 'It takes more than bread to keep a man alive'. Perhaps the graffitist's question was performing the same function!

As a seven-year-old boy I had been captivated by the message of the Salvation Army Band, and at an ecumenical service in St. James' Church,

Whitehaven in Cumbria, in celebration of the centenary of the Army's foundation under its original name, I made reference to the Exeter incident as one which could well have contributed to my spiritual awakening. In lighter vein I told the Salvationists that they could thus be sure that here was one bishop who would always look upon the Army, its witness and its work, with an admiration that the Bishop of Carlisle of a hundred years before – Samuel Waldegrave – would not have shared. They could, however, take heart. For whilst Bishop Waldegrave disliked the Christian Mission as the Army was then called, he also abhorred harvest festivals, surpliced choirs, and the Lambeth Conference – all of which survived. And the Army, too, mightily in its evangelistic witness to the truth of the Gospel and its practical demonstration of the demand of Christian love.

The only other incident from my early childhood which I can recall is equally significant, at least from hindsight. This again was in 1914, when I was taken by my father to the entrance of the Topsham Army Barracks 'to see the soldiers and hear the band' as he put it. The scene lives: the martial music and the marching men, the uniforms and the shiny brass buttons, the shouting of commands and the cheering crowds, the waving handkerchiefs – sights and sounds to excite a small child. But presently everything was spoilt for me when I saw two women near me sobbing bitterly. In later years I was told that I had then began a series of heart-rending questions: Why the tears? Where were the soldiers going? What's a war? Will you go away from us? Beyond that I can remember only that a small boy, frightened by what he had heard, clung more tightly than ever to his father's hand as we went home.

Was this the experience which made me as a schoolboy recoil with horror from those highly coloured pictures in history books which seemed to glorify war? Was it this childhood incident that planted in me the heart of a pacifist? And if the answer is 'yes', why has my mind ever resisted the heart's pull? There is, of course, the theory of the Just War but for me that has always called for clearer demonstration than the moralists could provide. I might well have been a pacifist had there not been a Hitler and a Stalin, a Buchenwald and an Auschwitz, a Czechoslovakia and a Hungary. For these names are written indelibly in the history books and they tell not only of evils past, but of evils present. Furthermore, from the moment when the atomic bomb bisected history, how fearfully difficult the weighing of values has been for the Christian whose concern is not only for peace but for truth, for freedom and for justice. The sanctity of these has not diminished even if the cost of defending them has risen. The new age may have circumscribed, but it has not rendered invalid, the age-old doctrine of the Just War.

Soon after the beginning of the First World War my family moved for a brief period to Torquay and thence to Newton Abbot, which was my birthplace. For a time we lived in a most attractive town house that we shared with my maternal grandparents. Its spaciousness, its many rooms, its walled garden, the intriguing hiding places in its outbuildings, all made of it a paradise for children. But the arrangement was temporary and I suspect that it was to my grandparents' immense relief that daughter and son-in-law, with their brood of four, left for a home of their own nearby. This was the home in which the rest of my childhood was spent and from which the young Bulleys went out into the world.

I was the third child and second son of Jethro Bulley and Lillie Caroline Luscombe, both of whom, as their names betray, sprang from West Country families. The surname 'Bulley' is rare, and its rarity has induced families bearing it to write to me in order to discover whether there is a common lineage. The correspondents have sometimes suggested that the family began its life in the Gloucestershire village of Bulley. Certainly it was from there, rather than from Devonshire, that a certain William Bulley went off to be a member of Edward the First's Parliament, but everything leads me to believe that he was an immigrant from Devon where the family indubitably had its roots in the village of Ipplepen near Newton Abbot.

The oldest monument in the parish churchyard of Ipplepen is the altar tomb of John Bulley who died in 1668 at the age of 81 and who, the inscription tells us, 'had the honour twice of being Constable of the Hundred of Hay Torre'. But the parish registers take the family back long before that date, for the first entry in the first register of Baptisms of 1558 records the baptism of Christopher, son of Rychard Bullighe, and from then through the years the name appears with different suffixes – 'ighe', 'eigh', 'ye', 'y'. Finally, in the very early seventeenth century, there appears the baptism of Richard, son of Samuel Bulley. Thereafter the spelling is all but constant in the registers of baptism, marriages and burials, though there was an occasional lapse to 'Bully' in the late seventeenth century – a lapse that I for one am glad was not sustained! The Rychard Bullighe mentioned in the 1558 Baptismal register might well have been the first of the line to drop the 'De' and change the spelling of his Norman–French ancestors – De BoLeigh. It would appear that the original suffix 'eigh', which survives in the names Bulleigh Barton, a thirteenth-century house in the parish, and Bulleigh Mill, which is marked on the first Ordnance Survey map in 1808, was changed to 'ey' in the late sixteenth or early seventeenth century. The Ipplepen registers record no less than 118 Bulley baptisms from 1558 to 1813, 24 marriages from 1616 to 1813 and 55 burials from 1671 to 1864. All this sets the family's origins firmly in the Devonshire village, rather than in the Gloucestershire village of Bulley where the registers have no such entries.

My grandparents, paternal and maternal, were godly people ever proud to have their grandchildren about them. Among the jolliest moments of a happy childhood were the great family parties which they laid on at Christmas time. They were, too, frequent visitors to our home as we were to theirs. My paternal grandmother, a diminutive lady of rare culture and great beauty, was no mean poet and although to my knowledge she never submitted any verses for publication, I recall the pleasure with which I heard her read some of her compositions in a gentle refined voice which fell upon the ears as softly as spring rains upon the ground. She was a quiet and diffident lady and I have often reflected that had someone been at hand to encourage her she might well have reached distinction in the literary world.

Her husband, on the other hand, was not the type to express himself poetically. He was of the soil, as it were, and ever more interested in the cultivation of the flowers and fruits of the earth, and in their names, popular and Latin, than in singing about them in poems. I picture him now with his vast mop of silver hair, his bright blue eyes and his huge beard which covered so much of his face that a small boy felt that there was no space left on which he could plant the kiss which eyes sparkling with affection invited.

The picture that I have of my maternal grandfather is again of a very old man, with stooping shoulders, white hair and beard, and a head which seemed always to be buried in the daily paper which he read avidly from beginning to end. A conversation with him revealed an alert mind, a ready and brilliant wit and a lively sense of humour. He was, too, a political animal, very well versed in current affairs and easily roused to anger if he believed that things were going contrary to the good of the country. I have seen him throw down the daily paper with anger, and lecture my grandmother as though she were a public meeting on what was needed to resolve the country's current problems. For her part, she would remain impervious to his tirades, continuing meanwhile to read her Charlotte Brontë, Trollope, Ryder Haggard or Marie Corelli. It was she who introduced me to Marie Corelli's *The Mighty Atom*, a book which impressed me as a young lad and prompted me to read other works of that writer who has been dubbed the most popular and worst Victorian author. While grandpa walked up and down stating what 'they' should be doing, grandma continued to read her novel. Neither took the slightest notice of the other during these sessions and both were apparently happy that it should be so.

From this background of culture, hard work, godliness and family affection came my parents, and on these same foundations our home was built. Battling against indifferent health my parents maintained the home on the material side by working prodigiously to ensure the best for the four children they had brought into the world. Only hindsight convinces me how great was their struggle to that end. The so-called working class of today enjoys a standard of living infinitely higher than that of the middle class, let alone the working class, of yesteryear. In our family, food was adequate but never more than adequate; luxury was out, vegetables were homegrown, backyard hens recycled every scrap of kitchen waste. Footwear was repaired at home; clothing was passed down from son to son and much was home made; holidays were by no means annual events nor do I ever recall the whole family being on holiday together.

The guidelines for the children's pocket money were severe in their end result if not in their very occasional percentage rises: 2d a week was the 'take home pay' but there were times when a 50 per cent rise was awarded on the condition that the collection in church on the following Sunday should rise by the same proportion. We were taught that giving was an essential element in living long before we could have spelt the word 'stewardship', let alone understood its full implications. Sunday collections were taken into account in our childhood budgets, and two boxes, inviting contributions for the Church Army and one of the missionary societies, were ever with us as visual reminders that the world was bigger than the small corner of it we inhabited. We learned that there were needs to be satisfied other than, and more desperate than, our own.

On the social and cultural side ours was a happy home where friends were welcomed, where there were books and games and music. When the marvel of the wireless burst upon the land, my father immediately mastered the know-how. He and my elder brother Leslie, who, unlike me, always compassed such intricacies with consummate ease, set about constructing crystal sets at once. I recall with affection the look of wonder on my father's face when he heard the first crackles on his crystal set.

Family games were entered into with zest. My parents taught us cribbage, insisting on our scoring in order to aid us in what academic jargon now refers to as numeracy. Post-Evensong gatherings around the piano on Sunday evenings were a regular feature of winter nights with my sister Doreen at the piano and my mother with her violin, accompanying the singing of the three brothers and my father whose flute-like alto voice I longed to inherit but didn't. I dabbled with the piano and later became sufficiently competent to play the organ for services in one of the mission churches in the parish of Wolborough and, very occasionally, in the church of St. Leonard where we worshipped. In the latter I played for a Sung Eucharist for the first time at the age of fifteen, standing in on that occasion for our brilliant blind organist, William Moran. I also tried my hand at composing and, in the mission church where I played, the canticles were not infrequently sung to chants composed by myself, though none knew it at the time.

Our association with St. Leonard's Church was long and close. The church itself is tucked into the main street in such a way that a passer-by would scarcely notice it, nor could it be said that it was ever all-glorious within. Nevertheless for me and my family it was a spiritual home and to this day I can recall treasured experiences within it that contributed mightily to my spiritual growth. The site of the original St. Leonard's was in the centre of the town where stands today St. Leonard's Tower, some 500 yards from the church itself. Old St. Leonard's, a tiny building, first mentioned in a document dated 29 May 1350 as 'Capella Sci Leonardi apud Nywaton Abbatis', was taken down in 1836 shortly after the consecration of the present church. The old tower has stood there for 750 years and from it in 1689 William of Orange declared, whether personally or through the lips of the Royal Chaplain, his resolve 'to maintain the liberties of England and the Protestant Religion'. I am sure that St. Leonard's was doing just that in my childhood days but the word 'protestant' was foreign to me then. Some people would have called St. Leonard's Church 'high'; it was in fact what I would call now 'catholic evangelical' in that it held a high view of the Church, presented the Word (especially to large congregations on Sunday evenings) with evangelical fervour, and ministered the Sacraments with meticulous devotion, making the Eucharist the central act of worship Sunday by Sunday.

The said William of Orange made his solemn declaration at St. Leonard's Tower following a night at Forde House, an Elizabethan mansion on the edge of town, where sixty years before Charles the First had been entertained sumptuously and with great splendour. In my boyhood the mansion was occupied by Lady Amy Bertie, a member of the Earl of Devon's family and an ardent member of the Church. Soon after my fifteenth birthday I had the temerity to call on her to ask for her patronage for a concert I was organising in aid of church funds. A footman received me courteously and bade me wait in the magnificent entry hall of the mansion. Feeling like Little Lord Fauntleroy, so small amidst things so vast, I walked slowly towards some of the oil paintings which excited my interest. Suddenly, advancing footsteps prompted me to turn quickly – and I did, but too quickly. I slipped on a rug, fell to the floor and in my recumbent position was greeted with laughter by Her Ladyship. Covered with embarrassment I stammered out my request and was put at ease immediately by her willingness to do more than I asked. As I rode home on my newly-acquired bicycle I reflected that not every boy of fifteen had had the privilege of kissing the very boards on which the feet of King Charles the Martyr had trodden.

The Rector of Wolborough at that time was Claude Alfred Wigglesworth Russell, subsequently a Prebendary of Exeter, and always a very fine parish priest. Normally he had a staff of three curates and both he and the curate in charge of St. Leonard's were regular visitors to our home. Occasionally, too, the curate who worked at St. Paul's Church would also call and one such, who called far more frequently than pastoral concern demanded, greatly amused the trio of brothers when they observed that he terminated his visits more speedily when my sister was not at home.

One priest who came to us at St. Leonard's was Richard Lionel Hussey, who subsequently left for the Manchester diocese in which he served for the rest of his notable ministry. He became known throughout the Church both as a powerful missioner and as a contributor to the debates in the Church Assembly and General Synod where his wit was appreciated even more than his wisdom. In Hussey's day the gallery of St. Leonard's Church would be well peopled with young folk at Sunday Evensong all anxious to hear the words of this lively young man who preached with such power and compelling sincerity. His influence in the town as a town councillor was equally effective and I recall his being carried shoulder high by ex-servicemen delighted at their success in getting him elected. It was Hussey who prepared me for Confirmation and who was at least partially responsible, albeit he never knew it, for nurturing my vocation to the priesthood. He left the parish of Wolborough in 1921 when I was fourteen and we were not to meet again until 1945 when we were both elected to serve in the Convocation of York.

The occasion could not but elicit from Hussey shafts of wit. Introducing me to one of his fellow proctors he described me as 'a piece of bread which I cast upon the waters of Devonshire twenty-six years ago'.

It was one of Hussey's successors, Kenneth Campbell Bickerdike, who came to the parish with a fine war record but whom the war had battered badly, who did most to help me realise my vocation. Even so it was more by his letters to me after he had left the parish than by anything he said or did for me in Newton Abbot that I was set on the path towards the realisation of my heart's desire.

Meanwhile, even in those early days, others were unwittingly helping to foster that vocation and not least my parents. We were never, as children, sent to church; we were taken and in that there is a world of difference. It was example rather than precept which helped us to see the relevance of Sunday to the rest of the week and of worship to the whole of life. My father, my brothers and I were all in the choir together, and my mother and sister taught in the Sunday School from time to time. My mother was deeply involved too in the work of the Mothers' Union (I knew that there was such a thing as the *Mothers' Union Journal* long before I met the *Church Times*!). A frequent visitor to our home in this respect was Violet Woollcombe whose husband Gerald was churchwarden of the Parish Church and a prominent solicitor in the town. Both of them were later to play a decisive part in the realisation of my vocation to the priesthood. Another frequent visitor to our home was Dorothy Bishop, who was a member of the Parish Church Congregation and was the area secretary of the Church Missionary Society. Since our parish was sufficiently catholic to support the CMS as well as the SPG and the UMCA, she felt free to enlist the support of the Bulley children in her 'Primrose Scheme' under which hundreds of bunches of primroses were picked by us during the spring and were despatched to the bleak towns of the Black Country and the North where they were sold in aid of missionary work overseas. To the same end I spent countless hours at a treadle fretwork machine cutting out jigsaw puzzles. My method was to beg from the tradesmen their empty tea chests, to paste pictures of the Cathedrals of England, of Devonshire and London scenes, of the Royal family, and of other subjects which were sufficiently colourful, onto the plywood boards and then to set to work cutting the pictures into interesting and intriguing sections designed to baffle the unfortunate person whose lot it might be 'to put Humpty Dumpty together again'. The finished puzzles would be neatly boxed and then marketed in aid of educational and evangelistic work in Kenya and Uganda. Visiting some schools in Kenya after my retirement, and discovering that many were built by the Church Missionary Society, I could not but toy with the notion that my boyhood hours at the fretwork machine were represented in the very stones around me.

These and similar activities were invariably encouraged by our parents who by word and example inculcated a sense of responsibility and caring which resulted in our being involved from time to time in all sorts of activities on behalf of needy people and charitable causes, ranging from visits to sick relatives and others to amateur dramatics and singing in charity concerts. How well I remember – I confess now with a shudder! – the four children presenting during the First World War a jingoistic children's drama entitled 'Made in Germany' which had, as its climax, the wild destruction of toys so marked. All this in aid of the Red Cross.

But individuals were our concern as well as causes, and one such in particular cannot be left out of my story, such was the impression contact with her made upon me. Indeed if my story had no mention of Lucy it would be incomplete, for Lucy was not only a colourful figure in her own right, she was a dear soul who in a strange way contributed to my understanding of what compassion is all about. Lucy was our 'daily' – a term which in her case described her function rather than the frequency of her attendances. She was a spinster of uncertain age, mentally limited – she could neither read nor write – but physically as strong as a horse. She did things about the house and grappled week by week with the considerable family washing. She was genial and helpful though I always suspected that her casual employment by my parents was as much to help her as it was to help them. Lucy was no oil painting. One look at her might suggest that the Creator had mislaid his recipe for physical beauty when he came to make her. Her awkward stance, her strange gait, her flat feet, her huge chin protruding almost at right angles from her face, her massive mouth with its five remaining teeth, all combined to make Lucy a figure of fun in the district, particularly among some of the children. But it was not so in our home. We were taught to respect her and to treat her kindly. It was, I doubt not, this kindly treatment, and the sense of security deriving from it, which made her arrive early and invariably made her show reluctance to go when the day's work was done.

'They'm be good boys,' she would say to my mother in her rich Devonshire accent, 'they be kind to me, they be.' The kindness which apparently impressed her was little more than our readiness to talk to her, to turn the handle of the great mangle as she toiled through the family wash, to joke with her, to play with her by hiding her equipment and even, on occasion, locking her into the back part of the house, and then telling her that there was a meal ready for her in the kitchen. When she laughed – and she would laugh till the tears rolled down her ugly face – her massive mouth opened to its full width revealing what to all intents and purposes might have been a cavern, complete with stalactites and stalagmites in the shape of her five remaining teeth. A mangling session might produce a dialogue such as this: 'Too fast, Master Cyril, too fast, you be turnin' that 'andle too fast. You'll be pullin' me een between them rollers.' A retort that that would make a fine lady of her, adding inches to her height, would produce another peal of laughter when the 'cavern' would open, and above it two lovely eyes would sparkle in a way which revealed her true character. When she was unable to find a piece of cleaning equipment one would hear a distant laugh and then, addressing herself, some such utterance as: 'It be that Master Cyril again, up to 'is pranks;

'e 'ides me soap, 'e ides me brush.' A little chuckle would indicate how she enjoyed the fun. If truth be told, as it must be, it was not invariably Master Cyril though he was by no means guiltless. The most insistent prankster in a trio of boys was Master Frank though he had an uncanny way of not being about when the prank was discovered. He remained a practical joker all his life and fellow officers in the Royal Navy told me years after that he was the life and soul of the Mess. When Bishop Eric Graham retired from the see of Brechin and came to reside in the Diocese of Carlisle his first comment on meeting me for the first time was: 'I used to meet a naval officer of your name in the Mess at Dundee in my diocese. He invariably kept the party very much alive and nearly gave me apoplexy with his stories and antics.' He had met my brother Frank.

I said that the story of my childhood days could not be complete without telling the story of Lucy since I am sure that my contact with her as a child taught me a great deal about compassion – the duty to offer it, the joy in offering it, and the thrill of seeing the effect of it on the one who experienced it. Poor simple old Lucy would leave our home when a day's work was done, always with something to cover a meal or two, but most of all with eyes which spelt gratitude, not especially, I am sure, for the pittance which was then the char's going rate and was indeed all that my parents could afford, nor for the meals she enjoyed, but for the warmth she experienced in contact with a closely-knit family whose members treated her with respect and compassion. So when she would say to my mother, as she did from time to time: 'When is the skule on 'oliday? I like the 'olidays. Them boys be kind to me,' I really believe she meant it. I know that we did something for her, so that when she left our home she 'walked tall'. She could not have realised how much she did for us. God rest her soul!

There was another exercise in compassion which I recall, though I am sure that none of us would have seen it as that at the time. Sunday afternoons were frequently, indeed regularly for a period, occasions for visits by my brothers and myself to an aged great aunt who lived alone and was housebound. There was a long period when she was unwell, but sick or well, we carried to her each week some little culinary gift. The economics of this puzzled me at the time since she was by repute more richly blessed with this world's goods than we were. But no matter, we were told, she was lonely and sick and someone must do something for her.

This little lady puzzled me greatly. Even from the child's approach to age she seemed to be very, very ancient. My younger brother was persuaded that she was 'at least a hundred'. The more sober estimate of my elder brother Leslie and one which I shared was that she was about eighty. She was wizened and frail; her skin seemed starved of moisture; her face was wrinkled; her beady eyes looked through you rather than at you. Each Sunday we would find her reading her huge family Bible, every word of which, I suspect, she accepted as literally true. On occasion she would fire a question or two at us and since these were frequently about a more abstruse part of the Old Testament we usually failed miserably in the test. She greeted us with a ceremony which never changed and which turned out to be strangely prophetic. We entered her presence – and presence is the right word for the awesome experience – with something approaching reverence, and she received us with a formula which became a joke among us in her absence, but was listened to with profound respect as she recited it. As my younger brother Frank, then under eight years of age, approached her she would say: 'Here comes the admiral'; my approach was greeted invariably with the words: 'Here comes the bishop', and my elder brother, then about eleven, was accustomed to: 'Here comes the lawyer'. None of us had at that time either to her or even within the home expressed any serious suggestion of what we intended to be or do, and if we talked among ourselves it would be about driving trains, sailing ships, delivering letters or keeping cows! But the little lady with the beady penetrating eyes which inspired awe rather than affection, had apparently discerned otherwise. And so it came to be, or almost.

Frank entered the Royal Navy, and was one of the fifty-seven officers who survived the sinking of the Royal Oak in the first days of the war, and who finished his naval career at the Admiralty. Leslie certainly went into the Law when he left school, and would have gone on to qualify had not his course been broken and his confidence shaken by the tragic death of the solicitor with whom he was working. He then abandoned the legal profession for teaching and remained in it to his retirement. Even so, in adult life, we have frequently spoken together of the uncanny way in which that old lady had peered into the future, rightly predicting the venue of service in which three little boys in stiff white collars, immaculately polished shoes, and impeccably clean faces, hands and knees, would one day take their places in the world.

With that description of our appearance I should hasten to add that the good lady saw us only on Sundays when cleanliness was not so much next to godliness as part of it. Not that Sundays were by any means Sabbatarian in our home. Public worship was certainly the rule of the day and good works were encouraged, but cycle rides on Sunday afternoons and rambles in the woods were permissible, and draughts, playing cards and other games were neither forbidden nor frowned upon if wintry conditions imprisoned us.

I must beware of asserting that the weather was much better when we were children, but looking back on those days my impression is that we were rarely so imprisoned. The open air called and its call was heeded early. Living as we did 'twixt Dartmoor and the Devon coast, with scenes of impressive grandeur at the back door as it were, and red sandstone cliffs and gorgeous beaches at the front door, 'the lot had fallen unto us in a fair ground'. Newton Abbot was richly served too with spacious parks, one of which was but a few yards from our home. So too were Bradley Woods through which the River Lemon, dividing the ancient manors of Newton Abbot and Newton Bushell, flows somewhat lazily. It was rarely deep enough to make it unsafe as a playground for children and I can recall hours of contentment messing about in its waters, catching tiddlers, eels and on one occasion an eight-inch trout which I carried

home with pride only to be lectured on breaking a law about which I had
never heard. Indeed I thought that I deserved reward not reproof for had I
not beaten, even belied, the old wives' tale concerning the local rivers:

> *The Teign for salmon, the Dart for peel*
> *Forde Leat for trout and the Lemon for eel.*

Through these lovely woods was a path to Ogwell Downs where primroses,
bluebells and blackberries grew in abundance, where the downland winds,
which blew wildly at times, could fill our lungs with clean air, and where
children could play unimpeded by querulous adults.

Family excursions to the moors or the coast were too costly to be frequent,
but as soon as the boys of the family reached the bicycle stage such beauty
spots as Becky Falls, Lustleigh Cleave, Widecombe in the Moor and the
lovely beaches of Maidencombe, Oddicombe and Babbacombe came within
our reach. My elder brother and I once ventured the long ride over Haldon
to Exmouth. It was a once-only trip made memorable by an incident we
never forgot. A bad wasp sting prompted me to call at a wayside cottage
for advice and treatment and I was doctored with a blue bag by an old
lady. As we were leaving, immensely relieved and grateful for the old lady's
help, she said 'It's funny you should have called sonny. I had a little boy
here last Saturday with a wasp sting and I read in last night's paper that
he died.' It was a shattering blow which frightened us so much that it left
us speechless. Not knowing whether it was the blue bag or the wasp sting
which had killed the boy it occurred to me that by rubbing off all the blue
which the old lady had put on I could at least reduce the chances of death
by half. There by the roadside and with a handkerchief wet with tears that
is precisely what I did. Both tearful we rode on in silence clinging to each
other for dear life and at length reached Exmouth. We dared not breathe
the possibility to our cousins but not even their eager and cordial welcome
could give me any assurance. How I prayed that night and when morning
broke I was never happier or more surprised than to find myself cycling
along Exmouth's wonderful sea front – an exhilarating experience frequently
repeated.

'Glorious Devon' was no mere holiday brochure cliché to the Bulley
children. We revelled in its beauties and its delights, and certainly there
grew in me through my childhood a passion for the sea, a love of picturesque
villages, of country lanes, of thatched cottages, of ancient parish churches, of
woodlands, of streams and of all the flora and flaura which are sustained in
and by them. Indeed nothing could be farther from the truth in my eyes than
Keats' description of Devon as 'a splashy, rainy, misty, snowy, foggy, haily,
floody, muddy, slipshod county'. Splashy and muddy perhaps in the winter,
for Mr. Macadam had not by then written his name over every highway in the
land, but the young Marcellus of our tongue does the county a grave injustice
by his catalogue of 'y' adjectives, and after all the 'slipshod county' was not

so bad as to preclude his completing his *Endymion* within its boundaries in 1818.

Thus whether in the home or out in the open, the environment in which we grew up was wholesome, congenial and conducive to balanced growth. Not that environment is the decisive factor in character formation nor is it the final determinant of human happiness or misery. Our good fortune was that with all this we had too a home where happiness was the by-product not of affluence but of affection, and where affection in its turn was informed, inspired and sustained by a solid if simple faith in the Living God. A sampler on the wall of our living room asserted:

> *Christ is the Head of this House,*
> *The Unseen Guest at every meal*
> *The Silent Listener to every conversation.*

I never sat down to a meal without seeing it in front of me. It was no mere wall decoration. Whilst I cannot recall my parents ever drawing our particular attention to its presence, or expounding its practical implications, I can say that what it declared was clearly the point of reference which governed our upbringing and made our home the happy place it was.

To say as much is not to imply that parents or children were pious paragons of virtue. Of course there were times when individual selfishness reared its ugly head. With four children at large there must have been quarrels, there must have been tears, there must have been occasional rebellions against parental authority, there must have been punishments, disappointments, failures and anxieties. But it is not these which break through the mists of childhood memories for me, but the caring, the contentment, the fun, the merriment, the sharing of interests, the birthday celebrations six times a year, and – especially when the London cousins came at holiday time – the hilarious games which momentarily turned the house into a bedlam in which my father was not averse to being a party.

If integrity demands that the story of a man's life should be a 'warts and all' saga, so be it, but I find it terribly hard to recall the warts of childhood at least in the context of home and family. Love, after all, is a fire which warms and lights, but it purifies too.

To the eternal credit of my parents to whom I owe so much, I dare to finish this chapter with some words of George Herbert which disclose the secret of our happiness as a family. 'God oft hath a great share in a little house,' he wrote. That 'great share' was the benediction which enabled us to pray, play and stay together.

2

Unfinished Symphony

I imagine that up to the 1930s the goals of education had rarely been a subject of public debate. Aristotle, Socrates, Ruskin, Dewey, Johnson, James, Huxley and countless others had had their say but what they said created no more than ripples in educational waters. They had said different things, but a synthesis of their definitions is not impossible, and would lead to an overall conclusion that education is both the imparting of knowledge and skills through systematic instruction, and the fashioning of character so that the educated become good people – good that is morally, spiritually, intellectually and socially and, I would add, technically. This last is an essential factor for a person should be good at something. A child should be helped to pursue excellence in some particular art, skill, academic or scientific discipline.

To Cardinal Newman education was thus something which was 'embodied', a tangible thing, something that could be handed on – a torch to be passed from teacher to pupil, from generation to generation. Then along came 'progressive education', so called. Education was no longer a torch to hand on, for learning was not by receiving but by experiencing, and only a multi-sensory approach – visual, auditory, tactile and, I suppose, gustatory – could enable a child to learn anything. Maybe it was not without educational significance, though I am not implying any pressure by the Ministry of Education on the Ministry of Transport, that the torch as the highway code sign for a school disappeared in 1957 and was replaced by a couple of children carrying school-bags. This in turn disappeared in 1964 and was replaced by a couple of children who, for all the world, might be out to play. Their school-bags have become redundant since homework was to be regarded as 'a bad thing'. Sitting in rows and listening must be abandoned; children must be encouraged to run about the classrooms 'discovering' and 'experiencing' – and thus, incidentally, wasting an hour learning what they could have been taught in five minutes. It was, not unnaturally, in the United States that all this was swallowed hook, line and sinker, but there has been enough of it in this country to give us the end result of erosion

16

of basic skills in many of our primary schools, thus impeding secondary and tertiary education.

All that as a prelude to a paean of praise for the system under which I received my primary education and for the teachers who talked whilst I listened and made me work when I might have preferred to play. I left my primary school with a firm grasp of the basics: able to read anything, able to write legibly – those copy books! – able to multiply, add, subtract and divide with ease, able to recite a good deal of the Church Catechism and to understand at least the sections dealing with Duty to God and Neighbour, able to rattle off the tables and to plant a stubby finger on a map of the world which could distinguish between Australia and America, Belgium and Burma, Canada and China. Nor was I different from the rest of the boys in the class. (But were we, I must ask myself in a shameful whisper, 'selected'?). They drove us hard those teachers and how we worked! It was not then deemed necessary to build igloos all over the classroom floor in order to discover how an Eskimo lived. We knew what stalactites and stalagmites were like without rushing off for a whole day to Cheddar Caves, though a visit in later years to Kents Cavern was confirmatory and exciting. We knew what an island was without experiencing 'islandness' by sailing around Lundy or standing on its highest peak! There was a rigid adherence to a curriculum covering not three R's but four, for religious instruction was deemed to be as important as reading, writing and arithmetic.

School was concerned with the accumulation of knowledge, with the handing on of the torch of learning, and it was not supposed that all that was being imparted should either be, or needed to be, immediately 'meaningful'. It was recognised, in other words, that education was concerned more with the fifty or sixty years of adult life than with the few years of childhood. Knowledge was indeed imparted, but those teachers knew that education was knowledge plus. There was not much glamour about it, and it was far from being fun in the classroom, but the systematic and hard work approach to the basics, and the strict discipline which was imposed, were themselves a preparation for adult life which cannot but be intolerable without self-discipline, which itself develops from imposed discipline, ideals of service, hard work and absolute standards of behaviour.

I say no more save that I am thankful that I left my primary school equipped not only with the basic skills of literacy and numeracy but, as I should express it now, with a keen sense of what life is all about. Those teachers who drove me in the classroom, played with me in the playground, prayed with me in the school assembly and in the parish church, helped me to grow 'in wisdom and stature and in favour with God and man'.

Soon after the end of the Great War I began what turned out to be a truncated life at the local secondary grammar school. The school had been in existence for only a few years, having developed from an institution for training pupil teachers. Since private enterprise had already established in the town a thriving school which was called the Grammar School, the State school had of necessity to call itself by another name. Thus it became, for the first years of its life, the Newton Abbot Secondary School, and so remained until the private school died and the word 'Secondary' in the title was changed to 'Grammar'.

Since Newton Abbot had begun its life sometime in the thirteenth century and for 700 years had been the natural centre almost the 'capital' – of a wide area bounded on the north by Moretonhampstead, on the west by Widecombe in the Moor, on the east by Chudleigh and on the south by the Kerwells – one might have anticipated the existence at some point in its history of an ancient Grammar School of Elizabethan or earlier foundation. But history tells of none and even when, in 1846, the town became an important junction of the South Devon Railway and gradually developed as an important railway centre for the west of England, the education authority had not roused itself to action in any special provision for secondary education. At the time I was enrolled the school buildings had been up for less than a decade and I recall their very 'new' look, and the existence of army huts on the school playing field still being used to house the preparatory department.

With high hopes I presented myself in September 1919, being led to the school by my elder brother who was then beginning his second year. From the boys-only primary department I was now not only in a co-educational school but also in a school which had been staffed largely by women throughout the years of the war, though as men came out of the forces the male teaching staff increased rapidly.

The headmaster in my time was one James Hembrough – tall, well-built, distinguished looking, kindly, every inch a gentleman, and with his shock of silver hair, clearly ageing. I picture his elephantine form lumbering along the corridors, frequently with a smile on his face as though his work was a source not only of satisfaction but of some amusement. I picture him presiding over the morning assembly, and frequently haranguing the school about gentlemanly behaviour, hard work and its rewards. These lectures followed the morning worship, always conducted reverently even though the hymn was invariably sung with what I regarded as indecent haste. The length of the subsequent and imminent discourse could be gauged by the introduction. The direction 'Stand on the ball of your feet and we shall see less people fainting' was always ominous. Hembrough himself was a scientist and from the first I gained the impression that any boy – and the lectures seemed to me to be invariably directed towards the boys – whose interests lay in the arts rather than the sciences was deemed to be a little odd. The new world in which we should grow up would be a world of science and the boy who could not come to terms with that would be gravely ill-equipped. There was also a refrain to his discourse to the effect that all he earned over £X a year was due entirely to the hard work he put in outside the school classroom and over his books at home. Undoubtedly the very strong science bias of the school, which was not to my liking, resulted in there being a glut of sixth formers going on to universities to read something in the science disciplines and an insignificant trickle on the arts side.

Around him Hembrough had gathered a staff of graduates as varied in temperament as in ability. Outstanding among the male members was a young maths master, Ernest Mount, who was not only the ablest of the male teachers but also the best disciplinarian. His immaculate appearance, his shock of red hair, his stern face and his peremptory commands, said a great deal about him. Any boy who was tempted to fool about in his lesson did not find it too difficult to resist the temptation after one experience of yielding. It was not that he personally ever laid a hand upon us, but that the flashing eyes, the red hair, the scolding voice and, I dare say, the apparent intrinsic integrity of the man, combined to reduce the transgressor if not to tears then to abject surrender. True, so firm was his discipline that he was the teacher whom the boys hated to love for I judge that had the gallup poll been invented in those days 'The Volcano' would have topped it for popularity as for professional ability. Even so, we could give vent to our feelings in the refrain:

Old Ernie Mount is dead and gone, his face you'll see no more. For what he drank for H_2O was H_2SO_4!

Schoolboys do not sing ditties like that, however seemingly disrespectful, about teachers whom they despise. They reserve them for teachers they admire. Ernest Mount was my hero! (I was privileged to meet him again in November 1979, for the first time since I left school, and delighted to find him hale and hearty. He took no exception to the couplet and knew of other nicknames foreign to me!).

Among the ladies on the staff who taught me at any time – and only those do I dare to judge – were two of rare culture and ability. Edith Wheeler was head of the history department, and could have won my warm appreciation without further qualification such was my love of her subject. But among her considerable gifts she had that of investing her lessons with a reality which might have suggested that she was giving an eye-witness account of events she was describing. When I first heard of Becket's murder from her lips I could picture the whole sordid scene in Canterbury Cathedral, even to the blood stains on the floor! With such contempt did she invest her voice as, for example, she told of the conspiracies of Titus Oates that I would gladly have headed a demo against the award of the pension given him for his bad old age. Of Henry VIII and his marital adventures she was perhaps a little more restrained, for after all it was only 1920. A great and utterly dedicated teacher was Edith Wheeler and, as I discovered to my joy, a great Christian too. So, too, was Florence Rainford who taught me French with consummate skill on her part and moderate success on mine.

My relationships with the staff were on the whole happy excepting perhaps with a certain art master who had not learnt the most elementary lesson for any teacher, namely that sarcasm must have no place in the teacher's armoury. I longed and struggled to achieve something in those drawing lessons, but at length surrendered before the sarcastic shafts of a crude man for whom in the end I nursed a hearty dislike.

Of extra-curricular activities there was one which I greatly enjoyed, and one which aroused in me a pathological hatred. The first was the school's Literary, Historical and Scientific Debating Society and the second was the school Cadet Corps which one was pressurised into joining. The occasional meetings of the former were informative and enjoyable and provided me with my first halting efforts in public speaking. Furthermore since I could absent myself with impunity when the subject under discussion was deeply scientific the society was invariably an amenable diversion which won my approval. But for the Cadet Corps and all its works I nursed a loathing which beggars description. Everything about it seemed to me to be so purposeless and futile – the parades and the puttees, the commands and the camps, the rifles, the field-days. I found the whole outrageous. The adolescent's adjective in these days would be 'obscene'. Such paraphernalia filled me with loathing. But there came a day when, mercifully, I was released from this abhorrent activity, but not until I brought the sergeant major near to death's door.

It all began so innocently, at least from my angle. One summer day I broke my arm playing cricket, and in those days that meant that one was off school for some time. When at last a return to school was deemed safe by the family doctor (who, by the way, used to arrive at the house in a chauffeur-driven Rolls Royce) only a week elapsed before I broke the arm again and was off for a further period. On my return I was ordered to attend a parade for rifle practice, and my fierce plea that my arm was not sufficiently steady to be 'messing about with a gun', as I put it, was dismissed. The sergeant major, a sixth former who clearly resented my describing such a sacred thing as firing practice in so impious a manner, insisted not only on my being present at the parade but also in my taking my turn at the target. I did, and with all but fatal results. The rifle rose and dropped on my weakened arm like a tiny boat on a rough sea and the target finished as clean as it was before I started. The squad had scattered with the first shot; the sergeant major, called by duty to stand by, escaped with his life but could never have been in greater peril. I was summarily dismissed from the corps with ignominy, a punishment which I received with the utmost alacrity. Never was I nearer a charge of manslaughter. The incident is embedded in the school records by reason of an article contributed by some wag who wrote of his contemporaries' misdeeds under the title 'Their favourite books'. 'Shattered Windows' was alleged to have been written by one David Pethybridge whose playful antics with a map pole resulted in smashing windows on opposite sides of a classroom in a single charge and retreat. 'Random Shots' was deemed to have been written by S. C. Bulley.

There was one other aspect of my school life that gave me sleepless nights. My hatred of the cadet corps and all its works was matched by a distinct distaste for chemistry and physics. Every Friday night I went to bed with the gloomy thought that from 9.15 to 12.15 on the following morning I should be imprisoned in a stinking laboratory, doing things which failed to evoke a spark of interest in me, and trying to learn things of which I could make neither head nor tail. There were, of course, other periods of similar purgatory in the course of the week which I found equally repulsive, among them something called, I think, mechanics. These, however, were spread through the week. I could tolerate these intolerable disciplines in doses of forty minutes, but an unbroken stretch of three hours proved to be wholly indigestible.

One such stretch proved to be a Waterloo for me. The habit was that experiments in chemistry were done in pairs. Tom and I were paired on a particular Saturday morning to engage in an experiment which it was evident he would enjoy and I should both detest and wreck. I decided therefore that the wiser course was to leave it to him, and to make progress with my maths homework since that was something I could enjoy and in which I could see some purpose. The arrangement appeared to be admirable. Tom was happy getting on with something in which he excelled; I was happy with my maths. So things remained for half an hour or so. Then came a voice over my shoulder, harsh and threatening: 'So you do your maths homework in my lesson you miserable little scoundrel.' I looked up penitently for the charge was indisputable. 'Why do you do your maths homework in my lesson, you wretched boy?' A pertinent question indeed from his angle, but not a little embarrassing from mine. I judged however that the question deserved an honest answer, and there came a moment of truth for the physics master: 'Because I am very fond of maths sir and I hate this stuff and do not understand it! He grabbed my book, ordered me to follow him, and follow I did like a whipped dog. Down the long corridor we went and at great speed, his gown blowing out like the sails of a dinghy. Clearly we were heading for the Head's room, he to expose my grievous sin, I to suffer the consequences. What should I say? 'I didn't think I was doing anything very wrong sir. I wasn't fooling about; I was working.' A bit hollow, but it would do as a first line in my defence. But no! The journey had taken a different turn, away from the Head's room, and up the stairs. Light dawned! Truly I was being led as a lamb to the slaughter but the slaughterer was to be not the Head but the maths master himself, my hero! The physics master entered his room courteously, and interrupted the lesson by handing me over, somewhat contemptuously, with a crisp: 'This boy prefers to do your homework in my lesson. I leave you to deal with him.' The hair of my hero master went redder than I had ever seen it; the eyes flashed with anger, the voice was stern and harsh. He spoke but five words and his accent on the last all but reduced me to tears: 'Bulley, I'm ashamed of you.' And then, across my neat work he drew two parallel lines in blue pencil and between them the word 'Cancelled. E.E.M.'. A very contrite boy walked from the presence of the master whom, least of all, he would have wished to displease. But he was still wondering whether perchance it was all a storm in a teacup. Suffice it to say that it was to the maths master that I apologised on the following Monday morning. What seemed like a peccadillo on the Saturday afternoon, and was being bolstered by solid arguments of justification on Saturday evening, became in church on Sunday morning what it really was, a sly breach of discipline, which left me with an uncomfortable feeling until I squared it on Monday.

I had by that time been confirmed, and that was an experience which impressed me deeply, touching as it did my spiritual perception and my personal behaviour. Preparation for that great day had in effect been going on under the guidance of my parents all my young life, and for several months before the event Richard Lionel Hussey, the assistant curate of Wolborough in charge of St. Leonard's Church, had been responsible for the intensive preparation. It was, in fact, in the course of that preparation that I began to think very seriously of offering myself for the Church's ministry. I dared not mention the thought to anyone at home or at church. It was not that I feared opposition to the idea from my parents. It was rather that I feared rejection of it by the clergy. After all none had ever spoken in my hearing of the way in which young men are called to the ministry, and none had ever sounded a call to young lads to consider the possibility. I tended to think of the Church's ministry as a 'closed shop', reserved for very privileged people, and there were thus moments when the thought, which I sincerely regarded as God-given, seemed to be so remotely possible of realisation that I ought to try to dismiss it from my mind. Somehow or other I did understand that the step I was taking at my Confirmation was a momentous one, and in a simple but sincere way I sought God's forgiveness for my boyhood sins and God's grace to come to Him that day with a heart and mind open to the indwelling of His spirit. Not long before, I had sung as a solo in that church Attwood's setting of 'Come Holy Ghost our souls inspire', and now that same hymn was to be sung at my Confirmation.

It is a salutary thought to me now, as a bishop, that I can recall very little that the Bishop of Exeter (Lord William Cecil) said in his address, though who could ever forget his request that we should stand without shuffling our feet since to do so would 'stir too much dust in this dirty church'. It was, in fact, an unfair gibe for the church abutted directly on to the main street from Newton Abbot to Totnes and in those days, long before tarmac had given us cleaner roads, that street was either muddy or dusty, according to the weather. That in turn meant that the bigger the congregation, the dirtier the church!

But the venerable and much bearded bishop said one other word which lived and lives with me. He bade us not to drink! Since alcohol found no place in our home, save perhaps in a bottle of wine at Christmas, that lesson was not immediately relevant. Even so I was not too young to have seen the evils of excessive drinking in the shape of drunken men lying on the pavements at night, and I shared with other children the fear of passing them. I knew too of homes which had been broken by drink – either by men spending the housekeeping money on beer or by violence committed under the influence of alcohol. Drunkenness was certainly more evident then, though I doubt not that there is in fact more of it today. The good bishop doubtless had drunkenness on his mind and took the opportunity to warn his flock against a besetting sin of the day. I have never been a teetotaller nor encouraged anyone else to be but I have seen enough of the dangers and evils of excessive drinking to counsel the same sort of warning which the Bishop gave to the young children at my Confirmation. I would happily support, against drinking, the sort of statutory legislation to discourage smoking with which we have become familiar and I would rejoice to see alcohol taxed to a degree so severe as to cut down its consumption markedly. But that, I fear, is a vain hope. Fearful of offending the so-called working man by taxing his pint of beer too severely and equally of upsetting the brewers and distillers, successive Chancellors of the Exchequer have done little more than toy with the taxes on a commodity which, however enjoyable in moderation, is a non-essential and a peculiarly dangerous one at that. A recent budget anticipated a yield of £288 million from increased taxes on alcohol. Had the increases been so substantial as to have anticipated four times that amount the end result would have been measured certainly in increased revenue but more importantly in incalculable social well-being. Taking into consideration the desirable reduction in consumption which higher prices would have effected, the increased revenue could be in the region of £800 million or more — a sum that could lessen cuts in the education and health services. On the credit side, too, there would be a noticeable diminution in the weekly adolescent hooliganism in our cities and trains which mars the image of soccer, a significant drop in the number of road deaths and hospital admissions arising from drunken driving, and an immeasurable contribution to the general welfare and health of the community. I have not forgotten the Bishop of Exeter's warning words at my Confirmation but if they meant little to me then I have, in the course of a long ministry, seen too many homes broken by drink, too many lives wrecked by it, too many deaths caused by it and too much misery occasioned by it, to be other than staggered by the complacency with which successive governments, so sensitive for example to the self-inflicted dangers inherent in drugs and in smoking, seem to treat this hazard both to the lives of others as well as to those imprisoned by it.

I have other memories of that great day in my life. Towering over us as he stood on the Chancel steps, with curly hair and long dishevelled beard, the Bishop was a somewhat forbidding figure who, as it seemed to me, had leapt straight from the Old Testament — as stern as any Amos. Even young children had heard and been amused by funny stories of his eccentricities, but standing before us then, he appeared to be too removed from mortals to permit a smile on his bearded face or a word from his lips which might evoke a smile from another. He was, in fact, remote. None of us met him after the Rite; none of us had the opportunity of speaking to him, nor was any opportunity made for him to speak to us individually. He came, he saw, he laid on hands and he went. I contrast this with present practice and praise God that things are different now. For my part I have always valued the opportunity of meeting the young people whom I have confirmed and of talking with them and their parents. Nor do I know of any bishop who would willingly adopt a different course.

It was about this time that I began to be aware of the somewhat perfunctory way in which religious instruction was treated in our school. Certainly it had its place in the curriculum, minimal though it was, though the lessons amounted to little more than the reading of a passage from the Bible, in sequence it is true, but without any serious or systematic attempt to expound or explain what was read. There was, of course, a staff of specialists, but there was none for the religious instruction which was left to the form teachers and positioned in the timetable at the beginning of the day. If my hindsight charge of perfunctoriness in the matter of religious instruction is valid, it could well be that much of the tabled time for the subject was pre-empted by the morning worship, which often embraced what might have been called moral instruction. Certainly every school day began with an act of worship which was constructed with care and led with reverence. There remains with me today the sense that that in itself was sufficient to make clear to us that school was not something apart from church, nor education remote from religion.

How different is today's approach when there are, within the teaching profession and without, some who would eliminate from our schools both the act of worship and the religious instruction. Frequently they disguise their true intentions by suggesting that the school curriculum should have within it what they call stances for living, in which they would set by the side of Christianity, Secular Humanism, Marxism and other social or political theories which by no stretch of the imagination could be regarded as having any place in religious instruction. How can philosophies such as these, which are based on the premise that there is no God and which deny the whole category of the supernatural, be a valid substitute for or be equated with Christian education? Certainly there is need for moral education which, as I recall, was associated with the morning worship in my school. Certainly we have a duty to respect and to provide for the needs of our non-Christian Commonwealth immigrants. Certainly a case could be sustained in our multiracial society for acquainting our senior pupils with other religions. None of these, however, should be regarded as a legitimate alternative to Christian education which, in schools, means among other things Biblical instruction. As I write this a judge, summing up a case in his court, has been describing those whom he was sentencing as being conspirators engaged in 'converting Birmingham into a municipal Gomorrah'. A week or so before, another judge had spoken in his court of a 'Good Samaritan action'. When I see such references, I ask myself how much longer they will mean anything if the Bible is to be banished from the schools as Hitler banished it when he came to power. The same is true of our rich heritage of literature, music and art which can scarcely be understood apart from the tradition from which they are drawn and by which they were inspired.

But this is not the most important consideration. Christianity is much more than a footnote which accounts for and explains our heritage, and the Christian faith is more than an attractive stance for living vying for a place among others. It is the historic faith embraced by our forefathers nearly 2000 years ago and which is in fact the cornerstone of our national history. Instruction of our children in that faith is an obligation laid upon us by our experience of its impact upon our common life. When our children come to adult life they can accept it or reject it, for Christ never compelled anyone to follow him. But for us to deprive them of instruction in it would be a grave abdication of our responsibility towards them. Those who, in the midst of the bitterest war in our history, calmly sat down to draft what on any reckoning must be accounted the greatest Education Act our statute book has ever seen – the 1944 Act – knew what they were doing and why they were doing it, when deliberately they stipulated that in every school there should be a daily act of religious worship and regular religious instruction with provision for non-Christians to be withdrawn should their parents desire. In its definition of what education is all about, the 1944 Act takes into account man in his wholeness – body, mind and spirit. 'It shall be the duty,' it declares, 'of the local education authority for every area, so far as their power extends, to contribute towards the spiritual, moral, mental and physical development of the community by securing that efficient education shall be available to meet the needs of the populace of their area' (Education Act 1944, part 2, para 6). So clearly was all this seen as a deliberate step to ensure the continuance of the Christian approach to education in our schools that even the one communist member of parliament at the time could not fail to see what was intended despite the absence of the word 'Christian'. Furthermore the same Act deliberately chose to sustain the partnership in education between Church and State even to the extent of offering grants to the Church to facilitate the much needed modernisation of Church schools. When therefore the National Foundation for Educational Research called, as it did in 1975, for the inclusion of 'the non-religious life-styles – Humanism, Communism, possibly Fascism and the counter-cultures – in religious education syllabuses in their own right', it was attempting to undermine the basis of the existing Education Act. Its suggestions were both mischievous and palpably absurd.

I find that when my eye stays on the glass of the present – to use George Herbert's phrase – I see things which are deeply disturbing in the present debate on education and not least in that part of it which concerns religious education. But when I look through the glass to what happened in my own school – and that was not a church foundation – whilst I do not discern perfection, I recognise that there was a sincere attempt to present the Christian Faith as lively and as relevant, and I believe that the morning acts of worship contributed to the development of my spiritual faculties. I have one other recollection, the contribution which members of staff made from time to time to the discussions and debates in our Literary, Historical and Scientific Debating Society meetings. Not infrequently those debates dealt with matters of faith and conduct, and for children from Christian homes to hear their teachers taking a Christian stand in such things was both enlightening and encouraging. Nor can I imagine that it did any harm to those whose parents sat lightly to the things of God.

But there were other anxieties filling my mind by the time I had reached my fifteenth birthday. In my own heart and mind I was by then resolved and, I felt, irrevocably, to offer myself for the sacred ministry. I recall a number of rich experiences of spiritual perception which so impressed themselves on my mind at that time that I could not but regard them as other than pointing the way. There was the moment, for example, when in a Lenten act of worship Bishop Walsham How's hymn '*O my Saviour lifted on the Cross for me*' confronted me forcibly with the message of the Cross and demanded of me a personal answer. There was, sometime later, a meeting with a group of young Church Army cadets who visited our parish during one of the Army's summer treks from their headquarters to Teignmouth. The fearless witness of those young lads, their sense of purpose, their dedication, their liveliness, their obvious fellowship in faith and fun – all evoked such a response in me that I followed them on my bicycle to Teignmouth to see and hear them bear their witness to the crowds on the sands. Furthermore I had had one or two desultory talks about the possibility of ordination with certain of the clergy but I recall experiencing a measure of disappointment at what seemed to me to be their lukewarm response, and their apparent inability to advise me how to set about it. I had begun to judge their lack of interest as a vote of no confidence until one Saturday evening, the Rector called at our home with a request which momentarily stunned me. One of the curates had been taken ill, and the Rector had come to ask me to conduct a service in St. Leonard's Church on the following day for the senior catechism – children from eleven to fourteen years of age – and to give them a short lesson or address. My obvious hesitation was immediately answered by the Rector's expression of confidence that I could do what he was asking, and an encouraging word from my father clinched the matter. I struggled into the night hours preparing for something which, with every passing minute, loomed before me as a frightening ordeal but at long last, the outline of the address completed, I crept into bed confident that all would be well and, if truth be told, somewhat elated at the thought that this must surely be regarded as a vote of confidence from the clergy which I had been disappointed not to have received earlier.

Morning came and the family went as usual to the Sung Eucharist at which I was one of the servers. What was to happen in the afternoon in that church had a special place in my prayers that morning. I had often lifted my voice in treble solos there but had not so much as read a passage of the Bible aloud. Lay participation in the conduct of worship was unknown in those days! To my father's home-going question as to what I was proposing to talk about in the afternoon I answered cryptically: 'Temptation, because I know a lot about it.' That then was the theme of my first address in a church and the notes of it survived for many years and were in fact used again in a little mission church near Durham seven years later.

The total experience of that day whetted my appetite and I became more eager than ever to find out how one trained to be a priest. Resolved not to approach the local clergy again directly I wrote to one of the monks at Kelham whose name I had seen in the *Mother's Union Journal*, and asked him what particular subjects I should be studying at school. A most encouraging and fatherly letter came back, but it was a letter which added fuel to the fires of dissatisfaction with my school which had been growing fiercer for some time. It was not that I was faring badly at lessons by any means, save perhaps in things like physics and chemistry, though even here there was the phenomenal occasion when I scored a 95 per cent in a terminal chemistry paper – a feat which drew from the headmaster the comment that I had restored his belief in the miraculous. (Surely he had been teaching long enough to know that that result was merely an indication that I had happened on the night before the exam to light upon the right things to swot!) It was not failure that fed dissatisfaction but impatience with the school's unreasonable bias towards the sciences, and the fact that I could see no prospect there of any advanced study in religious knowledge or in my getting any tuition in Latin which, from what my monk correspondent implied, seemed to be a *sine qua non* so far as ordination was concerned.

I became very restive. I found myself measuring the hours I was 'wasting' in physics and chemistry which could be put to better use. For a time I worked hard at the things I enjoyed and suffered the bitterest frustration over my inability to secure help in others. The frequent calls at our home at that time of one of the boarders at Newton College – a minor Public School – nourished a secret desire which had lurked within me for sometime for an opportunity to leave the Grammar School in favour of such a school as his, for as I talked with him on his visits it seemed that the College attached importance to just the sort of things I needed. That desire was never expressed in words, for I knew that the College fees would be utterly beyond my parents' capability. Furthermore I was beginning to be aware of the financial strain under which my parents lived, with three sons at school and a daughter constantly under medical care and unable to contribute to the family income. I could not but overhear from time to time whispered conversations which went on between them, concerning ways and means of making ends meet. All this worried me, as indeed it worried my brothers a great deal.

One night about that time, and during my prayers, I arrived at a make or break decision. When the academic year ended I would leave school, find some amenable job which might enable me to earn a little to help relieve the financial strain under which my parents were living, and go to the local night school to begin lessons in Latin. Stressing the latter point of my plan rather than the former, so as to avoid if possible causing them distress, I was able to persuade my parents to accept the plan, and fortunately they did so before I discovered the next frustration which was that the night school, like the

Grammar School, made no provision for classical studies of any sort. But by then the die was cast; I was to leave school at the end of the school year.

This was more in the nature of a crisis moment for my parents than for me, for they saw it as a grave set-back to my aspirations towards ordination, whereas I saw it as a liberating move which would enable me to get down to the sort of studies which were necessary, whilst at the same time helping them to continue helping me. It was a layman, not a priest, who came up with the most practical advice just then. Gerald Woollcombe, a partner in the legal firm of Watts, Woollcombe & Watts, was churchwarden of the Parish Church and his wife, Violet, who was Enrolling Member of the Mother's Union, was a frequent visitor to our home. I doubt not that my mother shared her anxieties with her and the outcome was that the good lawyer said that he could find a place for me in his office towards the end of the year and further that he had no doubt that he could find someone who would gladly help me in serious Biblical studies and in Latin.

Thus at the end of the academic year in which I reached the age of sixteen and without a Higher School Certificate (comparable with 'A' levels) I left the Grammar School, and with few regrets. My sojourn there had not been the happiest days of my life, but even so I would not go so far as to say with Bernard Shaw that my education had been gravely interrupted by my schooldays. Certainly I had been shown around the House of Knowledge and admitted to many of its rooms. Some I had explored eagerly and with profit; others I had explored less eagerly and with less profit. Some evoked no response; in others I had wilted. In a few subjects I had excelled, in others I had fared satisfactorily, in one or two I had failed miserably. My dissatisfaction arose not from what the school did for me but from what it failed to do. My relationships with the staff had been good and I respected even those whom I disliked. Even so I was never able to escape the conviction that those of us who could not excel in the sciences were registered as second-class citizens, and only those who would one day write after their names the magic letters B.Sc., A.R.C.Sc., which followed the Head's name, would reach the pinnacle of academic achievement. I heard of many such during my time but although the school was built in 1912 it was not until 1926 that the school could point to a graduate in arts among its old boys and he was an ordinand William John Bolt, who subsequently read further degrees in law and attained a London doctorate.

Like others of its ilk I suspect that the school has now become a victim of comprehensivisation – an ugly word matching an ugly development. The great Education Act of 1944 with the Norwood Committee's tripartite system of secondary education – Secondary Grammar, Secondary Modern and Secondary Technical – afforded opportunity for the best for every child. The Comprehensive idea is intrinsically at fault since it confuses equality of opportunity, which everyone desires for all, with identity of opportunity. In fact identity inhibits equality in this connexion. Just as physical disabilities – blindness, deafness, paraplegia – demand special schools to ensure that children so affected have, *ceteris paribus*, an opportunity comparable with that of their more fortunate fellows, so account must be taken of varieties of mental powers, interests and potential skills. It not being possible even if it were desirable to provide a special school for every child, though every child is different from every other, the tripartite system offered the best opportunity for equality, and rightly developed would surely have satisfied all whose motives were educational rather than political. Unfortunately the secondary technical side was gravely neglected and that put the system itself under suspicion. If, however, there had been sufficient political resolve to repair that omission, and if it had been recognised that eleven plus was too young an age at which to assess the right secondary school for a child, our educational system, so long among the best in the world, would not have been set back and impoverished as it has been by the Comprehensive development. For the most part the long-suffering teaching profession is making the best of a bad job and certainly in the smaller Comprehensives the graver disabilities are being overcome in the children's interests.

A greater question mark hovers over the massive educational factories which bestride the country. So vast is the financial commitment which is vested in them as buildings that they are doubtless here to stay, but I venture to prophesy that before the century is out each of them, like Gaul, will be divided into three parts, secondary grammar, secondary modern and secondary technical. Each will be under a separate head teacher who will know each member of his staff and each child in his charge. They may well share such facilities as playing fields, swimming pools and gymnasia, for that would make economic sense. 'Big is better' will give place to 'small is beautiful' and within the 'small' every child will rise to his or her full stature within own peer group – a peer group measured not by standards of class or money but by interests and potential. The school campus in a given area will be comparable in its set up with the collegiate university with its autonomous units each with a life of its own but sharing facilities for recreational, sporting and cultural activities. But no doubt that if something along those lines should come about some educational psychologist will come up with three different names, for 'Grammar', 'Modern' and 'Technical' are now dirty words! But we shall be back again to 1944! It was ever so. Village schools once consisted of one huge schoolroom. Wisely, as it seemed to most, these were divided into classrooms to facilitate concentration by the children, and possession by the teacher of a given area in which to work in privacy and around which to display visual aids appropriate to the age of the children. Then along came the 'open plan' idea and down came the walls. We were back to the village schoolroom! But never fear! The builders will be in those schools within a decade – up will go the walls again and once more we shall be back again to traditional classrooms.

Thus do the politicians, aided and abetted by the educational psychologists, drive us round in circles like children playing ring a ring o' roses. It's all very jolly, save that we might remember that the rhyme ends 'We all fall down'. It is well to remind ourselves that the Education Act of 1944 was the product of a National Government. Education was not then a football to be kicked around by political parties seeking party goals. It was a social service able to call to its aid the best brains in all the parties. Thus, uninhibited by party political dogmas, the National Government was able to devise a system of education concerned with a single aim – the spiritual, moral, mental and physical welfare of the nation's children. Clearly to assist in the preservation of this balanced programme and to avoid at all costs the rise of a grey uniform system of education which in Germany had shown itself to be so ready an instrument in the hand of the unscrupulous, it further reaffirmed its confidence in the Dual System, by which Church and State had for nearly eighty years been partners in the educational enterprise. Recognising too the varying needs, interests, abilities and skills of the child population, it produced a system of secondary education which, rightly pursued, would ensure for every child equality of opportunity. If and when a new Education Act is deemed to be necessary – a backward look would not be amiss.

3

Earning, Learning and Yearning

Thus in August 1923 I began to earn a living, not first in the solicitors' office, since the offer which Gerald Woollcombe had made to my parents was not open until the end of the year. In the meanwhile an estate agent in Teignmouth advertised a post for which I applied and to which I was appointed after interview. This meant that I became a commuter, catching a train each morning to the seaside resort seven miles distant. Since the train arrived well before office opening hours my love affair with the sea was satisfied daily by an invigorating morning walk along the sea front. That delight and the satisfaction derived from my being able to do a bit of useful study during the short journey each day predisposed me to accept whatever followed in the office. Short though the journey was it was long enough to begin to tackle the elements of Latin and I began to believe that the 'clickety-clank' 'clickety-clank' of the train's progress was genuinely conducive to the learning of conjugations and declensions. 'Amo, amas, amat, amamus, amatis, amant', 'bonus, bone, bonum, boni, bono, bono' – the rhythm of the wheels on the track made it as easy to learn these conjugations and declensions as the corporate recitation of table in the infant and junior school imprinted them indelibly on the mind. The daily morning journey was thus both pleasant and profitable.

The work in the office was interesting too and I had not been there many months before I had more than an insight into the workings of auction sales – which aroused my interest in antiques, inventories, business correspondence, accounting, typing, property descriptions, valuations, insurances, and bewildered people wondering which house to buy! I learnt too about time-keeping for on one particular morning, and one only, when the lure of the sea as I took my morning stroll along the front was particularly captivating, I arrived in the office five minutes late. I was summoned to the big chief's room which was not much larger, but distinctly more impressive, than mine, and there in less than twenty words I was given a lesson for a lifetime: 'This office opens at 9, and that is the time you must arrive, not at 9.05. That's all I have to say.' That

31

was enough, for it was not merely a salutary lesson for the moment but for life. From that moment onwards I became and have ever remained a stickler for punctuality.

The homeward journey each evening was not that of a student learning but of a young business man reading the evening paper, and in particular all the political news which was at that time beginning to feed my interest in national and world affairs. I took these daily journeys in my stride for some time, it never occurring to me that anything untoward or threatening could befall me. But on one of the homeward journeys, as I was immersed in my paper in the corner of a compartment in a corridorless train, the only other occupant, who was a stranger to me, suddenly said: 'You're a good looking boy, come here and talk to me.' I smiled – or did I grin? – at the compliment but ignored the invitation and said nothing. With that he pulled me diagonally across the compartment holding me tightly by the arms and glared at me angrily. For the moment I remained outwardly calm. No one had ever talked to me about the possibility of sexual assault and as for the physical assault on which I assumed he was bent, as I had ignored his invitation, I knew that I should be powerless. (In the school gymnasium I had on only two occasions been pressurised into putting on boxing-gloves and on each I emulated Mohammed Ali only in that part of his performance in which he dances out of harm's way!) After some smooth and flattering words the man began to tamper with my clothing. I reacted quickly and something like a battle of wits and hands ensued for I was still convinced that he was bent on beating me up. After a few desperate minutes I pulled myself clear and retired to my corner untouched but terrified. Never was the journey to Newton Abbot so long as I cowered in my corner, wondering from time to time whether pulling the communication cord would provoke him further or whether he, by protesting his innocence, would land me with the fine which was threatened for improper use of the emergency device. I said not a word about this on reaching my home for I suspected that the reaction of my parents might have been to make me give up the job and wait for something not involving me in a train journey, but I resolved that henceforward I would choose my compartment more carefully and find my safety in numbers. The world, the flesh and the devil had caught up with me and I realised that I was, as it were, on my own. I did feel, however, that I had won the first round!

As I progressed in the office work, and as the experience of meeting people and helping people in a modest way increased day by day, I began to know what is now referred to as job satisfaction. That, added to the joy of being able to contribute a little to the family income – I remember the pride with which I handed my parents my first pay cheque – yielded a return of personal happiness far exceeding anything I had experienced at school. The self-instruction in Latin was going on well too and when, prompted I believe by Gerald Woollcombe, one of the clergy offered to correct exercises for me and to help me with the rudiments of Greek, I felt that at last I was on the way to the fulfilment of my aspirations. The change of course from school to the world of work and the daily journeys to Teignmouth seemed in every way to confirm the rightness of my decision. And how I enjoyed my daily rendezvous vith the sea!

From early childhood I had seen the sea as something thrilling and invigorating, mysterious and majestic, and Teignmouth with its wide promenade, its busy port, its fish quay and its firm clean sands offered all I needed for the midday break from the office routine. Even on wet days, as I discovered, it was not difficult to engage an old salt, resting in his boathouse, in lively conversation about the history and mythology of the place. The French had plundered it more than once in its history I was told; the Devon granite used for London Bridge was shipped from its quay. But to hear an old Devon fisherman tell the story of the two rocks that can be seen from the shore, and which are known locally as the Parson and the Clerk, is an experience to treasure. So far as I can remember it 'the story goes like this. Years and years back, the Parson wi' 'is Clerk decides to go round that 'eadland, see, for collection, or summat like that. Well, the Devil stopped 'em one day and they were both drowned, and so as no more parsons should try it on, 'e turned 'em into rocks and there they be now!'

But Teignmouth had another port of call which used to attract me for part of the midday break and that was St. Michael's Church. It was always open, as indeed most churches were until vandalism and robberies forced a change of custom, and it offered a most wonderful atmosphere which even to a boy – and I still reckoned myself that in a day when one did not come of age until one's 21st birthday – could say: 'This is none other than the House of God and this is the gate of Heaven.' The Vicar of St. Michael's at the time was one Edward Gotto. I did not meet him and heard him preach but once and that to a gathering of the Guild of the Servants of the Sanctuary. The text of his sermon was, 'Who shall ascend into the hill of the Lord, even he that hath clean hands and a pure heart.' Had I heard that sermon before the train encounter I should have been more alert to my attacker's attentions and intentions.

These quiet moments in St. Michael's Church, and the meditations by the sea, answering as it ever does every human mood, were a rich bonus in my first months in the world of work. But by the end of the year a change was in sight as the vacancy in the Newton Abbot solicitors' office promised to me by Gerald Woollcombe was near at hand. I had been about six or seven months in the Teignmouth office and was so happy there and feeling so fulfilled that I would gladly have stayed longer. Three factors emboldened me to give in my notice: the initial kindness of the Woollcombes in their advice and proffered help, the higher salary which I should be receiving there and the fact that none of it would be expended in railway fares. But frankly it was with a heavy heart that I approached the change which came in February 1924. During the last mid-day break in Teignmouth there was a brief visit to St. Michael's and a walk along the promenade. The wooded hills which shielded the little town from northern blasts were mantled in light snow; the day was clear and bright and the sea was blue – the sort of day to bring to mind lines of Keats, who himself had lived in Teignmouth with his brother Tom, lines which I had learnt at school and which stand scored in the Palgrave's *Golden Treasury* which is one of the two school books which I still have:

> *The moving waters at their priest-like task,*
> *   Of pure ablution round earth's human shores,*
> *Or gazing on the new soft-fallen mask*
> *   Of snow upon the mountains and the moors.*

The ordeal of having to give in my notice had been over and done with for a fortnight and I had merely to bid the big chief goodbye. Even this I did with trepidation for I feared that I was letting him down. How thankful I was when he received me kindly and how surprised I was to discover that he was sufficiently human to be able to laugh. I had had only two close encounters with him before that day – the first in which he interviewed me for the job, the second when he remonstrated with me for being five minutes late. For the most part communication between us was by phone – he in his small corner and I in mine! But his parting word to the effect that he would speak well of me if at any time I wanted a reference to enter college, sent me on my way rejoicing.

The solicitors' office which I entered for the first time on the following Monday, was a much bigger affair. In Teignmouth there were but four of us including the boss. In Newton Abbot there were four partners in the very old-established firm and about ten or a dozen typists, clerks and accountants. The job itself was different too. I was in the enquiry office and that meant meeting all who called – simple people who poured out their problems over the counter, as though one was able to come up with a ready answer, frightened people who seemed genuinely surprised at any suggestion that they should consult one of the partners in the firm; angry people who had been, or imagined that they had been, victims of some injustice; worried people seeking out the Clerk to the Justices; and, of course, a continuing stream of people with appointments about property purchases, tenancy agreements, wills, litigations, copyright infringements and a host of other intriguing things which fill a solicitor's life. Correspondence about all those things passed through the enquiry office and it was indeed one of my jobs to copy the letters and make them up for the post. I had been counselled about the need for strict confidentiality but clearly I could not but help gathering to myself a store of legal knowledge touching human problems of many kinds. I have known more than one simple soul bring a letter back to the office and ask for it to be explained in words he or she could understand. I thought on occasion that what I was doing in this office could not have any ultimate bearing on the work which I hoped one day to be doing. I was wrong. Many times in the course of my ministry as a parish priest I was asked by some aged and sick parishioner whether a home-made will was 'all right'! I regarded the question as not an improper one to address to a priest, since the Book of Common Prayer enjoins him 'Often to put men in remembrance to take order for the settling of their temporal estates' and to 'Admonish a man to make his Will.' The answer to the question: 'Is this all right for my Will?' was usually that it was not a valid document. Since the person asking was frequently as poor as he or she was unlettered, and positively frightened of solicitors, on occasion I drafted a will in a sick room and arranged for its proper execution. As an archdeacon and bishop I have sometimes staggered a meeting by trotting out a bit of legal knowledge which I gained from that lawyers' office. In fact I found the whole experience there so enlightening and so demanding that once more I was happy and satisfied with this background to the pursuit of the goal towards which I was moving.

My colleagues in the office knew of my intentions as did the chiefs in the firm and whilst there was from time to time some gentle leg-pulling all of them were cordial, kind and understanding. Of the hundreds of people who passed through the office in the course of my two and a half years there, I can remember many, including clergy who came from time to time with troubles about something of which I knew nothing then but was to know a lot about in years to come. It was called Glebe! All of them were seeking the help of Gerald Woollcombe and all of them received it, for in ecclesiastical as in civil law, he seemed to know all the answers to all their questions. Dare I add, too, that I noticed that accounts to clergy for services rendered were frequently not rendered at all, and it was not long before I was to learn that doctors too had a habit of 'forgetting' to send bills to the clergy .

The transfer from Teignmouth to Newton Abbot as a place of work had many advantages for it meant that I saw a good deal more of my home, had more leisure for study and more opportunities to take part in the week-day parochial activities. Dr. James McIntyre, who was the priest-in-charge of St. Paul's Church and subsequently a Canon Residentiary of Gloucester, received me once a week and was of great help in my studies both classical and Biblical. Such progress did I make under his guidance that I began to think that there might be no academic impediment to my proceeding to a theological college, though I could still see overhead a very black financial cloud and, despite the reassuring words of Cowper's hymn, I could see no way in which it could break with blessings on my head. But I pressed on.

Further opportunities of testing were afforded by the Rector of Wolborough asking me to conduct services from time to time. None was more demanding, and as it proved more frightening, than a service he had asked me to conduct in what was then known as the Workhouse, the chaplaincy work which was in the hands of the Wolborough clergy. I went there but once, again owing to illness among the staff, and found the little chapel crammed with inmates – geriatrics most of them, some crippled, some senile, some merely old and feeble. The Rector had warned me that I should talk to them as I would to children and certainly when I saw my congregation I realised the wisdom of this advice. The occasion was memorable, first because the male nurse in charge of the chapel, if that was indeed his status, addressed me as 'Sir' each time he spoke to me, and this to a boy of seventeen plus, seemed at least a bit extravagant. Maybe, however, that was the sense of humour I discovered he had when he said, just before we went into the chapel, 'Don't you expect that man at the harmonium to play the hymns you give out sir. He won't know you're there and he'll play what he likes. If you give me the list I'll stand by him and make him play the right ones.' I did and the organist played them and very efficiently. The singing was hearty if raucous; the saying loud and clear; the Lord's Prayer in particular was offered as children would have offered it. I was beginning to warm to these poor folk and to love them for Christ's sake.

The moment came for the sermon. There was no pulpit and as the chapel was crammed to the doors the tide of people swept up to the entrance of the little sanctuary in which I stood. Only a yard separated me from the front row of chairs. I had decided to tell the old folk one of the parables and to draw a few simple lessons from it. I had been speaking for only a few moments when suddenly a man shouted out loudly and incoherently. Immediately in front of me, and but a yard away, two legs shot up in the air and the man collapsed at my feet foaming at the mouth. The incident left me speechless but it seemed that I was the only one to be concerned. The organiser of the organist walked over very calmly and, gripping the man by the shoulders, lifted him from the ground, planted him firmly on his chair and said, 'He'll be all right now sir, carry on.' I was not particularly reassured by that, but making sure from then on that I was three yards away instead of one, I continued the address. I took comfort subsequently in the recollection that St. Philip had precisely the same experience when he preached a sermon in the city of Samaria, but I suspect that he had had far more practice in the art than I had had and he would have taken this in his stride! However, that was my first sermon to an adult congregation and whatever it may have lacked in substance or orthodoxy it could never be described as having created no impact.

There was, however, yet another surprise awaiting me that afternoon. I stood at the door of the chapel to shake hands with all the old people as they left and it was obvious that they appreciated the gesture, so much so that one old lady refused my hand but threw her arms around me exclaiming, 'Isn't he lovely? We'll keep him here.' So tightly was she embracing me in her arms that I thought for a moment I should have to call the male nurse to my assistance, not this time as a nurse, but as a referee. He did in fact come over but before he could say 'Break!' she was pushed away by an old gentleman who followed her and was impatient to shake my hand.

Such experiences were rare but I was from time to time asked to help in the mission churches and in one of them, for a long period, I played the harmonium for its Sunday Evensong and heard the congregation and the little choir singing the canticles to chants which I had composed. The priest-in-charge of St. Leonard's drew my brothers and myself into the organisation of the children's and young people's work in that part of the parish and in particular asked us to be responsible for the choirboys' social activities, which included the running of a football team of which my elder brother became trainer and I became manager and secretary. As at that time my younger brother was captain of the team it became known in the district not merely by its true name – 'St. Leonard's Choirboys' – but also by the alias 'Bulley Boys United'. I don't think we were ever top of the schoolboys' or choirboys' league and I was certainly never a Bill Shankly or Brian Clough. What I do know is that the parents of the boys concerned were as grateful as were the boys themselves for the interest we took in them and that, at the very least, the boys learnt that the Church which expected much of them in service was ready also to give much to them in friendship and enjoyment.

Newton Abbot possessed a huge Market Hall and I attended some memorable meetings in it – for the most part political but occasionally religious. One such was addressed by the famous war-time padre Woodbine Willie – G. A. Studdert Kennedy. I had read a number of his books and been captivated by his devotional poems, and it was therefore with much excitement that I got hold of tickets for the meeting. He was a diminutive man, thin and as I recall rather haggard looking. He sat on a table on the platform, swinging his legs as he addressed a vast assembly of people of all ages, and riveting the attention of every one. He thundered out his message much as Amos and John Baptist must have done and there could have been few who were not stirred by it to think again about the person of Christ. Flashes of humour were met with peals of laughter but each led to a serious point which was pressed home pungently. 'David said in his haste that all men are liars,' he shouted, and added, 'and if he had had more time he would have said it at his leisure.' When the laughter subsided there came the point of the reference, as he developed his theme of God's holiness and man's perfidy, of God's answer and man's response. I went away from that hall strengthened and elated, more than ever determined to press on 'looking unto Jesus the author and finisher of our faith'. But I did something else. I went next day to Newton Abbot's well stocked library and took out two more of Studdert Kennedy's books. I know, of course, that he was no theologian in the way that academics measure theology, but I know too that he was a man of God – a pastor, an evangelist, a priest, a prophet – who in his day spoke fearlessly, decisively and with burning sincerity for His Lord and Master. That he won many to The Way there can be no doubt.

In that same year there was a General Election and at seventeen plus I was beginning to become politically aware, though I fancy that if anyone had suggested that within a year I should be qualified let alone entitled to vote I should have regarded the suggestion as ludicrous in the extreme. I still do. Voting in General Elections was something for adults only and adulthood began at twenty-one. However, I was sufficiently interested to attend the meetings of the candidates in that year as a learner and since what was still called the wireless had made no general impact up to then, the appearance of the candidates at public meetings provided the only opportunity the electorate had to hear them. Thus the meetings were invariably well attended and in my eagerness to discover what the parties stood for I was determined to hear each candidate even though my grandfather, the political animal in the family, assured me that the Liberal candidate would talk nonsense and the Labour candidate, the like of whom the Totnes constituency had never before known, would outstrip him in the exercise. I can remember nothing of the speeches of the Conservative candidate, Major S. E. Harvey, or of his Liberal opponent, Mr. P. F. Rousell, but the Labour candidate's speech and presence stick in my memory. She was one Katie Spurrell, a young school teacher with a mop of red hair, a voice which, in days before amplifying apparatus was available, was heard clearly through the large hall and an emotional appeal which brought tears to the eyes of the women. She would have had no truck with today's Labour left for she was clearly one of the old fashioned Christian socialists the like of whom are, sadly enough, very much in the minority in the party today where the strident tones of neo-Marxism too often drown the authentic note of Christian Socialism.

Katie was a commanding little figure and in those days something of a phenomenon, for the House of Commons had not, up to 1924, admitted many women into the Chamber and here was one who dared to try to break through those iron gates of Parliament Square via one of the safest conservative constituencies in the land. She failed in her attempt and not even the so nicknamed 'flapper vote', introduced in 1928, was enough to secure her election in 1929. Her speech was memorable to me for its frequent Biblical references and as her climax was, in effect, the Lord's Prayer, what she said clearly left me wondering whether I ought to abandon family loyalties and swear allegiance to the Labour party. Had I been eligible to vote at that time doubtless I should have voted for Katie but it would have been a vote for a person not a party, and of the heart rather than the mind. From what she said it appeared to me that the social gospel within the total Gospel of Christ was to be found in the manifesto of the Labour Party and in no other. I think I went on believing that for a time as Christian adolescents might well do, but gradually the illusion faded and I had to come to the conclusion that the Labour Party had no overriding claim to be the party for Christians, and that both in the Conservative and Liberal parties Christians could find policies wholly in tune with Christian purpose. Equally in all three parties they could find aspects of political policy with which they could not be happy. I remain so convinced and thus I hold that whilst the Church must concern itself always and actively with the fundamental dogmas of political purpose, it is not wise for the Church's leaders to ally themselves publicly with any one party since each must inevitably come under the Church's judgement from time to time, and each must from time to time win the Church's approval and suffer the Church's rebukes.

In articles I have written in the magazines in my various parishes and in the *Bishop's Comments* throughout my time at Carlisle I felt free to praise and criticise each of the parties as they appeared to me to deserve. This does not mean that I am incapable of exercising my ballot box rights intelligently when the moment comes. It means that, looking at the political scene through Christian spectacles, one judges policies not from the particular party think-tank from which they come, but from their merits or demerits in the light of Christian teaching and Christian purpose. The Church cannot give to any one party a blank cheque enabling it to fill in whatever policies it cares to promote. It must leave itself open to offer sanction to capitalism as to socialism - each has its acceptable as well as its unacceptable face – and to a combination of both if such affords the highest hopes for the greatest number in social justice and human welfare. But the Church can set its face against anything and everything, from whatever party, which diminishes the individual, and thus it must be unequivocal in its disapproval of every form of despotism whether from the far right or from the far left. A demonic evil resides both in Fascism and Marxism and no thinking Christian can lend his support to either. Each diminishes the individual to exalt the State, each denies personal and political liberty, each devalues Man, each flagrantly denies human rights. They are seen to be poles apart; in fact they are incredibly alike.

In theory Fascism leaves room for the Church and for the exercise of Christian Faith. In practice it so flagrantly denies all that the Faith stands for in its conception of the infinite worth of every individual, regardless of colour or race, that the apparent toleration of the Church is but a subtle and dangerous ploy. In the Christian book the individual is not merely an infinitesimal and transitory element in the social organisation who can be kicked around with impunity or eliminated at the State's behest. He or she is the child of God, an immortal soul, a unique person, precious and dear to the Creator, and as such holds a charter of human rights, sacred and inalienable – and all this whatever race, colour or creed. Thus the individual who says 'Yes' to God must say 'No' to Fascism.

But Marxist Communism, in its 'glass house', is in no position to throw stones at Fascism. It too demeans the individual and denies human rights, and the application of its philosophy, faithfully adhered to by Engels, Lenin, Stalin, Krushchev, and Brezhnev, demonstrates that whilst it talks of freedom it denies it to anyone and everyone who by its judgement, which may not be questioned, is dubbed an enemy of the State. If a man, foolish enough to believe in God, dares to set God above Caesar, then the State either writes him off as a lunatic and throws him into what it calls a psychiatric hospital or banishes him into a 'labour camp' or into exile. The recurring instances of denial of political and personal liberty, which we find so ghastly and repellent, are in fact the stock-in-trade of the Marxist Communist faith with its basis of materialistic atheism, its denial of the category of the supernatural and of the soul of man. Thus the Marxist sees the destruction of Christianity as of the essence of its ideology and to that end Lenin has told the world that Marxists should and would 'practise everything possible – tricks, guiles, illegal methods and be ready to suppress and conceal what is the truth'. Furthermore Brezhnev too has gone out of his way to make it crystal clear that his desire to pursue a policy of peaceful coexistence must not be interpreted to signify any departure from the ideological struggle. Thus, attractive though some aspects of the Communist social ethic may be – 'from each according to his gifts: to each according to his needs' – Marxism clearly offers no through road to their realisation. The love of neighbour which this demands, and which alone can overcome the greed and envy and selfishness and indiscipline that wreck societies, cannot be imposed by statute. It derives only from the true love of God. The conversion of individuals to faith in the Living God is therefore the decisive factor in the human dilemma. Thus, as in the case of Fascism, so in the case of Marxism, he who says 'Yes' to God must say 'No' to Marxism.

When our Lord bade his followers to be as harmless as doves he warned them to be as wise as serpents. Serpents hiss and doves coo. Confronted by Fascism and Marxist Communism, Christians cannot but hiss – Auschwitz, Buchenwald, Czechoslovakia, Hungary, Siberia – but confronted by Fascists and Marxists they must learn to coo, for Christian love has been known to convert where rational argument fails.

The good Christian Socialist, Katie Spurrell, Prospective Member of Parliament for the Totnes Constituency of Devon in 1924 and 1929, did a good deal of hissing and cooing in her impassioned appeal to the electorate. But Totnes persisted and persists in its allegiance to the Conservative cause. By the time the 1929 election came I was no longer in Newton Abbot, but the memory of my 1924 excursion into politics remains with me and at the time prompted me to read a good deal about the British Constitution and British social history beyond the doings of the Whigs and Tories to which I had been introduced at school. Indeed I became one of the Public Library's most regular customers both in its reading room and in its borrowing department, and although political reading was *ad hoc* and a transitory phase it stirred in me an interest in political and social concern which the years and the times have kept very much alive.

I mentioned earlier that the priest who did most to guide me along the path towards the realisation of my vocation to the priesthood was Kenneth Campbell Bickerdike whose ministry in the parish was centred upon St. Leonard's Church. Though of a somewhat nervous temperament – he had been severely wounded in the war – he soon endeared himself to the people and proved to be a priest with a singular ability to evoke a response from young people in particular. There were no mixed youth fellowships in those days, which was unfortunate, but the young folk at St. Leonard's contrived other ways of meeting within the fellowship of the Church's life. Certainly they were to be seen together at Evensong on Sundays – a strong phalanx in the gallery – but they worked together in organising socials, dances and what would now be regarded as 'Good Old Days' variety entertainments. The adults contributed more sedate opportunities for fraternisation such as whist drives (then very popular), tea parties, and even in those days, which some look back upon as hard and harsh, there was active concern for the sick, the aged and the housebound.

Some of the initiative for the work among the young people began to fall upon me but whether it was for the purpose of raising money for the church or, more frequently, to provide opportunities for the congregation, young and old, to meet together for fun and fellowship, I was happy to be used in this way. It may be too that some, outside the active life of the Church, were drawn within it when they saw how these Christians loved one another. I can indeed recall some such particularly among the young, but these social ventures were not seen as *ersatz* evangelism. Certainly the clergy took a lively part in them and were afforded the opportunity of meeting many people through them, but evangelism proper was not neglected and there were from time to time concentrated evangelistic efforts and parochial missions by which the faithful were strengthened, the wanderers were drawn back and the lost were found (I recall that prior to one of these, and without consulting the clergy, I sat down one evening and wrote letters to all the religious communities in the land asking them to remember in their prayers our mission throughout its duration).

I believe that a revival of such teaching missions could be a means of doing now what they did then – refreshing the faithful, awakening the apathetic, enlightening the doubter and answering the unbeliever. But it takes courage for the Church to turn its attention away from the easy peripheral tasks which have consumed so much of its time, energy and thought in recent years, to the hardest tasks of all – Christian education and Christian evangelism. Before us, as before St. Paul at Ephesus, there is today an open door of opportunity, but for us, as for him, 'there are many adversaries'. In my youth the greatest of these was possibly apathy. Now however there is opposition, overt and sinister, and it is time that the Church turned towards the essentials – to education and evangelism. New translations of the scriptures, and new forms of liturgical worship, developments in lay participation and discussions about re-union may be of a real help to those who are already 'looking unto Jesus' but they make no impact upon those who are crying 'Crucify him' – and there are today more in the second group than the first.

There never has been a perfect parish but the parish of Wolborough in which I was brought up, scattered as it was over the town and with five different centres of worship, was alert and alive spiritually and socially, and I look back in gratitude for the instruction in the Christian faith and in the purpose of the Church which I received from its clergy. The four individuals who were the greatest help to me were Claude Russell, Richard Hussey, James McIntyre and Kenneth Bickerdike; and it was the last who set me most decisively on the path to ordination. The night before he left the parish for a London vicariate he invited me to his home for what proved to be a memorable meeting He advised me first to set aside the plan I had been nursing for some years – that of going to a theological college, and to aim instead for admission to a university. And he produced there and then regulations for admission to Oxford, Cambridge and Durham. No one, clerical or lay, had ever made such a suggestion and although it had entered into my own head from time to time it had been as quickly dismissed as possibly academically beyond me and certainly financially out of the question. He overruled the first of these objections summarily and assured me that there were ways by which the second difficulty could be overcome too. He was leaving for London on the following day and giving me his blessing, he promised that he would keep in touch with me, adding, 'You must not go to the Altar offering one talent if you have been endowed with five.' Maybe he was right about academic talents, but I still knew that in terms of hard cash I had but one.

As the months slipped by I became more and more immersed in parochial activities and I began to realise that these were consuming much time which otherwise would have been devoted to study. A crisis was looming ahead; I must withdraw from many of these activities or progress in studies would be gravely impeded. A timely letter from Kenneth Bickerdike, an answer to prayer indeed, provided the answer. He had confirmed his view that I could get from a charitable source some limited financial help towards a university course and was persuaded that I should, without delay, complete my qualifications for university entrance. He further recognised that I had become so totally involved in the activities of the parish that he advised that it would be wise for me to seek some employment which would give me a break from Newton Abbot and all my contacts there. I had sufficient qualification by that time, according to him, to teach in a Preparatory School, and a resident post in such a school would help in many ways, giving time for study without distractions, opportunity to save some money, and experience in teaching that would serve me in good stead ultimately in the ministry.

With his help, and references from Gerald Wollcombe and the Rector, I was appointed to a Junior Master's post in a small school in Kent and thus in the summer of 1926 was making preparations for leaving home for the first time in my life. I was then nineteen. My elder brother had recently abandoned the law for the teaching profession; my younger brother was away in naval training and my departure would complete the dissipation of the young Bulleys from the scene of their upbringing. My parents did not look forward to the break but saw the wisdom of it and as, by this time, they were as anxious as I was that I should try for a university course, they did all they could to help me attain that immediate end. In fact, reducing the home from six to three in number would reduce the cost of running it, particularly as the three departing were the biggest consumers. We all saw this as easing the pressure on the family income and relieving some of the strain which was beginning to show in my father's health. Nevertheless the disintegration of a family which had been so closely knit, and whose members had not been apart from each other for more than a day since its inception, was a traumatic experience for all, and not least to my parents and my sister whose brothers had been her closest companions and playmates through the years. But the day had to come, and in mid-September the young country lad of nineteen plus set out for London for the first time in his life and arrived in the capital bewildered and somewhat frightened. Within an hour my wallet had been stolen, for no-one had warned me that you don't hang your jacket up whilst you wash your hands in a London railway cloakroom! Scotland Yard, which I was only too eager to visit, came to my rescue and provided me with enough money to complete the journey to Sevenoaks in Kent to begin the new chapter in my life.

I was welcomed at the school in Sevenoaks by the jovial headmaster and his wife and sensed immediately that this was to be another happy chapter which, if my hopes were realised, would lead me to university. The boarders did not arrive until the following day and there was thus ample opportunity to study my schedule of duties and my timetable, neither of which daunted me. The former embraced those of a housemaster and the latter the teaching of boys of eleven and twelve in subjects leading to their Common Entrance examination – including, I noticed with interest and particular satisfaction, their Latin. There were two other resident teachers – one who struck me from the outset as a rather strange old gentleman and the other a lively lady whom I came to admire immensely for her personality and teaching ability.

The headmaster of this school suffered a good deal of pain as a result of his war service and he was, in consequence, rather unpredictable – sometimes bubbling over with life and good humour, sometimes in the depths of gloom and despair, sometimes irritable and irascible. He was an excellent teacher, widely read and keen for his school to grow but in his contacts with parents he was never over-endowed with tact. To a naval commander complaining of his son's slow progress, he exclaimed 'The trouble is, Commander, your son, to put it bluntly, is thick.' The parental reaction was immediate, 'Well he's been here for three years so whose fault is that?' The commander did not know his man until he received the answer to his question: 'That surely, is between you and your wife. Ask her.' Nor were the headmaster's comments on the terminal reports always as tactful as they might have been. 'Wasting my time and your money' was succinct and probably true but proved to be wholly unacceptable to a proud parent. This tactlessness, or as he called it frankness, was hardly conducive to the growth of the school which was unfortunate for it was essentially a good establishment, with sound teaching and a happy atmosphere to which the headmaster's hard-working and able wife contributed richly. The school had indeed as many boarders as it could accommodate but the steady intake of day boys in an area which housed so many London commuters could have been stepped up considerably.

I found in teaching something deeply satisfying and rewarding. I was handing on the torch of knowledge which had been handed to me; I was opening rooms for exploration and windows for views, and the boys whom I was teaching, surely at the most eager age, were lively and responsive. Of course they varied widely in ability, but in the small classes which we had, there was opportunity to take account of the tardy without impeding the swift. Many of the boys were mischievous imps but this displayed itself in the dormitories, playrooms and playground rather than in the classrooms where they seemed to need little goading and responded quickly to encouragement. Most of them moved on at thirteen to Public Schools – Tonbridge, Monkton Combe and Westminster seemed to be the most favoured – and for the few not up to that standard provision was made for continuing education. Having to accompany cricket and football teams from time to time to other schools in the district I was introduced to the Garden of England to my great delight. Sevenoaks itself with its half timbered façades, its tile-hung walls, its ancient parish church and most of all its great house of Knole is a fascinating town with eight hundred years of history behind it. Knole House, once the residence of the Archbishop of Canterbury and subsequently a Royal Palace and the seat of the Sackvilles, is now owned by the National Trust. Within it there are as many rooms as there are days in the year, unless that year be a leap year. It is set in a vast park of the same name and this, with its trees and flowers and roaming deer, was the venue for the boarders', and therefore my, daily walk before lessons began.

I had planned a two-year stint at the school believing that in my spare time there – and as it transpired I had a generous share of free periods – I should be able to complete the necessary qualifications for university entrance and at the same time husband my financial resources to make the course possible. With Kennth Bickerdike's help and following a successful interview in London, I had by now been assured of a grant from the Ordination Candidates' Exhibition Fund. Although this grant, even augmented by my own savings and by any help which I could get from home, would not be sufficient to make possible entry to Oxford or Cambridge, I was assured that it would see me through Durham University where the fees were lower and the extras less demanding. The first year at the school had been abundantly happy and, in addition to the rich experience of teaching, I had made sufficient progress in my Greek studies to enable me to look forward with confidence to the final hurdle to be surmounted for university entrance in October 1928. But that was not to be.

The last day of the school summer term 1927 arrived and I was eager and ready for the homeward journey and for the opportunity of sharing with my parents the exhilaration which I felt at the end of a happy and successful year. There was but an hour of the term left before cars would be pulling into the drive to collect boarders, and day boys would be turning their backs on the school for seven or eight weeks. There was a restiveness far from conducive to serious work and I had invented a word game to fill the last hour. The excitement of competition and laughter was broken by one of the domestic staff arriving with a telegram for me. It read: 'Father died suddenly early this morning. Come home quickly.' I left the classroom, retired to my bedroom and sobbed bitterly. Just when the sun was in highest heaven and the way before me was clear the whole scene was shadowed by an impenetrable cloud of sorrow. The one to whom I owed so much in affection and love, in precept and example, in encouragement and support, was snatched from me by a premature death, and that before I would repay but a fraction of a massive debt. There in my attic bedroom, and through tears I could not restrain, I prayed – for my mother, my sister and my brothers and, hurled as I was from an exhilarating mountain in life to the valley of the shadow of death, I prayed for myself – for courage, for understanding and for light. Within an hour I was on my way home though the journey was never so long. At Newton Abbot station I was met by my elder brother who told me that my father had collapsed of a coronary in the street and had died instantly. An Officer of the Salvation Army, walking behind him at the time, was the first to minister to him. Distraught though she was my mother seemed to be braver than her children around her and to be fortified at that moment by an indomitable courage and faith.

Within the fellowship of the Church there were many to hold us up but I think that it was the character of the funeral service which we found to be of the greatest help. The clergy of the parish and the choir of St. Leonard's led a great congregation in a service in which the note of Easter was uppermost. Embracing as it did my father's favourite hymn, 'When all Thy mercies', the whole scene is very frequently brought to the forefront of my mind since Addison's hymn remains so firm a favourite.

By the end of the holiday it was apparent that my father's death would further delay my progress towards ordination. The breadwinner of the family was but fifty-two when he died and it was up to the three sons to devise means to keep the home together even though they were not themselves at home save for holidays. Thus I returned to Sevenoaks aware that my second year at the school would not be my last as I had intended, and that entrance to a university would be further delayed for at least another year.

Meanwhile I was to discover that the strange old gentleman who was my senior on the resident staff had decided not to return and whilst no one shed any tears about that, his departure left me as the only resident master. Since the headmaster had decided to increase his visiting staff most of the house duties would be falling on me. I was however to be rewarded with a rise in pay and my financial outlook was thus immediately improved both in respect of my obligations to the home and relative to my savings. October 1929 was now firmly inscribed in my mind as the new date for the university course to begin.

Heavier responsibilities fell on my shoulders from time to time by reason of the indisposition of the headmaster, but nothing seemed burdensome and always there was strength and wisdom to match the hour. Hard by the school was St. John's Church – a famed Anglo-Catholic centre – and I was able on Sundays and frequently on week-days, to steal out of the school before the boys were awake to receive the Sacrament there. The church was one of those rare churches where there seemed always to be someone at prayer and where the old verger, ever in attendance and a Simeon indeed, was so devout a holder of that office that his every silent movement conveyed to the visitor that this was none other than the house of God. He was a man upon whom was the Holy Ghost. His voice was long past its peak of musical excellence, but the fervour with which he sang was so obviously sincere, whether it vas 'Sweet Sacrament Divine' or 'O my Saviour lifted', that the choirs of angels to which he joined his songs could not but be oblivious to a few cracked notes.

On alternate Sundays it was my lot to take the boarders to Matins at Seal Church some two miles from Sevenoaks – St. John's being deemed to be 'too advanced' for them. This 'law of the Medes and Persians' had long been a sacred enactment which 'altereth not', until one very wet Sunday I flouted it and took the boys to St. John's High Mass. They were known subsequently to express the hope on a Saturday night that the following day would be wet at least in the morning. The music, the colour, the incense, the ceremonial were all such as to capture their attention and to kindle innumerable questions on the return walk to school. The assistant priest at the church – one Donald Pharoah, subsequently Rural Dean of Canterbury – became a confidant and firm friend of mine and we stretched our minds in theological and political discussions during occasional walks on summer evenings in the beautiful and spacious grounds of Knole House.

The work, play and atmosphere of the school were wholly congenial and I found myself as happy and even more fulfilled than I had been in the estate agents' and solicitors' offices. Thus occasional bursts of impatience for ordination that stemmed from a yearning which nothing could quench, were fleeting. I sensed in a way I had not done before that the work I was doing was in fact itself a training for that which I hoped to be doing in the years ahead. To observe the growing mind of a child, his reaction to newly-acquired knowledge, his enthusiasm for the attainment of new skills in the classroom and on the playing fields – all these are chapters in growth which I found to be more fascinating to watch than a novel was to read. Among those whom I was teaching were boys with lively little minds – receptive, creative, sparkling with imagination, and so inquisitive in their endless questions that they kept their teacher on his toes. The opportunities for pastoral care and for instruction in the things of God, particularly among the boarders, were ever present. To see the Christian faith growing in the mind and heart of a child, to answer his questions about the being of God and the words of Our Lord, to hear him say in effect 'Teach me to pray', were all opportunities to be grasped and experiences to be treasured. I remember many such, but perhaps none more vividly than when a boy whose conscience had been awakened by his night prayers, appeared at my study door, clad in pyjamas, to own up to a grave misdemeanour which he had spent the day stoutly denying. 'I had to own up sir, my prayers made me.' That was his way of saying that he had had a charismatic experience which is by no means the exotic phenomenon which some imagine it to be. The Holy Spirit, convincing him of sin, had driven him to own up and to unburden his conscience. One other occasion which lives with me was my breaking to a boy the tragic news of the death of his father and being drawn so completely into his sorrow as he threw his arms around 'sir' for comfort. Such moments could not but make me feel that I was in the right place at the right time. The yearning for the full-time ministry became ever more compelling, though there was a growing feeling that it had begun.

Just before the second term of my third year at the school I was interviewed by the Principal of St. Chad's College, Durham University (Dr. S. R. P. Moulsdale) in response to my application for admission to that college in the following October. The interview was everything I expected it not to be. It took place not in Durham but in a London hotel; it was very informal; it posed questions quite other than those I had anticipated and raised few of those for which I was prepared. But I warmed immediately to this jovial priest who was obviously so proud of his college and so completely dedicated to his work. There and then he accepted me for admission in the following October provided that I passed in the Greek paper which I had just taken. I returned to Sevenoaks that term with a heart full of joy, a breast full of hope and a case full of books which the Principal had counselled me to study by way of preparation. I cannot say that up to then I had never heard of Plato for he was not a gentleman with whose works I was at all acquainted. His *Republic* was however in the bag and since the Principal and Plato seemed to be such intimate friends I deemed it prudent at the very least to come to terms with him without delay. For me at that moment life was balm indeed. There was however still one fly in the ointment and that was shaped thus: £. Somehow or other not even the bland dictum of Plato himself that 'Nothing in the affairs of men is worth worrying about' was sufficient to swat that fly.

I recall that term particularly vividly since an epidemic of measles or some such obnoxious children's disease did me a rich service. The school closed for a short time thus giving me the opportunity which the two previous very busy years of school duties and private study had precluded, of seeing something of the Kent countryside farther afield than the immediate environs of Sevenoaks. These excursions were facilitated by the generosity of the headmaster in allowing me the use of what he described as his car when all was well with it, but impatiently dismissed as 'that car of my wife's' when, as frequently, it was temperamental. Nevertheless it behaved well in my hands and enabled me to see much of the woods, the hills and the valleys which surrounded the eight-hundred year old town.

Nothing, however, was more memorable than my first visit to Canterbury Cathedral, epic in stone of so much of our national history. To stand in its majestic nave, the pilgrim path of thousands who in years past made their way to the Shrine of St. Thomas, is to stand in a graceful forest of piers, and to reach the point where four such support the central tower is to stand on the spot which doubtless those pilgrims regarded as the entrance to their Holy of Holies. Augustine, Lanfranc, Arundel, Langton, Anselm, Cranmer, Laud – all these are names from the history books of men who come alive as one wanders and ponders in this great Church of Christ. But the name and the life and the death which capture the child in his history lessons, the artist at his canvas, the poet in his vision and the churchman at his prayers is that of

Becket, who in a day when religion and politics were inextricably intertwined, and archbishops were caught up in both, decided that he could be 'the King's no more' and was mown down by the King's men in the north transept of his own Cathedral. That was a murder which initiated a debate which still persists and ever will. The things which are Caesar's and the things which are God's have each to be taken into account in the Christian's dual citizenship, but when the demands of Caesar run contrary to the demands of God the Christian must take his stand. When Becket retracted his signature of the Constitutions of Clarendon on the refusal of the Pope to countenance them he believed that 'Caesar' was demanding something which was God's. By that belief he stood and for that belief he paid wih his life − here on this very spot. No wonder that poets and playwrights have seen in this tragedy the substance of high drama, historical and topical. Tennyson expressed it finely:

> *And all my doubts I fling from thee like dust*
> *And all the wisdom of the Chancellor,*
> *And all the heaped experiences of life*
> *I cast upon the side of Canterbury,*
> *Our Holy Mother Canterbury, who sits*
> *With tattered robes.*

So I wandered around this great Cathedral Church − its chapels, its transepts and towers, its strange little stairways, its choir and aisles and last of all into its crypt where a guide ran through the history of England with stories of archbishops, of scholars, of monarchs and saints, and of the French Huguenots who, under patronage of Queen Elizabeth the First, set up their silk-weaving looms among the squat Norman pillars. Inevitably the guide came to the story of Becket, of the King's vigil at the tomb, of his confession, of his lashing, of his absolution and amendment. The picture which Edith Wheeler had painted in the classroom of Newton Abbot Grammar School ten years before had suddenly come to life!

The summer term began with the school building garlanded as always with laburnum, its racemes of yellow flowers gracefully draping the entrance gates. There was swimming; there was cricket and that in the the town which boasts one of the oldest cricket pitches in the country − The Vine. But, as ever in this term, there were exams which somehow or other the boys accepted with a happy abandon that I had never been able to emulate. Among the newly enrolled was a little menace of eight years whose ingenuity to dislocate the whole establishment was matched by a slyness and skill of execution which belied his tender years. The headmaster saw him as specially provided by Providence to ensure that my last term at the school should be the most exciting, and if Master X − I dare not give his name lest he should be holding some high position in the realm! − recognised this as his mission, he could not but be praised for his devotion to it. Time would fail me to tell of his exploits but I picture him now holding the school to ransom by the simple device of locking its two main doors when all the boys were outside, hiding the keys and refusing adamantly to disclose their whereabouts. The whole school was caught up in a frantic search during what time Master X sat on the steps taking a malicious delight in the proceedings. After a thirty-minute search one key was retrieved from some bushes and Master X, knowing that his purpose was at last frustrated, promptly recovered the second. This was but one of his exploits designed to interfere with the orderly progress of the school. Dr. Spock was then only 26 and had not begun disseminating his wisdom about child care around the world either in its 'authorised' or 'revised' form. But Master X's parents were not the sort of parents to praise his impish initiative and when his conduct was reported to them they merely asked whether I had mislaid his slippers! Before the term ended I had however won Master X and I clinched my victory by directing his initiative and surplus energy into the end of term entertainment. It was one of those occasions when diplomacy demanded that every boy in the school should have some part, and Master X, the youngest in the school, was to recite a poem of some length about a dog. Having done this faultlessly and dramatically he won the unstinted applause of the Mums and Dads but was apparently uncertain what to do next. He stood bewildered and giggling in the middle of the stage. As official prompter I whispered 'Bow and come off'. His response was not what was intended but far more effective. He turned from me to the audience, growled 'Bow-wow, bow-wow' and made his exit to thunderous applause.

It was at that same entertainment that the school bade me farewell and showered upon me gifts, some still treasured, as reminders of three very happy and fulfilling years. I could not guess then that those years of teaching were in fact to exercise a decisive effect upon my future ministry and in many ways to direct its course. Meanwhile two holiday months were before me in which to make preparations for the degree and theological course at Durham which were to consume the next four years of my life.

4

Durham Days

When, early in October 1929, I set off from Newton Abbot's Great Western Railway station on the four hundred miles' journey to Durham, feelings of excitement jostled with forebodings. Here, at long last, was to be the moment of truth. Reaching it had been something of an obstacle race in which so many factors had conspired against me: the short-fall in matriculation requirements which resulted from a truncated secondary education; the subsequent battling, for the most part unaided, with Latin and Greek; my father's sudden death and the year's further delay which it caused to my plans; the financial uncertainty of the whole enterprise in a day long before the potential undergraduate was able merely to hold out his hand to the State for all that he needed – all these were the hurdles which had severely tested me but which had been surmounted, though not always with ease. As the train chuffed its way into what was for me unknown territory – geographically, socially, academically – I found myself surmising possible further hurdles which might yet impede me on the way, possibly academic, certainly financial. Moreover I began to feel old! I was twenty-two and I reflected that it was likely that all the other freshmen starting their degree courses would be eighteen-year olds straight from the sixth forms of Public and Grammar Schools. How should I relate to them – in age, in background, in ability, in interests, in financial viability? Should I be the odd man out? It was a fearful thought! But surely, I consoled myself somewhat naively, there could be no odd man out in a company of young men whose eyes were directed towards a common goal, and that goal nothing less than the sacred ministry of the Church. These and a thousand other thoughts ran through my mind as the train raced northwards towards the scene which I realised could make or break.

At York a priest came into my compartment and immediately engaged me in welcome conversation. Had he not spoken, I should have done, for I desperately needed at that moment someone with whom to share my more disturbing thoughts. (I was to discover in later years by the way, that contrary to popular belief, a clerical collar encourages rather than impedes

50

train conversation.) The priest proved to be a graduate of Durham who knew many of the answers to what for me at that moment were burning questions. He clearly sensed both my excitement and my fears, said much to encourage me, and as he left the train at Darlington calmed me with nine words which have lived with me since: 'When the will is dedicated, the way is directed.' The excitement within me rose as the train approached Durham and presently I saw for the first time a sight which seemed to me to be such that it should be counted among the wonders of the world – a sight which never fails to excite me even now. There was the great Cathedral Church of Durham balanced, precariously as it seemed, upon a rock, and towering over the city and the ancient castle in a manner which suggested at once the ascendency of the truths which it proclaims and the inviolability of the Faith which gave it birth. Now I knew why the University of which I was soon to be a member had chosen as its motto: *Fundamenta elus super montibus sonctis.*

The train pulled into the station and I had thought that it would belch forth immediately hordes of young men and maidens going to their respective colleges. I saw no more than a handful and that, I discovered on my arrival at St. Chad's College, was not surprising since I had arrived a day early. This proved, however, to be a happy accident for it enabled me to find my way around alone, to ensconce myself as comfortably as possible in the meagrely furnished room allocated to me over the front door of the college (immediately opposite – I saw to my delight – the ancient gateway to the Cathedral close), and also to meet some of the staff. The warmth of their welcome was reassuring and when Bell, the corpulent and ever kindly butler, came to tell me that despite my early arrival dinner would be served for me in the Hall, I began to feel that the College had been waiting for me for years. But first I must needs see the Cathedral. Up to that point in my life I had seen but three of England's great Cathedrals – Canterbury, Exeter and St. Paul's. To live for four years in the shadow of another was a benediction which I had not anticipated.

Durham Cathedral is in a class of its own. Its majestic setting is unequalled for grandeur and beauty. From the River Wear, which almost surrounds it, one can see how precariously it is perched on the summit of wooded cliffs, ready one might suppose, to tumble into the waters at any moment. Yet there it has stood its ground for nearly a thousand years. Whether viewed architecturally, theologically, romantically or historically, this great building, 'half Church of God, half castle 'gainst the Scot', as Sir Walter Scott dubbed it, cannot fail to stir the deepest feelings of all but the most impoverished philistine.

I was captivated by Durham Cathedral within an hour of my arrival in the city. On the south side, the ancient deanery and the canons' houses, shut off from the outside world at night by the great door opposite my room in college, and lit then by gas lamps, form an oasis of quiet dignity in a bustling world. Within that enclosure I was to discover that one could experience in the evening a sentient stillness and a solemn silence broken only by the sonorous strokes of the cathedral clock. On the north side was the Palace Green, the hub of the University which itself came from the bosom of the Cathedral. It was from there that I gained for the first time the true splendour of the great church, over 400 feet in length, with its magnificent central tower springing from its body and rising to 212 feet, and its twin towers at its west end 146 feet high.

I entered the Cathedral through the north door on which is a grotesque thirteenth-century sanctuary knocker. In early years frightened criminals would hurry to clasp its ring, seeking admission and sanctuary, and claiming the peace and protection of Saint Cuthbert whose shrine lay within. That may not have happened in real life since the sixteenth century but many an innocent undergraduate, putting on the face of a hunted criminal, has been photographed clinging to that same knocker – as indeed was I!

I stood spellbound in the Norman nave with its clustered pillars and massive cylindrical columns ornamented in various ways by channels cut into the stone, some zig-zag, some spiral, and some in a trellis-like pattern. The masses of solid masonry, decorated so delicately, brought to my mind a sermon which I had heard on words from the Book of Kings: 'He set up pillars, and upon the top of the pillars was lily work: so was the work of the pillars finished' (1 Kings ch. 7, v. 21, 22). The stern strong power of religious convictions must express itself in tenderness, in sympathy, in caring, in courtesy. I could hear again that preacher's refrain: 'First the pillars, then the lily work.' And do I recall that the verger told me that those strong pillars were each 23 feet in circumference, their girth being such that thirteen men must join hands to clasp one in their embrace?

I sought out the shrines of Cuthbert and Bede and other school history lessons came to life. It was but a brief visit that I paid that night and it finished with a prayer – some would say a selfish prayer – that what was beginning in my own life just then would so strengthen the pillars of faith that the 'lily work' of Christian living and Christian witness might never be lacking.

Back in college I set my study for action, shamelessly choosing the better part of a room which was to be occupied by two students, and then waited hungrily for some sign that dinner was at hand. Within half an hour a clanging gong sent me looking for the dining hall to which in fact savoury odours directed me. The table was set for two and suddenly there burst into the room with an aplomb which suggested either that he owned the place or was a prospective purchaser, an ebullient young man of about eighteen. He turned out to be a freshman who like me had arrived a day early. Within minutes I knew all about him – his home, his birthplace, his past scholastic achievements, his present hopes, his future desires, all came tumbling out from his lips – a veritable verbal Niagara. Appropriate gesticulations and flashes of humour added to what was for me a rich entertainment. Occasionally, when he paused for breath, I was able to inject into the torrent of words a modest contribution, which was sometimes informative but more often salutary.

Nevertheless that night there began a friendship which has remained unbroken through the years. Donald Nicholson, who christened his first vicar 'Mesech' because, as he explained to me in an early letter after his ordination, he was 'constrained to dwell' with him, has held down many important posts in the Church and there will be hosts of people in Darlington and Beaconsfield, in Oxford and London and in Edinburgh where for eight years he was vice-principal of the theological college, who owe much to his outstanding ministry.

Following dinner that night the conversation deepened as we went for what we later discovered to be a traditional post-prandial walk for undergraduates. Such is Nicholson's phenomenal memory that he was able to tell me recently that I reassured him that night as he expatiated on what he feared to be the imminent disaster which would befall the Anglican Communion if the scheme for the creation of the Church of South India went through. Later he and I were to become joint 'directors' of the college chapel – he as sacristan and I as succentor. It was our responsibility to produce the weekly service lists and as I adhered rigidly to the Anglican Calendar and he tended to introduce weird observances from some other publication, the lists rarely agreed. Since, however, I chose the hymns, and the collects, lessons, epistles and gospels followed, in those days, a clear course from the Book of Common Prayer, my list prevailed. But the sacristan could sometimes steal a march by dressing the Altar in colours in tune with *his* list!

Among those who joined the College when I did, Donald Nicholson and Alfred Webster-Smith, subsequently Dean of Lusaka, and Kenneth Warren who was to succeed me in the benefice of Ambleside in the Lake District, were those with whom I had an immediate and easy rapport. That is not to say, however, that my circle of friends was narrow. Both among men in my own year and in the second year I counted many friends, in particular among the second-year students Archie Davison, who became a much beloved priest in the Newcastle diocese, and a member of the Church Assembly, Eric Hammond with whom I collaborated in the production of college entertainments and in writing lyrics for the shows, and Eric Buchan who became Archdeacon of Coventry, and who in his eagerness to raise funds for the local hospital cajoled me into many money-raising ventures. He has since become known throughout the land and in many dioceses overseas for his ability to preach the Gospel of Christian stewardship in compelling and irresistible terms.

Despite any misgivings I might have had, I fell into the collegiate life with ease and revelled in every minute of it. The College Chapel, with its daily Eucharist and daily sung Evensong, was for me a continuing source of delight and spiritual strength. It was, too, my introduction to plainsong chant which made, and ever makes on me, a deep impression both for its suitability for use in a community of men and for its singular quality of interpretation of the poems of the Psalter. There was something supremely ethereal in the sound of sixty men reciting the old poems of the Psalter to the plainsong melodies.

So familiar did they become to me and so deeply did they impress me that even now as I read the psalms in isolation I find myself setting them to the melodies which my four years at St. Chad's imprinted indelibly on my memory.

With a resident staff of five under the principalship of the Reverend Dr. S. R. P. Moulsdale ('Dickie' to the initiated), the college was in admirable and adequate hands, academically and pastorally. The Vice-Principal, Professor of History Dr. C. E. Whiting (affectionately known as 'Pop') was a good priest and a lovable man with not a few of the eccentricities associated with professors. I met him on the first night of the term, when gravel was thrown at my window at about 10.30 p.m. and a voice came through the darkness: 'Get the keys from the Vice-Principal's room and let me in'. I had no idea whether this was common practice or law-breaking, but a freshman could not on his first night deny co-operation to a graduate. Going somewhat nervously to the Vice-Principal's room I made my request and was greeted with the words: 'Keys on that nail . . . who are you?' I declared my identity, took the huge bunch of keys and asked not unnaturally: 'Which one is it sir?' Taken aback by so practical a question the professor replied: 'Oh! Oh! now I wonder . . . well, it's the last one you try.' On another occasion a commotion at the High Table half way through dinner and a hurried exit by Dr. Whiting evoked from the Principal: 'It's all right, gentlemen, the professor is not ill. He's just remembered he should be dining at the Castle.'

The Bursar at that time was John Posnett Boden who had firsts in Classics and Theology and who served St. Chad's faithfully and ably for sixteen years. Ever immaculate in personal appearance, precise in utterance, sensitive in understanding, Posnett, as he was affectionately known behind his back, was in every way made to measure for St. Chad's of which he had once been a student. Both he and the Junior Tutor, the irrepressible Ian Pettitt who must, I am sure, be counted among the finest parish priests the Church has had in this century, contributed in no small way to the well-being, the success and the happiness of the student body. The fifth member of the staff was a layman, Lawrence Ambrose Body (and therefore known as 'Corpus'), the son of a priest who had made a name for himself as a missioner in the Diocese of Durham. He was a shy and reserved man, fearful of being engaged in any conversation which went beyond the Classics. He had, however, a devastating way of firing a question at a student in such a manner as to preclude anything but a definite answer, for the question always ended with the words: 'If so, why? If not, why not?'

But the moulding influence ever at work in St. Chad's from the day of its birth until his retirement was Stephen Richard Platt Moulsdale himself. He lived for the College, was ever proud of it and of the University of which it was a part and of which he became Vice-Chancellor, ever grateful to its founders and benefactors, and ever determined that it should continue to send out into the field men who would become dedicated priests, faithful pastors and fearless prophets. Dr. Moulsdale's sister, Minnie, was overseer of all things domestic, and under her supervision no Chadsman could ever complain that his material needs were neglected. Accommodation was simple but sufficient; food was substantial in quantity and superb in quality, varied and interesting. All this was so good that the most fastidious student would have found it very difficult to conjure up a legitimate grumble.

I concerned myself very little with the sporting side of college life though I have frequently been reminded of a memorable try scored by me on the only occasion on which I allowed myself to be cajoled into playing rugby football, a game for which, as opposed to soccer, I have ever affected a profound contempt. Nor did I ever do anything on the river save messing about in punts after the June exams were over. Nevertheless I recall one incident resulting from that sport which resulted in my disgracing myself in the Chapel. The College had bought a new scull, a boat rowed by one person, and it was duly named Ariel at 5.15 p.m. on a certain Friday afternoon. The simple ceremony was being performed by Dr. Whiting who launched it. One John Hardman, who rose to a height considerably over six feet, was to be the first to use it. He set off, shot over the weir and damaged the boat, I think irreparably, within minutes of its launching. It was, as I was to discover, my misfortune to read the Old Testament Lesson at Evensong that night and the ceremony by the river had consumed the time in which I would normally have been reading it through. Imagine my astonishment when I opened the Bible to read the first lesson to find that it was the passage from Isaiah 29 which begins with the words: 'Woe to Ariel, to Ariel . . .'. The College immediately collapsed into uncontrollable laughter and as the reader, though I tried hard to compose myself, I too fell to the laughter and the reading came to a halt. The Vice-Principal behind me tapped his stall and I was about to start again when he said: 'Gravitas, gentlemen, gravitas.' The effect of this was only to start further laughter and for a moment I stood helplessly by unable to start the reading again. It could not have been more than seconds but the lapse seemed interminable to me. The Vice-Principal summoned me to his presence after the service and I was prepared for a dressing down and ready with a profuse apology. But like the Prodigal Son I stammered out only half the prepared speech and the good Professor broke in: 'It's all right, son. I wouldn't have been in your shoes for gold.'

I was well content to give my spare time to other aspects of collegiate life, within the college and university: writing short plays for college entertainments, lyrics for revues (there was one about bishops which has frequently been hurled back at me by my friends since I became one). Music for the lyrics was provided by Ian Pettitt in whose make-up deep vocational dedication did not preclude a sense of fun and ability to create it. One notable occasion on which I appeared on stage was a presentation of *The Little Plays of St. Francis* which was put on by the dons and into which I was trapped, not unwillingly I would add, by being asked to stand in at one rehearsal for a don who was indisposed. He remained so, and I was thus counted among the blessed ones for the productions which excited the interest of town and gown alike. On the front row, on the first night, was the diminutive but imposing figure of the Lord Bishop of Durham, Dr. Hensley Henson, flanked by the massive and formidable figure of Dean Welldon, before whose presence both the earth and the Canons residentiary were wont to tremble, and for whom it was asserted two seats had been reserved, one being insufficient to accommodate him.

The College Debating Society of which I became secretary and subsequently President afforded a rich opportunity for practice in public speaking though the business of the hour was inevitably prefaced, and occasionally interrupted, by a little friendly barracking. On my first appearance as secretary I stood up to read the Minutes when some wag rose on a point of order that since the new secretary was a master of the art of plainsong the first two paragraphs of the minutes should be sung to plainsong chant. Obviously such a motion was carried with acclamation and the secretary was obliged to oblige. Thunderous applause for the effort was an adequate reward. The newly-appointed president began his term of office with a presidential address which custom demanded should be substantial in content and length. Even this potentially erudite, if not solemn, occasion could be interrupted by points of order. Only two such interruptions occurred when I gave my presidential address. The first was by Kenneth Warren with whom, at that time, I was sharing a room and much else who, to the unbounded delight of the whole college interrupted my first sentence with the words: 'On a point of order Mr. President, before you launch too deeply into so serious a topic, could you assure me that you are quite comfortable in my dress shirt?' The later interruption was as kindly meant if seemingly biting. It followed what might be called a purple passage in my address of which I confess I was rather proud. 'On a point of order sir, was that last sentence a quotation?' My answer: 'Not yet, sir,' won not only applause but immunity from further interruptions for the rest of the evening.

A further collegiate activity from which I gathered a great deal of experience was my contact with one of the Missions in which the college assisted in pastoral and evangelistic work. I became in my second year 'Dean' of Hett – a tiny mining village a few miles from Durham and within the parish of Croxdale. In particular we were responsible for the Sunday evening services in the village church and, as opportunity afforded, expected to take part in a certain amount of pastoral and evangelistic work. My two assistants in this were Alfred Webster-Smith and Kenneth Warren, one of whom normally accompanied me on Sunday evenings. After tea with a warm vicarage family but in the desperately cold vicarage house of Croxdale, we made our way on foot to the church a mile away. In a letter home I announced my appointment as 'Dean' with some pride and added that I had preached my first sermon in Hett. The comment in the letter was met with the seemingly discouraging, and almost caustic, reply from my mother suggesting that she thought it totally unreasonable of the College authorities to expect any young ordinand to make any impression in what she described as 'that particular environment'. The sentence hurt me somewhat and at first

I thought it was an unfortunate comment about a mining community though such a thought would be completely out of character for her. It was not until I read the postcript that light dawned. It read: 'When you mention further visits to Hett, remember to cross the t's!'

Hett was a small mining community and it thus brought me into contact with the Durham miner and his family. The tiny cottages which made up the village were all crowded, but if they were grim from without they were warm from within. The families were closely knit, and most of them were knit as closely to the Church by a simple but strong faith. 'The young gentlemen from the College' as we were invariably described were always welcomed and what we did was clearly appreciated. The little Church, lit by oil lamps and furnished very simply, was greatly loved by the people, and became each Sunday night a place where young and old gathered together to worship the Lord in the beauty of holiness. I do not use that phrase glibly, for though the prayers were recited in loud and deliberate tones and the singing was somewhat raucous, we knew that it was rightly directed to the Living and Holy God. Five memorable occasions spring to my mind as I write: one of rejoicing, one of sorrow, one of apprehension, one when I could have wished that the earth would open to swallow me up, and one when I was relieved that it had not done.

For our story the last shall be first. It seemed desirable to me that I should know something about the background of the people of Hett and as they were all miners I cherished a desire to spend a day in the pits. With the co-operation of the colliery manager this was eventually arranged and the news created no small stir among the congregation and not least among the miners themselves. The day came and donning the appropriate dress at the pithead I made my descent with a group of miners who were quick to detect the apprehension which doubtless betrayed itself in my demeanour. There was a good deal of jovial leg-pulling but as the shaft descended, and I became convinced that my stomach would reach the coal face before I did, I could manage only a weak smile. Hindsight suggested that in fact the descent was the worst part of the experience. A foreman showed me around for a while, and I was frankly appalled by the cramped conditions in which the men worked, but impressed by the good humour and determination with which they tackled what struck me as a most arduous and dangerous task. I came upon one man, working a very narrow seam and lying on his side as he hacked at the coal. The precision of his attack and the success which met every blow intrigued me and presently my questions to him, answered jovially and intelligently, were met with a counter question: 'Like to have a go sir?' Uncertain as to whether this was within the rules I hesitated and I suspect that no one was more surprised than he when I accepted the challenge I dropped to the ground, turned on my side, took his pick and began to do what I had seen him doing but with far from impressive results. My only reward was measured in tiny chips of coal, tokens of sympathy from a stern coal face which admired my cheek but despised my style. My instructor was at my side giving words of encouragement and suggesting strategy, but these did nothing to increase productivity. It was in fact chips with everything and nothing but chips, but suddenly an exclamation from the miner at my side changed everything. 'Hit the bloody stuff sir, don't just tickle it. Hit it and bloody hard.' Controlling my laughter I hit it and hit it hard – though whether it was 'bloody hard' I shall never know. The end result seemed to impress the miner as much as it excited me, for lumps of coal came tumbling down, huge lumps which glistened as the light fell on them. Bursting with pride I turned to my miner friend and said: 'Well there 'tis mate, but there's no blood on it.' By that time there was an audience of three to watch the amateur miner at work; they enjoyed the gentle taunt and appreciated my efforts. My tutor resumed his work and I pocketed a small lump of coal which subsequently I sent home with a note to the effect that it was mined by mine own hand. It never made a fire; it was a showpiece in the family for years.

Then there was the occasion for rejoicing. The people of Hett were constantly telling us that they looked forward to the day when their church could have electric lighting. The undergraduate staff got together to raise some money for that purpose and then encouraged the parishioners to do the same. After a good deal of delay the installation was complete and I persuaded Canon G. C. Richards, one of the residentiary canons of the Cathedral and Professor of Greek in the University, to dedicate the work and preach the sermon. We were convinced that he would talk far away above their heads but respect for his office was such that we knew they would appreciate enormously being noticed by one of the Canons. The greatly beloved Canon was noted in the University for his high pitched and rather squeaky voice as well as for his somewhat nasal intonation. He stepped into the pulpit, switched off the pulpit light leaving the little church in darkness save for the altar candles, and then announced his text with his customary nasal intonation: 'Every good gift and every perfect gift cometh down from the Father of LIGHTS,' shouting the last word and switching on the pulpit light simultaneously. The three students present could scarcely contain their laughter at this simple stunt by which a serious scholar riveted the attention of his congregation, but it worked, and if it were true that not the whole of his exposition of James ch. 1, v. 17 was intelligible to the folk present, the occasion was such that they never forgot it.

The occasion of apprehension confronted me as I approached the church on a dark winter night, alone on that visit as I remember. A distraught young woman ran out from one of the cottages pleading to me to 'Come quickly, the little baba can't live, will you Christen him.' The midwife believed that the newly-born child could not live more than a few hours. I knew, of course, that it was open to any member of the Church to baptise in an emergency of this kind, but suddenly to be confronted with the situation, and in the midst of family distress, was momentarily bewildering for a young man, ordinand though he was. However, water was brought, prayers were offered, and it was there in the tiny parlour of a miner's cottage and in the dim light of one oil lamp and a silence which could be felt, that I first said the words: 'I baptise thee in the name of the Father and of the Son and of the Holy Ghost.'

It was my practice to invite other members of the College to preach from time to time at the evensong service, though many to my surprise turned down the invitations. I recall, however, the reluctant visit of a graduate whose course had but a few months to run before his ordination. He got into the pulpit and after some hesitation announced his text: 'A sower went forth to sow his seed.' There was a long pause, a very long pause indeed, but at length he began: 'Obviously he must have done this many times before' – a further pause, longer than the first – 'but this time he sowed his seed rather carelessly . . . and a lot of it never came up.' A very long pause. 'There is a lesson here which we have to learn.' By this time I was perspiring. For a full minute nothing came, and at length the poor man turned round and left the pulpit, lost either for ideas or for words with which to clothe them. To be in and out of the pulpit in less than three minutes, two of them being silent, could be what some of the laity would prefer, but that night one or two of them could only say as they left the church: 'That was a funny sermon . . . he kinda didn't get going.'

The occasion of sorrow was the death of one of the young choirboys. I had had sorrow of my own but I had never been called on to go through the agony of suffering with bereaved parents. The community sense was so strong that the whole village was in mourning and I shall never forget the funeral of that little child. The blinds of all the houses around the green were drawn, the vicar was there, the students who regularly ministered to the people were there, and gradually the family mourners followed by almost everyone in the village, filed into the church for the moving act of committal in which Christian faith blended together the notes of sorrow and hope, of comfort and trust. The village children were there and we sang 'Loving shepherd of thy sheep' that they might discern that the love and care of the Living God for his children extends beyond the grave. We sang an Easter hymn that we might remind our sorrowing hearts and minds that death does not have the last word. We sang 'O love that will not let me go' to bear witness to our conviction that death, which breaks all the ties of sight and touch and sound has yet no power over love which lives forever since it is of God. Of all the things which the students did in that little mining village none was more appreciated by the community as it witnessed a number of young men ready to enter into and to share their grief, to weep with them that wept. That was indeed a preparation for much that was to come in our respective ministries.

St. Chad's was never a theological college in the ordinary sense of the term though we certainly had everything which such a college could give by way of training for the ministry. But the college is, and always has been, a constituent of the University of Durham, and was founded with the express purpose of enabling men wishing to enter the Anglican ministry to read for their degrees in whatever faculty they desired and to read subsequently for the Diploma in Theology. The Faculty of Theology has, in the course of the near 150 years of the University's life attracted men of great distinction as its professors and lecturers including scholars of the calibre of Oliver Quick and Michael Ramsey. In my day most of the professors were nearing the end of their time and some certainly betrayed their ages in their behaviour. I first met the well-known Professor of Philosophy, Dr. F. B. Jevons, for example, when walking behind him in The Bailey, I concluded that he was on the way to the bank since he was dropping cheques from the paying in slip book held loosely in his left hand. I picked up three cheques, caught him up and handed them to him with the words: 'You dropped these sir,' only to receive the surprising reply: 'What evidence have you that it was I who dropped them?' Fearing that I was about to be examined in logical positivism – verification by experience and all that – I answered swiftly and then saw to it that I was a good way in front of him. Towards the end of his time he was found lecturing to an empty room since the students, who had been clocked in at the door by the university policeman, had slithered silently away as soon as the coast was clear. The professor was a distinguished philosopher and in his day had been a brilliant teacher but since there was no retiring age for professors, and he himself was blissfully unaware of his diminishing powers, he sat firmly on his professorial Chair for far too long. But then, we all know people who have done just that – bishops, judges, politicians and university dons being among the chief sinners.

There were of course good, bad and indifferent professors and lecturers in the university in the thirties, as indeed there were good, bad and indifferent students. The benefits one derived from the lecturers depended more upon the efforts one put into the studies to which they directed us than upon the style or even the competence of the particular lecturer.

The University Union Society, with its headquarters on the Palace Green, was a social centre in which a few students certainly idled too many hours away drinking coffee and engaging in social chat. There were, however, from time to time stimulating lectures and debates arranged by the Society. Although the colleges were autonomous, inter-collegiate activities, sporting and cultural, were organised by the Union officials, and each college was encouraged to pull its weight in Rag Week when a stupendous effort was made to bolster the funds of the local hospitals. The week followed the end of year examinations and it was noticeable that most of the students were only too ready to grasp an opportunity for letting their hair down in a good cause. Students were to be seen about Durham and the surrounding towns in all sorts of guises and disguises. Unimpeded by conductors they jumped onto buses with impunity to collect money from passengers who were normally quite ready to enter into the fun. Dressed in all manner of garb and even, on occasion, painted in woad, students paraded the streets of the city and surrounding towns selling the Rag Week magazine and rattling their tins before all and sundry. There was no reluctance on the part of students thus to make fools of themselves for a good cause or of the populace to respond generously and with good humour. We for our part, I doubt not, found the exercise of therapeutic value after the strain of examinations, and they for their part knew that their hospitals would benefit from our efforts. In all this I was happy to take my part in dressing up, in begging, in selling and parading. Indeed thirty-five years after I left the University when my chauffeur, George Dixon, was driving me from Carlisle to Durham Cathedral where I was preaching, he posed the question, on going through Chester-le-Street, as to whether I had visited the town before. He received what to him was the surprising answer: 'Only once George, and then I wasn't in a cassock. I was dressed as an Italian ballerina!' His question had recalled a visit to the town by six undergraduates in Rag Week when, so dressed and so disguised, we entertained the populace and extracted from them much for the hospitals. Photographic evidence of that visit was destroyed only recently!

Although occasionally there would be a Union debate touching something akin to politics, for the most part the students were not political animals and the student political societies were the least supported of the many societies which flourished in the university. It was not that students were unaware or unconcerned with the world outside, as dinner talk would reveal, but that they recognised that their immediate responsibility was to prepare themselves for that world by making the best of the opportunity before them. There were never such things as sit-ins, lock-outs, boycotts and all the other adolescent activities by which a tiny minority of present-day students, more particularly and significantly from the non-collegiate universities, seek to voice their opinions. We were, and we knew that we were, *in statu pupillari*, there to learn, not to tell our teachers how to do their job, nor to instruct the authorities how to run the university or colleges. The massive conceit of the politically-motivated militant students of today – and it should be remembered that they are never more than an insignificant, though noisy, minority – born no doubt of the ease by which they are cushioned by public funds, and bolstered by philosophies which exalt rights over duties and privileges over responsibilities, can never be other than a disruptive influence in institutions of learning. I do not pretend that all was perfect in the academic world of the 1930s, but there was a real desire to learn and a recognition that to learn one needed the humility to sit at the feet of a teacher. Further it was accepted as axiomatic that the governing bodies of both universities and colleges knew what their respective responsibilities were and were both capable and desirous of discharging them in the interests of the student body. That, in my judgement, is a disposition which opens the way for a richer reward than the contrary concept which, under the guise of the blessed word 'participation', prompts young people to believe that they are competent to dictate what shall be taught and how the teaching institutions – school, college or university – shall be governed.

The National Union of Students has a membership of some 800,000. That sounds impressive until one discovers that every student in every university and polytechnic is swept into it without his even knowing, and any dues payable come not from his pocket but from the taxpayer's. The student certainly derives some material benefits from the Union but by no stretch of the imagination is the politically-motivated minority representative of the whole body. When therefore we hear of some monstrous resolution of the National Union of Students we need not think of 800,000 young people standing four square behind it. We can hazard a guess that it represents a number which, set beside the membership of the Union, is insignificant. There will always be a tiny minority which is wont to spend its time sniffing out areas of potential grievance and concerning itself with affairs extraneous to the studies for which the state is paying. Certainly young people must be encouraged to be socially and politically alert, but they must be taught too that there is 'a time to every purpose under the sun . . . a time to break down and a time to build up, a time to keep silence and a time to speak'. Fortunately the vast majority know that the immediate task before them is to equip themselves to the best of their ability for the job in life which lies ahead. It is 'a time to build up . . . a time to keep silence'. The privilege of higher education imposes upon them the responsibility for making the most of it and that in turn demands a degree of concentration which admits of neither time nor inclination for the sit-ins, lock-outs and other demos by which minorities in these days seek to impose their wills and by which they finish up by debasing the student image.

Time was when colleges were undisturbed by such idiosyncrasies as was the case, and happily enough is the case, at the University of Durham and at St. Chad's. My years there were abundantly happy and, I dare say, rewarding in giving me all that I had hoped for. Fears I had entertained at the outset about academic insufficiency were gradually dispelled by examination results, at least after the first term in which I floundered in unfamiliar waters. Terminal tests, known as 'collections', provided a guideline as to progress in our studies, though the ordeal of appearing before the whole staff of the college at the term's end was not universally or invariably welcomed. Criticism on those occasions was incisive; praise was sparse. I recall, for example, one occasion when my end of term results were, in my judgement, specially creditable, with two subjects at 'beta plus' and two at 'alpha minus'. (To the uninitiated I could translate that as two all but perfect and two moving in that direction!) I purred inwardly as the results were read out and I could have said to myself, 'Criticise that if you can, you carping dons!' But I was not encouraged to rest on my oars even with those results. 'Two beta plus, two alpha minus: symmetrical but monotonous' was the Principal's comment, but I admit that there was a twinkle in his eye as he gave his verdict.

In my third year, just when the financial cupboard was all but bare and I nursed alone a fear lest the last of my savings might vanish before the task to which they were dedicated had been accomplished, a modest bonanza came my way as a result of examination success. Van Mildert, who was Bishop of Llandaff from 1819 to 1826 and of Durham from 1826 to 1836, was a prelate who had always taken a lively interest in tertiary education and in particular in the proper training of ordinands. He had in his Llandaff days encouraged the Bishop of St. David's (Thomas Burgess) in the plan he was then formulating for the building of a college for this purpose at Lampeter, the foundation stone of which was laid by Burgess in 1825 shortly before Van Mildert's departure for Durham. His continuing interest in the project was sustained by the fact that Bishop Jenkinson, who succeeded Burgess, also held the Deanery of Durham. St. David's College began its life in 1827 and is thus the oldest of the colleges which now make up the University of Wales. Durham University was born in 1832, its founding father being Van Mildert. The good Bishop founded Open Scholarships both at Lampeter and at Durham and I was proud to become a Van Mildert Scholar, and only too glad to receive the financial boost which came to me as a benediction. Trivial enough by today's standards it was nevertheless enough to transform my budget. Surviving during the short vacations had been just possible but during the long vacations I had to devise means by which I could lift from the home the burden of my being there. There was no question in those days of walking along to pick up unemployment pay nor was it easy to find temporary gainful employment. But I found a way!

On three successive vacations I went with two other students to help in the East Kent Hop Pickers' Mission, organised at that time by the Church of England Temperance Society. The work itself was voluntary but since travelling expenses were paid, and lodgings were provided by the society, I was able thus to sustain myself and at the same time to gather invaluable experience in ministry. The house in which we stayed in Kent was primitive but cosy and we were welcomed by a dear old lady, short and round and always aproned, who for all the world might have been Beatrix Potter's Mrs. Tiggy Winkle. There was no bathroom; the loo was at the bottom of the garden; the stairs creaked and the bedroom floor was uphill. The old dear who welcomed us so warmly was arthritic, and only too happy for us to turn the tables as it were by preparing the vegetables before we left for the hopfields, and washing up after meals. I slept, I recall, in a four poster which I liked, and on a feather tie, which I disliked, not only because it embraced one far too cordially for summer nights but also, in this instance, because it provided too many routes of escape for the 'hoppers' which, in the course of a day's work, we had caught from the hoppers in the fields. I can recall now nights when, by the light of a flickering candle, and armed with a slipper, I fought many a losing battle with jumping fleas. However, when we compared our respective scores at breakfast mine was not invariably discreditable!

Every morning at about 11 o'clock we set out to the hopfields by bicycle to talk to the pickers as they worked, and to teach and to entertain their children. In the evenings we conducted open-air lantern shows which always concluded with a service of worship. We threw onto the screen some really ghastly pictures the brilliant colours of which captivated adults and children alike. We sang hymns and on one occasion one of the three missioners – an undergraduate from Oxford – accompanied them very professionally with a concertina. Among the slides two or three were authentically 'magic' in that they were early 'movies'. All this, and not least the specifically mission aspect, was clearly appreciated, and I have no difficulty in recalling now the wonderful atmosphere which pervaded our congregations gathered together with one accord in one place and that beneath the stars. For us it was a rich experience in pastoral care and evangelistic enterprise; for them it was a demonstration of God's caring love mediated by the Church. Problems, anxieties and tensions frequently came our way, many beyond our understanding and ability to resolve, but that we listened and we cared was itself helpful and when, at length, the camp broke up and mums and dads came to bid us farewell, the hearty handshakes and the occasional tear in the eye said what they clearly found too difficult to put into words. The children on the other hand were uninhibited, and grubby though they often were, spruced up for the journey home they presented themselves with some pride as though to assure us before departure that we had never seen them at their best. From them were waves and indeed kisses from the youngsters before they boarded their home-going coach with happy abandon and much chatter.

We had lectures in Pastoralia in the University of Durham of course but up to that point in my life I had learnt the art far more through my contacts with people than through my hours in the lecture room. The boys in the Kent school, the people in the solicitors' office who tended to pour out their troubles over the enquiry counter, my contemporaries in college, the miners and their families in Hett, the hordes of hop-pickers and their children from the East End of London – all these had been my teachers.

The years at Durham passed incredibly swiftly and when in October 1932 I began my last year at College thoughts were being directed towards my Admission to the Diaconate timed for Trinity 1933. My unexpressed intention had always been to begin my ministry in the East End of London towards which my imagination had been fired by Kenneth Bickerdike, Rector of Shadwell, with whom I had stayed on two occasions and who had taken me round several parishes. But before I began to make any enquiries to this end, letters from various clergy whom I did not know began to reach me with invitations to consider curacies here and there. Not being tied to any diocese I was able to consider seriously any and every such approach but by the time the second term of the year began I became anxious to finalise something, since the many letters I was receiving were beginning to distract my attention from the work still to be done to complete my Diploma in Theology. Thus I firmly set aside suggestions which came from Gateshead, Leigh-on-Sea, Littleport, Southend-on-Sea, and several other parishes in different parts of the country, and decided to follow up a postcard sent to me by a priest whom I did not know and which bore only a couple of sentences. He was himself an assistant curate of Newark-on-Trent and by sending the card he was apparently trying to do a good turn for the vicar he was just leaving. The card merely said: 'You might like to consider going to Newark where I have been very happy.' I knew nothing of Newark save that King John had died in its Castle and that it had been the royalist stronghold near which Charles I ultimately surrendered in 1646. I wrote a brief note at once and addressed it to The Vicar, The Vicarage, Newark, knowing full well that despite its lacking any indication of the County in which Newark was situated (which, frankly, I did not know at that time) it would in that halcyon postal age reach its destination on the following morning. I count the reply which I received among the most gracious and kindly letters ever to be addressed to me. I warmed immediately to the writer both for his detailed and exciting description of the opportunities for a full and demanding ministry which the town offered and for what lay between the lines of the letter. I accepted immediately his invitation to pay him an early visit and within a week I found myself in the study of Canon William Kay, himself a graduate of Durham, who had emerged from the first world war at the age of twenty-six with a DSO and an MC with two bars. He told me everything about the parish and the work of the Church within the town; he showed me its lovely Parish Church, its schools, its mission churches and its Song School. In fact my mind was all but made up, and that to accept his invitation to join his staff, when I first met him at the station and sensed his lively, dynamic and utterly dedicated approach to his work. When I first stepped inside Newark's magnificent Parish Church I offered an immediate prayer that I might be granted the privilege of working under the guidance of so impressive a parish priest and of serving in a church of such surpassing beauty.

On the afternoon of the same day I was in the study of Bishop Henry Mosley, Bishop of Southwell from 1928 to 1941. Within half an hour of my meeting him he said: 'If Canon Kay wants you and I know that he does, then I will ordain you at Trinity. This kindly man of God then talked to me of many things – of Newark's vicar, of Newark's church, of my background, of his background, of my hopes and of his desires. I had never been near a bishop since the day of my Confirmation thirteen years before and that was long before bishops made themselves 'open' to people let alone young people. Somehow or other I cannot imagine that Lord William Cecil, Bishop of Exeter when I was confirmed, could have engaged any of us in a meaningful conversation. Here was an approachable man of God; I discerned that I could be happy in his diocese. Everything being completed I made to leave only to be met with the question as to what my immediate intentions were. Replying that I was hoping to get back to College that night, he said peremptorily: 'Impossible, my dear boy, you'll stay here for the night and I'll take you to Nottingham for a train in the morning.' After an early meal he set off for an evening Confirmation leaving me in his study to raid his library, and as he put it, to write at his desk and generally to pretend that I was a bishop for the evening. I did just that: read a few chapters, pulled out a piece of notepaper, wrote a letter to the student with whom I was then sharing a room in College to the effect that he would realise 'from the above address' (Bishop's Manor, Southwell) that things had moved far more swiftly than I had anticipated. I signed the letter 'Cyril Southwell' and went out to post it. For the next two hours I wondered whether there was any way by which I could recover it! However, the Bishop returned by about 9.30 and in response to his question: 'How have you spent the evening?' I answered truthfully: 'Behaving like a Bishop as you suggested, my Lord.' I thought that a sufficient confession for my misdeed particularly as he received it so well. We talked into the night and there began a friendship which was to be sealed ever more deeply in years to come, but that is another story.

The next morning, as soon as breakfast was done, the Bishop swept me into a particularly opulent car, the breed of which eludes me, and took me to Nottingham Station. I remember his apology for the expensive car. 'You may be surprised, dear boy, that I go around in this but the very rich layman who gave it to me insists that I can do a better job as Bishop if I can move around in a reliable and comfortable car.' Suffice it to say that you will not be likely to see any bishop, or archbishop, in anything so luxurious today – though I have had the experience of seeing a Rolls among the staff cars outside one of my church schools in the diocese of Carlisle!

I returned to St. Chad's with a light heart and an eager desire to speed up the attainment of an ambition which I had nursed for fourteen long years. In the Easter vacation before my last term at Durham I spent a week at St. Deiniol's Library, Hawarden, reading, meditating and writing essays for my deacon's examination. I confess that I rather resented the last of these exercises since it seemed to me that when one was working hard to secure theological qualifications at University level, to have to write further examination papers on similar subjects was an unnecessary burden. When I became a bishop I made it clear from the outset that no such burden would be imposed by me on men who had already equipped themselves to the best of their ability in theological studies.

The months slipped by and when I finished the last paper of the last examination in May 1933 and was fairly confident that all would be well, there was nothing left to do but to relax and to await my admission to the diaconate. Examinations had always been a fearful experience for me and I never entered one without the feeling that I must inevitably fail it. My fears were invariably proved groundless by success but I invariably took each success only as an indication that it would be the next exam which I should fail. But now there were no more and all was joy. I recall that that night about a dozen of us went to the cinema and saw a film, the title of which eludes me but not the theme. It contained a song which was being sung by a number of office girls who operated their typewriters in rhythm with the music. The song had within it the words: 'I don't know why I'm happy, so happy, so happy.' We did, and we felt it permissible to join in for it was almost as though the manager had chosen the film to coincide with the conclusion of the year's exams. However, our chorus was so hearty that he came to us and respectfully suggested that he would have to ask us to leave if we insisted on singing. We desisted. There was no antipathy between town and gown in Durham, no student hooliganism, and no student vandalism. A dozen gowned graduates and ordinands at that, could not let the side down, but being on top of the world we could not resist that chorus. Nor could the manager as he told us after – but he added: 'I joined in backstage.'

The last days at Durham were very precious. Firm friendships had been forged, mind had been enlarged, vision had been kindled and, speaking for myself on a subject about which no man can speak for another, faith had been mightily enriched, religious convictions had been strengthened, the sense of vocation had been deepened and commitment to Our Lord and His Church set in a widened context. All that and more I had gained, partly by my contacts with professors and lecturers and with the staff and students of the college, but mostly by the hours which had been spent in the college chapel in public worship and in private meditation and prayer. The Chapel is a simple wooden building, erected only a few years before I joined the college, and looking from without like a Scandinavian village church. It is less ornate now than it was in my time at Durham but it still holds for me precious memories of spiritual awakening and renewal and of what worshipping the Lord in the beauty of holiness really means. On my last Sunday morning there the Missa de Angelis seemed particularly moving and the hymns, chosen by myself and including that most wonderful of Eucharistic hymns 'Lord, enthroned in heavenly splendour', sung to the lovely Welsh tune *Bryn Calfaria*, all conspired to make of that day one of the most memorable as well as one of the hardest to see through.

There was one last duty to discharge. That same evening Kenneth Warren, Alfred Webster-Smith and I went together to the mission at Hett for the last time, they to conduct the service and I to preach. The little church was crammed to the doors, with the young children having only the sanctuary step on which to sit. The Hett community was there in force – young men and maidens, old men and children and the old women whom the Psalmist somewhat ungallantly forgot. We worshipped as we ever did but in the prayers there was the consciousness that we should not be all together again. The service over, the people lingered, awkwardly, shyly. Then the churchwarden, a retired miner, expressed his desire to make a speech – a speech which doubtless had cost him hours of preparation. Having done so he whisked from beneath a pew three small filing cabinets of oak and solemnly handed them to us as 'our way of saying thank-you for all you have done for us'. I assured them that they had had a large share in 'teaching us our trade' and for that we too would always remember Hett, its people and its little church. We parted and I heard nothing of Hett or its people for fourteen years when, following a broadcast from my church in Mansfield, a letter signed by a great many members of that congregation came expressing their joy at being able to worship with me again. That is the sort of gesture which one does not forget.

The following day I packed my goods and chattels, bequeathed some philosophy notes to a friend in need, sold enough textbooks to raise my train fare to Newark, and set off from the College with but a pound in my pocket and less than five in the bank. Even so I was rich and I knew it. Durham and St. Chad's had in four years bestowed on me treasures which use would not diminish and time could not erode. As the train pulled out of Durham station there was a last lingering look at the mighty Cathedral perched on its rock, and I fancied I could hear again the Psalmist's song *Fundamenta eius super montibus sanctis.*

Had anyone prophesied to me just then that I should return one day to receive from my University a Doctorate of Divinity (*Honoris Causa*), and to become Chairman of the Governing Body of my College, I should have dismissed the words as idle talk. My mind just then was set on the immediate future and I doubt not that as the train hurtled its way south to the beginning of the work upon which my heart had been set for nearly fourteen years, I followed the practice which I began with my Confirmation of shooting an 'arrow prayer' that I might be given wisdom and courage to meet whatever opportunities or challenges lay ahead. I had no illusions about the demands of the dedication I was about to make. More than once I had read and pondered upon the *The Form and Manner of Ordering of Priests* in the Book of Common Prayer and each time found myself wondering how any man could dare to enter upon so challenging a way of life. But the moment had come for me to put my hand to the plough and there was never a thought of turning back. *Ad te levavi oculos meos!*

5

Spiritual Climacterics — Newark

Southwell Minster is the village Cathedral of the Midlands which the sightseer is apt to miss. It does not throw a gracious tell-tale spire into the sky as does Salisbury; it is not a city set on a hill like Lincoln; it does not dominate the skyline from afar like Durham and it does not impose itself on the scene like St. Paul's. Southwell Cathedral hides itself, but he who sees it has the richest reward. Not until the visitor stands face-to-face with its west front does he realise that the modest little township which is Southwell hides within itself something so vast and so splendid. If he is a connoisseur of Cathedrals he may well marvel first how it comes about that anything so old can be so clean. Southwell has never had to contend with anything approaching the 'dark satanic mills' of industry and one gets the impression that its stones are as clean as when they were set in position some eight hundred years ago. The Minster has a striking west front with two Norman towers capped by conical — some would say comical — spires like pepper pots, and a central tower so squat that it might suggest that its founders really were determined that it should not be seen from afar. Like the King's daughter of the Psalmist it is all glorious within, with a bold Norman nave, an elegant thirteenth-century quire and a chapter house decorated with a veritable riot of magnificent carving, in which birds and foliage abound and which tells of the imagination and skill of some master carver who though unknown is certainly not among those who have left no memorial.

It was in this loveliest of settings that on Trinity Sunday 1933 I was made a deacon in the Church of God. I recall that whereas those ordained with me were surrounded by near relatives, I stood alone. My younger brother was at sea; my elder brother was a housemaster and unable to leave his post; my mother was recovering from an illness and unable to make the long journey from Devon to Nottinghamshire. By the courtesy, however, of the Dean and Chapter of Exeter, she and my sister were given places in the quire of Exeter Cathedral where there was an ordination on the same day and at the same time. Thus they were with me in spirit, in what was for me a tremendous and all but overwhelming occasion. The road from the moment when, as I firmly believe, the good Lord put it into my mind and heart to serve him in this way, had been long and frequently uphill. I confess that there had been times when I had all but surrendered. But now, at long last, I was actually laying before the altar such gifts as I had, and was receiving through the Bishop the Church's commission to use them within the sacred ministry to the glory of God and the welfare of His people. At that time there was no 'Bulley' in *Crockford's Clerical Directory* nor had there been since the death of Dr. Fred Bulley, President of Magdalen College, Oxford, who died in 1897 and who had been ordained in Christ Church Cathedral, Oxford on Trinity Sunday 1833, precisely a hundred years before me.

The Ordination was preceded by a short retreat held, at the invitation of Bishop Mosley, in the Bishop's Manor and conducted by one of the honorary canons of the Cathedral. I cannot recall the theme of his retreat addresses nor that of his sermon in the Cathedral, but I recall vividly the address of the Bishop of Willesden (The Right Reverend Guy Vernon Smith) at my Ordination to the Priesthood in Newark Parish Church a year later. Based on the three words: 'Holy, Holy, Holy,' it was a most moving address in which the Bishop spoke of the transcendence of God before Whom those offering themselves for the sacred ministry must, on that day of all days, prostrate themselves. He spoke of God's holiness, of the meaning of holiness, of the bankruptcy of a merely secular Christianity affecting to concern itself only with this world's affairs and this earthly life, of our duty as ministers of the Word and Sacraments to lead our people to God Himself and to show them how, by reflecting God's holiness, their secular concerns could be so purified as to become sacred. Whether the general congregation understood an address which searched so deeply into the mind, the heart and the soul, I do not know but I know that for my part, and I doubt not too for those ordained with me, that the address, coming immediately before our ordination was an awesome challenge both personal and vocational.

My admission as a deacon in Southwell Minster in 1933 and my acceptance of the Order of Priesthood in Newark Parish Church a year later were for me spiritual climacterics which transcended in importance everything I had ever done in expression of my commitment to Our Lord. I was deeply conscious of the totality of dedication demanded and acutely aware of my need of divine grace to meet it. How often I had offered the simple prayer: 'Here am I, send me.' Now, exhilaration that the prayer had been answered, that I was now being sent out as a 'messenger, watchman and steward of the Lord', was tempered with trepidation lest I should fall lamentably short of the Bishop's charge in the Ordination Rite: 'See that you never cease your labour, your care and diligence, until you have done all that lieth in you, according to your bounden duty, to bring all such as are or shall be committed to your charge, unto that agreement in the faith and knowledge of God, and to that ripeness and perfectness of age in Christ, that there be no place left among you, either for error in religion, or for viciousness in life . . . Have always printed in your remembrance how great a treasure is committed to your charge.' Were men ever more solemnly charged? No priest, looking back across his ministry can, in the light of that charge, do other than beat his breast for shame for his failures – and I judge that no priest, looking back across his ministry, can fail to lift up his heart in thanksgiving that God has so accepted his offering, though imperfect, and used his gifts however modest. I was soon to learn that in this business of commitment to Christ what mattered most at any given moment was not where you were but which way you were looking. 'Looking unto Jesus, the Author and finisher of your faith' was the sure recipe for swift translation from the valley of dismal failure to the high road of new endeavour.

Ordained as priests, at the time I was made deacon, were two men with whom I was to be closely associated in the days ahead. Philip Butterfield was already on the staff of Newark Parish Church and we worked side-by-side for three years. Reginald Foskett was to be closely associated with me in the educational work in the diocese of Southwell, more particularly in that among adults. Our ways parted in 1948 when he became an incumbent in the Derby diocese, but we came together again twenty years later in the Diocese of Carlisle. Philip Butterfield's early death from cancer was a great loss to the Church on earth, though his strong witness to his faith as he approached his death must have been a strengthening testimony to the many to whom he had ministered, both as a parish priest and as a confessor. We were so closely knit together in the three years during which we worked cheek-by-jowl that we could afford to disagree – frequently on matters touching the ordering of worship, often on the interpretation of a scriptural passage, rarely on any aspect of classical theology. When, in 1936, Philip left to become Succentor of Blackburn Cathedral, he gave me a book of prayers – bearing the inscription: 'To S.C.B. from P.D.B. in memory of the Great War, 1933 to 1936.' The legend was typical of the mordant, though never unkind, wit of which Philip was a master, but it also said much about the esteem in which we held each other. During a brief respite in his last illness we met after many years and that by the waters of Windermere. He knew then the nature of his illness as I did and we talked about it, but there was no hanging of the harp by the waters nor any tears – but radiance, confidence and virile faith. I do not know whether I helped him that day, but I know that he helped me.

Following the Ordination service in Southwell the Bishop entertained those who had been ordained, their immediate relatives and a number of canons, who looked incredibly aged, and other clergy. Recalling my fifteen hours in his home at the time he accepted me as an ordinand I was once more struck by his easy rapport with people and his fatherly interest in his clergy, ancient and modern. Here was a Father-in-God who not only laid his hands on us but embraced us cordially within the spiritual family of the diocese and demonstrated a real concern for our material welfare. On this latter score I was able to tell him that Newark had arranged to pay me £208 a year, that I had found adequate accommodation for £9 a month and, noting that the

Parish covered a wide area of the town, I had bought a somewhat decrepit bicycle for thirty shillings with a promise to pay when I had my first month's stipend! Of course it would be a tight budget, but it was nevertheless with high spirits I left Southwell that day to begin the work on which I had set my heart fourteen years back. At Evensong in Newark Parish Church that night the new curate, still feeling somewhat awkward in a clerical collar, broke himself in by reading the Lessons.

Through the centuries travellers up and down the Great North Road – Dick Turpin for example, along with monarchs and great officers of Church and State – cannot have missed the spire of Newark's Church rising as it does to a height of 252 feet. From the main King's Cross to Newcastle railway line the 750-year old spire can be seen above Newark's highest roof-tops pinpointing a spot of England on which for a thousand years the Gospel has been preached and the Sacraments have been ministered. True there is nothing left of the Old Saxon Church which must first have staked God's claim on the Newark of a thousand years ago, but what is there for all to see is a gracious building of great splendour. Almost as long as the spire is high it betrays in its varying styles Transitional, Early English, Decorated and Perpendicular – nine hundred years of civic pride and pious dedication. The end result is a massive parish church of singular beauty and magnificence which, when it was completed in the sixteenth century, could have accommodated the whole of Newark's population, at that time two and a half thousand. That is, of course, remembering that our forefathers did not count on getting a seat, save for the weakest who went to the stone seats along the walls.

At the time I joined the staff of Newark there was seating for about 1800, and I have many times seen the church full, and uncomfortably so, particularly for those great national and civic occasions for which it is both the responsibility and privilege of the parish church of a community to provide opportunities for thanksgiving, dedication and remembrance.

On my first appearance in the church on that Trinity Sunday evening I was immediately impressed by the dignified ordering of the worship, as well as by the very high standard of the music. Both were comparable with the best I had seen and heard in Durham Cathedral, and in Southwell Minster that same morning. As to the singing it was not merely the thundering of the anthem – on that occasion Dvořák's 'Holy, Holy, Holy' – but the sensitive chanting of the psalms which enthralled me. Behind this splendour of stone and sound there must, I thought, be a fascinating story of preservation both of fabric and endowments. And so it had been!

In common with most of England's Cathedrals and Parish Churches, Newark suffered the sort of desecrations and deprivations which were the inevitable consequences of the vicissitudes of our violent history. Both at the Reformation and, notably for Newark, in the Civil War when the town was garrisoned for the King, and under Cromwell, much damage was done to the fabric of the church and undoubtedly many endowments were lost.

As to the fabric, the seventeenth and eighteenth centuries were centuries of decay; the nineteenth and twentieth were centuries of wise and worthy restoration. Endowments had disappeared in the course of centuries, but one, remarkably and happily, survived all, and that one lends to Newark something distinctive.

In 1534, Archdeacon Thomas Magnus, whose name is preserved in Newark's Grammar School, left an endowment 'for a Song School Master and six singing boys to maintain Divine Service in the High Choir of Newark Church'. How faithfully the good archdeacon's desires were fulfilled in the earlier years history does not tell, but certainly Divine Service was being maintained, at least in the mornings, in the eighteenth century, and from 1888 Evening Prayer was offered too day-by-day. How far the 'six singing boys' made any contribution to this we do not know, but I know that in my days in Newark the archdeacon's wishes were being faithfully fulfilled. The office of Master of the Song School was filled adequately and admirably, by one Francis Woolley, an old boy of Lancing College and Stewart of Rannoch Scholar of the University of Cambridge. He was a more than competent organist who served his apprenticeship as deputy organist of Lincoln Cathedral, but undoubtedly his prime interest was in choir training and in that he excelled. I was to discover to my great joy that Evensong was sung daily in the church, though in 1939 Hitler deprived us of that delight, at least in the winter months, since it proved to be impossible to use the church after dark. Nevertheless the choir of 'singing boys', four times as many as the sixteenth-century archdeacon envisaged, and a dozen lay clerks maintained the Sunday Services — a Sung Eucharist, Matins and Evensong. The musical tradition did not wilt.

Throughout his twenty-three years as Master of the Song School, Francis Woolley gave himself totally to his office, concerning himself — in a way and to an extent which the general congregation never realised — not only with the training of the men and boys of the choir but also with their spiritual and material welfare. His work was his vocation and he gave himself and much of his substance to it unreservedly. He found time too for composition and the fact that only a few of his works have been published reflects, in my judgement, not on the quality of his work but on his reticence. One short anthem in particular, now unfortunately out of print, written by him on the death of his brother who was a priest, and embracing the words 'The souls of the righteous are in the hand of God', always struck me as superbly sensitive in the ethereal quality of its melody and in the simplicity of its harmonies. It is the sort of anthem which can be used with effect at All Soul's Tide, on Remembrance Sunday and on similar occasions on which the elaborate is inappropriate.

It was one of my responsibilities to assist Francis Woolley in the recruitment of boys for the choir, to prepare them for confirmation and generally to work with him in ensuring that the Church's interest in them and care for them was motivated not only for what they did but for what they were. From our work together there began a friendship which was sustained long after

I left Newark and was cemented by two touring holidays which took us all over the United Kingdom, to every Cathedral in the land (including the highlands of Scotland), except, strangely enough, the Cathedral in the Lake District which was destined one day to be 'mine'.

Saturday was traditionally my free day and although, more frequently than not, it was sacrificed for weddings or other urgent work, when it was free we occasionally met up with one Michael Ramsey, then sub-Warden of Lincoln Theological College and later Lecturer of the lovely Parish Church of Boston, and dined together in Stamford or Grantham.

Francis Woolley was the man who first opened up for me the vast treasury of English Church Music and stimulated a particular love of the gems which have been preserved for us from the sixteenth century onwards. The conservation of this music is not the least service performed by our Cathedral choirs and by choirs in our great parish churches.

This prompts a glance at the present. I reflect that time was when every little parish church in the land, village and town, could count on having a few men and boys to lead the singing in worship. A variety of factors have contributed to the wide demise of church choirs. Social structures have changed, priorities have turned turtle, discipline is lax and there is frequently no one willing or competent to accept the task of training. It must be said, however, that the work of the Royal School of Church Music has greatly enhanced the standard of the choirs which have been sustained. At risk of being charged under the Sex Discrimination Act I would dare say that choirboys have diminished in numbers as choirgirls have been recruited. The end result of 'no choirboys' could be 'no choirmen'. Maybe there is something to be said for the advice which I once gave to an incumbent who asked whether I thought it wise to augment his fast diminishing but splendid choir by introducing girls. My advice was 'Let there be parity. Have twelve of each and tell them all that that proportion would be as the 'Law of the Medes and Persians which altereth not'. That seemed to me to offer at the least the possibility of avoiding what I had seen going on in boys' choirs in many parishes – male shortage, female augmentation, male leakage, female numerical domination, male disappearance.

In the course of my nine years on the staff of Newark the continuing worship, day-by-day, Sunday-by-Sunday, and on the great occasions when the whole community gathered together, was ever uplifting. Both the incumbents under whom I served, William Kay and Alfred Parkinson, set an example of discipline and fidelity by their daily attendance at the Eucharist and the daily offices, and all of us found these to be both the well-springs of grace for the discharge of our common ministry and the sealing of our fellowship one with another in the service of our Lord and His Church. The responsibility of preaching to considerable congregations was both a challenge and a privilege. I recall in particular that the south aisle at Evenson would always hold its considerable phalanx of youngsters, largely from the local Grammar School and our church youth organisations; how on Sunday afternoons I met approximately 100 children of 11 plus to 15 gathered in church and these represented but one section of our religious education programme for young people. The Body of Christ was undoubtedly strong though I have an uncomfortable feeling that at the Monday morning staff meeting we seemed to be less concerned to praise God for what under Him had been achieved than to grumble about failures to break through here and there. But strong it was and that was a reflection of the day-in and day-out work which went on unceasingly.

Holding for the moment to the church itself and what happened within it, I recall the fearful experience of mounting the seven steps of Newark's high pulpit to preach my first sermon at Matins on an August Sunday morning. There was what by today's standards would be reckoned a vast congregation, swollen a little by visitors perhaps, but not very different from a normal Sunday morning, particularly remembering that even in those far-off days Newark also had a Parish (or Family) Communion at 9.30 a.m. every Sunday. For my first sermon I had chosen a text with which I thought it impossible to go far wrong: 'By their fruits ye shall know them.' The script was written in full – a practice to which I adhered rigidly for the first twenty-five years of my ministry and thereafter for any and every occasion which might be one attracting the special attention of the media so-called.

The testing moment came when I was pokered to the pulpit by Frank Cook the verger, mounted the steps, announced my text, and was immediately conscious of movement in the front pew. To my dismay I saw that one churchwarden was looking at his watch and the other had picked up and was consulting his Greek Testament. What was more frightening to a beginner, it seemed to me that neither was going out of his way to do what he was doing surreptitiously. As if that were not enough to put a novice off his stroke I then espied one Canon Charles Steel Wallis, Principal of St. John's College, Durham who for four years had been lecturing me in Church History in the University. The Canon appeared in Newark Parish Church once a year and invariably on the same Sunday. For three successive years I happened to be preaching on the occasion of his visits and, in my youth, was greatly encouraged by his complimentary remarks and amused by his parting quip: 'I can understand why nobody preaches here but you.' My unspoken reaction to the quip was that he had not heard my Vicar – a compelling preacher indeed.

However, having survived the ordeal of my first sermon in the great church I soon found myself only too eager to take my turn in the preaching ministry to a congregation which was both receptive and critical. Not all of them looked things up in the Greek Testament but enough of them were sufficiently intellectually alert to demand of their spiritual guides strong and solid instruction in the things of God. All of us were kept on our toes! Furthermore, in days long before sound amplifying systems had progressed from Cathedrals to Parish Churches, one learnt that it was useless to spend long hours – and they were frequently night hours – preparing a sermon, and a further twenty minutes delivering it, unless one made oneself heard in the distant parts of the Church. For the experience of having to do that I have been ever thankful. Nowadays, when people seem to be incapable of hearing the human voice except through a loudspeaker, every parish church seems to have thought it necessary to install such apparatus. Hensley Henson, who spoke of typewriters as 'writing machines', dubbed such apparatus as tending to 'make unintelligible sermons aggressively audible'.

Newark Church was sufficiently well known, and invitations from William Kay were sufficiently irresistible, to ensure that we had eminent special preachers from time to time. I recall visits from William Temple, then Archbishop of York, and from two Deans – Inge, the 'gloomy' Dean of St. Paul's and Hewlett Johnson, the 'Red Dean' of Canterbury. Temple spoke at a public meeting on 'Democracy'. Without a note of any sort, without the slightest hesitation, with sentences so well fashioned that one might have thought he had learnt the whole thing by heart, he spoke for exactly an hour. Then, looking at his audience with a smile, he added: 'I don't know any more,' and sat down to thunderous applause.

The Deans preached at Evensong and those two occasions were such that 'standing room only' notices might have been displayed. Inge, who was then regularly contributing popular articles to the London *Evening Standard*, the spicier parts of such articles appearing subsequently in the national papers, could be guaranteed to draw a great crowd. I must not here speak for the Vicar, but I confess that two of the curates chuckled naughtily when they observed the frayed manuscript which Inge extracted from his pocket as he left the return stalls to be pokered to the pulpit. We had more than a suspicion that it was very old and possibly very learned. The vast sermon-tasting congregation, anticipating no doubt, some of the Dean's *Evening Standard* tit-bits, were subjected instead to a lecture on an aspect of Pauline theology which even the Lambeth Conference might have found daunting. It was about that time that Hensley Henson asked whether he regarded Inge as one of the pillars of the Church of England replied: 'Not so much a pillar of the Church of England perhaps as a column of the *Evening Standard*.'

Hewlett Johnson's discourse was much more homely and more predictable. Nothing that he had said could have been beyond the understanding of the simplest people present; none could have doubted his sincerity; all would have been surprised and perhaps disappointed, had there not been a 'red' streak here and there in the picture which he painted. One of the choirboys posed me a question before the service: 'Is a Red Dean a sort of Cardinal?' – a definition which the Dean himself greatly enjoyed when I passed it on to him afterwards. Following supper in the Vicarage and that, by the kindness of Canon and Mrs. Kay, was a weekly assignment for the curates, where the Dean extolled *ad nauseam* the achievements and glories of Soviet Russia. After an hour or so of this, unable to possess my soul in silence any longer, I was the fool who stepped in where the angels feared to tread and commented: 'But

Mr. Dean they would have shown you only their drawing rooms, wouldn't they?' I was immediately, but gently, crushed with a counter question: 'Yes, Mr. Bulley, of course, and if you come to Canterbury what shall I show you, the Cathedral or the slums?' Crushed as I was I kept still silence, that is, until we met again, I as Bishop of Carlisle and he in retirement, when an opportunity arose to pursue the conversation. I was surprised to discover that the Dean's son-in-law was a priest in the diocese and not knowing that I had met him he invited me to his vicarage to meet the old gentleman over tea. On being introduced I ventured to recall the incident in Newark vicarage of thirty years back. He listened intently as I told the tale, concluding it humorously with some such remark that he had put me firmly in my place with one pungent question. Then lifting his bowed head, still covered with the ample supply of long white hair which prompted people to confuse him with Cosmo Gordon Lang, he said, 'I remember Newark and I remember my visit there. As to the rest of your story, is it too late to apologise?' I then understood why all who knew him and who criticised bitterly his utterances and his views invariably tempered their indictments with a remark to the effect that he was nevertheless a very gentle and gracious person.

In Newark's great parish church the ministry of the Word and the sacraments was offered daily and in and about the parish itself a vigorous pastoral, evangelistic and teaching ministry went on day by day under the inspiring and dynamic leadership of William Kay. Every Monday morning the staff met in his study, four clergy and for a time, two ageing nuns. Visiting books were produced and examined, pastoral problems were discussed, plans were prepared for courses of lectures and for confirmation preparation, and at the beginning of each term, for weekly visits to the three church schools which had been preserved and modernised by the vision and financial expertise of the Vicar himself. Our days began before the Altar at 7.30 each morning and sung Evensong at 6, attended regularly by the Vicar and his staff and seldom without a handful of the laity, was more frequently the interlude between the afternoon's visiting and the evening's lectures or youth work, than the end of the day's work. In the course of the day there would be the pastoral care of the sick and the aged, in the local hospital and in the Bede Houses hard by the church. Here there was a weekly service for the old people in their own tiny chapel. I picture as I write one of the old men in his small sitting room, an open family Bible always on his table. His ambition he told me, was to read every single word of the Bible before he died. When first I learnt that, he was in the middle of the Book of Daniel, and I assured him that as he had managed to get through Leviticus, not to mention the sixth chapter of 1 Chronicles, I rated his chances of making his goal very high.

I cannot resist relating an incident in the home of an old Alderman of the Borough of Newark who was bedridden and well past his ninetieth year. He was very deaf and I always took with me one of the old but very effective speaking tubes in order to have an intelligible conversation with him. I administered the Sacrament to him every month, and chatted with him for a bit afterwards. On one occasion he told me to take from a drawer a bundle of letters and to read the bottom one to him aloud. It proved to be a letter from Charles Dickens to the old alderman's father, replying to an invitation from the Newark Liberal Party to the novelist to stand as Liberal candidate for the constituency which Gladstone held from 1832 to 1846. I remember only the last sentence of the letter in which Dickens gave his reason for declining the invitation. It was to the effect that he was persuaded that he could do 'more for humanity by continuing my literary work than by joining that motley assembly at Westminster'. The broadcasts of Prime Minister's Question Time to which we have recently been subjected might have prompted him to add further adjectives to qualify the noun 'Assembly'!

When recently I destroyed my Newark visiting book I discovered that I had visited an average of 38 homes each week in the first three years of my ministry, and a perusal of some of the names and comments by the side of them opened up a flood of memories – memories of bereaved people, enquiring people, desperate people, lost people. Here and there in the book a more substantial note of incidents I had forgotten – sad, tragic, frustrating, amusing. No parish priest can ever complain that his job is dull!

The first entry in the book records a visit to a simple home on Newark's only hill, remarkable not for the cordial welcome I received but for a quite different reason. A small boy took an interest in me as soon as I sat down. He climbed on my knee and, becoming more and more intimate, he cuddled into me warmly. The moment came to leave and the toddler followed me to the door and held out his arms to be lifted up to say goodbye. I obliged and planted a kiss on his cheek, whereupon Mummy said, 'I hope you don't mind his clinging to you like that, but he has got the measles!'

Another note in the book recalls a pastoral call which achieved more than one would have thought possible in the peculiar circumstances. I was about to get into my little Austin Seven, which I had acquired on the instalment plan for £18, to go home to tea, when at the far end of the street in which I had been visiting for most of the afternoon, I noticed a furniture pantechnicon pulling away from a house which had been empty for some while. It was clearly not an occasion to expect entry but clearly an opportunity to welcome newcomers to the town and parish. A knock at the door brought a man in his shirt sleeves and I greeted him with a smile and 'Welcome! Peace be to this house and all who dwell in it.' His eyes goggled with surprise and, before speaking to me, he shouted to his wife within, 'Alice it's a parson; we've been in Coventry ten years and never did one darken our door. Well I'm damned!' I assured him he wasn't and that produced the laugh which resulted in my being invited into the house. There among the packing cases they entertained the parson, told me something of their lives, their long neglected church membership, their sons and their hopes for them, their yearning to recover what once they had – spiritual perception, and their recognition of the opportunity which lay before them for a new start. We knelt among those packing cases and prayed God's blessing on the new home and the new start. Alice and her man became regular members of the congregation and the sons, two of our faithful servers. When I hear of clergy dismissing parochial visiting as an effective part of the pastoral ministry that is but one of the incidents which I recall as supportive of the contrary view.

Among the sad entries of those early days in my ministry, perhaps the saddest of all, is one which recalls the death of twin brothers at the age of nine. There was a note of the morning call which told me that one had died and of the evening call when I learnt that they were united again in death. Entering into the agony of a family in deep sorrow is never easy for a parish priest, however experienced he may be, and often he feels so inadequate as indeed I did then. The day of the funeral came. A large congregation gathered to weep with them that wept and to commend the little children to the hands of God. When the two small coffins were set on their resting place in front of me and the music ceased, for the first time in my ministry, and it has happened only once since, I was too overcome with grief to start the service. I knelt down; everyone followed me. We kept silence, and in the silence we found the courage needed to open our mouths. Nearly a quarter of a century later, when I was about to be consecrated to the office of bishop, one of the hundreds of letters which I received was from the sister of the two small boys. The letter began: 'You will not know me by my married name but I remember you well from your days in Newark. Do you remember . . . ' Remember? A parish priest could never forget so poignant a moment in his pastoral ministry.

On the teaching aspect of our ministry, in the winter months we arranged courses of lectures after the pattern of the Church Tutorial Classes Association and I recall three such which I gave in the winters of 1933, '34 and '35 on Creed, Code and Cult – all attended by about fifty people. Other members of the staff did similar work and all this, plus lively youth organisations, centred around the parish church and the daughter church of St. Augustine, kept us on our toes pastorally and intellectually.

Since Canon Kay was Rural Dean of Newark, the Ruri-Decanal Chapter normally met in the vestry of the Parish Church, and it was at such a meeting, shortly after I joined the staff, that I first met a gaggle – if that can serve as a correct collective noun! – of clergy. They were an interesting group with varying gifts, all eager to extend the hand of fellowship to the new boy and, as it seemed to me, all speaking from immeasurable years of experience. There was the solemn evangelical who gave the impression that it was impious to laugh; there was the opulent squarson whose leggings shone so brightly that they could have served as mirrors, who visited his parishioners on horseback and never failed to be in Newark on market days; there was the disillusioned country parson with the Good Friday face whom I found it hard not to slap on the back with a resounding '*Christos anesti*'; there was Elijah (as in my mind I christened him), grey, gaunt and garrulous, of whose age I could only safely say that he was post-Reformation; finally there was the jovial Tractarian, most devout and excessively courteous, who had a recurring dream which he thought that a young man who had done some psychology should be able to interpret for him. Individually they were kindly men and dedicated. Collectively they were worried men and dispirited. I recall how at my first chapter meeting all with one accord groaned about the difficulty of raising money for the diocesan quota. I must needs keep still silence, of course, for as a new boy I knew nothing about the financial problems of running a parish or a diocese, but I came away from that first chapter meeting not a little disturbed by their preoccupation with 'things' and their failure to discuss any of those subjects which to a young man seemed to be the pressing issues of the day. I concede that it was the impatience of youth which prompted me, following a similar dismal chapter meeting shortly after my ordination to the priesthood, to write to the *Church Times* under the pseudonym 'Young Priest'. I know not whether it was cowardice or sensitivity for the feelings of the gentlemen of the Newark Chapter which made me conceal my identity, but at least I refrained from signing the letter 'Disgusted'! There had been a rather critical article in the paper on the subject of the newly-ordained and this had added fuel to the – I hope – righteous anger within me. In defence of the newly ordained I wrote, *inter alia*:

'Your recent leader concerning the newly ordained is as provocative as all good leaders should be. Might we have one next week concerning those who have been in orders many years, who have convinced themselves that their people will not respond, that they have ceased to make effort to win them for the Kingdom? Sweeping assertions are liable to grave misinterpretation but there must be many young priests who set out on their ministry with a glorious vision of the kingdom that is to be built, but whose vision derives small encouragement from the example of the older brethren with whom they must come into contact... He is a fortunate young priest who has not, very early in his ministry, heard such remarks as: 'I've given up visiting. It does no good.' Is the grace of Orders something which fades with the years?

Many a young priest might be encouraged to hold fast the vision which he saw at his Ordination, if some of the elder brethren whom he meets in the ruri-decanal Chapter would display half as much zeal for the Kingdom of God as they display in efforts to reduce their diocesan quota assessment, or in persistent destructive criticism of anything which calls for greater and renewed effort.

This represented an early and somewhat immature intrusion into the letter columns of the press but it should not be concluded that I have ever been an eager or persistent writer of 'letters to the paper'. Both the *Church Times* and *The Times* have in fact published letters of mine from time to time, but unlike my first intrusion, they have been provoked by the utterances or letters of others. Religious education and politico-religious matters have been subjects on which I have kept a close watch but contributions to the correspondence columns of the press have been rare and rarely sustained save for a brief encounter with Mr. Enoch Powell. However, more than once I have been invited by editors to take part in some controversy in the correspondence columns and one such invitation arose in what for a young curate was a strange circumstance.

In the early days of my ministry the only way in which I could afford a holiday was to act as a locum for a holidaying priest in return for the use of his vicarage, and this I once did in a parish near Weston-super-Mare. On my last Sunday in the parish one of the lessons at Matins prompted me to preach on the problem of suffering. The theme is one which taxes any preacher, but with time on my hands I was able to prepare the address with special care, dealing with the Christian approach to the problem and with answers to it which were unacceptable to the Christian – but remembering all the time Baron von Hugel's salutary word of warning and encouragement that in facing the problem of evil and suffering we go out into darkness 'with but one little candle in our hands'.

On the morning following that address I returned to Newark and at the weekend was astonished and exercised by the arrival of a local paper from Somerset with a banner headline reading: 'Holiday Preacher attacks Christian Science.' Unbeknown to me the editor of the paper had been in church on the previous Sunday morning and had apparently taken a shorthand note of the address, including my references to Christian Science. In his editorial he spoke of the preacher as 'a comparatively young man with an earnest manner and a pleasing voice', and added, 'There is no doubt that it was a very helpful address . . . though pungently critical of Christian Science.' The local paper followed a week later with a letter from a Christian Scientist in it and an invitation from the editor to answer it. I did so and I recall that the correspondence persisted for a while. When it ended there reached me, anonymously through the post, Arthur Mee's book on Somerset inscribed: 'From friends in Somerset,' and a note 'In appreciation of the address on suffering and of your subsequent stand in the press.' When a man is in his first curacy he cannot help finding such a gesture encouraging.

Although I have never courted controversy, there have been, occasions when the priest who exercises his prophetic, ministry responsibly, whether in public address or in writing, finds it thrust upon him. On such occasions he must, in the current jargon, stand up to be counted, for to sit down, impotent and dumb, is to abdicate his responsibility. The incident I have recalled is phenomenal in that it finds no parallel in the first twelve years of my ministry and that it arose in a parish where I was only a visitor. More was to come later when I was enticed into such fields as Sunday games, Sunday cinemas, astrology, apartheid, humanism, Marxism, drugs, comprehensive schools, transplant surgery, abortion, euthanasia, and many other such which tear the Christian conscience, and exercise the minds and hearts of those who seek guidance for what Richard Baxter called 'their walk with God to life eternal'. Inevitably the walk is through and not around these areas of human concern and although the priest must never pretend that the Christian Church has ready and easy answers to any and every controversy, he must never withdraw to the sanctuary as though the Christian gospel has nothing to say about the complexities of the human situation.

In Newark the local papers were never slow to report the activities of the Church, and what the vicar said about the impact of the Gospel upon current affairs, domestic or national, was accounted newsworthy. Certainly when the moment came for Canon Kay's departure there was a paean of praise for what he had done for the Church and the Borough, and for the influence he had exercised. I have ever been grateful for the good fortune which was mine to have begun my ministry under his inspired leadership.

After three years our team was broken up. William Kay went off to be Provost of Blackburn Cathedral; the senior curate, the genial Harold Fores, went to a church in Paignton; and Philip Butterfield followed the Vicar shortly after to become Succentor of Blackburn. I was to become senior curate and to move from the small flat in Newark which I had occupied with my sister for the greater part of my three years to the Vicarage in Coddington, the village two miles from the centre of Newark, which was at that time held in plurality with Newark. No sooner were these things settled than the Bishop summoned me to his home and to my vast surprise, asked me whether I would take over the direction of the education work of the diocese whilst remaining senior curate of Newark and priest-in-charge of Coddington. The suggestion was one that I had not remotely anticipated, and he explained it on the basis that I had had three years' teaching experience, albeit not in a state school, and that he had heard something about the educational work which I had been doing in Newark itself. Since the work which he was asking me to do would, as I realised, take me to schools all over the diocese, involve me in courses of lectures to teachers serving under both the County and City Education Authorities, and demand of me the general direction of all the educational work, in collaboration with Miss Grace Bartlett, the diocesan Sunday Schools organiser, I could see that acceptance would mean very long days and very little leisure. The day would begin, as it had done from the time when I was ordained, in the Parish Church at 7.30 a.m., I should then need to get to schools anywhere in Nottinghamshire by 9 a.m., to inspect the work of religious instruction both in church and county schools, and on some afternoons to give courses of lectures to teachers. On the other afternoons and evenings I should be free for work in Newark and Coddington.

Added to this field work there would be the supporting desk work – compilation and typing of school reports, preparation of lectures to teachers, correspondence with local education authorities concerning church school buildings, and the revision of syllabuses of religious instruction both for church and county schools. All this, at least in term time, would demand something like a fourteen-hour day. But it was not this somewhat forbidding prospect which made me ask the Bishop for time to think about his proposal. Nor was it any feeling of inadequacy. I was young and fit, and since my ordination I had come to realise that the years of administrative and legal experience in the solicitors' office of my youth, and the three years teaching experience in the Kent School, had not been, as I at once supposed, stop-gap years of frustration, but years of valuable training. It was not the character of the work nor the immensity of the task which made me demur, but something more fundamental.

The Bishop, all unwittingly, was confronting me with a momentous decision. Up to that point in my life I had by no means set aside the possibility of marriage and, if truth be told, my thoughts were beginning to turn more frequently to my native county where lived the sweetest and most gentle girl I had ever met. We looked at life through the same window as it were, and although I had resolved that I could not and would not contemplate marriage until I had been in Holy Orders for three years, in my heart I had decided that the period of self-imposed discipline had been reached, and that maybe the moment had come for me to make a move to which, rightly or wrongly, I suspected she would respond favourably. Now what I was being invited to undertake seemed to me to be well within the compass of an unmarried man but well beyond what was reasonable for someone who might be committed to a wife and family. Thus the problem which racked me, and which I shared with no one, was one which seemed to be resolving itself into a conflict of vocations. I wrestled by day and by night against the Bishop's deadline but suffice it here to say that there came the moment when I chose celibacy since the possibility of vocation to marriage seemed so clearly to threaten the totality of my vocation to the ministry. I have never regretted that decision though I cannot conceal the truth that it became easier not to glance back to what might have been, when a certain young lady in Devonshire announced her impending marriage.

I do not record this to suggest any value judgements regarding the respective merits of a celibate or married clergy. Happily the Church of England, by grace of Henry VIII and we like to think of God too, has been well served by both married and unmarried priests. It will remain so, and I suspect that before this century closes this will be yet another of our ordinances which the Church of Rome will copy. Having said as much I must in honesty add that parochial church councils, exercising their rights under the Benefices (Exercise of Rights of Presentation) Measure 1931, almost invariably express a strong preference for a married incumbent, although I discovered, as an archdeacon and as a bishop, that under test this preference was no more than a crude attempt to get a free assistant curate — two for the price of one as it were. I was interested to note too on more than one occasion during my episcopate that where a parish had had an unmarried incumbent, there was often a note to the effect that it had no objection to another! More seriously I have from time to time detected an episcopal bias against the unmarried priest for certain appointments, to the office of rural dean for example and to higher offices. Again on examination the bias proves to be founded on nothing more than a supposed inability of an unmarried priest to entertain his brethren and their wives. Such a ludicrous notion prompts me to close this subject with a reference to my good friend Russell Barry, Bishop of Southwell from 1941 to 1963. Addressing a quiet afternoon for clergy wives he made them all purr with satisfaction as he opened his first address with the words: 'Half the clergy of the Church of England are made by their wives,' and after a pause for that wholly agreeable assertion to sink in, he added: 'and the other half are ruined.' Rumour has it too that once upon a time the clergy of the Lincoln Diocese nicknamed their Bishop's wife 'The Lincoln Handicap'.

I moved from Newark to the Vicarage of Coddington in March 1936 and in the light of the personal decision which I had made, and my moving from a two-bedroomed flat to a commodious vicarage, I suggested to my mother that she might like to give up her home in Devonshire and join my sister and myself in Nottinghamshire. This she did, and with alacrity, entering immediately into the life of the village of Coddington both as enrolling member of the Mothers' Union and as a lively participant in everything which concerned the village and its welfare – Mothers' Union, sewing parties, socials and such like. From that point in my ministry wherever I went, she and my sister went, and until she reached the age of 80 my mother's active participation in parochial activities did not diminish. She endeared herself to everyone and continued to do so until her death in her 91st year.

Meanwhile, Canon Alfred Parkinson, Vicar of Retford, had been appointed by the Bishop to the benefice of Newark with Coddington, and that appointment made history in that he became the first Vicar of Newark to be appointed by the Bishop since, following the dissolution of the monasteries in 1534, the patronage had passed to the Crown. Since Coddington, which was in the Bishop's patronage, had been united to the benefice of Newark in William Kay's vicariate, patronage of the united benefice was exercised alternately by the Crown and the Bishop. Since the Crown had appointed William Kay, his successor was appointed by the Bishop. Newark knew Alfred Parkinson well as he had once been Vicar of St. Leonard's, Newark. He was received cordially, different though he was in every way from his predecessor. 'Parky', as he was affectionately known throughout the diocese, was pre-eminently a pastor. He laid no claim to scholarship nor to power in the pulpit, nor to administration, but as a pastor and a priest few could match him. In meetings he was hesitant and slow to reach conclusions and in that a striking contrast to his predecessor whose quick and perceptive mind analysed situations swiftly and accurately. On this point one of the wardens at the time described the contrast between the two men as 'like sleeping on a spring mattress for seven years then changing to a feather tic'. To say as much was to say nothing derogatory of the new vicar. Parky was cosy, warm, affectionate, ready to embrace all and sundry, and that alongside his shining integrity, deep devotion and piety, endeared him to everyone. He loved Newark, its church and people, maintained its traditions and exercised a tireless pastoral ministry. He found the preaching very demanding and we came to an arrangement by which I did at least one of the three sermons in the parish church every Sunday and more often than not two, whilst he went to the daughter church of St. Augustine's or to the village church at Coddington.

My educational work started up in earnest in the autumn of 1936 and it soon became evident that I had not over-estimated the demands on time which it made. With Bishop Mosley's approval Grace Bartlett and I set up a diocesan Council of Education, believed at the time to be the first of its kind in the Church. It was to concern itself with the development and co-ordination of the work of religious education among adults, among young people, in Sunday Schools and in lay Schools. Grace Bartlett was the only full-time officer in the field and she concentrated on the Sunday Schools. The development of the youth work and that among adults was in the hands of clergy holding parochial appointments. Everything touching Day Schools, whether Church or County, and contacts with the local education authorities and teachers, was to be my responsibility as was the co-ordination of the whole field. So keen were the local education authorities that religious instruction in their schools should be of the highest quality, that they not only invited me to inspect regularly what was being done in their schools in this field, but also sought the help of the church in the production of an adequate syllabus, and invited me to give courses of lectures to their teachers to assist them in this part of their work. This was a service to the community which the Church offered voluntarily, the authorities paying only my travelling expenses. I found amusement in the fact that journeys I made for work in primary schools were paid for at a lower rate than those made for secondary schools, and at a lower rate still for any ventures into the field of adult education. Thus rated were important discussions I had with Principal Wortley of the University College, Nottingham, about hopes which were gradually being brought nearer to realisation for the College to become a University. My concern was that if and when that happened there should be a Faculty of Theology in the University and this was a hope which Wortley came to share. A great deal of water was to flow under Trent Bridge before the University was born, and Principal Wortley did not live to see it, but those earliest moves which I had made, supported mightily, and vigorously furthered by Dr. Barry when he became Bishop, are among the factors which helped to establish what has become a most distinguished Faculty of Theology.

The visits to the schools, often made in the incredibly difficult driving conditions which Trent valley fogs created, would on occasions demand a whole day from 9 to 4, but most could be completed in a morning. It was exhausting but rewarding work, often amusing, but sometimes perilous in touching susceptibilities of clergy and teachers. Even so only on two occasions did I receive petulant letters following the despatch of reports on the inspections I carried out. One was from a Headmistress berating me for everything I had said and done and written. The force of this was nullified shortly after by a letter from the managers asking my assistance in securing her removal. The other was from a parish priest in whose school I discovered that the Roman Catholic Catechism had replaced the Anglican which was, of course, a part of the Diocesan Syllabus. Criticism of this practice in the report met with a caustic and abusive letter from the incumbent with a declaration that he had no intention of 'training up a herd of Protestants hostile to the Mother Church of Christendom'. I sent the letter to the Bishop for it seemed to me to demand episcopal attention. He returned it to me with a note which said 'Send me the sort of letter you would send to the old man if you were Bishop'. I drafted it thus:

Dear Father X,
Mr. Bulley has handed me a letter which you addressed to him recently following a report he sent you after an inspection of the religious instruction in your school. I have seen a copy of that report and I can only confirm the comments he makes in it with regard to the teaching of the Catechism. I am delighted to know that you have no intention of 'training up a herd of Protestants hostile to the Mother Church of Christendom' since such an exercise forms no part of the Diocesan Syllabus of Religious Instruction. I must however ask you to have another look at the Trust Deed of your school where you will see that you are required to provide religious instruction in accordance with the principles of the Church of England and specific mention is made of the Catechism. Whilst therefore I admire your determination to eschew hostility to the Church of Rome I must ask you to cherish that loyalty to the Church of England to which you are bound by oath and which in this particular reference, demands that you should fulfil the terms of the Trust committed to your charge when you were instituted to the benefice of Y.

The Bishop sent the letter. It was not acknowledged but I was invited to preach in the old man's church before the year was out and I took that as a sign of grace and as an indication that he would amend his ways.

The great Neville Talbot, Bishop of Pretoria from 1929 to 1933, was at that time Vicar of St. Mary's, Nottingham. On one occasion I spent a whole day in his schools and was indeed much impressed by what was happening in them. My report to the Managers was a glowing one, save for some rather pungent criticism of one particular class at the top of the school which seemed to have but a sparse knowledge of the syllabus they had been studying. Having despatched the report I heard through the ecclesiastical grapevine that the class which I had berated had been taught by the great Neville himself, and I began to wonder how an assistant curate, albeit director of education for the diocese, would fare at the hands of the assistant bishop of the diocese. I waited nervously for the storm to break! A week elapsed and then there came a postcard from St. Mary's Vicarage bearing the legend 'Dear old man, my word you've caught me bending, but I'll do better next year, I promise I will. Yours N.' That was Neville – great in mind, great in stature, great in heart and not, alas, the only great man whom the Church of England has failed abysmally to use to his full capacity.

It was some months following this incident that Bishop Mosley said somewhat casually to me over one of our many working dinners: 'Neville would like you to join him at St. Mary's,' and I answered equally casually, 'Not on your life, I admire Neville but preferably from a distance.' No more was said but I was to discover that the naughty Bishop told the great Neville my reaction to the suggestion and told him in my words. My next visit to St. Mary's Vicarage was far and away my most memorable. The 6' 6" monument of episcopacy answered the door himself, put his hands under my elbows, lifted me bodily to a corner and wagging his forefinger demanded, 'What did you say to Father about me?' I replied with such dignity as I could in the circumstances command, 'I told him I admired you at a distance and that was never more true than just now.' The great bishop drooped like a dying daffodil and I felt miserably small, but still unable to yield to his persuasions. But that disagreement did not destroy our relationship. A few years later we both found ourselves in the same hospital, I for something minor, he for something major. His room was over mine and we corresponded with one another via the nurses. My first communication to him was in rhyme and his reply, lengthy and modelled on the poetical rhythm of the Psalter, began with the words, 'I went down like a tree in the blitz: but the Lord lifted me up.'

From Alfred Parkinson's arrival in 1936 to the summer of 1939 the parochial programme and the diocesan work consumed me totally, so much so that there was frequently a tearing of conscience as to whether any one of my three fields of ministry – the diocese, the parish of Newark (which paid my stipend) and the parish of Coddington – was failing to get a fair share of my time and attention. Certainly the village seemed ever to be given the evening hours, and the night hours, very frequently until 1 a.m., were reserved for the compilation and typing of school reports, for reading, for sermon preparation. It was all very demanding but equally fulfilling and when, very recently, I destroyed bundles of letters from teachers, from parishioners and from clergy whose schools, churches and parochial church councils I had visited in those far-off days, I realised again how richly blessed I was in the opportunities which were mine throughout the Newark period of my life.

But soon everything was to change, or so it seemed. On 31 August 1939, Francis Woolley and I set off on holiday for a visit to Salisbury Cathedral and a tour of the west country, but not with any confidence that what we had planned would be realised to the full. Two nights later we sat in the Cathedral Close and pondered the serious turn of events. In that inspiring environment and in the quiet and stillness of the summer night, what was going on in Europe and might break upon our own country at any moment seemed utterly remote. But the news on the following morning was such that we made at once for home. Hitler's war was upon us and the mood of the nation was that nothing would ever be the same again. But very quickly the mood of the people stiffened and if the news bulletins did nothing to encourage it there began to creep into minds and hearts the spirit of defiance which made them determined to adopt a 'business as usual' attitude. Whilst it could not be quite like that, there was nevertheless a remarkable determination to grin and bear it, and with Rob Wilton assuring us that he and 'one other bloke' were guarding the east coast, all of us tried to carry on with our appointed tasks. The work of the Church was not by any means halted though many of its patterns were inevitably changed by restrictions which were imposed. Teachers became soldiers along with others and schools were deprived; clergy became chaplains and those who were left had, of necessity, to take more upon themselves; journeyings around the diocese, although provided for by extra petrol coupons, were somewhat restricted; and only churches which were capable of being blacked out at night could be used to hold evening services in the winter.

Of necessity the number of school inspections was reduced; courses of lectures to teachers were less since the diminished staffs precluded the release of teachers during school hours. But as parishes blacked out their vestries and halls, and people learnt to live under the difficulties, much of the evening work to which we were accustomed was restored – tutorial classes, youth organisations, confirmation preparation, study and prayer groups, all gained new momentum, and it was as though we were in business again. The slight diminution in my travelling around the diocese imposed by the restrictions enabled me to do more work in Newark itself, and in the village of Coddington where the population of young people was swollen by the arrival of children from Lowestoft Grammar School. These were quickly absorbed into our youth fellowship, and town and country children prayed and played together to their mutual advantage. Australian airmen were stationed in the village, and to welcome them and knit them into the community, the Church took the initiative in arranging gatherings of a social nature – Saturday night hops being particularly popular both as a way of entertaining the troops and of raising money for the Red Cross.

A great many of our war-time visitors joined us in worship and on Sunday nights in particular, when many churches could not be used, Coddington Church with its home-made blackout frames, was filled to capacity week by week. Ringed by airfields as we were we had many frightening experiences and not infrequently the piercing air-raid siren would cut through the very prayers for peace and happiness, truth and justice, which were being offered. There were moments too when the shadow of war rested heavily on the homes of the worshippers and every parish priest in the land must have faced in those days the unenviable task of breaking bad news to parishioners and the heavy responsibility of sustaining them by his presence and prayers.

Vivid in my own memory is the announcement on the one o'clock news bulletin on Saturday 14 October 1939, of the sinking of the *Royal Oak*, 'with great loss of life' we were told. My younger brother was an officer on that ship, and his wife and three-year-old son were with my mother, my sister and myself in the drawing room as the announcement was made. We held our own through the announcement until the little lad broke out with, 'I know what's happened; the Germans have sunk my Daddy's ship.' In the midst of all the tears I had to leave them to conduct a wedding at 1.30 p.m. Never have I found it more difficult to concentrate on the service as I did on that occasion, and never did I leave a church with such indecent haste when the service was over. Not until late in the evening was our personal anxiety relieved when the Admiralty rang to say that my brother was among the 57 officer survivors. I went immediately to the village to ask the most astute person who had been at the wedding whether everything I had said and done was normal. (The couple concerned, who knew nothing of the strain under which I was working at their wedding, assured me subsequently that they detected nothing of my anxiety.) On the following night I met my brother at Nottingham station – unshaven, penniless, dressed in scraps of clothing given him by the Red Cross, desperately sad at the loss of colleagues including two seamen whom he had twice rescued from the cruel sea. Of the ship's company of 1,234 no less than 810 lost their lives. The local press recorded my brother's survival, and his arrival at my home, and this prompted telephone calls from two or three bereaved relatives who were anxious to talk to him. A Newark doctor then rang him to say that he would be doing a real service if he would call on certain of his patients who had lost relatives in the disaster. I passed the requests to him and he answered with tears in his eyes, 'I can't. I really can't – but I must.' So I took him on these sad pastoral visits. He comforted the bereaved and being himself a man of faith passed on the Christian message which, at that moment, was probably more powerful through his lips than mine, and we prayed together.

This was the sort of situation in which every parish priest must have found himself, and too often in those dark days, and I record it, not merely because these are personal memoirs, but because it highlights the truth of that doctor's subsequent comment to me in expressing his gratitude for my brother's co-operation. 'I suppose you have to go round looking for trouble just now and bringing comfort where you can.' But the faithful pastor did not, in those grim days, have to look very far. As soon as the period of phoney war was over, sorrow and suffering, anxiety and grief were all around us and the pastor's privilege was to enter into them and speak the word of the Lord.

Grim though the days were, they had about them too a touch of the glorious, for was it not true that so often they elicited the best in human nature in the sharing and the caring which we then experienced. In the face of a common peril there was a common concern of each for the other. How vast the contrast of today, when envy and vulgar greed has brought us to the brink of national disaster, averted only by satisfying its ever increasing demands again and again and again. Neither politics nor economics has the ultimate answer to this for our malaise is more fundamental. Nor is it enough merely to sing 'Forgive our foolish ways.' What is needed is for individual Christians to stand up and to declare 'I have all I need, enough is enough.' If that means that an individual Christian works when others strike for more and more, he will accept the title 'Scab' as one of honour. The claimed right for a man to withdraw his labour has been disgracefully abused and without a change of heart will continue to be to our common distress. Compulsory arbitration of industrial disputes could yet be the only way by which the corporate blackmail which the strike has become might be eliminated as a redundant weapon. It was not, we should remember, the passing of any law about sharing and caring which made these virtues manifest in the heart-breaking days of the war, and it cannot be that national salvation could come overnight by some change in the structures of society. The evil which weighs us down is not inherent in our system; it is endemic in our hearts. It was Krushchev indeed who once lamented that the failures he saw and admitted in communism lay in its inability to make a selfless man. The inability is beyond the power of capitalism too, though at least, unlike Marxism, it does not begin by denying the reality of the Source of the Love which can overcome selfishness. A certain tune had to become top of the pops before many heard about 'Amazing Grace', but it is just that power, channelled by the Living God into hearts and minds ready to receive, which can so transform men and women that their natural self-centred motives give place to caring and sharing and daring. Whatever else happened in those war days there was undoubtedly an upsurge of dedication and prayer and this, I believe most profoundly, resulted in what I have called 'a touch of the glorious' which shone through our relationships one with another through the darkness of that hour. 'Adversity doth best discover virtue,' wrote Francis Bacon in his *Of Adversity*. That was true in those grim days and may be is ever true, but it must follow that its discovery, or disclosure, in prosperity, if the more testing is yet the more glorious.

The war years were so prolonged that it began to be accepted that despite all the difficulties each man must find it possible to do his job with an unremitting zeal. Excuses for doing less than that were ever at hand but none was regarded as valid. There was a war on and the hour demanded maximum effort from everyone. Thus my programme of work in the field of education throughout Nottinghamshire, and in the parishes of Newark and Coddington, did not diminish though it was of necessity re-planned so as to complete as many tasks as possible using the smallest amount of petrol! Furthermore for the parochial work the bicycle came into its own. The days were still long, the nights were shorter and frequently disturbed, but there was ever an inner satisfaction that under God one was able to bring to people in their hour of need a message which enlightened, which strengthened and which comforted. The care of the pastor was warmly appreciated, the voice of the prophet – the man of God – was welcomed, the ministrations of the priest in ties of sacrament and prayer and counselling and comfort were sought and accepted. No parish priest could ever have felt unwanted or unused in that dark hour of our history.

Towards the end of 1940, in one of the working lunches or evening meals which I had at intervals with the Bishop, he imparted the secret of his intention to retire in 1941 and temporarily filled me with gloom. The seven years I had served under him and in particular the last four, in which I had been privileged to enjoy his closest confidence, had for me been immensely happy and satisfying. Something like a Paul–Timothy relationship had been established between us, I valued his counsel and friendship; he appreciated my efforts and put before me innumerable opportunities for extending my experience even, on occasion, being his ghost writer for some articles for the press. I found myself wondering whether it was by some initiative of his that I was invited to preach in Lincoln Cathedral in the first year of my priesthood. I find it amusing on reflection that my first 'Bishop's Letter' to the Diocese of Carlisle was, in fact, my second 'Bishop's Letter'. The first was written on an urgent request from Fulham Palace where Bishop Mosley was staying. 'Write a letter for me on some educational theme or what you will and send it to the printer by tomorrow.' I recall that I quibbled by suggesting that I would prefer to send it to him 'for vetting and possible deposit in some ample wastepaper basket at Fulham'. He would have none of it! The printer must have it without delay. Subsequently I received an appreciative note in his all but indecipherable handwriting. I appreciated the wisdom of his decision to retire to make way, as he said, for a younger man, but I viewed the prospect of the parting of the ways with apprehension.

A day or two before he left he called me to The Manor for a chat and a meal. As we bade each other farewell at the door I had the temerity to ask him who his successor might be. His sense of fun, and at this stage teasing, prompted the reply: 'Tell me the rumours among the clergy.' I listed five whose names had been thrown around the diocese in recent weeks. 'It's one of those,' he said with a chuckle as he waved me good-bye.

I was not to wait long before I knew which of the five had been appointed the 5th Bishop of Southwell, and that in a surprising way. A telephone caller having established my identity said: 'You won't know me. My name's Barry and they've asked me to be Bishop of Southwell, I'm staying for a couple of nights incognito in a pub in Southwell and I wondered whether I might cycle over to see you to learn something about the educational set-up in the Diocese.' The 'you-won't-know-me' part of his introduction amused me as my eyes lighted upon two of his books which I had long before read with profit and the 'I'll-cycle-over' astonished me as I supposed that the Bishop-elect might with reason have summoned me to see him. However, that was my first contact with Frank Russell Barry who was to bring to the diocese of Southwell great gifts of scholarship and prophecy and to serve it with ability and distinction for twenty-two years. Our first meeting presaged a further period of very close contact with the diocesan Bishop. His lively interest in what was being attempted in the educational field in Nottinghamshire at the primary, secondary and tertiary levels, and in the voluntary and statutory fields, was immediately apparent. But what interested him most of all were the moves which were afoot for the foundation of a University of Nottingham. I was able to tell him that I had already established contact with Principal Wortley, the Head of the University College and sown seeds which I hoped might mature in the shape of a Faculty of Theology. This excited a lively response on his part and it was noticeable that one of his earliest moves was to establish a relationship with the college. In his *Period of My Life* he notes that he was 'able to ensure that the Department of Christian Theology was incorporated in the original Charter' of the new University. He would not resent my saying on my own behalf what in his autobiography he says on his. 'I shall always be glad to have taken some part in the birth of the Nottingham Faculty of Theology,' even though my part was no more than preparing the ground and sowing the seeds.

Bishops Mosley and Barry came to the diocese of Southwell with different gifts and from different backgrounds. Each of them contributed richly to the life of the Church in Nottinghamshire, and each recognised that the other had talents to lay before the altar which he lacked. Barry knew well how close my relationship with Henry Mosley had been and how great was my admiration for the work he had done. I therefore appreciated his asking me to write a brief appreciation of Mosley for the *Diocesan Gazette* following the Bishop's death in 1948. Since to my knowledge no memoir of him has appeared I think it worthwhile to repeat here an extract from the brief reference which appeared then.

Before coming to Nottinghamshire Henry Mosley's experience had been confined to the work of the Church in the East End of London – first as a parish priest, then as Bishop of Stepney, in which office he followed in a line of great personalities – Cosmo Gordon Lang, subsequently Archbishop of Canterbury, Arthur Foley Winnington Ingram, the great Bishop of London and Luke Paget, subsequently Bishop of Chester. Bishop Mosley made no claim to scholarship – 'I can leave that safely to Neville,' (Bishop Talbot), he once said to me – but throughout his long ministry in the East End and his thirteen years in Southwell he showed himself as a humble and dedicated priest, a devoted Father in God, a great Pastor and an able administrator. For his work as a Bishop to which he gave himself unsparingly, he was able to draw from the treasures of his long experience as a parish priest, and all over Nottinghamshire there will be those for whom his passing will stir up visits to their parish church, of his fatherly interest in all their affairs, of his geniality and warmth of heart. My first night in this county was spent beneath his roof and in his study on that evening began a friendship which grew ever stronger with the years. From the time in 1936 when, at his request, I took over the educational work in the diocese, I found myself very frequently in his presence. The man I got to know so well and to revere so sincerely was a man of wise judgement, of deep spiritual perception, of stern self-discipline, of great heart and kindly disposition, a 'good man full of the Holy Ghost and of faith', that was Henry Mosley.

Within five months of his Enthronement Bishop Barry, recognising that I had done a six-year stint as Director of Education and an even longer one at Newark and Coddington, asked me whether I would like to consider going to St. Anne's, Worksop, as a first benefice. Just at the time he approached me about this I was giving a course of weekly lectures in Worksop for the Nottinghamshire Education Committee, these involving an early morning drive through Sherwood Forest each Thursday. On the day following his mention of the possibility of my working in Worksop my windscreen was shattered by a stone flying from a workman's pick and I had of necessity to continue the journey without a windscreen and in a blizzard. On the following Thursday another mishap impeded me – a flat tyre, and this was repeated yet again on the next Worksop journey. The Bishop rang me at night to ask whether I had as yet made up my mind about St. Anne's. I related the incidents which had befallen me and added jestingly that all the signs were therefore that I should not go. 'On the contrary,' said the Bishop, 'all the signs are that the devil is determined to put you off. Tell me you will go before he tries again!' I did just that, at the same time acceding to his request that I should become chairman of the main education committee.

Thus a fortnight before Easter 1942 the time came to bade farewell to Newark and Coddington and to the Directorship and to set my face towards my first benefice. Handing in the education portfolio was not difficult, not that I had in any way tired of the work but rather that having held it for six years I looked forward eagerly to the opportunity of giving myself wholly to the office and work of a parish priest. Leaving Newark and Coddington after nine years proved to be a painful uprooting. The nine years I had spent there had afforded me vast opportunities of ministry in all its aspects and the people had taken me deep into their hearts as I had taken them into mine. The farewell gatherings and the gifts they showered upon me were testing emotional experiences as news cuttings, long preserved, remind me, but the moment which is recorded only in my memory was the evening before my departure for Worksop when, for the last time, I took my stall in the quire of the great Parish Church for the weekday Evensong. 'Oh how amiable are Thy dwellings, O Lord of Hosts' we sang and I reflected that I was to turn my back on that lovely parish church which had given me so much and in which there had been for me so many experiences of communion with the Living God. That ground had been hallowed by a thousand years of prayer. The stones around me were impregnated with the devotion of centuries. The stall in the quire which was mine had been the seat of countless priests before me. There in that building under the mighty hand of God I had learnt how to be his messenger, his watchman, his steward. Must I turn my back now on my spiritual home? When the office was over and the choir had left, I lingered in my stall to offer a private prayer of thanksgiving for nine of the happiest years of my life. I read the Psalm we had just sung once more. 'How amiable are Thy dwellings: thou Lord of hosts', or as the Jerusalem Bible has it: 'How I love your palace!' Newark Parish Church had become a part of me and I of it . . . and now I must leave it, and little Coddington, and all those to whom it had been my privilege to minister these past nine years – and who had given me their friendship and encouragement. I must go from the known to the unknown, from friends to strangers. I was not fearful to go, but tearful to leave. But here in the Psalm was the answer: 'They will go from strength to strength . . . the Lord God is a light and defence, the Lord will give grace . . . and no good thing shall he withhold.' With that assurance I put a wet handkerchief into my cassock pocket and left for the Song School. Do the laity realise, I wonder, how traumatic an experience the parish priest passes through, after serving and loving his people for long years, when the moment comes for him to leave?

6

First Benefice — Worksop

Worksop in Nottinghamshire has many claims to fame and at least one which could be unique. It is, so I learn, the only town in the world so named and since the spelling has changed some fifty times, between the Werchescope of Saxon days to the Worksop of to-day, one might have supposed that some home-sick emigrant to distant parts might have pounced upon one of the variants as a name for his newly founded settlement. I knew the town well before the Bishop of Southwell invited me to consider working there, for its Norman Priory, founded by Sir William de Lovetot in 1103, had given it one of the more splendid churches in Nottinghamshire and that church had, in its turn, given the town schools which were highly regarded. I had visited the Priory and the schools on a number of occasions and had been lecturing to teachers weekly at the local Technical College throughout the winter of 1941–42.

Even so, I knew nothing about the town's history and little about its industries, its people and their interests. I had discovered in Newark that the burgesses of an ancient country town were very proud of their heritage and knowledgeable too about its history, and they expected those who came among them to share their pride. Thus I deemed it prudent to delve a little into Worksop's past, to acquaint myself with the townsfolks' occupations and interests — to discover if I could what made the town 'tick'.

Worksop had by then been an industrial centre for more than a hundred years and from its inception the accent had been on mining. But this was not a place where any 'dark, Satanic mills' had left their scars. Fringed as the town is by Sherwood Forest, the Dukeries and the vast Manor Estate, Worksop is a pleasant town set in a framework of trees and parklands. When its historian John Howard wrote in 1826 of its 'records of departed grandeurs' it must have been people and events rather than buildings that he had in mind, since Worksop's noblest 'grandeur' in the latter context, the Priory Church, though now bereft of its monastic buildings save for the Early English Gatehouse, stood then and stands now presiding over the town in quiet dignity. Doubtless

Howard had in mind the long procession of great men and women, who, in one way and another, had touched its history, from the founder of the Augustinian Priory to the men of his own day. From the late fourteenth century successive Talbots, Earls of Shrewsbury, had made their mark on the town and its life, including the apparently brilliant but fearsome member of the family John, the first Earl, described in Shakespeare's *King Henry VI* as:

> *'Where valiant Talbot, above human thought*
> *Enacted wonders with his sword and lance,*
> *Hundreds he sent to Hell, and none durst stand him,*
> *Here, there and everywhere, enraged he flew.'*

Other less frightening characters visited or lived in the town in the course of its history – King Stephen, Cardinal Wolsey, Elizabeth the First, 'Bess of Hardwick', Mary Queen of Scots, James the First, Charles the First, Walpole and others. All these were entertained – though 'entertained' is scarcely the right word for Mary's 'house arrest' – in The Manor, a mansion which in its hey-day had more rooms even than the great house of Knole in Kent with its 365. This Manor, which witnessed so many occasions of royal pomp and splendour, was largely destroyed by fire in 1761 and although its owner-occupier, the Duke of Norfolk, intended that it should be succeeded by a mansion no less splendid, the death of his only son immersed him and his wife in such grief that they abandoned the project long before the plans were completed. Their Graces were content to live in The Manor as it was. It was subsequently sold in 1840 to the Duke of Newcastle who in turn sold it to Sir John Robinson in 1890. Sir John was in effect the father of St. Anne's Church and thus the name of Robinson comes much into the history of the church and parish.

Before, however, the story of my incumbency of St. Anne's proceeds, mention must be made of one eminent visitor to that part of Worksop which became the parish of St. Anne who was not received cordially by the townsfolk nor given the respect which ecclesiastical historians might regard as his due. On St. Peter's Day 1780 John Wesley, then aged 78, paid his only visit to Worksop and the day was made memorable for him – and this on his own admission – by his being pelted with 'sheep's garbage'. Furthermore only a handful of people followed him from Bridge Street to the little chapel on Castle Hill, and they were not impressed by him or his message. It would appear that as Athens was to Paul so Worksop was to Wesley. Perhaps it was his failure to get the message through that added to the garbage attack which he suffered at the town's centre, which prompted him subsequently to describe the Worksopians as 'the most stupid people that I ever saw'. I suspect that the charge of stupidity related to the people's failure to respond to his call, rather than the garbage attack, which drew from him his acid comment on the simple Worksopians. Other places must have staged their 'Wesley out, Wesley out!' demonstrations if not with 'sheep's garbage' then with other missiles.

Anxious to think the best of the ancestors of those to whom I was to minister I found myself wondering whether they were rejecting not Wesley as a person but Wesley – so it might have seemed to them – as the renegade priest. Were they, in Worksop then, such dedicated children of Mother Church that this peripatetic preacher, not content to pursue the ordered life of a parish priest, aroused their suspicions and resentment? If, as he claimed, the whole world was his parish, were they on their own behalf and in defence of a parish priest whom they revered, making a unilateral declaration of independence? The question merited some research into the fidelity or fickleness of the local Church at the time. The parish priest just then was one Philip Howard, a scion of the Norfolks who owned the advowson. He seems to have been a very faithful steward of the Word and Sacraments and one who directed his ministry not merely to the gentry, the yeomen and the merchant classes but to all and sundry of his parishioners, even to the hurlers of garbage. I asked the present Vicar of Worksop, Canon Peter Boulton, to be kind enough to confirm or question this conclusion by searching into his parish records to assess the quality of ministry afforded by the Church in Worksop at the time of the Wesley visit, and the measure of response, as far as it was possible to do. He did just this, and with great care, reaching the conclusion: 'All in all here was a classic parish carrying out both its religious and social obligations with a balance and restraint which might well have been upsetting to Wesley who was as capable as any revivalist of mistaking a steady continuous faithfulness for apathy and ignorance of the Gospel.'

A discerning judgement? I think so. Master Wesley should withdraw his stupidity charge, and the eighteenth-century Worksopians should apologise for their hooligan behaviour by which they thought they were defending things surely believed amongst them. Like modern protestors who have behaved similarly with eggs, tomatoes, flour, and tin-tacks on cricket pitches, they were bringing into disrepute the very cause they were seeking to defend. And these things happened in that part of Worksop which in 1912 became the parish of St. Anne's!

When Sir John Robinson bought the Manor and its estates in 1890 the Duke of Newcastle reserved the Lordship to himself. In similar circumstances elsewhere that might have had little consequence. In the case of the Worksop Lordship, however, it deprived the new owner of The Manor of a privilege which had been attached to it since 1542 – the privilege of 'finding for the Lord the King for the time being on the day of his Coronation a glove for his right hand and supporting the right arm of the said Lord the King on the same day, so long as he shall hold the royal wand in his hand'. Worksop had treasured for centuries this link with the monarch's coronation. When, however, Queen Eliabeth the Second was crowned, and the Duke of Newcastle was no longer resident in the United Kingdom, the Court of Claims, strangely insensitive to the feelings of the town, accorded the privilege to someone unconnected with it – a decision which not unnaturally provoked disappointment, even anger.

If, however, privileges were withheld from the sale of The Manor and its estates, Sir John Robinson was very conscious of the responsibilities which lay upon the shoulders of the town's largest landowner. Worksop had been growing in population steadily since the closing years of the eighteenth century. A new parish had been carved out on the northern side of the town in the mid-nineteenth century when St. John's Church was built. Early in the twentieth century it became evident that the town would grow rapidly on its western side – towards the Manor Estate – and no one was more conscious than Sir John of the need for further provision to be made for the spiritual needs of the newcomers. In 1911 The Bishop of Southwell sent the Reverend Hamish Gray to begin work in the new area on the western side of Worksop where there were already about 5,000 people in residence and plans in existence for many more dwellings. Mr. Gray did not find it difficult to enlist the interest and support of Sir John and Lady Robinson and very soon plans were formulated for the building of a new church on land which Sir John provided. Meanwhile Mr. Gray began his work in the small Mission Room on Castle Hill near which John Wesley had spoken to his tiny congregation and in which during my vicariate scouts and cubs held their lively meetings.

The new Church, described by Sir Edwyn Hoskyns, Bishop of Southwell at the time of its consecration, as the finest modern church in his diocese, began its life on 24 November 1912. Both the ground and the building were given by Sir John of whom it was said at his funeral that 'he planned it, watched it growing stone by stone, and in it worshipped humbly, quietly and reverently from the day it was consecrated'. His widow, Lady Maude Robinson, continued to take a lively interest in the church and the parish even after she left the town, and throughout my time as Vicar she was keen to be kept aware of our work and plans, ever ready to encourage them by her interest, and supported them by her generous giving. As at the time of the Bishop's approach to me about succeeding the Reverend Percy Leeds as Vicar, I was concerned with a Bible study group which met in her home at Kirklington Hall, I was at the outset privy to the problems and possibilities of St. Anne's and I knew that I should be able to count on her support in exploiting the possibilities and resolving the problems.

Thus I went from the two ancient churches of Coddington and Newark to a modern one, and from the old vicarage of Coddington to a new one which was superior both aesthetically and functionally. Worksop parish was outstandingly good – a gracious church of fine proportions and richly appointed, a well-built and attractive vicarage provided in 1929 and set in the church grounds, a Primary School founded by the Priory and handed over to St. Anne's in 1923, and a commodious and functionally adequate Parish Hall ideally situated in the heart of the town yet within the parish. I recall now my chagrin on learning that this hall was under requisition. It remained so for the major part of my incumbency. Once back in our hands, however, it became the scene of a number of memorable parochial and town meetings of an evangelistic and educational nature, of many lively dramatic presentations, of musical evenings and of a massive arts and crafts exhibition by which we sought to demonstrate that the rigid line between the sacred and the secular – religion and music, religion and art, etc. – is a line drawn of man's ignorance rather than of God's wisdom.

With a nucleus of worshippers and workers such as I found on my arrival, the way was open for what I believed would be an exciting and demanding ministry. All manner of projects and plans began to race through my mind. I recall vividly, however, the conflicting advice offered me by an informal meeting of the church officers. There was the treasurer, deeply concerned at the parlous financial state of the parish – annual income £390, annual expenditure £520. In his judgement the priority for the new vicar was to grapple with that problem. There was the superintendent of the Sunday Schools – and I was soon to discover that no parish could have boasted one more able and dedicated – pleading for leadership, in particular for a rather distant enclave of the parish known as Crown Street. There was the concern of the more aged of the wardens for a renewed effort to win back to the Church those who were once among its most regular worshippers. There was the young secretary of the council bewailing the loss to the parish of its assistant curate who was forced to leave 'because we hadn't enough to pay his monthly stipend'. Finally there was the still small voice, if I may so describe it, of the deeply committed but somewhat formidable head teacher of the day school who said: 'What we need most is teaching, and teaching and more teaching.' I warmed to her response especially and immediately for in my view she sought that which, offered and received, could mean that what all the others sought could be added unto them. I tried to take account of all their 'priorities' in my first letter to the parish:

> There are two words which must be writ large across the operations of the Church today – two tasks before you and every worshipping community. They are 'Education' and 'Evangelism'. I hope that these may be the keywords of my ministry among you, that in the power of the Holy Spirit we may together strengthen our hold upon the things surely believed among us, and proclaim them with such assurance and conviction that others will see in them an irresistible appeal.

The church officers had clearly felt that they were doing their duty in indicating weaknesses in the life of a church and parish which clearly meant so much to them, but when my ministry began I discovered several pluses to set against their minuses. One of these was undoubtedly the church's outreach to young people. St. Anne's, Worksop was the only one of my parishes in which the Scout and Guide Movement was strong, not merely in numbers, which could be matched elsewhere, but in Christian witness and Christian purpose. The numerical strength was demonstrated for the non-worshipping community when, with colours flying and bugle band awakening the sleepers, they paraded very frequently to church. The witness and purpose were demonstrated by the close integration of the two movements into the witness and purpose of the Body of Christ in that place. That was the natural outcome of dedicated leadership, for both Fred Thompson the scoutmaster, and Becky Greaves, the guide captain, did what they did for and with the young people out of a true concern for their balanced growth. The spiritual and moral values which formed the primary motivation of the two movements, but which tend to be pushed to the periphery under leaders of lesser calibre, were always well to the fore. The scouts and guides of St. Anne's were firmly within the Body of Christ – as regular worshippers, as workers – singing in the choir, serving at the altar, teaching in the Sunday Schools, and a great many remained so, long after scouting and guiding days were over.

Furthermore a parish which in 1942 could boast a Junior Parochial Church Council, structured on similar lines to the statutory body, watching over the work amongst young people in particular but taking an active part in every aspect of the Church's witness and work, could hardly be indicted for neglect of the young. Within their experience and ability our lay leaders played with the young folk and prayed with them. The 'playing' expressed itself in the things which are normally associated with the movements – camping, working for badges, games, acts of social service and, I recall too, many dramatic presentations of singularly high quality. The 'praying' was within the adult worshipping community at the Eucharist Sunday by Sunday, and although neither the scoutmaster nor the guide captain made this compulsory, such was their own example that the youngsters came to regard being 'in the Lord's Own House on the Lord's Own day at the Lord's Own service' as part of their Duty to God. Before going to St. Anne's I had often questioned the efficacy of the scout and guide movements as instruments in the hand of the Church in its contribution to the balanced growth of the children of the Church. My experience there convinced me that given the right leadership the two movements could take an authentic and powerful place in the parochial programme of voluntary religious education of the young.

The young people were there in force on the Thursday before Passion Sunday in 1942 when I was instituted to the benefice by the Bishop of Southwell and inducted by the Archdeacon of Newark the Venerable Percy Hales. The Bishop, never at his best with children (though brilliant with students) commented on their presence and captured their attention by speaking simply about their part in 'writing the next chapter in the continuing story of St. Anne's'. There was a great congregation from Newark and Coddington as from Worksop itself, and the presence among the dignitaries of Victor Turner, the Archdeacon of Nottingham who had been St. Anne's second Vicar, afforded special pleasure to the Worksopians and indeed to me since I had been working closely with him in the educational work of the diocese for so long.

'Sir, we would see Jesus,' said a Greek tourist to Philip in the Temple, and in my first address on the following Sunday morning I asserted that request as the one which any congregation might address to an incoming parish priest as indicative of their need and his task. So my ministry at Worksop began. Passion Sunday, Palm Sunday, Holy Week, Good Friday, Easter Day – there was no searching for a theme for those early addresses. It was Jesus – the orb of God's truth, 'yesterday, today and forever', Jesus the Way, the Truth, the Life, Jesus the Mediator, Jesus the Crucified, Jesus the Redeemer, Jesus the Living Christ. If, as I had been told, their need was for 'teaching, and teaching and more teaching', it could start nowhere but there, and so it continued – from the pulpit, at the altar, in the parochial church council, in the day school, in the youth groups and through the parish magazine to which I attached immense importance. A widely-distributed and well-produced parish magazine affords a rich opportunity for systematic teaching and since for the most part it is the only piece of specifically Christian reading matter which is put through the average letter-box I have ever regarded it as a potential instrument of evangelism and education. The average parish treasurer's only concern is that it should 'pay its way'. My concern has always been that it should make its mark. To that end whilst it can present those parochial tit-bits beloved by parishioners, its real value lies in its use as a medium for religious instruction in the Christian Faith and the Christian way. If it does that it is an investment whether or not it satisfies the Treasurer.

Eighteen months later this teaching ministry was mightily augmented by the arrival in the parish of a young assistant curate who proved to be a brilliant expositor of Christian theology, a sensitive pastor and a disciplined priest. His arrival on the scene so soon took the parish by surprise since I had so frequently stemmed the impatience of the church council in their desire to augment the staff. I had been told that the monthly stipend of the last curate had on occasion been raised by the holding of an *ad hoc* whist drive and whilst these entertainments were not without value I counted the labourer to be more worthy of his hire than that his reward should depend upon anything so fortuitous. At my first meeting with the church council therefore I made it clear that much as I would welcome a colleague, I could not contemplate taking any serious step towards augmenting the staff in the way that they and I desired until a substantial portion of the necessary stipend could be secured by some capital investment which would yield a continuing income. Since no one in the church council displayed any alarm at the promulgation of so expensive an idea, there and then – and this had not been planned before the meeting – I added: 'We must raise for this purpose a capital sum of something like £3,500.' To my astonishment, and I believe to the council's own surprise, someone proposed a motion to that effect adding that the substantial collection from the service of Institution should form the basis of the fund. The appeal to this end was launched in June 1942 and the £3,500 was raised before 1944 ended. Subsequently it was increased by the addition of a legacy of £2,000 under the will of Lady Maude Robinson. In the late summer of 1943, by which time the Council and the parish had demonstrated their determination to fulfil their resolution, I met for the first time — it seemed fortuitously but the adverb is inappropriate in the context of the prayers I had so frequently offered — one Thomas Wood, who with a first-class degree in English, a degree in Divinity and Mirfield training, seemed to me to have much what the parish needed at that moment in its history and I needed at that juncture in my ministry. My decision to offer him a title and his to accept it were immediate! Within a month of our first meeting Thomas Wood was ordained at Southwell and we became colleagues. In fact we worked cheek-by-jowl for some 15 years and our friendship has persisted for 35 years, though for the last 21 years he has been in the Province of Wales and is at the moment Head of the Department of Theology at the University College of St. David's at Lampeter.

No sooner had the parish completed the Assistant Curacy Endowment Fund than there came a call from the Bishop of Southwell in a Pastoral Letter which drew attention to the spiritual needs of people in the new areas of Nottinghamshire — a call to those whose forefathers had provided them with churches to help those who had none. The call coincided with the issue of new regulations of the Ministry of Education concerning school buildings which, with the implementation of the Education Act 1944, would make heavy demands upon St. Anne's and other parishes, which were fortunate enough to have church schools. The Bishop's Call and our own needs were set before the annual parochial meeting and a decision was made to raise £1,000 for the Bishop's Reconstruction Fund and £1,000 as a first step towards the sum that would be needed for the construction of new classrooms at our church school. The task was completed within a year, and that not by a few gifts from wealthy people but by generous, even sacrificial gifts by the whole worshipping community and by hard work by young and old alike.

This meant that in addition to the stabilising of the parish finances and the increase of giving to our overseas work, £5,500 had been raised for our own and diocesan purposes and that within a period of three years. But recalling the life of the parish at the time, both from memory and from the detailed diary of events in the parish magazine, it is clear that money-raising was by no means the dominant theme of our corporate life nor even a time-consuming factor in our parochial programme. It was rather that St. Anne's congregation — a happy mix of manual and professional workers in a proportion of approximately five to one — responded so willingly to the teaching about Christian stewardship of money. Nor was there any lack of enthusiasm on the part of the youth organisations in carrying through efforts which they sponsored. The women's organisation, which met weekly in the vicarage and under the inspiring leadership of my mother, worked hard for our own and overseas enterprises.

This aspect of parochial life prompts a look at the present position of giving in the Church. Thirty-five years ago it had scarcely occurred to the Church that the taxpayer putting his shilling into his free will offering envelope week by week could, by covenanting his gift, all but double it. The great national charities had long been availing themselves of the benefit of the statutory provision by which the government had in effect declared its intention to assist or at least not to impede charitable work. The Church, which by its very message keeps charity alive, had been slow to avail itself of the privilege, and the ordinary churchgoer, despite knowing about Deeds of Covenant, assumed that they related only to those with cheque books. Certainly the suggestion was received cautiously by St. Anne's Church Council, but it was received and acted upon by a few. I am sure though that St. Anne's was not the only parish in which there were godly people who had an uncomfortable feeling that by being asked to covenant their giving they were being invited to take part in a tax 'fiddle'.

Many years were to elapse before Christian Stewardship campaigns found their way into English church life, the earliest being conducted by secular fund-raising organisations many of which managed to secure for their staffs men who were able and willing to inject into their training programmes a sense of Christian purpose. Adventurous parishes, prepared to do and dare, blazed the trail of the pioneer; others looked on askance; still others wrote the whole enterprise off as a base thing devoid of any degree of spirituality. It soon became abundantly clear, however, that under the right leadership such campaigns not only resulted in a vast increase in parochial income, but in renewed interest in the parish church and in its worship and work. The discerning saw such campaigns as an aspect of mission and it was this approach which prompted dioceses to appoint Christian Stewardship directors who could both organise campaigns within the diocese and educate clergy and laity alike in their potential. Christian commitment was seen as demanding the dedication of time and talents and material possessions, and its fulfilment lay in sacrificial giving. There can be no doubt that this movement within the Church has wrought nothing but good, but since it is not by any means a 'once learnt never forgotten' lesson there is need for revision courses at regular intervals in which the church council can give account of its stewardship and in which the meaning of Christian commitment is spelt out anew. That this should be done in the context of something like an *agape* or parish supper seems all to the good since it provides an opportunity for those who meet in worship to meet in *koinonia*.

One of the most enthusiastic exponents of the spiritual and material value of the Christian Stewardship campaign, and one who is known in a great many dioceses both in England and overseas for his work in this connection, is Eric Buchan, sometime Archdeacon of Coventry. Recent research by him in which he compares significant statistics in a group of parishes loosely designated as 'Christian Stewardship parishes' with a comparable group of parishes which have not adopted this method of teaching is so startling as to command the attention of the most sceptical. Far from de-spiritualising the Church's work and witness such efforts heighten it. It is, in fact, an aspect of mission which kindles in people an awareness of their membership of the Body of Christ, of their fellowship one with another in the service of Our

Lord and His Church, and of the cost of Christian commitment – and which challenges them to face up to the consequential demands.

This leap in my story from the past to the present is not to imply that the parish of St. Anne's, Worksop had developed its giving anything like so efficiently or effectively as is done by a Christian Stewardship campaign. But the faithful there had learnt something about the need of the Church for planned giving, and by refusing to segregate giving (money raising if you like) from worship and witness, they had set their feet at least a little way on the right path. Under the impetus of stewardship campaigns a great many parishes have gone far since then but many still lag behind. In consequence the Church's work is so often gravely limited by its meagre resources. My conviction is that before long we shall see something in the nature of what the world is wont to call a religious revival. There will be once more a recognition that life has a spiritual dimension, and men will look again to the Church to explain and expound, to direct and sustain. Many more men will be offering themselves for the sacred ministry and be ready to dedicate their whole lives to service of God within it. Will the Church, which in this particular context means the laity, be ready to meet that situation by ensuring funds for their training and stipends for their services? Only, I believe, if there is everywhere an understanding of what Christian commitment means in terms of stewardship and that gospel cannot be preached without reference to what a man does with his material possessions. The man who asked Our Lord what he should do to inherit eternal life received an answer which he neither expected nor welcomed. Maybe he anticipated a nice philosophical discussion concerning the term 'eternal life' in relation to the keeping of the Law. What he got was a peremptory command to get working with his cheque book! Shackled as he was by his 'great possessions' it was no wonder that 'he went away sorrowful' – unwilling to face the challenge of giving. Religion was all right but it must not be allowed to interfere with his private life in that way. Yet there it was: Eternal Life, Our Lord told him, was life which is characteristic of the Living Loving Caring Giving God. To live is to give and to give is to live – not haphazardly but thoughtfully, not meanly but generously, not constantly counting the cost but sacrificially.

Just before I left the parish of Mansfield I came across a parish magazine nearly a hundred years old. Curious to discover what vicars were saying in their parish letters in those days I turned to the appropriate page. The letter I read was one of the most apologetic any parish priest can ever have written. The good man was expressing his profound regret that he and the squire could no longer sustain the work of the church alone and that he must, as from a fixed date, institute a collection in church which he promised would be at one service only each Sunday. We have gone a long way since then, but we still have a long way to go.

As a footnote to this plea for acceptance of the Christian Stewardship approach to direct giving in parishes I would say that I have never seen its development as ruling out the parochial programme events such as working parties, bazaars, garden parties and fairs, or even fayres! These bring opportunities not only for the exercise of God-given talents sometimes by those who have little more than the widow's mite, but also for the Body of Christ in a given place to work with hand and heart and head for the work of Christ. More importantly, perhaps, they draw together in common purpose those who gather together in common worship and in that sense they can be seen as an extension of that fellowship one with another which is sealed in Holy Communion. We can assume that the Lord of the Dance of Life never looks askance when he sees his people 'altogether with one accord in one place' whether that place is the parish church, the parish hall or the vicarage lawn.

St. Anne's, Worksop knew something about direct giving and practised it with devotion – but how they enjoyed themselves working together for a common purpose and that the noblest of all! Garden parties, sales of work, whist drives, jumble sales, pantomimes, dances, dramatic presentations were all opportunities for fellowship and fun as well as for raising money for the Red Cross, the Church Army, for our Church school and other laudable purposes. Happily, so strong was our band of workers, numerically and in enthusiasm, that my colleague and I could never complain that the organisation of these events drew us away from our specifically pastoral and priestly work, though we did demonstrate once a year that we were not unwilling to take our place in 'serving tables' when the need arose. The annual Vicarage Garden Party was the great social event of the parochial calendar and the preparation for that, and its carrying through, very properly demanded direction by the vicar and hard work on the part of the vicar and curate alike. The spacious vicarage lawn was on that occasion trampled by a thousand feet and more and from the moment of its opening by, among others, the much loved Winifred, Duchess of Portland, idolised by the Nottinghamshire miners and their families, to the last streak of daylight, there was merriment, laughter and fun.

Meanwhile the 'teaching, teaching and more teaching' pressed ahead in a variety of tried and novel methods. There were courses of sermons based on the liturgical readings, the answering of questions submitted by members of the congregation, the initiation of a parish library, articles in the parish magazine and, from time to time, special projects for intensive instruction. One of the last mentioned – a Teaching Convention, spread over a week – was designed to break new ground by encouraging some of the committed Christians to evoke the interest of their agnostic or unbelieving friends. It was to be held in the only accommodation available to us which was capable of being blacked out – namely the vestry with its limited space. My introduction of the plan to the Parochial Church Council began with the words, 'I want 25 Christians to seek out 25 non-Christians – agnostic, atheist, Marxist or what you will – and bring them here every night for a week that we may teach them and that they may raise their own problems and questions.' When the time came we fell a little short in the numbers but among the forty-four who came each night there were indeed agnostics and secular humanists, for the most part relatives of members of the council itself. Several individuals subsequently presented themselves for Confirmation and the son of one of them is now a priest. It was a daring venture which achieved less than we hoped but certainly broke new ground as we planned.

When at length our hall was restored to us we arranged a series of public lectures designed to expound the Christian approach to certain controversial issues of the hour – Communism, Industrial Relations, Sunday Entertainment, Sex and Family Life, Politics – and these aroused a good deal of interest in the town and provoked lively discussions. But perhaps the most memorable meeting in the Hall, advertised as 'for men only' in the hope that winning the attention of father might alert the whole family, was one addressed by Dr. Cyril Garbett, the Archbishop of York, and attended by the Bishop of the Diocese and by men from Worksop and the surrounding parishes. The Hall was full to capacity and Dr. Garbett's evangelistic call was vigorous and compelling. I recall that he was accompanied on that occasion by his domestic chaplain, one Gerald Ellison, who was to become Bishop of Chester and subsequently Bishop of London. Neither he nor I could have foreseen when we talked about the final arrangements for that great meeting in 1946 that we would find ourselves working together again as members of the Northern Bench of Bishops. At that meeting copies of *Towards the Conversion of England*, which had just been published by the Church Assembly, were distributed to everyone present, and from that meeting a number of enterprising exercises in evangelism began in that part of the diocese.

Towards the Conversion of England was in fact an admirable document, received with enthusiasm all over the country at the time, but not followed through with the courage and daring which the hour demanded. Although the report was initially welcomed, it did not arouse what would now be described as the on-going response which it deserved and demanded. Nothing comparable with it has been ventured since, though the Northern Province did, in the early seventies, and under the impetus of the then Archbishop of York and Bishop of Liverpool, sound a *Call to the North* which was to be a concentrated effort in evangelism and renewal. Inevitably there was some defeatist talk but many were roused to special ventures in evangelism and education. The truth is, however, that the Church of England is too suspicious of enthusiasm to allow itself to become deeply involved in anything approaching mass evangelism – and that I say to our discredit. We desperately need to recognise what is good in methods adopted by those whose endeavours we tend too easily to dismiss. Billy Graham, for example, is an evangelist who excites reactions ranging from unbridled enthusiasm to cold suspicion. But he is an evangelist and if, as such, he can speak to those who have not hitherto heard, or having heard have not hearkened, if he can lead towards Christian commitment any of those who have not been touched by more traditional methods, then undoubtedly the Spirit of God is at work through him, and who are we to gainsay the Spirit? I know of course, that your unbeliever cannot in a single evening be brought to love God with heart and mind and soul and strength, for spiritual growth is not mushroom growth. He will not on a single evening learn all there is to know of the Christian Faith and the Christian Way of Life, nor compass the demands of total commitment to Our Lord Jesus Christ, for commitment is a matter for the intellect and the will as well as of the emotions. Yet if, in a single evening, the light breaks through his darkness in any degree, how great is the resultant opportunity for the Church to draw him into its fellowship so that through communion and prayer he may become a lively member of the mystical Body of Christ. It is, in fact, just at that point that the Billy Graham campaign method is lacking. It kindles the emotions, confronts unbelievers with the Christ, and evokes a response to a degree that they mount up with wings as eagles, and then they are left to their own resources. The erstwhile unbelievers soon discover what the committed Christian knows only too well – that the mounting with wings as eagles is the easier part of our surrender to Christ. Far more difficult and demanding is it 'to walk and not faint', to endure and persevere, and for that we desperately need to be within the fellowship of the Church, active in worship, active in service, drawing encouragement from those who like ourselves are 'in Christ' and receiving supplies of grace from the Lord of the Church himself.

I do not write this as in any sense a commercial for Billy Graham or as an expression of whole-hearted approval of his methods, but as a salutary reminder that in this matter of evangelism we need the courage, the boldness, the thrust which he and others like him – not forgetting the Marxists – have for their respective causes. Evangelism is an area in which the Church of England has been too timid, too fearful of failure, too shy. It has ever been the subject which is pushed to the bottom of the agenda. The revision of Canon Law, the concoction of new liturgies, the creation of a system of Synodical Government, the compilation of little schemes for joining little churches to little churches – all these are easier and more engaging. Yet whilst all of them may do something for the person who is touching the hem of Christ's garment, and holding on somewhat tenuously, none is likely to challenge the person at the edge of the crowd or the person who has long since turned his back on Christ or never been encouraged to confront him.

My faith in the parochial system convinces me that the best hopes for rebirth and renewal reside within the parish, and the key person is, as ever, the parish priest who is the 'messenger, watchman and steward' of the Lord. However faithfully he delivers the message to the faithful, watches over his people as pastor, and ministers the sacraments of which he is steward, he must hear and hear again the command 'Go out to the open roads and invite everyone you meet to the banquet.' For that he needs the help of the laity to work with him in special evangelistic efforts. From time to time there is room for the help which the old-time Parish Mission could bring – aggressive evangelism which under the impulse of the Spirit renews the faithful, alerts the apathetic, encourages the doubter and challenges the unbeliever. I have seen great things happen in and through such efforts. I am not disposed to accept any easy thesis that the method of the Parochial Mission is outmoded. There is a time and place for such ventures now. Christians must awake to the need of the hour. Nor must they be content to do less than drawing people into the fellowship of the worshipping community. I have heard priests – and even a bishop! talk scathingly about 'treating people as pew fodder'. To suggest, as the quip does, that public worship is of small moment, is to do God a dishonour and man a disservice.

I find in my records notes of the vast gatherings of people in St. Anne's on National Days of Prayer and in particular a reference to one such when nearly 1300 came in the course of one day. To suggest for one moment that all these were regular worshippers would unfortunately be remote from the truth, but in the monthly parish magazine letter following that day of prayer I called the faithful again to the task of helping them to become so. I wrote *inter alia*:

We must not weary in our efforts either individually or collectively to draw others within the fellowship of the Church, since the Church as the guardian and exponent of the Gospel is the only society which can point men to a Light strong enough to pierce the darkness of the time. Can you remember the last time you personally encouraged someone to come along to church? Or is this something in which you have been reticent and timid? Whilst it is quite possible to cherish quite high moral standards and even religious beliefs without worship, I cannot but contend that their endurance is imperilled and their potential power minimised so long as their holders keep themselves aloof from the worshipping community. When people queue for worship as, just now, they queue for fish, then we may begin to hope that the somewhat nebulous respect for God and the things of God which come to the surface of our national life on, for example, days of prayer may, by being thus clarified, defined and secured, prove to be a factor far more cogent in the ordering of our international and national affairs than men may yet know or dare to hope.

In this connection my colleague and I took up King George the Sixth's call in August 1944 for a Revival of Spirit and in a series of addresses touching the nature of God, the nature of man, God's initiative and man's response, we sought to point the way for such revival in the individual and through the individual to society. To make the readers of the parish magazine aware that such things were being talked about not merely by bishops and priests no opportunity was lost of quoting significantly Christian utterances of statesmen and military leaders – Smuts, Dowding, Montgomery and other such men unafraid to bear their Christian witness.

The utterances of many such eminent laymen were often the starting point of my discussions and debates with two military units in the parish – a Pioneer corps stationed in a building not far from the church, and some

Royal Engineers in a camp on the periphery. Treating them as parishioners I offered my services, which were warmly accepted. The officer in charge of the Engineers said that they would like an occasional Sunday church parade and a 'padre's hour' – the latter, incredibly, early on a week-day morning. The Headmaster of Worksop College kindly allowed me the use of the College Chapel for the church parades, and the padre's hour gatherings were on the camp site, attendance being voluntary and invariably good. For these men submitted questions in writing and my answers led to lively discussions. This arrangement continued for some time without let or hindrance and without thought on my part of payment, for the men were in my parish and therefore within the 'cure of souls' which I received at the hands of the Bishop when I was instituted. It was therefore something of a surprise to me when on one of my visits the quartermaster-sergeant handed me a cheque for what to me was a considerable sum – something like £60. I recall his look of astonishment when I put it back on his desk saying that I could not accept it since I was already being paid by the Church itself for ministering to my parishioners. Living where they were the soldiers were within the 'cure of souls' entrusted to me by the Bishop. There ensued a very lively but friendly argument, he contending that an extra Sunday service and early morning visits to the camp for padre's hours merited extra payment and I contending that mine was a vocation in which there were no strict hours of work. He sought to close the argument with the assertion that I was not allowed to work for nothing for the Army, and with that he thrust the cheque into my hand again. I persisted in my refusal to take it whereupon he put it under a paper weight on his desk with a flourish: 'There it is, and you will be the one to lift it from that weight. Mark my words!' A jocular comment touching the unwanted cheque fell from his lips or mine on my weekly visits, until at length he caught me, in the course of a procedural discussion, slyly pulling the cheque from beneath the weight. His prophecy had proved to be correct for having been appointed meanwhile an Officiating Chaplain to the Forces, I was being challenged by His Majesty's Inspector of Taxes for not declaring on my return the amount of the cheque resting contentedly on the sergeant's desk. My determination 'to work for nothing', as he described it, was frustrated, not for the first time, and as it transpired not for the last.

Meanwhile the soldiers on our doorstep were not our only concern. We were at pains to keep in touch with men from the parish, and indeed some women, who were serving in the forces. They were remembered in our weekly prayer group and kept informed of our remembrance of them by our sending to them from time to time news of their parish church and its activities. Thomas Wood, who worked assiduously with the Fellowship of Youth, saw that those leaving the parish to join the forces were, so far as their frequent movements made it possible, kept aware of their Church's constant remembrance of them. But early in 1945, when it became apparent that the war in Europe was nearing its end, we began to conceive plans for the welcome home for those who had been parted from their homes, their friends and their parish church for so long. Thus in my April letter to the parish I made a plea for careful consideration of ways and means by which we could ensure that the Church's main task of drawing its sons and daughters back into the fellowship of the worshipping community should not be overlooked in the midst of the social events which, quite properly, would mark their return. Again with the active help of my colleague we gathered together about twenty of the younger end of the adult congregation to form themselves into a 'cell' whose purpose it would be to establish immediately a fellowship of spirit with those who were away, and to have in being by the time they returned, some organisation made up of men and women of comparable age into which they could feel their way back into the full fellowship of the Church. Thus there was born the 'Twentieth Century Club' — an *ad hoc* arrangement designed to meet a situation which all of us were coming to believe would arise within weeks rather than months. The mounting excitement at the possibility of an early end to the war lay behind the last sentence in my April letter to the parish in 1945:

> May I remind you all that on the day when hostilities with Germany are officially declared to be at an end there will be a service of Thanksgiving at 7.30 in the evening (unless that day be a Sunday when the service would be at 6.30). Any who are moved to come straight to the House of God immediately following a public announcement of the end of the war in Europe will find the clergy there ready to lead them in a short act of thanksgiving whatever the time of day — or night.

When the moment came some weeks later they did just that in their hundreds, and very moving indeed it was as crowds flocked into church to join in prayers of thanksgiving and hymns of praise for the deliverance.

But the war in the Far East was still with us and even those who returned to their homes quite quickly after the cessation of hostilities in Europe were soon off again. Our Twentieth Century Club had been initiated none too soon. Their meetings were held in the vicarage drawing room and I recall one — I think the first — when those who came sat wearing their overcoats and in some instances gloves! The coal ration did not extend to extra fires though subsequently a fortunate miner would arrive with a small basket of coal enough to keep our extremities from freezing, our minds from torpidity and more than enough to warm the cockles of our hearts. It would be idle to pretend that the club achieved all that we hoped for from it, but less than honest to underwrite the contribution which it made in knitting within the fellowship of the Church once more very many of those whose association with it had been so gravely interrupted.

Suddenly the war in the Far East came to an abrupt end by a means which none had foreseen. The atomic bomb marks one of the great divides in history. Atomic energy had been harnessed and its first use had been to eliminate an entire city. Everyone was relieved that the war was at an end but as the reports of its awful climax reached us minds were tortured, hearts were broken and consciences were deeply disturbed. 'Say something Vicar, please, about the moral and spiritual implications of this atomic energy thing,' said the lady who three years before had told me that what was needed was teaching and more teaching. And when that lady spoke the Vicar dare not stand by impotent and dumb! Far into the night on Saturday, 11th August I struggled, tearing up manuscript after manuscript and at Evensong on the Sunday I did my poor best to draw out 'The Lesson of the Atomic Bomb'. Much of what I said appeared in the press and subsequently the short address was printed in full in the magazine.

It was in 1945 too that three honours were thrust upon me, the acceptance of which took me away from the parish from time to time, though only for brief periods. The first was my election to the Convocation of York, the second my appointment as Chaplain to the High Sheriff of Nottingham and the third my appointment to the Honorary Canonry of Oxton Prima Pars in Southwell Cathedral.

Although I had always kept myself informed of the discussions and debates of the Church Assembly and of the Convocations, I had never entertained the thought of seeking membership of those bodies and when, from time to time, members of the clergy suggested that I should do so I invariably brushed them aside with the plea that I had no stomach for ecclesiastical politics. My heart was in the parish and I had no urge to be extracted from it. However, the pressure was increased as the war was nearing its end and when Bishop Barry himself commented that he thought I should show willing to serve as a proctor I yielded and submitted myself for election. When it appeared that I had done what my brethren wanted, for I came top of the poll, I was reassured. (In subsequent elections I remained top of the poll until Nicholas Allenby of the Society of the Sacred Mission, then a tutor at Kelham Theological College and subsequently Bishop of Kuching, stood for election and pushed me into second place. Very properly he cornered all the first votes from the monks of Kelham!). From 1945 to the day of my retirement I took my place regularly in the Convocation of York, in the old Church Assembly and in the Synod and there were times when I thought my journeys thither were worthwhile. I confess, however, that the initial reluctance to be involved in ecclesiastical politics was never quenched and as a parish priest, as an archdeacon and as a bishop I found myself begrudging the time which the meetings consumed and longing at each session for an early return to the parish or the diocese. Nevertheless in the web of my total experience there are valuable – and colourful! – strands which could not have been there but for my membership of those bodies.

Resident at The Manor throughout my vicariate was John Farr, a nephew of Sir John Robinson and a local magistrate. On his appointment as High Sheriff of Nottinghamshire he invited me to be his Chaplain – an office which involved my attendance at the Nottingham Assizes for the sessions during his year of office. More than one friend quipped at the time that to be Chaplain to the Sheriff of Nottingham was vastly superior to the same office for 'any old sheriff elsewhere' for I could not but meet Robin Hood, Maid Marian and other interesting people. 'My socialist inclinations prompt me to ask you to put in a kindly word for Robin Hood,' wrote one. Fascinated as I have always been by the judiciary and by the Bar I accepted John Farr's invitation with alacrity and in the course of the year met at close quarters Mr. Justice Charles, Mr. Justice MacNaghten and Mr. Justice Birkett. My daily meetings during the Assizes week with the last mentioned were the most memorable. In the course of the drive from St. Mary's Church to the Court, Judge Birkett was kind enough to comment generously on my Assize Sermon and said that he would like a copy of it for his records. I regarded this request, however, as no more than a kindly gesture to a young priest, something not to be taken literally, but when I called at his lodgings for the drive to the Court on the third morning and once more failed to produce the copy of the sermon, he stood before me, looking splendid in his robes, and said grandiloquently but with a rich smile, 'His Majesty's Judge of Assize hereby orders the Reverend Mr. Cyril Bulley to produce by tomorrow morning a full and authentic copy of the sermon preached by him in St. Mary's Church, Nottingham at the opening of this Assize, on pain of . . . ', and he broke off with a laugh adding that his request was sincere. The copy was duly produced on the following morning. In the course of the main trial on that day the Judge suddenly pushed in front of me a bundle of American comics produced by the counsel for the defence in the trial of some youngsters who had held up a cinema cashier and who had said that the idea for the crime they committed came from the comics. 'Have a look at these,' the judge said 'and use your influence to stop them coming into the country.' I recall vividly how, in his summing up of that case, Judge Birkett turned frequently to the young lads and addressed them in a manner which might have been that of a father concerned for the future of his sons.

By the end of a long Assize I had spent many hours with the Judge and had been deeply impressed by his mastery of words, by the brilliant way in which he summed up the various cases and by what I can only describe as his pastoral concern for the young people who had gone astray and for those who had been hurt by their crime and by the crimes of others. When we parted we were destined not to meet again for fifteen years. By that time he had been created Baron Birkett of Ulverston and I had been consecrated Bishop of Penrith. We met then as chief speakers at the annual dinner of the St. George's Society in Barrow-in-Furness at whose Grammar School Birkett had received his early education. The Mayor was about to introduce us to each other when I stayed him with the words: 'We know each other well. We studied American comics together in our youth.' Lord Birkett enjoyed the recollection and, remarkably I thought, recalled the case being tried at the time. We were never to meet again, but four years later I was glad to be invited to a little ceremony on Ullswater when the fell known as Nameless was renamed Birkett Fell in memory of the Baron's vigorous opposition to a bill promulgated by the Manchester Corporation. The implementation of the waterworks clauses in that bill would undoubtedly have destroyed the scenic beauty of Ullswater and damaged irrevocably a lovely part of the Lake District.

It was Birkett's espousal of that cause in the House of Lords on 8 February 1962 which saved the day, his brilliant speech winning the support of a substantial majority. Two days after this triumph he died and there were many who felt that his last speech was his greatest, not forgetting his brilliant performances at the Bar or those sadly unrecorded war-time radio speeches which he made anonymously as 'Onlooker'. The Ullswater Preservation Society conceived the idea of putting a plaque on the rock face of Kailpot Crag, near Howtown, and of renaming the fell, but the project was not fulfilled until July 1964. Major E. W. Hasell (Chairman of the Preservation Society hired a Lakeland steamer which carried members of the Birkett family, the Baron's biographer (Mr. H. Montgomery Hyde), myself and about a hundred or so guests to a point on the eastern shore of the lake. There in what was subsequently described by Mr. Montgomery Hyde as 'a simple but remarkably moving ceremony' I dedicated the plaque to the memory of one 'by whose vision and labours the values of this beautiful spot were discerned, defined and defended to the common welfare of all who seek here refreshment of body, mind and spirit'. (I am indebted to Mr. Montgomery Hyde for recalling my words at the dedication).

Though in his early days Birkett had been destined for the Methodist ministry, in his later life he claimed to be no more than '*a Christian agnostic*'. Yet in a *Face to Face* television interview with John Freeman in 1959 he was not hesitant to assert that his knowledge of the Bible and of the hymns of Wesley and Watts were among his 'greatest possessions' and that he looked back on the religious training he had been given as the most formative influence of his life. 'I would call myself a Christian,' he said, 'but the great doctrinal things rather perplex me and trouble me.' Knowing the man as I did, and remembering how when I called for him at the Judge's lodgings in Nottingham each morning of the Assize week I found him reading his Bible, I fancy he might well have heard some words spoken to another who in his day was an expert in the Law: 'Thou art not far from the Kingdom of God.' I count it as a privilege that my path crossed his in 1945 and although we met but rarely I was able at the end to pay my respects to the man and his work in that simple ceremony on Ullswater.

With the war over 'reconstruction' was the word on the lips of states-men and churchmen alike in the closing months of 1945 and throughout the following year. A German academician re-opening the University of Heidelberg was quick to indicate where in his view his people had gone so tragically wrong. 'Each individual man is an infinity,' he said. 'No scientific conception can embrace him as a whole, for man is always more than what is known about him. Hence there belongs to humanity a 'picture of man' that over and above what is knowable, envisages what man is and may become . . . There is no true picture of man apart from God and our task is to recover the true picture of man.'

I quoted that German's words in the parish magazine of January 1946 with the plea that we should hear them as applicable to our own country and people too. At the annual parochial meeting that year plans were laid for the more effective discharge of the clergy's pastoral responsibilities by the appointment of 'district links'. Members of the congregation were to be invited to be responsible for disseminating in their own district information about the church's work and for passing on to the clergy information of circumstances calling for pastoral ministry. Further arrangements were made for the extension of the Freewill Offering Scheme and for further special efforts in the field of evangelism. These last took place during the Lent of 1946. The Easter which followed was particularly significant for me for I nursed in secret a suggestion which I knew could result in its being my last Easter at St. Anne's.

A Confirmation had long been planned for Rogation Sunday 1946 and it was on the previous Sunday at Evensong that I announced that after a great struggle of heart, and mind and will, I had decided that I could not do other than accept the Bishop's invitation to me to take up the office of Vicar and Rural Dean of Mansfield. The Bishop had made his approach to me some weeks before and in the somewhat casual manner to which those who knew him well became accustomed, His comment 'I should like you to go to Mansfield' met with the equally casual answer from me 'Never!' Then we both got down to serious talk. The peculiar circumstances of the vacancy were such that I had been inclined to say at once that I would wish to be excused. The fact was that Mansfield, which was the largest town in the diocese next to the city of Nottingham itself, had been without a Vicar for six years, for its incumbent, Canon F. L. Hughes, had been serving as a Chaplain to the Forces throughout the war and unlike most chaplains he had not resigned his benefice. The parish had been in the hands of an assistant curate since September 1939 and indeed for a period in 1938. At the end of the war, when it was anticipated that the Canon would return to his parish, he was appointed Chaplain General, doubtless at the instigation of Field Marshal Montgomery with whom Canon Hughes had served in the Eighth Army.

Inevitably there was a division in the town 'twixt those who thought that the Canon should have resigned the benefice many years before, and those who saw nothing amiss, in the peculiar circumstances, in his continuing to hold two appointments for so long. The internal tension was so sharp, and so public, that it was not a situation into which a priest would jump eagerly, and the Bishop was sufficiently sensitive to appreciate my hesitation. Undoubtedly, however, there was a great work waiting to be tackled in the borough and the deanery, an ancient parish to be Vicar of which was high privilege, and a sphere with responsibilities that could not but be demanding and exciting. Yet I hesitated. Whether by episcopal design, or by his having picked up an inspired leak about the Bishop's offer, the Diocesan Surveyor (Mr. Nat Lane), who was a member of the Mansfield Parochial Church Council, called at St. Anne's Vicarage in the midst of my turmoil of mind, ostensibly to survey the vicarage but actually, as I soon discovered, to persuade me to accept the Bishop's invitation. I thought long and prayed earnestly, and it became my profound conviction that the finger of God was pointing me clearly that way and that I dare not say other than yes to the Bishop's request. Thus a benefice rejected by Cyril Garbett in 1909 was accepted by Cyril Bulley in 1946. In so doing I could see a thrilling and exciting task before me but I could see, too, a parting of the ways for myself, my mother and my sister, which would need to be faced with stiff upper lips. We had been mightily encouraged and supported by a considerable and loyal army of workers at St. Anne's. Turning away from them after so short a pastorate would, it seemed just then, savour of desertion. But they were big enough to see it differently.

When I left Worksop in September, taking with me to my great joy the love and affection of the people of St. Anne's, I had the satisfaction of knowing that the parish would be having a new vicar within a month of my leaving and that meanwhile the parish would be in the hands of Thomas Wood who had been a loyal and able colleague for the last three years and upon whom my eye was already set as a possible member of the staff which I should need to build up at Mansfield as soon as that proved to be practicable.

7

Picturesque Memories – Mansfield

The move from St. Anne's Church, Worksop to St. Peter's the Parish Church of Mansfield was for me a reversion to the ancient, for both Newark and Coddington Parish Churches have plenty about them to certify their antiquity. Newark, however, has nothing to show for its undoubted Saxon origin whereas Mansfield has both its entry in Domesday and its clear evidence of the existence of the original Saxon Church in the lowest of the three weatherings on the east side of the tower. But, as in most of our ancient parish churches, and so at Mansfield, successive generations of citizens demonstrated their fidelity by restorations, extensions and enrichments as need demanded or piety dictated. Thus the little Saxon Church, doubtless wattled with a roof of stone slabs, was given a Norman tower by about the year 1100 and it would seem that for about fifty years Saxon nave and Norman tower sufficed as the parish church of Mansfield-in-Shirewood. The tower, built by the Romans maybe as much for security as for the curfew bell which it would house, stands today and within it eight bells bearing dates from 1603 onwards. It was indeed in that year that 'ye belles were rong', so the old Register tells us, to mark King James the First's proclamation at the Market Cross and the ringers were each paid half-a-crown for their trouble. The probability is therefore that the metal in the present bells, even of those bearing eighteenth-century dates, is at least in part pre-Reformation.

By grace of William Rufus, Mansfield had long been a Royal Manor and the proximity of the Court in the Forest encouraged the townsfolk to enlarge their church in the last years of the twelfth century. Through the centuries, motivated now by piety, now by necessity, the church grew in stature so that now, approaching it from the road on its north side, known significantly as Toothill (i.e. Watchtower) Lane, it presents to the keen observer a history of English architecture. There is the Norman tower, strategically placed at the cross roads and betraying within it signs of Saxon workmanship, and there the Early English lancet and doorway of the same period. There are windows in the Decorated style, Perpendicular chapels and a Classical spire of the seventeenth century. All combine to tell a story in stone of the Church rising to the needs of each day and generation, accepting and blessing the arts and skills of man, and baptising as it were successive changes in styles of architecture which the years brought. One wonders whether there were among our forefathers recurring and bitter arguments as to whether the succeeding changes in architectural styles were 'in keeping with our church'.

The excesses of the Reformation and the bleak years of the Commonwealth saw in Mansfield, as in parish churches everywhere, those acts of deprivation, destruction and desecration the like of which, centuries before, had broken the heart of the Psalmist: 'They break down all the carved work thereof with axes and hammers . . . they have set fire upon the holy places and have defiled the dwelling-places of thy Name.' Mansfield lost all its stained glass and a great many of its treasures in the course of such spoliations, but managed to preserve some of its tombs and, surprisingly and happily, its chapels. At some point, however, and I doubt not but with the best will in the world, the inside of the church was gravely disfigured by the addition of galleries. A nineteenth-century restoration relieved the church of these and opened up to view again architectural beauty which had long been hidden.

The 38th Vicar of Mansfield — the first was Ralph, Clerc de Maunsfield appointed in 1280 — was Canon Alfred Prior who was bold enough, in a short history of the church published during his vicariate, to challenge civic pride by suggesting that a visitor to the town 'might be pardoned for thinking that nothing of interest can be embedded in so unpicturesque a town'. The adjective is in truth one which could spring to the mind of the passer-by, as it sprang to mine as I frequently hurried through the town en route from Worksop to the Church House in Nottingham. Indeed it is alleged that on one such journey I uttered an injudicious comment to my passenger, subsequently quoted back at me, which was in the nature of a sigh that 'wherever the Bishop sends me next may he never send me here'. But he is a naive traveller who assumes that things of interest, historical, or architectural, reside only in the picturesque. As Canon Prior asserted in his reference: 'As the oyster has its pearl, so Mansfield has its parish church.'

The 'pearl' is truly 'embedded' in the town, standing as it does at its heart with the busy and bustling world whirling about it. Taking a stance by the main gate of the Parish Church it was difficult to picture Mansfield as once it had been, a place — to quote an unknown admirer of the last century — 'with the sylvan beauty of a typical old world agricultural town'. The 'sylvan beauty', still to be enjoyed in what remains of Sherwood Forest nearby, has long since been banished from the town itself by the industrial and commercial development which inevitably followed the discovery and exploitation of the rich mineral resources which had long lain hidden beneath the glades of the Forest. In the Mansfield of my day the 'ancient' was represented only by the Parish Church and by the remains of some cave houses hewn out of solid rock and inhabited until the latter half of the nineteenth century; the 'modern' was represented by the eighteenth-century Moot Hall and the nineteenth-century Town Hall both in the spacious Market Place. The town was a hive of industry with coal mining as merely one, albeit the major one, of dozens of lively and prosperous industrial concerns. In that respect Mansfield was living up to the motto which it adopted when it received its Charter of Incorporation in 1892 – *Sicut Quercus Virescit Industria!* I was quick to discover though that it was not only Mansfield's industry which flourished 'as the oak'. There was, too, a strong community sense and a lively social concern which expressed itself not least in fine secondary schools – modern, grammar and technical, in public libraries and in a museum and art gallery with its old water colours recalling the Mansfield of yesteryear.

Thus when on 26 September 1946, by which time I had done my best to discover something about the history of the royal town and of its ancient parish church, I was instituted and inducted as the 44th Vicar of Mansfield, it was with a sense of pride, tempered with something like awe, that I held the episcopal seal on the Deed of Institution and heard the Bishop's solemn words: 'Receive the Cure of Souls which is mine and thine.' At such a moment a priest cannot fail to be acutely aware that so great a privilege must be paid for by the ready acceptance of concomitant and great responsibilities. Some mathematical wag had noted in the current parish magazine that 243,090 days would separate my institution as vicar from that of Ralph's in 1280. The information, arrived at before the day of electronic calculators, was doubtless intended to arouse the interest of the young people of the congregation, remind them that there was a Church of England long before there was a State of England and that there was a Vicar of Mansfield over 600 years before there was a Mayor of Mansfield. But at that solemn moment in my ministry I was concerned to look forward rather than backward, more especially as difficulties immediately ahead had been set out so sternly and starkly by the priest-in-charge in that same magazine. He had written about serious divisions in the congregation – those very divisions which had initially inclined me against accepting the Bishop's invitation. Such phrases as the need 'to present a united front to the outside world', 'to lay aside the narrow vision of the past', along with his urgent call to desist from sabotaging the work of Mansfield Parish Church, and his battle cry, 'Death to the fifth columnist in each of us' – all these were at the very least somewhat off-putting to a young man setting out on the biggest job he had ever been called on to undertake.

The vast congregation in the church that night and the welcome accorded me and mine in the gathering afterwards, the presence of all the clergy of the Rural Deanery, of representatives of Free Churches, of the Mayor and members of the Borough Council – all invested the occasion with an importance and significance of such magnitude as to be frightening for the young man at the centre. But the ceremonial and ritual of the service itself were such as to reassure me and, added to the cordiality of the welcome, sent me to bed that night with high hopes and a light heart. I confess that I awoke in different mood. I could think only of those ominous words which kindly clergy had said to me the night before, touching what one of them called 'the mighty job of reconciliation' which lay before me, and of those grim phrases which peppered the article that the departed priest-in-charge had embraced in his farewell article. Soon after nine I was back in the church again, this time to be met only by the faithful old verger Frank Trevis, and he too all unwittingly touched the same sore spot as he spoke, in his rich Dorset accent, of the need 'to pull St. Peter's together again'. I went to the Lady Chapel to read the office of Matins, but I found myself sitting and wondering instead whether I had made the mistake of my life in leaving a parish where there was peace and concord for one where apparently there was strife and division. A 'mighty job of reconciliation' they told me the night before. But why pick on me to do it? I reflected on this and turned over and over in mind the article in the current issue of the magazine which called so urgently for a 'united front' that it betrayed equally pungently the presence of deep and acute division. Suddenly, momentarily, I felt unequal to the task and desperately lonely, wondering to whom I could turn for an objective assessment of the root cause of the troubles. Somewhat mechanically I opened my Office Book to read Morning Prayer, and there in the first verse of the first psalm for the day was a reminder of what I should have been doing:

'When I was in trouble I called upon the Lord: and he heard me.'

I read it and re-read it and a sense of guilt crept over me. I read on, only to find in the last verse what sounded like a deliberate reminder of a grim possibility:

'I labour for peace, but when I speak unto them thereof they make them ready for battle.'

But the Psalm persisted in rubbing in the lesson which I most needed just then:

'Our help standeth in the Name of the Lord . . . The Lord himself is thy keeper: the Lord is thy defence upon thy right hand.'

When I rose from my knees that morning I was at peace, confident that under God those immediate difficulties would be surmounted and that there lay before me years of happy and creative ministry. And so it was!

The Borough of Mansfield had at that time a population approaching 50,000, and the Deanery with its 24 parishes accounted for one third of the total population of Nottinghamshire with which the Diocese of Southwell was coterminous. Although St. Peter's parish had only 10,000 within its boundaries, it was inevitable that the church, as the old Mother Church of the town, should have extended its influence over the whole area and should have drawn into its life and worship and work dedicated churchpeople whose spiritual home it had been before they moved out from the town centre to the newly-developed areas. There were no hospitals within the parish boundary, but the clergy of the parish church had long been responsible for chaplaincy services to the Harlow Wood Orthopaedic hospital on the town's outskirts. The task of the Vicar and Rural Dean of Mansfield was therefore a mammoth one on any reckoning and without a colleague it was inevitable that some parts of it must receive less attention than they merited. The war years had left their mark on the parochial life of the church everywhere and that was nowhere more true than at Mansfield which the war had deprived of its vicar for over seven years. Thus on setting my foot in the parish I faced not merely the task of reconciliation, of which so many reminded me, but that of reconstruction — material and spiritual. In that first year of my vicariate it was only the presence of a lively band of lay workers who rallied round magnificently which made it possible for me to begin to repair what the war years had laid waste and to give to the parish and town the spiritual leadership which it rightly expected of its vicar, and to the clergy of the Rural Deanery such counsel and help as they needed. Even so I was conscious that I was touching but the surface of the work — fishing in the shallows as it were — and although I longed to launch out into the deep in ways which the hour demanded, I was acutely aware that the winds were contrary.

All over the world just then victors and vanquished alike were confronted with massive and intractable problems which were the inevitable aftermath of war — material problems of reconstruction, social problems of rehabilitation, of broken homes, of shattered hopes, of shortages of food and raw materials and, in countries other than our own, of desperate poverty, of hunger and starvation. Certainly the hour demanded that the contents of the Gospel should be applied to the world's wounds. The 'social Gospel', intrinsic in Christian theology, could not be muted. But the hour was such that it demanded something more than a 'watered down' secular Christianity. Unless the Church presented to the world the Living God the trumpet would give an uncertain sound and the real battle for the souls of men would not even begin. Statesmen, politicians and philosophers were getting to the heart of things and adding their testimony to that of spiritual leaders throughout the world. 'Only a revival of the spirit of religion,' President Roosevelt had said, 'would meet the needs of the hour.' He declared too that he could not conceive 'any problem' — social, political or economic — that would not melt away before the fire of a spiritual awakening'. In our world of politics the confidently Christian voice of Sir Stafford Cripps was talking of the 'selfishness and pride which has ever been inherent in human actions and human institutions' and to which the only answer was a religious one. Dr. Joad, of Brains Trust fame, whose rationalist creed had taught him to regard evil as merely a by-product of circumstances, confessed that he too had come to the conclusion that he had been wrong all along. 'I see now,' he said, 'that evil is endemic in man, and that the Christian doctrine of original sin expresses a deep and essential insight into human nature.' He declared publicly that he had abandoned rationalism and his so-called Life Force Philosophy as manifestly impotent and shallow and that he had embraced Christianity, which he had come to accept as both true and relevant. Add to all this a word from the editorial column of *The Times* to the effect that 'men are slowly and painfully re-learning the eternal truth that the unsupported human will can never finally prevail against sin and therefore unsupported human effort can never make the new world for which we all yearn', and we have something like a summary of the deepest thoughts and desires of thinking people in that post-war period.

But was it all wishful thinking? Were men really re-learning that Eternal Truth? There was evidence to the contrary. The National Day of Prayer, for example, called by King George the Sixth for observance on 6 July 1947, evoked a noticeably less enthusiastic response than similar calls in the days of the war. It was as though men reasoned that the God who, as they had declared so lustily, had been 'our help in ages past' was now merely to be held in reserve as 'our hope for years to come'. Sheltered as we were from the worst effects of 'the stormy blast', they could afford to move God from the centre to the periphery of their lives to await a further summons for help. It was not the opposition of atheists, either of the secular humanist brand or the Marxist, which the Church had to confront with its Gospel just then. Atheists were rare but apathy was rife. The war ended, the task of the parish priest thus became immeasurably more difficult and demanding. In the grim days of the war his was the message which comforted and consoled, his was the ministry which inspired and strengthened, his was the word which embraced eternal truths about Life and Death at a time when life seemed so tenuous and death was so near. But when the stormy blast had ended, many were content to set God aside along with the gas mask and the identity card.

But there was not only apathy; there was also bitterness in the hearts of many. The answer of some people, in Mansfield as elsewhere, to the sorry plight of the people of Germany for example, sunk as they were in the abyss of despair, poverty and hunger, was merely to shrug off appeals for money and practical help with the heartless jibe 'They brought it on themselves.' In the face of this the voice of the Church had to be sounded in protest and the love of the Church had to be seen in action. At Christmas 1948, we sought to alleviate a little of the suffering and to dispel some of the misery of our erstwhile enemies by inviting people to leave parcels of clothing, blankets, etc., by the Christmas Crib in the church. To this there was an impressive response from the congregation of a hundred or so substantial parcels which were subsequently sent to Germany. Some of the garments had sewn into the sleeves short greetings written in German, or texts from Scripture and the names and addresses of the donors in the hope that they might receive letters from the recipients. A number of very touching letters came expressing gratitude both for the gifts and the thoughts which prompted them. Could anyone deny the healing power of such gestures? Yet we had to meet our critics. One such I remember vividly – a lady whom I met in the church on Christmas Eve. The church was in darkness save for a light over the Crib. I approached the stranger and discovered her to be a foreigner. Although her English was as limited as my French I discerned that she was anxious to know the origin, the contents and the destination of the parcels. When to the best of my ability I made her understand that they were gifts from the congregation for dispersal in Germany her eyes opened wide in astonishment. With typical French gesticulations and in a shrill and agitated voice, which cut through the darkness and silence of the church, she betrayed her anger and bewilderment. In an excitable mixture of English and French she exclaimed: 'Ah! Les Anglais, les Anglais! Quel drôles de gens – 'ow you say it, 'funny people'? Oui? Ils combattent les Allemands. Les Allemands les tuent – tuent, comprenez vous? – kill you say? avec leurs bombes. (This sentence was illustrated!). Still, zey fight zee Germans. Ils combattent, ils combattent – alors ils vainquent les Allemands – et puis – ils leur donnent leurs – 'ow you say it vetements?' I dutifully interjected, 'clothing – coats, dresses.' She shrugged her shoulders – whether in disgust or bewilderment I could not tell – as she added, 'Les Anglais – drôles de gens – conduite étrange' – here a long pause and a smile on my face as on hers as she reached her climax – 'mais c'est magnifique'.

I saw the outburst as one of self-analysis culminating in surrender to the claims of Christ.

Some eighteen months before this the Government had decreed that the prisoners of war might be allowed outside their camps at certain times and on certain conditions and this humanitarian gesture in its turn evoked angry opposition in many quarters. It was reported, for example, that the Millwall Football Club had refused to allow prisoners to watch their matches and had done so 'with detestation and loathing'. The management of some of the cinemas adopted the same line. Their action, applauded by many, demanded a challenge. An article which I wrote in our newly-fashioned monthly journal *Forward* entitled 'The Next War – Sportsmen Sow Seeds', embroiled me immediately in a fierce controversy and when parts of it appeared in the local and national press a shower of letters – some abusive, most supportive – descended upon me. I was asking no more than that Christians should take the only stand open to them as Christians – that hating the sin they should yet love the sinner. The supreme task before us then was to heal the world's wounds, and the first and greatest contribution to that end at that moment was to foster in the Name and by the power of Christ the spirit of forgiveness and mutual goodwill. I cannot resist recording here three simple verses which I quoted in the article which were found by a British soldier scratched on the wall of a filthy blood-stained prison in Singapore, clearly the work of some British or Australian prisoner of war:

> '*If I must face the firing squad*
> *Though harm I did nobody,*
> *Teach me to love thee still my God*

As bullets strike my body.

If I must die a lowly spy,
        Though spying did I never,
Stay in my heart, O God, and I
        Will love them more than ever.

Forgive them all the tortures done,
        My thirst and my starvation,
For who could suffer more than One
        Who died for our salvation?'

Would that our latter day graffiti had but a fraction of the didactic value
of that of the unknown soldier poet!

Since what I called at the time the rumblings of hatred persisted I put to my
church council a suggestion which, to their credit, they accepted immediately.
It was that we should invite prisoners of war from a camp nearby to join us
at Evensong on the following Sunday and to meet the congregation over
refreshments in our commodious Parish Hall after the service. A German
padre and a German student teacher read the Lessons – and did so admirably
though they had never read English in public before. We provided the 40 or
so men who came with copies of the Book of Common Prayer in German,
though I discovered subsequently that most of them knew enough English to
follow what was being done and said. The worship together and the fellowship
one with another in the hall afterwards broke down the barriers and was itself
an act of witness which did not go unnoticed in the local paper. 'Altogether
with one accord in one place' all of us were very much aware of the Presence
and Power of the Spirit of God at work that night, and the evening brought
to the hearts and minds of those young German soldiers, long separated from
their loved ones, a joy which was reflected in their faces and in their eager
attempts to engage in intelligible conversation. Furthermore friendships were
formed which lasted long after the men returned to their homeland.

It was only later that I discovered how it came about that the prisoners
were for the most part well versed in the English language. They came from
a camp in which men were continuing their training to be either pastors or
teachers – a camp embracing in effect a Theological College and a Pedagogical
(Teachers' Training) College. In January 1948, when the students of Ridley
Hall, Cambridge came to spend a week in the Deanery of Mansfield, we
began the week by entertaining the theological section of the German camp
to lunch with the British Ordinands. Since many of the students had only
very recently been discharged from the forces they found themselves sitting
cheek-by-jowl with those whom they had been in combat not long before.
It was a historic occasion and present at it with the students and prisoners
were the Bishop of Southwell (Dr. Barry), Pastor Dr. Daaman, himself a
POW, Falkner Allison (Principal of Ridley Hall and subsequently Bishop

of Winchester), and Cyril Bowles (Vice-Principal and subsequently Bishop of Derby). Seated at the table were churchmen from the United Kingdom, from Germany, Burma, Africa and Iran – symbolic of the world-wide nature of the Christian Church and of the reconciling power of the Risen Christ to 'break down the middle wall of partition' between nation and nation.

Something else had been happening over the past months of these efforts to sound the Christian Gospel of forgiveness. The congregation itself had become united in a way which they had not known for a long time. Seeking reconciliation with those who had been their common enemies they had themselves become reconciled. At last there were evidences that the first sermon which I preached in Mansfield Parish Church on the words: 'We are ambassadors for Christ; we beseech you on behalf of Christ to be reconciled' (2 Cor. ch. 5, v. 2), was, under the hand of God, 'bearing fruit a hundred-fold'.

I cannot, however, disguise the fact that the first twelve months of my Mansfield vicariate were months in which one part of the work of a parish priest was of necessity gravely neglected. Certainly the sick, the dying and the bereaved were visited in home and hospitals. One such ministry within a matter of weeks of my institution lives in my memory in graphic detail. Among the Girl Guides on parade that night was a little eleven-year-old by name Ruth to whom, as I was to learn later, the coming of a new vicar was a matter of great moment. Very shortly after, she was taken seriously ill and I met her for the first time in hospital. Seldom can a child have spoken so naturally of her faith, of her prayers, of her love of the Lord Jesus and her affection for her parents as did Ruth to me during that first meeting. I visited her daily for a week and I suspect that she knew what we knew, that those were the closing days of her short life on earth. Though she was but eleven, and not confirmed, she asked whether she might 'take the Holy Sacrament with Daddy and Mummy'. She did so to her and their great comfort and joy. To be with, to talk with and to pray with that little child in those last days of short pilgrimage on earth was to see an old text in a new light – 'A little child shall lead them.' Here was a Christian soul whose sanctuary had remained unsullied and that in a world which, throughout her short life, had been torn with strife, embittered with hate and besmirched with falsehood. Here was a little child with a burning faith and with that perfect love which casts our fear. Such a one must our Lord have had in mind when he stood a little child in front of his disciples and warned them, 'I tell you this; unless you turn round and become like children, you will never enter the Kingdom of Heaven.' No parish priest could be other than richer for such an encounter with innocence.

But beyond this ministry to the sick and the suffering, the dying and the bereaved, there was very little opportunity for visiting over a wider area. Fortunately the church council members were aware of this and as conscious as I was that the parish desperately needed further priestly help. Mention had been made at the first church council meeting over which I presided of the 'tangles, difficulties and intractable problems' which needed the vicar's attention and by that the churchwarden undoubtedly meant church properties calling for major repairs following the neglect of the war years, the peal of bells needing restoration and the Church House needing renovation. I deemed the last of these to be the most important and realising that the council was as eager as I was to augment the staff I made it clear that as soon as this house was ready to receive clergy I would bring two assistant curates to the parish. Nothing could have spurred them to action more quickly. The branch of the Mothers' Union, the Men's Society, the Ladies' Working Party, nurtured very devotedly by my mother, dedicated themselves to the task of raising the new money needed for the renovation and remodelling of the house. Within eight months the work had been put in hand and within twelve months it was completed and paid for. Thus in the August following my Institution I was able to announce that Thomas Wood, whose work with me at St. Anne's had marked him out as a priest of great distinction and dedication, would join me again as senior curate, and that John Milner, who had graduated at Durham, served in the Royal Navy and received his training for the Ministry at Lincoln Theological College, would join us as a deacon at the end of September. Thus a year from the opening of the new chapter in the history of Mansfield Parish Church, the major material problems touching the repair and renovation of the church properties and the recasting of the bells had been resolved, the tensions within the congregation had evaporated and an adequate staff had been brought together. That was the Lord's doing and it was marvellous in our eyes. I was confident that with the arrival of my two young colleagues the impact of the Church upon the life of the parish and the town would be immediately and immeasurably strengthened, not least in the area of those pastoral contacts between clergy and people which not only present the Church to the people as a caring Church but prepare the way for the Church to be accepted as a teaching Church.

To say as much is not to suggest that nothing in the sphere of spiritual growth by way of evangelism and education had happened in those first twelve months, but merely to acknowledge that in proportion to the need the accomplishments looked miserably small. Even so, since the inner circle of the congregation had responded to leadership swiftly and lifted from their vicar's shoulders the 'bricks and mortar' aspect of his overall responsibilities, I was able to give the major part of my time to pastoralia and to teaching within the existing parochial units of young people and adults and, of course, in the didactic ministry which the pulpit offers. Furthermore, I persuaded a group of men – though they quipped that the word should not be persuaded but 'bulleyed' – to put themselves under instruction designed to equip them for lay evangelism, to go out indeed and 'compel them to come in'. Not all the bread they cast upon the waters returned but their efforts did result in drawing within the fellowship of the Church a score of people prepared to declare their commitment to Christ and who subsequently received the gift of the Spirit in the laying on of hands in the first 'adults only' Confirmation which older members of the congregation could ever remember. Indeed, the Bishop of the diocese was drawn to the parish three times in that first year of my Mansfield ministry, twice for Confirmations and once to preach the sermon on Industrial Sunday. The last mentioned visit established in Mansfield a precedent which was to have encouraging results beyond our imagining.

For about a hundred years or so the Church of England had become accustomed to the annual harvest thanksgiving service which was seen as taking the place of the observance in mediaeval England of Lammas Day (August 1st) when bread made from the newly-harvested wheat was used in the Mass. (Etymologically the word 'Lammas' would appear to derive from loaf and 'mass'). This was clearly in the nature of a thanksgiving for the harvest. But 'Industrial Sunday' so called was conceived in this century by the Industrial Christian Fellowship as a way of focusing attention upon the truth of Christ's Lordship over the whole of life and in particular upon the application of Christian principles to the nation's industrial, and economic concerns. Since Mansfield was bristling with industries it seemed to me that this was an observance which its Parish Church should not overlook.

We made of the occasion an industrial harvest thanksgiving (broadcast by the BBC on Industrial Sunday 1949), affording an opportunity to say something about the Christian philosophy of work and renew in the minds of all, and of representatives of management and the shop floor in particular, both the truth of man's dependence upon God as the source of all raw materials and that of man's dependence upon his brother man for fashioning those resources for the common welfare. Leaders of the local industries co-operated by allowing us to have in the church on that Sunday products of the labours of Mansfield men and women and it was encouraging that managers and men in goodly numbers 'followed' their products to church: a metal box worker, a miner, a boot and shoe operative, a radio assembler, a cotton doubler, and a transport worker – each laid before the altar some token of his work making clear to the listeners the nature of his contribution to the needs of the human family. The Mayor of the Borough then invited the congregation to pray for God's blessing upon the town and upon all who worked within it for the common welfare. A 'harvest thanksgiving' it was, but instead of corn and fruit and vegetables, there were boots and shoes, wireless sets, metal boxes, cotton bobbins, coal, machine tools, ale and children's toys. In a shower of appreciative letters which followed the broadcast from far and wide was one which struck a discordant note, and that from a local resident who sent his letter also to the local paper. I was severely scolded for allowing a basket of hops with three bottles of ale nestling in it to be brought into a place of worship. I surmise that the Indictment was not induced by any thought on the part of the writer that someone might slyly seize them in the course of the service – a feat which would have been difficult since they were at the foot of the pulpit! – but because, as a teetotaller, he regarded such things as the work of the devil. Furthermore he posed what I am sure he regarded as a searching question for the vicar: 'If by the time the next Industrial Sunday comes round some Mansfield factory has made an atomic bomb, will the Canon have one on display in the Parish Church?'

In subsequent years I invited Members of Parliament whom I knew to be Christians to come to Mansfield to preach for the occasion and one such, whose words and witness were particularly appreciated, was the Member for Cardiff Central, now the Right Honourable George Thomas, Speaker of the House of Commons. So memorable was his address, and so deeply was I impressed with the strength of his Christian commitment, as we talked together late into the night, that I confess that it was with a twinge of disappointment that I saw him elevated to his present high position. That a man of his wisdom and integrity should have been chosen for an office demanding such strict impartiality was not surprising, but that a statesman so deeply committed to the Christian Faith and the Christian Way of Life should be thus prevented from making his voice heard in the Councils of the nation, and indeed in the Labour Party itself, is a deprivation which the country can ill afford. I doubt not that his resonant 'Order! Order!' was more immediately effective in the classroom of this ex-teacher than it appears to be in the Palace of Westminster.

The recollection of those close contacts between the Parish Church and the town's industries and workers prompts me to venture a comment on the development within the Church of the appointment of 'Industrial Chaplains', 'Agricultural Chaplains' and the like. Clearly there must be specialist chaplains in certain fields – in prisons, in the large hospitals, in boarding schools, in the Services – but to go beyond these residential situations to appoint specialist priests to station themselves in, or to run in and out of, factories is in my judgment, a wholly mistaken policy. The unit of society is not the factory but the family and the Church's ministry to people should be a ministry channelled through the home and by the parish priest. This is not to suggest that the Church has nothing to say about industrial conditions as they affect both management and labour, or to deny that there are within the Gospel certain 'therefores' which bear reference to social as well as personal behaviour. It is to assert rather, that the Church's ministry is to men as men not to men as miners or machinists or mechanics, and it is a ministry most effectively offered by the parish priest in the context of men's homes. Of course there is a place in the factory for the social worker as there is a place in the court for the probation officer, and the wise parish priest will get to know each, and be ready to co-operate with each, in resolving any personal problems of his parishioners of which they may become aware. He will, too, eagerly accept invitations to visit factories within his parish or to attend a Magistrates' Court if by doing so his ministry to a parishioner can be so furthered. Beyond that the priest should stick to his last – the parish – and the Church should phase out the so called Industrial chaplains and others of their ilk and plant the men back into the parishes where they belong. It was twenty years ago in his *Vocation and Ministry* that Bishop Barry warned the

Church against a 'specialised type of Ministry' motivated by 'the stratification of society along functional and occupational lines'. In a vigorous defence of the parochial system and the office of parish priest he saw the reorientation of Ministry to 'functional or occupational man' as 'a surrender by the Church to a sub-Christian doctrine of man' — a heresy which we should repudiate. 'Life is far more than livelihood so a man is far more than his occupation.'

I like to think that what my colleagues and I were trying to do together in our contacts with the industrial concerns of workers in Mansfield ten years before our Bishop wrote those words helped him to foster that conviction. We saw the Parish Church standing as it did at the town's centre as a place which proclaimed by its very existence the sanctity of human personality, a place to which all could come to find in their common relationship to the Living God, a fellowship which transcended the divisions created by 'function' and 'class'. I recall that our church council, which in conversation with the Bishop I described as a 'ministry of all the talents', did just that. Miner sat with lawyer; shop assistant with architect; transport worker with teacher; factory manager with factory 'hand'. 'Function' did not divide, for all were complementary in their service to God and his Church. The church which they served and in which they worshipped proclaimed a Gospel which whilst it spoke to man's present condition spoke too of things eternal — of Salvation, of Life and Death, and Love which is indestructible. Certainly we penetrated the world of industry, of education, of drama, of politics and local government. Not everyone could understand why the Vicar spent time chairing the Borough Youth Committee, founding a branch of the United Nations' Association, encouraging the establishment of a Marriage Guidance Council, sharing with his colleagues an active interest in the town's schools — but we knew what we were doing and in whose Name we were doing it. The Church was the power house of a redemptive mission and, 'unprofitable servants' though we might well have been, we did our best as 'missioners' to carry the message out and to draw those who heard it into the fellowship of Christ's religion.

From the moment of my colleagues' arrival in the parish we established a daily meeting at the Holy Eucharist and in the course of that and the daily office of Evening Prayer we set before the Living God the needs of our people and sought his blessing on our ministry to them. We planned together and we worked together, each of us having some special responsibility for the oversight of one of more of the parochial organisations for adults, for young people (not then be it noted known as 'teenagers'), and for children, and all of us sharing fully in the priestly, pastoral and prophetic aspects of Ministry offered in the homes and in the church.

One early result of this more intensive care and shepherding of the parishioners was a quickening of interest in the church, its worship and its work. The congregations at the Sunday services, in which the singing was led by a particularly fine choir under the able leadership of Dr. George Allen the organist, grew rapidly and at Evensong in particular the average age of those attending was manifestly lowered by a great many young people from the local grammar schools who, as a result of the growth of the Fellowship of Youth, were taking an eager interest in the Church and its work. There was a lively response to courses of addresses and to experiments in teaching which from time to time replaced the traditional sermon. One such was the answering of questions which the congregation submitted, generally anonymously. These came from young and old alike and touched a range of subjects — Biblical interpretation, Church history, Church doctrine, prayer and worship, and — even in those days — inter-church relations. I can recall but one of those questions submitted, I discovered, by the head choirboy at the time. It was: 'Why do you think God became Incarnate in the male sex rather than the female?' That the answer did nothing to impair his faith stands proven, I submit, by the fact that that erstwhile head choirboy is now a priest. (Shortly after writing this paragraph there came to me news of the death of the Reverend Roy Boole who was the choirboy mentioned.)

It was good for the Church in Mansfield generally that the two local papers, the *Mansfield Reporter* and the *Mansfield Advertiser*, counted the Church's activities as newsworthy. Thus our experiments in teaching as well as our social activities, our garden parties, Christmas sales, Gift Days as well as experiments in evangelism and education were all reported regularly and handsomely. Indeed in the spring of 1948 one editor ventured an editorial on the size of the congregations in the Parish Church, adding a delicious press exaggeration to the effect that only by early arrival could anyone be sure of a seat. This in turn prompted a note in *Forward*, which by that time was going into about a thousand homes in the parish, to the effect that would-be worshippers need not take the quip too seriously for although the church was comfortably full Sunday by Sunday we could find room for more in the Lady Chapel.

One of our dramatic efforts which created a deep impression was presented as an act of worship and meditation on Good Friday evening in 1950. The theme was provided by a play in prologue and two acts entitled *The Prisoner of Hope* by M. Creagh-Henry and D. Marten, itself based on the incident in the Gospels of the restoration of his sight to the man born blind. The Hall, which seated nearly 400, was full to capacity and the great congregation responded to the occasion reverently in the prayers which the play prompted and in the hymns which were in tune with the theme. The choir was at its best as they contributed between the acts and scenes Wesley's *Lead me Lord*, Orlando Gibbons' *Jesu grant me this I pray* and Anton Dvorak's *Blessed Jesu, Fount of Mercy*. I count the evening as one of the most memorable in my ministry as a parish priest and when finally the congregation dispersed in silence I saw it as one during which many deepened their commitment to Christ and His Church and many were encouraged to think again.

From time to time, and in particular during Lent, we used the medium of drama in the church itself, though it must be admitted that there were a few murmurs of dissent when the suggestion was made, it being thought by some that such an idea was impious. However, when it was explained that the Christian Church had used drama as a method of evangelism and education in past centuries and that possibly the first plays ever produced in Mansfield were in the parish church, and the first group of players members of the congregation, the murmurs ceased. Our intention was to present to all who were prepared to learn the lessons to be drawn from one of the world's greatest allegories – *The Pilrim's Progress*, and we decided to present the story stage by stage in the words of the author himself and to follow each part with a short address which would expound the religious truths inherent in it. Thomas Wood, who among his other qualifications had a first-class honours degree in English, used his expertise in dividing the classic story into six manageable parts. Further he trained members of the youth fellowship to read them dramatically, and over the six Sundays in Lent these were relayed with sound effects from the vestry to the church following the third collect at Evensong. The office ended, the church was plunged into darkness save for the lights on the altar and the excerpt was introduced by one of the choirboys singing from the vestry the first verse of Bunyan's well-known pilgrim hymn. It was a modest effort produced wholly within the family even to the electronics but there was no doubt that it evoked an appreciative response, provided a powerful medium of incisive instruction and involved the younger members of the spiritual family in a way which helped them to realise both their place within it and the Church's ready acceptance of their time and talents. As we approached the following Lent there were many requests from the congregation to repeat the experiment but in that year we turned our attention to *The Little Plays of St. Francis*, which again were powerful indicators of profound truths, and which again enabled us to establish contact with 'seekers' and 'doubters' drawn to the church by what they thought to be a novel approach but which we knew to be a medium of instruction as old as the hills.

The members of the congregation were as happy as were their clergy to see the church comfortably full Sunday by Sunday but the clergy themselves eschewed any suggestion that they could rest on their oars. A call was made for volunteers to put themselves under instruction for a visitation of the whole parish house by house and for that purpose something like fifty people would be needed. Here was a test, for it was clear that the very thought reduced the majority even of the most faithful, to a state of fear and trembling. The question was posed to the Vicar, 'Could we go in two's' and the vicar replied that there was adequate precedent for just that way of evangelising since our Lord himself sent seventy disciples 'two and two before his face' (St. Luke 10, verse 1), but that in that event we too would need seventy disciples to undertake the work. It was a long time before the clean white chart awaiting signatures of volunteers had as much as a scratch on it. A reminder of its presence in the porch became a weekly announcement in the church services until at length I added to the notice words which, in another context, they were accustomed to hearing in church. The announcement that week was 'I await still in faith and in hope for someone to sign the chart in the porch.

This is the sixth time of asking.' When I left the church that night there was one signature and that the signature of the meekest little man in the congregation, albeit one of the most dedicated. Though we never reached the biblical number many others followed and quickly the list closed at just under fifty.

I could not resist asking some of my most faithful worshippers why they had been so hesitant in offering their services, but the answer one of them gave me should not have surprised me as much as it did. It was to the effect that they were fearful of not being able to answer the communists whom they would meet on the doorstep. Their fears were exaggerated for although the not insignificant cell of Marxists in the town were not slow to write to the local papers to challenge anyone who uttered a critical word about their philosophy and politics, they were not so thick upon the ground as to be encountered in every street. My reluctant evangelists reminded me that I myself had been the object of their attacks on more than one occasion in recent months, and more particularly following the appearance of a press report of a lecture on Marxism which I had given to a group of men which bore the headline 'Vicar's Sweeping Denunciation of Communism'. Those five deep black words, thrown across four columns of the local paper, had beneath them a report of the talk in which I had endeavoured, in as objective a way as for a committed Christian was possible, to expound to a gathering of men of varying intellectual capacity what the Dialectical Materialism of Marx, Engels, Lenin and Stalin was all about, and how that no one wedded to this philosophy could find room for God in his thinking. The word 'sweeping' in the headline was unfair since the lecture, which cost me many hours of research and preparation, was closely reasoned. The adjective doubtless referred to the categorical assertion in the summing up that a Christian, being one who believes in God who, *ex hypotnesi*, is changeless and eternal, could never embrace a philosophy which is essentially atheistic, which rules out the category of the supernatural and diminishes man by the denial of the soul. 'From each according to his gifts, to each according to his needs' did indeed express a sentiment which Christians and Communists could utter in unison, but since it is only by the compulsion of love rather than by the compulsion of force that this desirable end can be achieved, it is the Christian alone who is in touch with those divine resources by which the noble end can be realised.

The account of this meeting did not escape the watchful eye of the local communist cell. Would that Christians were as alert! There followed a letter from one of their number in which the writer was good enough to exonerate me from any suggestion that I might be a Fascist, but he saw me as a threat to the spread of Marxist Communism. A further scolding from the same direction was meted out to me at the time of the General Election in 1950 when I invited all four candidates — Liberal, Labour, Conservative and Communist — to attend the Parish Church on the Sunday before the poll. I did indeed hesitate in sending the invitation to the Communist candidate but decided that courtesy demanded that he should be included even if, as I surmised, the invitation would be rejected or ignored. Neither reaction proved to be the case. I received a stern rebuke from the Communist for daring to invite him, and that left me wondering what I should have received had I ignored him. However, all four candidates attended a meeting in our Hall which, as chairman of the local branch of the United Nations' Association, I had called to afford to the electors an opportunity of hearing the several candidates' views of the sort of foreign policy which their respective parties would pursue. Each speaker was to address the vast audience – the biggest which any of them had seen in the campaign – for 15 minutes precisely. Warning was given that any one transgressing, either by introducing domestic issues or going beyond his 15 minutes, would be counted out! The communist candidate who refused to stop at his third time of asking resumed his seat only by my pulling his coat tails and forcing him to sit down. This was my first and only experience of chairing a political meeting and my rough handling of the Communist, determined to steal more time than his opponents, evoked the only laughter of the evening. When, subsequently, that gentleman himself proposed the vote of thanks to the chairman, in most generous terms, a meeting which at times had been heated and very noisy, closed with satisfaction all round that justice had been done and had been seen to have been done. Whilst disclaiming any credit for the decision of the nation it is perhaps worth recalling that in that General Election the Communist Party contested 100 seats and were defeated in 100 constituencies.

To revert to the reluctant evangelists and the visitation of the parish to which they had committed themselves, clearly our intention had always been to prepare them for the task by prayer and instruction and this we did. Furthermore a small card which set out the Church's place in the community, which spoke of its ever open door, of its anxiety to serve all and sundry and of the ways in which we were trying to do just that for the children, the young people and adults alike, was prepared as a way of opening the doorstep conversation. When at length the visitation began the visitors were both surprised and delighted at the cordiality of the welcome they received. What they started diffidently, they carried on confidently. There were, of course, the brusque dismissals here and there, and interesting doorstep encounters during which the visitors heard strong avowals to what may now be called a religionless Christianity, but there were also invitations to 'Come in', and from some of these the visitors saw rich rewards for their witness. The experiment was perhaps an enterprise in lay evangelism which may well in total have done more for the visitors than the visited, but certainly it produced results in bringing within the orbit of the Church's ministry of worship and teaching many who had long been impeded by doubts, inhibited by sloth or estranged by ignorance of the Church's faith and function. As I write this I think of one family in particular who by this lay initiative were won for Christ and his Church. Tentatively their children were sent to the Sunday School; a son joined the choir; Mum and Dad came to worship, fitfully at first, at length regularly. Dad, a miner, stood for and was elected to the Church Council. Not all the seed which was sown bore fruit but that it was sown in faith was surely counted for righteousness. As I wrote to those valiant visitors at the time, 'God asks of us not success but fidelity'.

A further result of this visitation was a further increase in the circulation of our monthly journal which my colleagues and I regarded as a potent instrument of evangelism and education. Since it was a book of some twenty pages we were able month by month to embrace in it not only instruction on those things which sustain faith but also Christian comment on current affairs. Thomas Wood, a moral theologian of no mean stature, contributed articles touching subjects which teased the minds of Christians during the post-war years – Sunday games, Sunday cinemas, Euthanasia, Gambling, and Disestablishment among them. Such was Wood's mastery of his field and his reputation in it that no one was surprised when he was invited to preach in Westminster Abbey within a year of his joining the Mansfield staff. The congregation, purring with pleasure and determined to bask awhile in reflected glory, saw to it that they were represented in the Abbey for the occasion by the churchwardens and others.

A perusal of the parochial records and press cuttings over the years reveals references to national and international problems some of which were then clouds no bigger than a man's hand but which now hang over the whole world with menacing ferocity. As far back as May 1949 our monthly journal published an article of mine on a theme, then unheard of by most people, under the heading 'Putting the Clock Back'. The Prime Minister of South Africa, Dr. Malan, had begun to reverse General Smuts' slow but decisive moves towards an enlightened racial policy. The word 'Apartheid' was heard in our land and Christians were being summoned to ponder the policy it connotes in the light of the New Testament. It was a recurring theme for in future years articles with such headings as 'South African Regress' and 'A Festering Sore' appeared.

If I add that I wrote frequent articles on politics, on trades unions, on drama and the arts, on radio, on rumour, on secular humanism, on existentialism, on education *inter alia*, it might suggest that our concern was wholly with the social implications of the Gospel. Nothing could be further from the truth. Indeed I suspect that the so-called 'trendy theologians' of today reading the articles fed to the congregation would write them off as 'old fashioned and insular'. The truth is that through the years we pressed home ever and again both the Gospel which must be applied to these facets of our common life and, even more so in the written word, the essential place of those acts of piety – prayer, Bible reading, public worship and regular reception of the Holy Sacrament – which can alone sustain a virile Faith. For some reason beyond my understanding it has become unfashionable to press upon the community the essential place of public worship. It is Christian action which is shouted from the house-tops. Christian contemplation is muted even within the churches. Cranmer knew better when in that rarely used prayer for the High Court of

Parliament he taught us to pray that 'peace and happiness, truth and justice, religion and piety may be established among us for all generations'. The peace and happiness for which we yearn are not self-poised; they are derivatives of truth and justice. But they too are not self-poised for they in turn derive from a religious view of life, and without the exercise of piety they cannot endure. I have heard Russell Barry say more than once, 'If you keep your Christianity inside the churches you will soon find that it isn't even there'. A fair indictment of pietism perhaps, but those who knew him well knew that what in his *Period of my Life* he called his 'old fashioned personal religion' – expressed for example in his Confirmation addresses – set the Church, public worship and the ties of sacrament and prayer very high in his scheme of things. My colleagues and I knew that our growing congregations were not the result of any singular expertise on our part, but rather of our consistent preaching and teaching in the church, in our pastoral ministrations, and in the several parochial organisations. And that it was only by communion with the Living God in worship that lives can be regulated by divine truth and sustained in the pursuit of Christian duty. 'Without knowing anything of your past habits,' I wrote in my first letter to the people of Mansfield,

I call you all to re-examine your rules of prayer, of communion and of corporate worship. See that they are commensurate, insofar as we can make them so, with the abounding love of God. See that you cling to them, devotedly, not only because they represent your acknowledgment of God's deserts, not only because your spiritual life must atrophy without them, but also because so much depends upon the example which you give and the spiritual and moral power which, through you, God can bring to bear upon his world. The simple duty of going to church assumes in these days a tremendous significance. There is an idea abroad that somehow or other Christianity can persist apart from the Church – that 'all these things', which Christ promised should be added to those who 'seek first the Kingdom of God', can be secured by some under-the-counter method. In fact they are promised to those whose first interest is not in them at all, but in yielding to God both the honour due to Him and the service of our lives. Christianity is religion in fellowship. The Church is therefore not an 'optional extra'; it is of its essence. That is why St. Luke regards it as worthwhile recording in the Church's first history book that the earliest adherents of the Christian religion 'continued steadfastly in the apostles' doctrine and fellowship, in the breaking of bread and the prayers'. Such activities are set aside by the world as pedestrian and paltry. They are in fact the source of that spiritual and moral power which alone can wrest the soul of man from the forces of materialism. When you are strengthening your hold upon the Christian faith, when you are saying your prayers, when you are worshipping in church, when you are making your Communion – you are doing 'big things'. Be meticulous about them and use all

your powers of influence and example to help others to see them as
you do.

It was a simple message but it was pressed home ever and again, and at
the same time everything was done to ensure that the acts of worship in our
church should lack nothing in beauty and dignity and should be such as to
invite and encourage congregational participation and understanding. I was
able, a month or two before I left the parish, to write in the monthly journal
a comment which reflects something of the people's response to what I dare
to describe as our pressure to 'think on these things'.

> I hear a good deal from time to time, in conversations and in letters
> about the beauty and dignity of the services in the Parish Church. It
> is good to know that these qualities, which are there only because they
> are consciously contributed by so many who assist in the ordering of
> our worship, are found by so many to be conducive to the spirit of true
> worship. Words so often said to me are that 'people who stop away
> do not know what they are missing'. I believe that to be profoundly
> true. Worship is an end in itself. We do not offer it in order that we
> shall get something out of it, but because we owe it to God. But just
> because worship, which is in fact the total offering of our total selves to
> God, is the primary purpose of our being, there is something singularly
> satisfying and strengthening about an act of pure worship such as we offer
> in church. That is why 'going to church' must play so vital and large a
> part in our lives. That is why we should never miss an opportunity to
> introduce others to the fellowship of our worship and strive by every
> means in our power to help them to establish themselves in it. Though
> our congregations are large, we are far from satisfied. I am persuaded
> that there could be a good deal more activity on the part of regular
> members of our congregation in encouraging other people to join in
> our acts of worship. What do you do about this? It demands first that you
> should look to your own habits and further that you should recognise
> your Christian duty in the matter of evangelism. A congregation which
> makes no attempt to evangelise has within it seeds of decay.

None of our great team of workers – clergy, church council, Sunday
school teachers, youth leaders, choir, servers, sidesmen, Mothers' Union,
Men's Society, Women's Working Parties – would have been so simple as
to believe that our words, spoken or written, would invariably bear fruit. It
was always by 'line upon line, precept upon precept, here a little and there a
little' that progress was made. But that, under God, it was made was a constant
joy which expressed itself in a congregation which was no mean advertisement
for the Church Militant. There were the great and memorable occasions in the
church itself – the many broadcast services, in both the home and overseas
programmes, the 'touching of the bells', the frequent episcopal visits among

them that of the Archbishop of Grodno and of the Bishops of Southwell, of Derby, of Nassau, of Singapore, of Grantham and of Newfoundland. There were the inspiring Gift Days when an annual day-long vigil by the clergy received gifts from over 700 homes adding nearly £500 to the direct giving through the free will offering scheme. There were the memorable dramatic presentations in the Hall, and summer garden parties, the Christmas Fairs – all of which attracted vast crowds and rejoiced the hearts of those who had put in long hours of service to ensure their success. There were the Royal visits of the Princess Elizabeth and Duke of Edinburgh and later of Her Majesty the Queen – visits in which the Church played its part with its welcoming bells and its loyal acclaim. There was the visit of Field Marshal Viscount Montgomery who opened our summer garden party, snapping out in his customary manner a 'straight from the shoulder' speech bearing witness to his faith whilst professing profound ignorance of how one opened a fête. I recall that subsequently he nevertheless displayed great skill in a sideshow devised by the men of the congregation, which they had called 'Monty's Tanks'.

Added to all these was the fun which belied the notion that the unknowing cherish that the Christian religion inhibits gaiety and laughter, that religious folk despise merriment and mirth. None of the 80 or so men and women, boys and girls, who joined the clergy of their church in what came to be known as 'Operation Cobweb' in 1950 will ever forget the real enjoyment which we derived in giving the church its great spring clean. Everything movable was pushed outside, and with the help of equipment loaned to us by industrial concerns we scaled the heights. Roofs, walls, pillars, windows were all brushed and treated; every square inch of woodwork was polished, floors were scrubbed three times; carpets and hassocks were treated to violent beatings by the scouts, and at 10 o'clock on a Saturday evening the operation which had lasted a week was completed and someone posed the question, 'Why is it that we always enjoy doing work we aren't paid for far more than the work we are paid for?'

Then there were those delicious harvest suppers when the good Winnie Baggaley produced her rabbit pies, so many that the Forest of Sherwood must have been temporarily denuded. Mickle melody followed the meal and that in turn gave way to hilarious farces and speeches in which clergy and church officers, dressed up for their respective roles, reduced the assembled company to uncontrollable laughter. There were, too, the innumerable Christmas parties in which no one was forgotten and the chartered train which carried 500 members of the congregation, young and old, each year to Skegness where the clergy were not averse to battling it out with the choirboys on the dodgems. The Shrove Tuesday social and dance was the signal for a temporary Lenten halt to these frivolities – not because they were 'wrong' but because the Church marked out a season for special efforts in self-sacrifice and self-discipline. All these social occasions served to bring together the whole congregation and gave expression to and further nurtured the fellowship one with another which those who are in Christ find and seal in the Eucharist. The incredulous world looking in on any of those happy occasions might have been disposed to utter, maybe with envy if not surprise, 'See how these Christians love one another'.

But all these – the highlights of our worship, the excitement of our learning together, the joy of giving, the exhilaration of working together for so high a purpose, the parties the games, the fun – all were but the more brilliant flashes of colour in the mosaic of our corporate life. Within that mosaic, represented by what perhaps did not so quickly strike the eye, were the ordinary day-by-day activities of the Church – its daily prayers, its unceasing ministrations to the sick, to the suffering, to the anxious, to the bereaved; its instruction of the young in schools, in Catechism, in youth groups; its benedictions upon the happy intimacies of family life in baptisms, confirmations, and marriages; its administration of the Blessed Sacrament at the altar and at the sick bed; its comforting of the bereaved and its laying to rest the mortal remains of the bodies which had been temples of the Holy Spirit and in so doing declaring ever and again the message of Eternal Life. Could any man in any vocation find anything so satisfying, so purposeful, so demanding, so exhilarating, so rewarding, as the parish priest finds in the life to which he has given himself? My answer is unequivocal.

Thus when on a certain November day in 1950 the Bishop of Carlisle (Dr. Thomas Bloomer) button-holed me in a corridor of Church House, Westminster, to ask me to join him in his diocese as Archdeacon of West-morland and Director of Religious Education for the Diocese of Carlisle, my immediate response was to say that I had no desire to give up the office of parish priest for purely administrative work. He was quick to say that his plan was to ask his Archdeacon to become Vicar of Ambleside and to make that his base for Archidiaconal and educational work. Never having met the Bishop before, but warming to his engaging personality immediately, I could then do no other than promise to consider his suggestion seriously and to discuss the matter with my own Bishop. There we left it, and if the truth be told what happened during the next two days of the Church Assembly was certainly not sufficiently exciting to take my mind off the possibility that the Mansfield chapter of my ministry was reaching its conclusion, as I thought, all too soon.

On returning to Mansfield I shared my problem – for it was certainly that since I had anticipated being in Mansfield for seven years or so – only with my mother and sister and my colleagues, and tried to adopt inwardly the policy of 'business as usual' which I certainly followed outwardly. I wrestled with the problem for a few days – and nights – and decided that I could not give the peremptory negative answer which within my mind I had formulated in the course of the journey home from London. I would seek the guidance of the Bishop, though not forthwith, for maybe ten days' contemplation of the pros and cons might enable me to go to him with a quieter mind. I recalled the dictum of the priest who joined me in that journey from Newton Abbot to Durham University twenty-one years before — 'When the will is dedicated the way is directed'.

Meanwhile there were other things to occupy my mind and time, not least the preparations for the Christmas Feast and the implementations of recent church council decisions concerning our school and our long disused churchyard. The latter had been a sad eyesore for years — a disgrace to the church and to the town, and whilst I had from time to time decided that something should be done to make it presentable it was a paragraph in a *Mansfield Parish Magazine* of the year 1871 which I had recently discovered in our archives that made me spring into action. Even in those far-off days, I was to discover, Mansfield had a Church Council nearly 60 years before the Enabling Act made such a body a statutory requirement. In one June 1871 magazine I read that the Church Council had resolved that 'sheep are no longer to be allowed to feed in the churchyard'. I read the words with a smile. Sheep grazing in the middle of Mansfield! What a sight for sore industrialised eyes! They had been banished, I read, as part of a plan to 'transform a melancholy scene of neglect into a pretty and tranquil place'. But can anything be more 'tranquil' than an old sheep having its lunch, I pondered. I determined in my own mind not that the sheep should be reinstated but that the closed churchyard on the south side of the church which was still a melancholy scene of neglect should not remain an eyesore any longer. It must be transformed into an attractive garden worthy of the sacred purpose for which it had been consecrated in years past and providing, not a grazing place for sheep, but a tranquil retreat for the aged and seats where they might rest awhile.

The plan was put before our church council in December 1950, it being explained that whilst the control of the churchyard remained within their hands the liability for its maintenance rested with the Borough Council, though it was not within their power to alter its layout in any way. Thus it was at that meeting that we resolved that action should be taken under the appropriate Local Government Acts of 1894 and 1933 to level the ground, remove and rearrange the gravestones (most of which were broken), to construct footpaths, create lawns and flower beds, and to provide seats. The suggestion was received cordially by the Borough Council and our expressed hope that the work might be done in the course of the Festival of Britain was noted with approval. It was so done though I have never been back to see the result.

The weeks leading to Christmas seemed, as ever, to move more rapidly than others and following my talk with the Bishop of Southwell and with others whose counsel I valued, I decided to accept what I was beginning to see as the Bishop of Carlisle's challenge. I resolved not to mar my Christmas or my people's Christmas by announcing my impending departure until the festival was over. According to the *Nottingham Guardian* 'a gasp of surprise came from the congregation' at Evensong on 31 December 1950 when I told them that I would be leaving Mansfield in the spring. It was a difficult announcement to make, the more so since the parish found it difficult to accept. We were indeed a very happy family and, under God, we had done great things together. We could say in all humility 'Not unto us O Lord but unto Thy Name give the praise' – but that made it no easier to realise that that chapter in the long story of Mansfield Parish Church was coming to an end.

Since I was going to the far north-west the announcement won me not only congratulations for what the laity described as my promotion but also sympathy that it involved my having to go 'up north' and, from those who had holidayed in the Lake District, there came promises of gifts of umbrellas! I had to assure them that my experience of the north in Durham had convinced me, an immigrant from the deep south-west, that the people no longer painted themselves in woad, that their land was not permanently covered in snow and that, if it were true that the Lake District had more inches of rain than elsewhere, my information was that it probably had no more hours of rainfall than the average. When, ultimately, I found myself in Carlisle it was not unusual to receive letters, even on one occasion from a government department, which were addressed to 'Carlisle, Scotland'! Altogether the advantages and disadvantages as between residence and work in north and south are in my experience pretty evenly distributed.

Nevertheless, as the time of my departure drew nearer the thought of the distant move weighed heavily. It mattered not where the breaks had been – Teignmouth, Newton Abbot, Sevenoaks, Durham, Newark, Coddington, Worksop – the experience of leaving places and people had always been traumatic. It was not merely that each move meant separation from so many who meant so much to me and who had always been touchingly grateful for what I had tried to do with them and for them. It was, I doubt not, that in each place where I had worked, I had found a job satisfaction which made severance unpalatable, and under God, a fulfilment and achievement that prompted a desire to be left alone on ground familiar to me, for further exciting ventures in pastoralia and evangelism. Leaving Mansfield would add a new dimension to the trauma of farewells since I was going into 'foreign parts'. I had never visited Cumberland or Westmorland and I knew but one person in the whole Diocese of Carlisle, namely Victor Turner, who had once been Vicar of St. Anne's, Worksop and subsequently Archdeacon of Nottingham. Furthermore I was, with not a little hesitation, going back on my tracks as it were.

Bishop Bloomer had explained to me that his diocese had made very little progress in the negotiations which the Education Act of 1944 required, that the Church should enter into discourse with the local education authorities concerning the Church Schools, and he was anxious that his new archdeacon should take up this matter urgently and vigorously, and further that he should bring new impetus and vision to the whole field of voluntary religious education in the diocese. This was precisely the sort of work which I had left behind in 1942 and I had never anticipated being caught up in such work again. Since, however, in the intervening nine years. I had been chairman of the Southwell Diocesan Committee responsible for overseeing such work, any hesitation which I had was not motivated by any feeling of inadequacy in that sphere. It derived rather from the fact that once more I should find myself tackling a three-pronged job as Vicar of a parish, Director of Education in the diocese and Archdeacon of Westmorland.

Altogether the assignment was a formidable one and from the moment I accepted it, I began to see ahead the tearing of conscience which I had frequently experienced from 1936 to 1942 when, as senior curate of Newark, priest-in-charge of Coddington, and Director of Religious Education for Southwell, I had had to serve three 'masters'. Contriving a programme of work which ensured that each of those 'masters' had a fair measure of my time and thought and energy had not been easy, and now that I was nearly ten years older might be more difficult still. All that, added to the fact that I was abundantly happy in Mansfield and richly blessed with two colleagues who contributed their respective and considerable gifts to the total ministry we offered with dedication and enthusiasm, made some of the 90 days between the announcement of my appointment and my subsequent departure days of tortuous questioning. Sometimes I wondered whether I might not have been wiser to answer the Bishop of Carlisle's invitation with words which in those days young men advertising for a change of curacy frequently used – 'Not North'.

The last Sunday Evensong in Mansfield's ancient parish church and the vast gathering on the following Tuesday, when the congregation along with the clergy and people from the deanery, civic representatives and members of Rotary, UNA, and other associations in the town filled the parish hall, were indeed rather overwhelming. The gifts showered upon me and upon my mother, the speeches by the Wardens, the Mayor, the Chapter Clerk, and the Free Church representatives prompted me, so the local paper reminds me, to say in the course of my reply: 'But I really cannot understand all this adulation for I'm just an ordinary fellow who has tried to do the job of work for which eighteen years ago he gave himself to God and His Church'. I left that Hall with not a single umbrella but with many gifts and with a lump in my throat. But Mansfield was determined to have the last word for the ringers, whose belfry I used to visit once every Sunday, decided that they must send me on my way rejoicing and this they did the night before I left the town by ringing 2520 changes of Grandsire Triples. I am no campanologist and have little idea of what that means, but I know a merry noise when I hear it. 'As the bell clinketh, so a man thinketh,' says the old proverb and that night it rejoiced my heart to know that as we were doing our last packing in the vicarage, the bells were turning the thoughts of Mansfield people towards us and I knew my people well enough to know that many would turn their thoughts into prayers.

8

Hills of the North – Ambleside

Let me begin this part of my story by shattering some illusions. To those of my Mansfield parishioners whose only knowledge of the Lake District was its meteorological reputation, the move from the bustling borough of Mansfield to the tiny township of Ambleside was seen as a passage from life unto death, though those among them who had spent holidays among the mountains and lakes would have conceded that such a 'death' could not but be a 'paradise'. The notion of rural tranquillity is part of the stock in trade of the urban mind and I was very soon to discover that among the hordes of people who flock to the Lakes in the summer were many who nurtured it. 'What a quiet little place Ambleside must be in the winter!' said a visitor to me before I had spent a winter there. He pictured its streets bereft of their holiday crowds, its lake without its steamers and boats, its hotels and boarding houses closed, and its inhabitants, exhausted by the summer invasion, settling down tortoise-like for their winter hibernation. One return visit in mid-winter would have dispelled for ever any notion that Ambleside 'dies' every November. I was not long in learning that as soon as the last visitor had piled into his car all the family's goods and chattels and secured his boat firmly to the car's roof, the last hiker had stuffed his already over-loaded rucksack with mementoes and the last steamer had hooted its end-of-season farewell as it left Waterhead for its winter sojourn at Lakeside, Ambleside picked up again the threads of a lively community life. True there were no neon lights, no theatres, no night clubs, no glittering dance halls and a cinema operating only on four nights a week, but as the autumn leaves began to fall the little town came alive to its own concerns and throughout the winter months it seethed with activity. Scouts and Guides, Cubs and Brownies, YM and YWCA, Choral Society, Drama Group, Field Society, Dancing Classes, Soccer and Rugby Clubs, Mothers' Union, Women's Institute, Young Wives' Group, Workers' Educational Association lecture courses, and rarely a week passing without one or more 'Coffee Mornings' to help forward the work of this Charity and that, and incidentally to provide a rich opportunity for turning a locality of

141

a couple of thousand into a lively and caring community.

But there was – and maybe is – another fallacy fostered to some extent by the media, and one which lay behind one of Russell Barry's many classic and amusing exaggerations as he gripped my hand in farewell on his last visit to Mansfield Parish Church before I left. 'You've never stopped working here,' he said 'but you'll have to up there. Everything shuts down from November to April.' A few reports of torrential rains and of consequent floods here and there, a few pictures on television of snow-covered mountains and snow blocked roads, and a terrifying weather syndrome for Cumbria is imprinted indelibly on the minds of those who know it not. Let it be recorded that in my 21 years service in Cumbria, as peripatetic priest and prelate, only on five occasions did the ice and snow and the frost and cold and flood which enjoy honourable mention in the Benedicite, prevent me from fulfilling engagements, and on at least three of those occasions the whole country was locked in the same arctic conditions. I do not deny, however, that some of the journeys were perilous and on one such indeed I feared for my life.

Attempting to reach Bampton on the eastern side of Cumbria in the winter of 1963 for the institution of its new vicar – an occasion be it remembered which normally gathers the whole village community together – and finding that Shap Fell had long been solidly blocked by snow, I tried to ascend Dunmail Raise but failed miserably as indeed the motoring organisations had predicted. One hope remained and that was to tackle Kirkstone Pass. Uncongenial though the conditions were I passed through Troutbeck and began the ascent. Gradually the storm became fiercer and the snowfall heavier, and at length the car would take no more. I was forced to abandon it and within minutes saw it engulfed in snow up to its windscreen. Against a biting wind and driving snow I set off back to Troutbeck and within yards I realised as never before the power of a violent snowstorm and blistering and biting wind to interfere with breathing. Several times in the two-mile trek I stopped exhausted, turned my back to the wind and filled my lungs for a few more steps. Each time I did this I felt more reluctant to start again and I became vaguely aware that the bitter winds and driving snow which were freezing hands and face and feet were also numbing the will to carry on. I thought of Capt. Oates and unashamedly confess that I was frightened. But I struggled on in what was an up-hill fight against a down-hill gradient. Never was I more thankful, nor more exhausted, than when I rang the bell of Troutbeck Vicarage to seek shelter and to thaw out within and without. From there I phoned the Vicar-to-be to apologise for my inability to get to the parish for the great occasion only to receive the answer: 'There's no need to worry, my lord, nobody else can get here either.' Three weeks elapsed before I could fulfil the engagement and even then, unable to complete the homeward journey, I was forced to spend the night in a hotel – my rochet taking the place of pyjamas! On another memorable occasion, when the Rothay burst its banks only half a mile from my home, it was only by pushing the car door open against the on-rush of the water and climbing onto its bonnet, where I stood in several inches of water, that I could escape the worst furies of the flood. That, fortunately, was on a homeward journey, but impeded by floods on another occasion and arriving at one of Cockermouth's churches five minutes late for the morning service, the organist displayed either a sense of humour or a strange insensitivity, by choosing Handel's Water Music for the episcopal processional entry. I could not help but reflect that even Handel would have been incapable of writing anything so pleasing had he had water squelching in his shoes as at that moment I had in mine.

But it is the very rarity of such climatic conditions which has imprinted these experiences so indelibly on my memory. No such mishaps befell the two coach loads of Mansfield and Worksop parishioners who had made the journey from Nottinghamshire to Westmorland for my Institution to the benefice and Collation to the Archdeaconry in the week after Easter in 1951. They saw Lakeland at its best — the spring sunshine sparkling the snow-capped hills, glistening on the waters of the lake and heightening the varied colours of the spring flowers. They saw in all its splendour what Charlotte Brontë, writing a hundred years before, described as 'a glorious region of which I have only seen the similitude in dreams waking or sleeping'. They joined about five hundred of their fellows in the service of Institution in praising the 'Immortal, Invisible, God only wise' and the eyes which were lifted to the mountains as they walked to the church were raised to the Creator within —

> *Unresting, unhasting and silent as light,*
> *Nor wanting, nor wasting, Thou rulest in might,*
> *Thy justice like mountains high soaring above,*
> *Thy clouds which are fountains of goodness and love.*

Rising early from their hotel beds on the morning following the service all with one accord joined me with many of my new parishioners in the Eucharist, after which my erstwhile parishioners set off for a tour of the Lakes as a prelude to their homeward journey. Despite any misgivings they might have entertained about their vicar's departure to the far north, with all its hazards and blizzards, they went home fully persuaded that the lot had fallen unto him in a very fair ground.

As I had done before taking up my Worksop and Mansfield appointments so too, before going north into what for me was *terra incognita*, I made it my business to delve a little into the history of Ambleside and Rydal and to discover something about the Cumbrian mountains and lakes. But this time I found myself mixed up, as it were, not with industry but with nature and with art, not with royal and ducal personages but with authors, with poets, and with ecclesiastics. I was reading again poems vividly or vaguely remembered, beginning to look forward, for example, to a sight of Arnold's 'blue, haze-cradled mountlins', to the opportunity of sharing with Southey the experience of seeing these mountains don 'their wintry garments of unsullied snow' and of living with Wordsworth under the 'more habitual sway . . . of meadows, hills and groves'. Arriving in the spring I could expect to be welcomed by Wordsworth's 'jocund company . . . a host of golden daffodils'. Certainly I looked forward to the new work with its three-pronged challenge in parish, archdeaconry and diocese with eager anticipation, but I looked forward too to living in a part of England unparalleled in its natural beauty by any other.

The name Ambleside, originally spelt Hamelsate or Amelsate – and I was to discover that the oldest locals pronounced the name of their town much like the sound of those spellings – appears in records as far back as the thirteenth century, though archaeological discoveries leave little room for doubt that the first settlement was way back in the Bronze Age, and no room for doubt that the district was occupied by the Romans from about 70 AD to 400 AD Among the Roman soldiers who were stationed in the Borrans Fort at Ambleside there were doubtless some who were Christians, and indeed in the course of excavations on the site of the fort in the late eighteenth century a brass crucifix was one of many interesting and informative finds. Some Romans soldiers may well have held the Faith in those early years but it was not until about 1550 that Ambleside had its first place of worship, which was possibly dedicated to St. Anne. It was that little chapel with its unceilinged roof, its earthen floor and crude benches, its walls white-washed without and decorated within with texts from Holy Scripture, which in effect became the parish church of Ambleside in 1676 – though the existence of registers in the form of long narrow parchment scrolls dated from 1642 onwards suggests that the Chapel had already been serving the purpose of a parish church for more than thirty years. By the end of the eighteenth century, however, it had become 'mean, decayed and damp' and in 1812 it was rebuilt on the same site, and the treasures which it had gathered to itself through the years, among them Ambleside's famous early seventeenth-century Steeple Chalice and its first edition of the Authorised Version of the Bible, were carefully preserved. Mysteriously however, the Bible disappeared at the end of the seventeenth century. As it was one of the very rare '*he*' Bibles – that is a Bible in which Ruth ch. 3, v. 15 reads 'and *he* went into the citie' whereas subsequent versions read 'and when she went into the citie' – Ambleside was thus dispossessed of a valuable treasure until, two hundred years later, it was recovered for the town by some public-spirited resident who found it in a Huddersfield Bible Warehouse.

The little mountain Chapel of St. Anne ceased to be used regularly for public worship towards the close of the nineteenth century, but not before men who figure in the history of Church and Nation had preached and ministered in it. Among these were Thomas Arnold, Headmaster of Rugby, F. W. Faber, curate of Ambleside before he followed Newman into the Roman Catholic Church and author of a number of our favourite hymns, Dr. Spooner who bequeathed to us the Spoonerism 'Kinquering congs their tatles tike', and less authentically 'You have deliberately tasted two worms and you can leave Oxford by the town drain'. Other famous signatures appear in the 'Strange Preachers' Book' – among them A. C. Tait (93rd Archbishop of Canterbury) W. F. Hook (Subsequently Dean of Chichester) and F. D. Maurice the noted Christian Socialist. At the time of the Coronation of H.M. Queen Elizabeth II, Canon Charles Smyth then of Westminster Abbey was kind enough to draw my attention to a note in Dean Stanley's *Historical Memorials of Westminster Abbey* in which the Dean says: 'For the best expression which has perhaps ever been given of the full religious aspect of an English Coronation, I cannot forbear to refer to the sermon preached on that day' (i.e. the day of the Coronation of Queen Victoria) 'in the parish church of Ambleside by Dr. Arnold.' The Canon's kindness enabled me, at the time of our Queen's Coronation, to summarise, for the parishioners of Ambleside to read in 1953, a sermon which had been addressed to their forbears at the time of the Coronation of another young Queen in 1837.

It was very early in that young Queen's reign that Ambleside began to grow in fame and in population. What might be called its 'Industrial Revolution' began in the late fifteenth century and for nearly two hundred years the woollen trade flourished. According to Clarke's *Survey of the Lakes* the inhabitants were 'very industrious: the women spun wool, the men weave linseys, kerseys and other course cloths' and fulling mills and corn mills alike were busy. Even so very many less than a thousand people lived in the district and it was after this industrial activity had declined and the district began to attract the attention of artists and men of letters that Ambleside became famous for its natural beauty. Stage coaches, drawn always by six horses, were the precursors of today's motor coaches bringing visitors to a part of the country whose praises were being sung by men like Coleridge, Wordsworth, Southey, Faber, de Quincey, Clough and Arnold. When these came to live among the hills of the north the Lake District grew both in public esteem and in intellectual and cultural stature. It was not long before Ambleside outgrew its 70' by 21' mountain chapel and, encouraged by the Poet Laureate (Wordsworth), by Mrs. Arnold (widow of Thomas), by Mrs. Clough (widow of Arthur Hugh), and perhaps most energetically by Dr. John Davy famous as a surgeon, geologist and anthropologist and brother of Sir Humphrey of the 'Davy Lamp', that the townsfolk, numbering then about a thousand, bent themselves to the task of building a new church which they did at a cost of £6,000. This was consecrated by the Bishop of Chester on 14 June 1854 in the presence of a vast congregation which embraced the rich and the poor, the learned and the simple, the unknown and the famous, including among the last mentioned Mrs. Wordsworth, then 84 years of age and, according to de Quincey, still a lady of 'supreme expression, of sunny benignity, and of a radiant graciousness such as in this world I never saw surpassed'. In the congregation were Mrs. Arnold and Matthew Arnold, Dr. John Davy, then Inspector General of Her Majesty's Military Hospitals, W. E. Forster, the great Liberal statesman and architect of the Education Act of 1870, and Agnes Nicholson, postmistress of Ambleside and friend of the Wordsworths and the Arnolds.

Thus did St. Mary's, Ambleside – still being referred to as 'the new church' when I arrived just before its 97th birthday – begin its life. Within was a memorial window to the man who not only contributed generously to its building but who, more than that, had helped people to discover the glory of England's lakes and mountains – the Poet Laureate, William Wordsworth. The window is significant in that it is held to be the first cultural object to which our American cousins were invited to contribute, and to which they did magnificently, on the initiative of Professor Henry Reed, the poet's American publisher, who wrote of Wordsworth as of one who had brought to the world 'so great a moral and intellectual good'. It was John Keble who chose the scriptural subjects for the window and the Latin inscription at its base is his composition: 'MDXXXLIII In Memoriam Gulielmi Wordsworth, P.C., Amatores et Amici partim Angli partim Anglo-Americani'. The presence of that window earned for the north-east corner of the church the title 'Wordsworth Chapel' but it was not so furnished until 1952 when once again Americans, as well as people throughout this country, responded to my appeal to make it in fact what it had long been in name. From that date of its consecration as such, and that in the presence of the Senior Fellow of St. John's College, Cambridge (Wordsworth's college), of the well-known Lakeland poet, Norman Nicholson, and of other lights in the literary firmament, the Chapel was used daily for the Divine Offices and for the week-day celebrations of the Holy Eucharist.

Nearly thirty years were to elapse from the building of the church before the parishioners could face the task of raising the money needed for the provision of a vicarage, but this too was accomplished in 1883 at a cost considerably exceeding that of the church. Three vicars were to come and go before one arrived who, with his family of eleven sons, could make full use of its 22 rooms. The vicarage is a splendid example of the Victorian builder's concept of a house built to blend in with its surroundings and to last for ever! Gloriously sited on a knoll hard by the church its main windows afford a panoramic picture of Loughrigg Fell, and set as it is in the heart of the little town it is readily accessible to the parishioners. I dismissed on my arrival murmurs which were circulating touching the possible disposal of a house so well built and so well placed. Maybe the first use of my archidiaconal powers was to over-rule the diocesan surveyor's initial rejection of my suggestion that division rather than disposal was the way to meet the legitimate complaint that a house which, as I used to say, had 22 rooms, 51 doors and 153 draughts, was too large and too expensive to run on a parson's stipend which was then about £520 a year. 'Divide and conquer' was the proposal I set before the church council and in due time that is precisely what happened with the end result that the house was divided into four parts – an adequate vicarage, a small cottage home for a retired priest, a top storey flat for a curate and a sizeable Vicarage Room for use by the parish – the last two with entrances from the back of the knoll on which the house was set. As the entrance to the top storey flat was across a bridge spanning a chasm between the knoll and the house the flat was named 'Kirkbridge'. In the vicarage so planned I lived happily for nine years and my two immediate successors between them for twenty. I cannot forbear to add that the speed with which the church today disposes of its over-large parsonage houses, thereby frequently offering speculators opportunities of making vast profits on their subsequent modernisation or conversion into flats, is in my judgement a short-sighted policy. The redundant vicarage of today could well be the needed vicarage of tomorrow, and the modernised and minimised sturdy Victorian house of today could well be standing its ground through the life of several of its twentieth-century successors.

Added to the Church's 'plant' within Ambleside itself – the Parish Church, St. Anne's Hall which the old church had now become, the vicarage and two church schools, there was the little church of St. Mary at Rydal built in interesting circumstances thirty years before Ambleside's 'new' church. Although the hamlet of Rydal had but twenty dwellings and a population of scarcely a hundred it had enjoyed the full-time services of an incumbent until 1942 when it was wisely decided to unite the benefice with that of Ambleside. Like Ambleside, Rydal as a manor and township reaches back to very ancient times for the secrets of its origins. Readers of Miss Mary Armitt's 800-page volume entitled *Rydal*, published in 1916, will find there a fascinating chronicle of the Celts and Romans, of the Angles and Normans and their successors who in their turns peopled the mountains and dales, wrangled over the forest and timber rights and the green-hew, hunted the deer, and traded the wool yielded by their flocks of Herdwicks and the char and trout from mountain streams and lakes. But for Rydal's ecclesiastical origins it is to Grasmere that we turn and it must have been to the Rector of Grasmere in the early nineteenth century that Lady le Fleming of Rydal Hall first confided her desire to build a place of worship in what she might well have regarded as her village. (The pedigree of the Flemings of Rydal reaches back to the early twelfth century, and when Squire Daniel entered into possession of the manor and lands in the mid-seventeenth century, Rydal House, as it was then known, became a mansion of stature and the Lord of the Manor a gentleman highly respected if not feared by some). Lady le Fleming took someone else into her confidence concerning the plan she cherished – namely William Wordsworth, her tenant and nearest neighbour, and it appears that in the choice of a site for the church his was the decisive voice. The Wordsworths had been living at Rydal Mount since 1813 and they were clearly at one with Lady le Fleming in her pious desire, even though there had at times been some friction between tenant and landlady concerning the dilapidated state of the house. Apparently the poet found it difficult to persuade her ladyship to effect the necessary repairs and in an extant letter there is a sharp reference to the fact that the long-awaited repairs and renovation had been 'from time to time delayed and as we are now informed, are not to be done at all'. However the house was in due course renovated, the breach was healed, and when the foundations of the new church were at last laid in 1823 the poet was moved

to express his joy and his hopes in a poem which he dedicated to Lady le
Fleming, and in the last verse of which he utters a prayer for God's blessing
on the enterprise:

> *Heaven prosper it! may peace and love*
> *And hope, and consolation fall,*
> *Through its meek influence, from above*
> *And penetrate the hearts of all;*
> *All who, around the hallowed Fane*
> *Shall sojourn in this fair domain;*
> *Grateful to Thee, while service pure*
> *And ancient ordinance shall endure,*
> *For opportunity bestowed*
> *To kneel together, and adore their God.*

In fact the 'hallowed Fane' proved not to be altogether to Wordsworth's
liking. 'It has no chancel,' he complained, 'the altar is unbecomingly confined,
the pews are so narrow as to preclude the possibility of kneeling in comfort,
there is no vestry and what ought to have been first mentioned, the font,
instead of standing at its proper place at the entrance, is thrust into the farther
end of a pew.' I note the reference to the altar and the font and I discern in
it Wordsworth's recognition of the primary place of the Gospel Sacraments
in the life and worship of the church. But what would our modern liturgists
make of his references to kneeling since they seem so determined to prevent
us from kneeling before the Lord our Maker? Though the church was not
all that Wordsworth had hoped for, its deficiencies – in fact remedied in
1894 – did not drive the family back to their parish church at Grasmere.
They worshipped regularly at Rydal, and in the school holidays they were
joined by the Arnolds, then living at Fox How, and for a time Wordsworth
was himself the church warden.

This then was the 'plant' to which I was introduced at my Institution to the
united benefice: two parish churches, the one seating just under a thousand,
the other a hundred, a commodious vicarage of 22 rooms, a parish hall in the
shape of the old mountain chapel and two church schools one of which called
for extensions and the other for ultimate replacement. I was soon to be made
aware that whatever the potential of the 'spiritualities', the 'temporalities' to
which I was inducted into the 'real, actual and corporal possession' were not
all as fair as they seemed. Everyone agreed that the vicarage was so vast that
it could not possibly be maintained on an incumbent's stipend and mine
was not augmented by my holding two other offices. Furthermore, the
bells of Ambleside and the tower in which they hung presented the new
vicar with an immediate and costly problem, and it was evident too that
the extensions to the infant school could not long be delayed. Even the old
church, serving as the parish hall, which I met for the first time following
the service of Institution, called loudly for modernisation and redecoration. It

seemed indeed that only Rydal's little church was quiescent midst the general clamour for immediate and considerable expenditure. The Ambleside Church council was certainly alert to all these needs and as anxious as I was to hand on to the future unimpaired, and if possible enriched, all that had been handed down to us from the past. But fortunately a keen and responsible nucleus of dedicated worshippers needed no pressure from their new vicar to accept the thesis that first things must come first and that the building up of the worshipping and witnessing Church and the adequate provision of the spiritual means to that end must over-ride all else.

I arrived in Ambleside shortly before the holiday season began and I could therefore assume, in a way not possible from May to October, that every one I met in church or in the streets was a parishioner. Within a month that was no longer the case for from May onwards Ambleside's populatiin of 3,000 rises gradually to its August peak of about 10,000 and in mid–September begins to drop less gradually to the end of October. Over the same period Rydal would add several hundreds to its winter population. There was therefore a dual ministry to discharge – to the residents and to the visitors. Counted among the residents were the students and staff of the Charlotte Mason College, a Teachers' Training College founded by the lady of that name who was herself the Founder of the Parents National Educational Union whose headquarters were in Ambleside, the girls of Fairfield School, a boarding school of the same foundation, and the boarders of King's School, an independent school for boys. As soon as the College and schools had disgorged their students and pupils from the pews they normally occupied, these were filled by visitors from all over the United Kingdom and indeed the world. Thus throughout the year there was an opportunity which I treasured – that of exercising a powerful teaching and preaching ministry in the context of a lively congregational worship. Our normal 'out-of-season' congregation, which included our own young people as well as the children from the schools and the students and staff of the college would range in age from 8 to 80, and in our summer congregation were representatives of every age group, of many countries, of different churches and, from time to time of black and brown and yellow from the so-called Third World.

I was soon to learn that the sort of people who came to the Lakes for their holidays were generally the sort of people to whom corporate worship meant a great deal, and also that many who sat loosely to the claims of God in their work-a-day lives were by no means averse to following the crowd into church on their holidays. With the pressures of work temporarily set aside they were able to give some serious attention to the things of the spirit and not a few testified to the spiritual enrichment they received from their being 'altogether with one accord in one place' in acts of worship so planned as to evoke lively congregational participation. Thankfully I can recall now many long conversations with visitors anxious to find again during their holiday that dimension of life which once they had and which under pressure of the world they had lost. Among letters recently destroyed were many from people whose signatures meant nothing to me after so many years but whose gratitude for the privilege, as they put it, of joining in those great acts of worship meant a great deal to me at the time and to those around me who contributed so richly to the Church's work and worship. Not the least important among these were the churchwardens and sidesmen who were meticulous in welcoming visitors and finding seats for them difficult as it often was, and the organist and choir whose contribution in leading the singing of vast congregations was outstanding. Sydney Lewis, who shortly after my arrival succeeded the aged Ernest Skelton after his 60 years' service to the music of the church as chorister and organist, worked enthusiastically with me to build up a choir strong in numbers and of a standard infinitely higher than might have been expected in so small a parish. Though the emphasis was on congregational singing, each member of the congregation being provided with a pointed psalter as well as a hymn book, few Sundays passed without the contribution of an anthem, though I recall that on one or two occasions when this was the intention the sudden depletion of the men's ranks by an S.O.S. from the mountain rescue team of which some choirmen were members, called for cancellation of something which had involved many hours of preparation. The biggest congregations of the year were in August when although the church could seat comfortably 800 people, sidesmen had frequently to encourage members of the congregation to 'contract' somewhat to admit another in a pew here and there! Throughout August the picture of a church porch littered with rucksacks before the early morning celebration of the Eucharist, and the altar rail thronged with young people appropriately clothed for the day's fell walking or climbing, was one which could not but lift the heart of any parish priest.

For nearly ten months this dual ministry to residents and visitors, along with the responsibilities attaching to the office of archdeacon and to the education portfolio, were carried on alone. Thus, satisfying and exhilarating though the work was, I was conscious that much on the parochial side was inevitably being left undone. It was only by raiding my old diocese of Southwell and winning the co-operation of its good bishop that I drew to my aid Vernon Clarke who was my colleague for three years and who with his wife Cicely made a significant contribution to the pastoral side. His departure three years later left me once more on my own for a further six months after which a further subtle reconnaissance of Nottinghamshire led to my plucking from the city of Nottingham Tony Wharton who had been a layman in my Mansfield congregation and who with his wife Marjorie brought valuable gifts to the service of the Church both in Ambleside and Rydal.

The teaching ministry – clearly so important an aspect of the total ministry in a church which, in winter as in summer, gathered so varied a congregation – was extended through all the customary parochial organisations for children, for adolescents and for adults and by means of a carefully-tended bookstall from which Christian literature to the value of £250–£300 was sold year by year. In all this the assistant curates and their wives, along with many dedicated layfolk, with my mother and, for a very short time my sister, played their parts magnificently. Rather more persuasion was needed, however, to convince the church council that the ministry could be even further extended by the written word provided that they agreed to the re-casting and enlargement of the parish magazine. They had for years been accustomed to the normal type of magazine which faithfully records baptisms, marriages and burials and, I have found to my dismay, almost invariably omits the records of confirmations. It has been found that such a production, embracing a few choice words from the vicar, makes a palatable if modest meal and spiced up by the commercials normally gladly paid for by local tradesmen can 'pay its way', albeit but only just.

So here, as in Worksop and Mansfield, there was mild astonishment in the council when enlargement and refashioning of the monthly magazine was suggested, and here as in Worksop and Mansfield there was the cry 'it will never pay'. However when I readily agreed that in terms of pounds, shillings and pence they could well be right, but that I could nevertheless assure them that measured in terms of Christian evangelism and education, and of the life and witness of the parish church in the community, there would be handsome returns, reluctantly they allowed the vicar to have his way. I recall an amusing discussion in the church council concerning a name for the new journal. My suggestion was *Prospect* meaning 'an extensive view', 'a long view of things'. Others suggested *The Cresset*, defined as 'a burning torch on a beacon' and this seemed particularly apposite for a parish set among the mountains. However when another dictionary told me that a cresset was 'a receptacle containing combustible material', I retreated hastily and settled for *Prospect*.

Thus *Prospect* was born in January 1952 and happily it has survived to this day. It quickly blossomed into a sizeable monthly journal and within eighteen months of its first appearance it was going into eight out of every ten homes in the parishes of Ambleside and Rydal. It proved to be not only a means by which the whole community was made aware of what was happening in and about its parish church, but also, by means of a faithful band of distributors, it became a way of establishing regular pastoral contacts between church and people whether or not they were regular attenders at worship. Furthermore it attempted month by month to provide some systematic instruction in the Christian Faith and Christian way of Life – to expound, to explain, to guide, to awaken, to encourage, to appeal, to alert, to summon, even to amuse as when stories were inserted to tell of the opening, by children, of the annual autumn fair in which the Pied Piper of Hamelin, Winnie the Pooh, Elizabeth the First and St. George and his Dragon and their respective entourages appeared. Choristers gave their lively impressions of their annual corporate holidays in London, Edinburgh, Jersey, Northern Ireland and the Isle of Man. I doubt not that the time and energy and money spent in that monthly production, never the work of one man, was reflected in the growing interest of the two communities generally in their Parish Churches, by the growth in the congregations, and by the lively response to the inevitable appeals which were made for the maintenance and improvement of the church's buildings. Conversions are not effected by typewriters or parish magazines, but the written word of the parish priest, addressed to all his parishioners, whether committed or not, can be a powerful instrument in opening the way towards them is, in my experience, indisputable.

I must revert to the words above which assert that my sister helped in all this for 'a very short time'. The fact was that soon after we settled in Ambleside she was taken seriously ill and it became clear to my mother and myself that she was unlikely to recover. After a distressing period in which she was bedridden she died on the Feast of Stephen 1951 when she was still under 50. Having then been in Holy Orders for 18 years I had seen, in the course of my pastoral ministry, many people cross the horizon which we call death – the horizon which is but the limit of our sight – but never one of my own kith and kin. The experience, personally heart-rending though it was, was one which helped me enormously thereafter in sympathising – which means 'suffering with' – the bereaved in my pastoral ministry.

My sister had never been robust and consequently was always rather introspective, and that made her far from at ease in a vicarage house where inevitably there is little privacy. Attached as we were to one another – and no one discerned that better than Russell Barry whose letter to me following her death is one that I remember with deep gratitude – she died leaving me with a guilt feeling that I had failed her, not consciously or deliberately but out of my dedication to the demands of my vocation. I recall that in the course of her terminal illness I suffered many hours of self-questioning. Had vicarage life been too much for her – the constantly ringing doorbell in the town vicarages, the incessant telephone, the invasions of the house by people for this committee and that, the women's working parties, the entertaining and the anxieties of budget balancing? Had I been wrong in involving her? My mother had taken all these in her stride; my sister frequently wilted beneath them. Was this an instance of *mea culpa, mea maxima culpa*? But as the light of life in her began to flicker on that Christmas Day, and I sensed that she shared a peace which seemed to mock my anxiety and challenge my faith, my mind leapt back to our childhood days when three brothers protected their frail sister, played with her, carried her around the house on their shoulders singing impromptu ditties which embraced their pet name for her, and evoked from her squeals of childish delight. I thought of the jolly holidays which we had had together since she came to share my home in 1933 and of her shafts of wit about my various far from second-hand cars. ('If this thing's going in part exchange, you'll get more for it if you take it round to the garage in the blackout!' and – as the rain began to drop onto her head as we motored over Dartmoor, in a truly frightening storm, the quiet voice which asked 'They didn't by any chance give you a free umbrella with this car did they?'). And on that Christmas Day I reflected on the warmth of our home, and the rare peace and quiet which generally possessed it at Christmas time when for a day or two the doorbell was silent, the telephone died, and the house, bright with her decorations, glowed with the happy intimacies of family life. In the morning, on that last exchange of Christmas presents, a smile defied her pain as she gave me hers and accepted mine, and a trembling hand had been lifted to receive the Holy Sacrament at my hands. I stayed at her side through the night, and the next morning, as I held her in my arms, she moved into what Matthew Arnold in his *Requiescat* calls 'The vasty hall of Death'. I knelt at her bedside and commending her soul to the gracious keeping of the Living God I recalled the words sung at my father's funeral 28 years earlier:

> *Through every period of my life*
> *Thy goodness I'll pursue*
> *And after death in distant worlds,*
> *Thy glorious theme renew.*

And I stood by the bedside waiting for the courage with which to break the expected news to my mother.

That's how it came about that one of the earliest entries in the burial records in the new *Prospect* was that of Amy Doreen Bulley, aged 49 years. It was a heavy blow but one to be borne and one, moreover, which could not be allowed to impede 'the King's business' which then as ever 'requireth haste'. In the parish it was the season of parties – the little children's, the choristers' (first the boys, then the men), the Mothers' Union, the Vicar's and many others. And the parish priest must be with them in their merriment despite his personal sorrow, even though preference urged withdrawal for a space. Within the vicarage there was a quiet and a stillness, in the parish outside were the parties – fun and games, feasting and dancing, the excitement of little children, and the merriment of adults becoming such. Here were contrasts, but the one did not deny the other. As the night brings out the stars, so sorrow enhances joy.

It became clear to me towards the end of 1952 that what had become known as 'The Steeple Problem' could no longer be burked. Rumours, quite unfounded, were in circulation that Ambleside's new vicar was bent on removing the spire of the church and these, infiltrating the press, were prompting 'Disgusted' and others to write to me. The fact was that according to no less than three architects the spire of the church was exercising a crushing effect on the tower whose masonry was clearly overloaded and the ringing of the bells, though not the cause of the damage to the structure, could only aggravate the situation to the point of possible collapse of tower and spire. The architects whose advice had been sought before my time had given the most ominous warnings – the first to the effect that only the removal of the spire would prevent a disaster. Ambleside generally regarded it as all but sacrilegious to deprive lakeland of so unique a picture – a spire against the backgrounds of the mountains. A second architect advised the retention of the spire, and the removal of the organ from the base of the tower so that an internal concrete structure could be built within to carry the spire. The first architect's scheme was to cost something approaching £5,000 and the second architect's £20,000. The Department of Technology at Manchester University could offer no greater comfort. Consequently I counselled our approaching Mr. Stephen Dykes-Bower, surveyor of the fabric of Westminster Abbey and many cathedrals, for some clear and decisive guidance. He described the spire as having considerable architectural merit and as 'helping to counter what might otherwise be undue oscillation'. He it was who produced the scheme which, following a public meeting attended by several hundred people and a debate which lasted just under three hours, with 'down spire' and 'retain spire' speakers following one another rapidly, was accepted by an overwhelming majority. A further resolution to raise the necessary £5,000 was similarly passed.

Fortunately for us the controversy spilt into the national press and pictures of the church against its familiar Loughrigg background prompted people in different parts of the country to send gifts even before the appeal was launched. It was noted that 14 June 1954 would be the one hundredth birthday of the church and I expressed my hope that by that day all the work would be completed including the work on the bells themselves, and all the money needed to pay for it would be in hand. When that day dawned one thousand three hundred and sixty gifts ranging in size from £50 to 1/- (with one of £250) had been received and we were short of something like £400. A gift day for the hundredth birthday celebrations had already been arranged and I had told the community that they would hear their eight bells after the years of silence if by 7 p.m. the remaining money had been offered in full. £100 shortfall would silence one bell, £200 shortfall would silence two bells etc.

It was a happy gimmick which drew to the church on centenary day, as I sat awaiting the gifts, reporters and photographers and even the BBC gathering material for a talk on the church's centenary to be broadcast in North America. Centenary day saw special services and between them came men and women, boys and girls, and 'mixed infants' bringing their gifts, and many of them doing their best to extract from the vicar how near we were to hearing all the bells. The ringers gathered in the belfry at 6.30 p.m. I joined them at 6.45, and imparted to them first the secret that our gift day had yielded £439.0.5d. Together we offered prayers of thanksgiving and then there crashed from the belfry the news for which the whole community was waiting, many standing in the churchyard anxious to be among the first to count the ring. Following Evensong 300 people repaired to the church hall for a supper dance – with speeches and good humour, good fun, good exercise and everyone tasting all to the full.

A few days later the verger reported that the boiler had burst, and because that struck some people as highly amusing and others as singularly unfortunate once more we spilt into the press whereupon a gentleman in Bournemouth, concerned lest I should dally over this sad state of affairs in a way which had all but caused the downfall of my predecessor as Vicar a hundred years earlier, sent me a cutting from the *Illustrated London News* of 12 January

1856. I record it as a salutary warning to all church councils confronted with problems relating to church heating systems. Headed 'A Congregation nearly suffocated', it reads:

> The new church at Ambleside has recently been warmed by means of flues leading from the coke fire. Owing to some imperfection of the flues a deleterious gas issued into the body of the Church during the morning service last Sunday. Young children, being nearest the floor, were first affected and about twenty of them followed one another out before the adults took the alarm. At about the middle of the sermon the congregation rose in a body and went out, to the apparent astonishment of the preacher, who, in his elevated pulpit was unaware of the mischief. He was left entirely alone in the church. The scene in the churchyard was singular for a day in January — numbers of persons were laid on the grass, fainting, convulsed and moaning. None altogether escaped injury. During the afternoon the druggists shop was crowded for stimulant medicines — debility and headache prostrating the population like a plague. None of the cases have terminated fatally, but the danger to several must have been imminent. Repeated warnings had been given to the authorities for weeks past by the ringers and others who had suffered from the fumes of the coke, but no notice was taken; and on Sunday last the doors were shut and kept shut by the churchwardens, whose practice it is to go to the inns during prayers to see whether any drinking is going forward, and who will allow no admission of air during their absence, or on their return. By the latest accounts some of the invalids were rather worse than better, while others had nearly recovered.

What exciting times our forefathers in Ambleside had lived through! And what choice language the press used to describe the catastrophe! A Series 2 revision would turn 'deleterious gas' into 'noxious gas' and Series 3 would further amend it to 'harmful', and in neither would anyone have 'terminated fatally' even though one had died. But it is interesting that 'young children', even in those far off days, were 'nearest the floor'! I am as intrigued now as I was when the Bournemouth gentleman sent me the cutting to know why the churchwardens were so anxious that there should be 'no admission or air during their absence or on their return'. Far be it for me to call into question the motives of those faithful church officers but their behaviour could at least suggest that they were bent on asphyxiating the whole congregation in their absence and themselves on their return. However, having drawn the attention of the parish to the church's desperate need for a new boiler before winter should come, and the awful possibilities of our retaining a faulty heating system, I for my part fled to Minneapolis for the Anglican Congress. But that is a tale which belongs properly to the archidiaconal third of my working life in Ambleside and shall be dealt with later. Suffice it here to say that as I wilted in the nineties of a Minnesota summer I had news that the faithful Amblesidians were, on their own initiative, organising a garden party for 'the boiler fund'.

But that was not to be the last of the 'bricks and mortar' problems which would call for resolution. It was quickly followed by essential work on the schools including the extension of the Infant School, long foreseen, and expensive work on the 'old church', unforeseen. The latter had long served as a parish hall with every possible inconvenience. This had been tolerated but when the ceiling began to fall, closely followed by the roof caving in, this proved to be the last straw for one or two of the faithful who counselled allowing the old building to fall into ruin, one even suggesting that as such it would not be unattractive standing as it did on its hill complete with 'yonder ivy mantled tower'. But by then the Ambleside community had the bit between its teeth and having triumphed so magnificently over its earlier trials was not to be daunted by another. So the old place was re-roofed and re-ceiled and so delighted were the parishioners that 'the old church' was safe that we promptly conceived plans by which it could become a presentable parish hall with all the mod. cons. which it had hitherto lacked. This time it was to be by indirect giving and to this end the proceeds of our annual autumn fairs, each lasting a whole day and each opened in the morning by some Lakeland personage having the welfare of the Church at heart, and re-opened in the afternoon by the children of our church schools and of the independent boys' and girls' schools whose staffs were always eager to help.

No sooner had Ambleside's material problems, at least on the ecclesiastical side, been resolved at a total cost of something like £20,000, than disaster befell little Rydal in the shape of dry rot which an architect discovered had affected the whole roof. Once again there was talk of closure and arguments adduced in support of that were the minuscule winter population (less than a hundred), the small winter congregations which nevertheless represented in fact about 20 per cent of the resident population, augmented by a choir of girls from Fairfield School. My own desire, however, was to hold on to the church, a desire nurtured by an innate reluctance ever to see a church closed but in Rydal's case a conviction that we could not overlook the Church's ministry to the summer visitors. Deep in my mind too was a secret desire which at that moment I shared with none but the realisation of which would I know, be impeded by the death of Rydal church. What that secret was will later be revealed. Meanwhile once again I must face the tiny church council with a 'to be or not to be' decision. It was a memorable meeting held in the church that evening when, following prayers, I stood within the pew once used by the Wordsworth family, and beneath the pulpit in which Thomas Arnold and Fred Faber, among others, had proclaimed the Word of God. I put before an anxious group of a dozen parishioners the stark alternatives – either we set out to raise £2,000 or the church, no longer safe, must close. The Rydal folk decided unanimously to try, we knew not how, to raise the money, and I went home that night feeling that we had given God the glory and by so doing must have pleased the spirits of those faithful servants of His who had worshipped in Rydal Church in the past. Once again the work cost far more than the original estimate and once again the money came, never in large sums, but 'here a little, there a little', chiefly from Rydal itself but from Ambleside too, from England, Ireland, Scotland and Wales, from the United States, from Canada, from New Zealand, from Australia; and from the Arnolds and Wordsworths, le Flemings and Fells, from Forsters and Fletchers, from Wordsworth's College (St. Johns, Cambridge), and Arnold's school (Rugby), in pounds and in dollars, and in all £2,988 2s 3d. When the work was completed and paid for a small balance of under a £100 remained. For me that was a victory not merely for the present but for the generations to come.

Meanwhile something was happening which might have surprised some but did not surprise my colleague and myself. The need to direct the parishioners' attention to the 'bricks and mortar' problems, and to encourage them to meet them with their gifts and hard work, far from impeding our pastoral and teaching ministry kindled the interest of many who hitherto had taken the Church for granted. Many were led to a new understanding of the place of a church within a community and of the Church within their own lives. The word 'stewardship' was not then as current in the Church's vocabulary as it is now but it was beginning to impress itself on the minds of many and to indicate an approach to the use of time, of talents and of material possessions which had a marked effect on the Church's work and witness and worship. Through the years the number of people presenting themselves for Confirmation had greatly increased and significantly there were several Confirmations for adults only. We were privileged to broadcast several services on the Home and Overseas programmes of the BBC, and such broadcasts had the effect of strengthening the corporate life of the worshipping community and of enabling us to convey to listeners something of the vigour and fellowship which marked our church life. There were also the great national occasions when the church was crammed to its capacity by those who came to mourn the death of Queen Mary, and of George the Sixth, and to pray for Her Majesty the Queen on the day of her Coronation. There was an Ordination and a memorable visit to Ambleside of the Primate of England (Dr. Cyril Garbett) for which purpose a massive marquee seating 2,500 had been erected in the park hard by the church which proved in fact to be inadequate to accommodate all who came. Hundreds who could not get in listened to his address seated on the grass outside and on the top of Loughrigg. But all these were but highlights within a continuing offering of worship day-by-day, with always a few to join the clergy in their prayers and praises, and Sunday by Sunday with always a representative congregation of young and old to receive the Ministry of the Word and Sacraments. There were times of course when the parish priest and his colleagues would have reckoned themselves unprofitable servants but many more times when they rejoiced together to see what great things the Lord had done.

Were I to conclude this part of my story without reference to two significant Ambleside occasions entered into year by year by thousands of visitors I should be indicted and rightly so. The Rock Service and the Rushbearing, the former in May and the latter in July, were local festivals which involved the whole community but which attracted the attention of thousands of visitors every year.

Just beyond the boundary of the parish of Ambleside is the hamlet of Clappersgate and therein is a house known as White Craggs, which seventy years ago was set in the middle of woods which ran down to the road by the side of the River Rothay. Time was, in the days of the bobbin trade, when such coppices provided valuable raw materials for a lively industry but that industry had all but died and such little coppices were no longer of commercial value. The house was the home of a well-known surgeon C. H. Hough whose brother, William Hough, was Bishop of Woolwich from 1918 to 1932. Dr. Hough and his wife conceived the notion of clearing the coppice and creating an alpine garden on the rocky slopes. True to Wordsworth's counsels in his *Guide to the Lake* he and his family worked at the task 'in the spirit of Nature with an invisible hand of Art' and throughout the back-breaking but fascinating enterprise they were at pains to see that 'Antiquity, who may be styled the co-partner and sister of Nature' was not denied 'the respect to which she is entitled'.

The work extended over many years and the end result is a Rock Garden with thousands of alpine plants from every corner of the globe, and with beds and rocks blazing with innumerable colours. The rocky promontory on which the house and its gardens stand is a spur of Loughrigg Fell which itself towers behind it. Standing with one's back to the Fell one faces a panorama of great beauty with the glistening waters of Windermere in the distance, the winding waters of the Rothay at the foot of the hill and on the slopes a profusion of plants and flowers and berries covering the irregular and precipitous rocks with a carpet which embraces every colour of the rainbow. Half way up the hill and cut into the rockface is a shrine commemorating members of the Hough family. This was consecrated on the Feast of Corpus Christi 1934 by then the Bishop of Carlisle (Dr. Herbert Williams). From then until recently an open-air service has been held each year and as the years have passed the congregation at that service has risen from a hundred or so at its inception to something like three thousand coming from far and wide. As far back as 1919 the Houghs had put a notice on the gate 'Anyone is welcome to walk around the Rock Garden' and I recall the Misses Hough, who occupied the house during my time in Ambleside, telling me that the privilege was not abused and that people not only walked around without disturbing the garden but contributed to charitable work for which voluntary contributions were invited.

It was my privilege in May 1958 to preach at the Rock Service on the 25th anniversary of its inception and that to a congregation exceeding 2,500. No one who has ever attended the service could have been other than deeply moved by the atmosphere created by the procession of clergy and choir moving slowly up the hill towards the shrine — 'with the cross of Jesus going on before'. Two choirs, one of them unseen, sang antiphonally the psalm 'Levavi oculos ad montes'. The vast congregation joined in the prayers and the hymns, and listened to the address, delivered in front of the shrine and 'thrown out' by rocks rising perpendicularly behind it to the people in the grounds below and even, as a policeman on duty told me, heard on the bridge over the Rothay another crowd of people further below. Writing a foreword in the third edition of *A Westmoreland Rock Garden*, written by Dr. Hough in 1929, the 61st Bishop of Carlisle (Herbert Williams) described these open-air services as 'a potent instrument of evangelism'. From my own experience I endorse his judgement for I know from comments made to me by visitors, and indeed by letters following the services, that many who came merely to look at natural beauty were helped to perceive within it something of the divine mystery and so perceiving to discern in it the countenance of God.

On the west wall of Ambleside Parish Church is a mural painting of the Rushbearing ceremony, put there by one Gordon Ransom who during the Second World War was in Ambleside studying art under Dr. E. W. Tristam. It covers some twenty-six feet of the wall and with its sixty-two all but life-sized figures, including the Vicar and the Verger of the day (Canon H. A. Thompson and Mr. William Robinson), and many of the local children, it depicts aspects of the local festival during the celebration of which all Ambleside is agog with excitement.

The rush-strewn earthen floors of the churches in pre-Elizabethan days had of necessity to be renewed from time to time — in the sanctuary frequently, in the nave probably not more than once a year. As the time for renewal approached, the old rushes would be taken out and burnt and whilst the adult population busied itself in making the church once more sweet and clean and tidy, the children would gather the rushes to provide the new floor. Entering into the fun of the occasion they would pile the rushes onto a dray in as decorative a way as possible and then drag it to the church to the accompaniment of the village fiddler's merry music. The new rushes would be strewn on the floor by the adults and when the floor was fully carpeted all would join in singing praises to the Lord of Earth and Heaven following which all would repair to the village green for feasting and merry-making. In later years, to add to the colour of the occasion, children began the practice of weaving rushes into all manner of garlands and decorating them with flowers, and these 'bearings' — harps, crosses, crowns, shields — would be carried in procession to the church and there lodged as offerings. The whole ceremony was in fact not merely one of 'spring-cleaning', but of the community voluntarily accepting responsibility for the care of the House of God within the parish. The invention of carpeting and other ways of covering earthen floors resulted in the custom falling into desuetude but it appears that certain Cumbrian parishes were not to be so easily deprived of an opportunity for making merry. Ambleside and Grasmere are two of the five parishes in the land in which the rush-bearing ceremony has continued without break through the years.

The Ambleside festival takes place on a Saturday near the feast day of the patron saint of 'the old church' and it begins with a procession through the town in the early evening on Saturday and concludes with tea and sports for the children in the park on Monday afternoon. The children make their own bearings, doubtless with not a little parental help, and these, along with more ambitious examples by the adults on frames which appear from year to year, are carried around the town in a procession headed by the town band. As in earlier years the bearings recall many biblical themes and symbols, though I found to my dismay, in my first experience of the great occasion, that the one symbol missing was that which throughout all Christendom, and for sixteen hundred years at least, has been the most sacred of all to Christians – the Cross. In subsequent years during my vicariate that omission was repaired by the good Hough sisters who prepared a very beautiful processional cross which was carried at the head of the procession as it wound its way through the narrow streets of the town. On reaching the market place, where anything up to fifteen hundred people would by then have gathered for the colourful spectacle, a great hush would come upon the crowd as the band played the opening bars of the Ambleside Rushbearing Hymn written by Owen Lloyd, friend of the poet Coleridge and assistant curate of Ambleside in the early nineteenth century, with its first verse linking the present with the past:

> *Our fathers to the House of God*
> *As yet a building rude,*
> *Bore offerings from the flowery sod,*
> *And fragrant rushes strewd.*

The simple hymn ended, the procession moved from the market place back to the parish church followed invariably by inhabitants and visitors alike and producing together a congregation so big that many were left standing. With restless and excited children ranging in age from two or three upwards, with people crushed so closely together in the pews that they could scarcely be comfortable, and with others standing restlessly in the aisles, the occasion was for the preacher the most difficult one of the year, and I wondered many times how F. W. Faber, whose 1840 Rushbearing sermon was published, could possibly have held the attention of such a youthful and excited crowd with such phrases as 'tenacious of keeping the ancient festival of the green flags of the pool-side and rushes of the field', and whether Ambleside took his descriptions of them as 'slow to change like the mountains that surround them' as complimentary or otherwise. But I know this: that any parish priest of Ambleside who might dare to suggest that the historic Rushbearing Festival had had its day or that its ordering should in any way be modified, would be met with an immediate and decisive vote of no confidence. T'Reysh Bearing is not to be tampered with! To any reader of this who finds himself in the

Lake District at Rushbearing time I would say, 'Ya mun ga an see't, a ya mun ga te't kirk,' and if you are young enough you will be given your piece of gingerbread as you leave the church. The service will not be as tuneful as at other times nor will there be stillness, or peace and quiet, but becoming as little children for a while you may perchance conclude with Wordsworth, who went to many a Rushbearing, that 'to be young was very Heaven'. It is to that poet we can turn for the most sensitive description of the festival and its purpose in his *Rural Ceremony* —

> *Closing the sacred book which long has fed*
> *Our meditations, give we to a day*
> *Of annual joy one tributary lay;*
> *This day, when, forth by rustic music led,*
> *The village children, while the sky is red*
> *With evening lights, advance in long array*
> *Through the still Churchyard, each with garland gay,*
> *That, carried sceptre-like, o'ertops the head*
> *Of the proud bearer. To the wide Church door*
> *Charged with these offerings which our fathers bore*
> *For decoration in the Papal time,*
> *The innocent Procession softly moves: —*
> *The spirit of Laud is pleased in heaven's pure clime,*
> *And Hooker's voice the spectacle approves!*

Needless to say so colourful a festival invariably attracted the attention of press and amateur photographers in their legions and during my time I was invited by the BBC to speak of its occurrence and significance on the radio and on one occasion at least it was televised. Even simple things such as these evoke letters from people asking interesting questions and affording opportunities for a little postal evangelism. But of all the broadcasts from and in connection with the Church during my vicariate none drew more letters from troubled people than an address I gave at one such service on 'Conscience'. We rarely see in these days as we used to do in *The Times* an acknowledgement of the receipt by the Treasury or by a business concern of 'Conscience money'. I suspect from letters I received following that broadcast address that some such sums were handed over, that some long delayed apologies were offered and broken friendships mended. Only one of our broadcasts from Ambleside went overseas and among the letters which followed that, was one from a missionary doctor in Central Africa, who rarely set eyes on another European and even more rarely had an opportunity of joining with others in Christian worship. She wrote enthusiastically and appreciatively about what she described as our 'lively service' and added that it had 'done something great for my vocation, my vision and my vigour'.

Following a broadcast service which embraced the sacrament of holy baptism — certainly the first ever and possibly the only such broadcast —

there were letters from parents and godparents who had been moved by the occasion and among them a heart-rending one from parents whose only son had left home to join the Royal Navy and whom they had failed in not encouraging him to be confirmed as the baptism service directs: 'You are to take care that this child be brought to the Bishop to be confirmed by him . . . '. Some months later the parents wrote again and this time were overjoyed to tell me that their son had written to tell them of his impending confirmation in Portsmouth and urging them to be present for what he described as 'my great day'. They were not to know that they and their son had been remembered in our prayers in Ambleside Church and that I had written to the naval chaplain to enlist his pastoral concern for the lad. I found that the broadcast services both from Mansfield and Ambleside invariably opened up rich opportunities for evangelism and pastoral care and for that reason I believe that religious broadcasting, both radio and television, though not something which can do the Church's job for it, can be a potent factor in the proclamation of the Gospel.

Digressing for a moment from the parochial scene I think it worthwhile commenting with satisfaction on the generous amount of time devoted to religious broadcasting both by the BBC and the ITV. It is easy to criticise adversely, and some of the programmes offered invite such criticism, but on the whole the standard is high and so far as it is within its power to do so the Church should strive to ensure that it continues to be. This is not to suggest that the Church's only interest is in religious broadcasting. The medium is so powerful in the extent and depth of its influence that the Christian's concern goes beyond the quality of programmes like *Songs of Praise, Stars on Sunday, Sunday Half Hour* and many other quite excellent programmes by which the Christian Gospel is proclaimed and the Christian stance for life is presented. In a plural society we must alas anticipate that not everything broadcast will be 'lovely and of good report'. Other gods than the Living God will infiltrate the system and bring with them attitudes to life and standards of morality unacceptable to Christians. Broadcasting House was described in 1931, as a 'Temple of the arts and muses . . . dedicated to Almighty God' and Sir John Reith's prayer 'that all things hostile to peace or purity may be banished from this house' to the end that 'the people inclining their ears to whatsoever things are beautiful and honest and of good report may tread the paths of wisdom and righteousness' was a pious dedication to which the whole nation would then have uttered a sincere 'Amen'.

Those sentiments were re-echoed by Sir William Haley in 1948: 'We are citizens of a Christian country,' he said 'and the BBC – an institution set up by the State – bases its policy on a positive attitude towards the Christian values. It seeks to safeguard those values and to foster acceptance of them. The whole preponderant weight of its programmes is directed to this end.' According to Sir Charles Curran that 'positive attitude' has been abandoned since broadcasting must play a neutral role in society. 'It is not our job,' he said 'to adopt a particular morality and then persuade everybody to follow it.' It nevertheless remains part of the job of the Christian Church and if it is our lot to live our lives under the pressures of a plural society we must beware lest the world squeezes us into its mould (see Romans ch. 12, v. 2) and we must be alert and vocal when our values are denigrated and debased. If it is true, as the defenders of violence on television frequently tell us, that broadcasting cannot but mirror society, have not those who pay for it the right to suggest that the mirror reflects its bloodiest aspect far too often and far too crudely? If the protest of one who has been known also to praise attracts the more serious attention, let me close this paragraph as I opened it, noting the numerous 'slots' for 'religion' both in the radio and television programmes, acknowledging their generally high quality and expressing the hope that the Latin dedication in the entrance hall of Broadcasting House may continue to exercise an influence over those who direct what is planned within it and goes forth from it.

9

Diocesan Peregrinations

Woven into the colourful and exciting fabric of parochial activity in Ambleside and Rydal, from the time of my arrival in 1951 to the end of 1958, were the multifarious responsibilities attaching to the office of Director of Religious Education for the diocese. Whilst these included the general oversight and co-ordination of the church's educational work in spheres other than the statutory, my time and energy had of necessity to be directed chiefly to the working out of the implications of the 1944 Act. Since this aspect of the wide educational field was itself so demanding it was good that the work touching the Sunday Schools and the training of teachers for them was in the able hands of Miss Veronica Medd, who had already served the diocese in that capacity for three years before my arrival and continued to do so throughout my time in it. The Youth Service work was well directed by Walter Ewbank who, many years later, I was to appoint as Archdeacon of Westmorland; work in the field of Adult Education was led by Canon Aidan Hervey, who organised training courses for teachers of religious instruction both in the Church and County schools.

The 1944 Education Act, be it remembered, was the work of a National Government. Thus whilst the course of its debate was not marred by the grinding of party axes there were not lacking, inside Parliament and outside, a few voices of people determined to put an end to the long-standing partnership of Church and State in the statutory field of education, which had persisted from the time of the Forster Act of 1870. However, the clear desire of the commonalty, as of Parliament itself, was that the voice of the Church in the educational counsels of the nation should not be silenced, and the active interest of the Church in the education of the nation's children should be sustained. This meant, *inter alia*, that the Church schools would not be outlawed, and that in order that they should not lag behind the 'State' schools in building standards, grants would be made available for them, under certain conditions, to facilitate improvements, extensions and, where necessary, replacement. The 'certain conditions' embraced a willingness

164

of the Church on its part to provide its share of the necessary funds for the modernisation of its school buildings. Where there was no such willingness the Church schools, whilst remaining the property of the Church, would become 'Controlled' – a term which clearly implied that the Church would lose the complete control of them which it had enjoyed hitherto. The schools which were to be retained as Church schools in the sense in which that term had been used hitherto, would be designated 'Aided'.

When I arrived in the diocese I found that the Church owned by far the greatest number of the village schools in Cumbria, over two hundred in fact, and my task was to meet and give guidance to the managers and trustees of these schools and of the parochial church councils in the parishes in which they were situated, and other similar bodies in the city and urban areas where there were larger church schools. Clearly the desire of the diocese was to preserve as many of its schools as possible as full church schools but to ensure at the same time that they should match in quality, educationally and structurally, other schools within the statutory system. This was a costly and exacting exercise which as Canon Kenneth Harper in his *Story of the Lakeland Diocese 1933 to 1966* rightly says, involved me in 'many and long journeys and protracted meetings with incumbents, managers and parochial church councils'. He rightly discerns too that these meetings were often difficult since they concerned a new approach by the Church to the care of its schools, an approach which must inevitably call for new money. In those parishes where there was a determination to hold on to the schools at all ccsts there was a ready acceptance of the so-named Barchester Scheme as a means by which that determination could be declared in a way acceptable to the Ministry of Education and by which funds to cover ultimate costs could be husbanded. The Scheme, invented by John Todhunter, a civil servant in the Ministry of Education, himself a devout Roman Catholic concerned for the preservation of Church Schools, had been taken up in a big way by myself and by Leonard Hawkes who succeeded me in the educational work in Southwell diocese and who subsequently became Archdeacon of Lindisfarne. Expounding the scheme to canny Cumbrian farmer churchwardens called for infinite patience on my part and a measure of fiscal credulity to which they were unaccustomed on theirs. Nevertheless 102 parishes accepted it and signed agreements to that end.

Other excitements were aroused by my determination to regain control by the Church of certain of its schools which, to put it crudely, had been 'filched' by local education authorities, either by sleight of hand on their part but far more frequently, by default of action on behalf of the local church. Canon Harper, writing of the voluminous correspondence which this part of my work involved, sums up years of intricate research of trust deeds, of legal battles and triumphant recoveries to the Church of properties which had been lost to it, in his incisive note that 'the Director made sure in every case which he could find that no money or rights to profits from the sale of diocesan schools were lost or overlooked'. Inevitably there were differences from time to time with one or other of the five local education authorities with whom I had to deal and in resolving these I found that my early insights into Law proved to be useful. The researches resulted in uncovering irregularities which called for delicate handling: a privately-owned school building, for example, whose rightful owner did not know it was his and which the education authority had all unwittingly been using as its own for long years, and an amusing instance of a parish receiving from the education authority an annual payment in recognition of a privilege accorded the authority many years before but which had long since lapsed. As in this instance the parish was Ambleside, the Director (Archdeacon Bulley) found himself writing to the Vicar (Archdeacon Bulley) to inform him of this irregularity and to suggest that his church council should refund to the County Treasurer a sum of £30 or thereabouts. To keep the file straight it was subsequently necessary for the Vicar (Archdeacon Bulley) to write to the Director (Archdeacon Bulley) saying that this had been done!

I am again indebted to Canon Harper for the information that I had completed the main negotiations concerning the status of our church schools by the end of 1954 by which time 110 schools had opted for Aided status and 87 had been content to allow the schools to become Controlled. Of the 110 it was known at the time that some were scheduled for closure since rural depopulation had resulted in there being too few children to justify their continuance. These closures of schools, two or three with less than ten children, had been effected by 1971 and at the time I left the diocese there were 79 Aided schools, and 73 Controlled. According to the *1974 Carlisle Diocesan Directory*, the number had by then been further reduced to 39 Aided and 53 Controlled. Thus in twenty years 86 rural primary schools had been closed in Cumbria alone and in the country as a whole the figure could be over a thousand. It is in my judgement impossible to regard this as other than 'a bad thing'. Certainly there were here and there schools with less than a dozen children and in those instances a strong argument based on economics rather than education could be made for closure, but the Plowden Report *Children and their Primary School*, which in effect regarded 90 children as the minimum number for a satisfactory school, has resulted in the closure of a great number of primary schools and since most of these have been village schools it has dealt a severe blow to rural England. Even Lady Plowden herself has come round to the view that 'small village schools should be kept open because of the continuing community involvement they provide'.

I 'stay' my eye for a moment on this important matter. It had been contended, and by some still is contended, that the small village schools were not only economically burdensome but educationally disadvantageous to the children attending them. The economic argument for wholesale closure, which on the surface seems to be so decisive, has itself been called into question, for whilst it is true that in hard cash terms of staffing, cleaning, heating and equipping, the education of a child in a small rural school is very much higher than that for a child in a large urban school, there are other factors in the equation which cannot be ignored. Against the 'saving', for example, should be set the cost of transporting children to the towns, which can be measured, and the undoubted but immeasurable costs to the local community of 'urbanising' its children to their and its impoverishment, and to the nation of jeopardising the survival of the village and village life. One educational argument adduced in favour of closures is that the small number of children in rural primary schools results in the lack of what is called peer group stimulus. It is held too that such schools must suffer from limited resources, and from an inevitable restriction of curriculum which I take to mean that there can be little instruction in such subjects as science and music though the latter, to my knowledge, is frequently successfully provided by peripatetic teachers.

Against all these objections to the maintenance of the small schools can be set certain advantages which they enjoy. The favourable teacher/pupil ratio, for example, facilitates individual attention which helps both the gifted and the less gifted child. The family atmosphere which is a feature of such schools, the ease of parental involvement in the schools's activities, the preservation of a close relationship of parents and teachers, the concern of the village for its school and the school for the village, all these making for ease of discipline, are weighty favourable factors which cannot be overlooked. Furthermore where the village church and the village school walk hand-in-hand there is a union of purpose which is reflected not only in the lives of the children but in the quality of life in the community as a whole.

There can, of course, be bad village schools as there are bad urban schools, but by the measure of academic achievement there is no decisive evidence that the small village school is in any way inferior to the larger school and, in the days of the much maligned 11 plus examination there was indeed evidence to the contrary that the individual attention possible in the small school paid a special dividend.

Throughout my educational work in Nottinghamshire, as in Cumbria, I lent my support wherever it was reasonable to do so to the retention of the village primary school. I believe still that it is in the interests of young children, socially, physically, emotionally, educationally – and I dare add morally and spiritually – to receive their early education within the village in which their homes are set. I believe further that it is in the interest of the village itself to see its church, its school and its village hall as essential factors in the wholeness of its life. I believe yet further that it is in the interests of the nation to recognise that whilst it may be true that the village school makes greater demands on its fiscal resources than the urban school, the demise of small rural schools must result in the decline of village life and rural communities generally and that to the impoverishment of us all.

By no means all our Church schools in the diocese were in the rural areas. We had such schools in Carlisle, in Whitehaven and Barrow, in Ulverston and Dalton in Furness, in Kendal and Kirkby Lonsdale. These were all handed down to us from the past, but we built new schools too and in particular one which involved me in months of consultation and debate in the course of which seemingly intractable problems had to be overcome.

This school, which had been mooted before my arrival in the diocese, was to be a secondary school for the children of eleven plus living in the Grange-Cartmel area, but as Bishop Bloomer told me soon after my arrival, the will to see it built had withered sadly as the anticipated cost to the Church mounted. The Bishop readily agreed with my suggestion that we should revive the proposal which from the angle of the local education authority was not difficult since it was still within their official Development Plan. I began by eliciting the interest of Mr. Richard Cavendish of Holker Hall and that was probably the easiest task of all those confronting me since he was ever ready to help the Church in its work and did so generously. It was he who offered us a site for the school in the village of Cartmel and it seemed to me that there could be nothing more appropriate than our founding a new school within a short distance of the ancient Priory Church, though at the time there were those who resisted this in favour of establishing the school at Grange-over-Sands.

Having kindled the interest of the clergy of the nine parishes from which the school would draw its pupils, I addressed a public meeting chaired by the Bishop in which I expounded the plan to the laity. Having whipped up their enthusiasm I asked them to raise £5,000 towards its cost. This they undertook to do – and did – and on 27 October 1956 the Bishop laid the foundation stone of the new school which two years later was duly opened by the Princess Margaret. (I recall that as I handed her the key Her Royal Highness quipped that she hoped it would not snap in the lock and on my putting in a word in praise of local workmanship, she added that one such key had done just that at the opening of a library by her father George the Sixth.) The school was duly christened (and I use the word deliberately for what was done in the context of an act of worship) Cartmel Priory School and under the headship of George Hargreaves it began to flourish immediately winning the respect of the community which it served. Within a year or so this school catering, be it remembered, for children who had in the unfortunate common parlance, 'failed 11 plus', was entering children for GCE 'O' levels and achieving such creditable results that pupils were occasionally passed on to the Grammar School at Ulverston for 'A' level work. I saw the school as the Secondary Modern school par excellence, living and working in the closest association with the Church and the local community, stretching the children to the limit of their capacity, intellectually and physically, and achieving for them and with them academic results which might well have eluded them in a Grammar school context. Over the next fourteen years I visited the school regularly for meetings of its Governing Body, for Consultations with the Head Teacher and his staff, and for prize-givings and other school functions.

Perusing press cuttings covering that period of my ministry within the educational field I caught sight of one of those deep black banner headlines by which, as it seems to me, editors seek either to endorse a view or to invite correspondence about it. It reads 'Archdeacon deplores slaughter of the Grammar Schools' and I record it merely to indicate my long-standing conviction that the tripartite system of secondary education – Secondary Grammar, Secondary Modern, Secondary Technical – offered the best in equality of opportunity. In that conviction mine was not by any means a lone voice twenty years ago but the forces of bureaucracy, encouraged then more by economic than by educational argument, had their way and one by one were joined together Cumbria's ancient Grammar Schools and fine Secondary Modern Schools for better or for worse, for richer or for poorer, and will so remain until a higher wisdom puts them asunder.

The educational work, taking me as it did all over Cumbria for evening meetings which frequently held me in some parish far from Ambleside until very late at night, was exacting, exhausting, exciting and occasionally exasperating. Presenting the case for the retention of their school as a church school to a group of Cumbrians was easy enough until one began to talk money. It was never the desirability of what they were being asked to do but the price of doing it which extended the discussion into the night hours and from time to time introduced me to facets of country logic which were new to me. However, the travelling midst the mountains and fells and vales, the lakes and tarns and rivers, was as attractive by moonlight as by daylight and since I could tie much of it in with my archidiaconal duties there was in it all an economy of time. But those archidiaconal duties became clear to me only as I began to perform them – by which I mean that the Church has a habit of appointing a man to a task without providing him with what might be called a job specification. As in 1951 I journeyed from Mansfield to Ambleside, I knew full well what the parish would demand of me and experience had taught me how to meet the demand; I knew what the office of Director of Religious Education involved for I had done it all before, but nobody had given me a run-down of the responsibilities and duties of an archdeacon. 'You'll pick them up as you go along,' said Russell Barry with an engaging smile. That, plus a few desultory glances at the ecclesiastical section of Halsbury's *Laws of England* was the only tutoring I had as I took up the office of Archdeacon of Westmorland.

Up to the ninth century an archdeacon was, as the title implies, the chief of the deacons who in their turn were at the beck and call of the bishop to assist him in his work. Gradually, however, he became an officer of some distinction, the *oculus episcopi*, the eye of the bishop, over a defined area of the diocese. It was the archdeacon's responsibility to discharge on behalf of the Bishop some of the governmental aspects of the episcopal office and in time this resulted in his becoming responsible for the care of the Church's properties within his archdeaconry. Thus the archdeacon admits churchwardens to office and in doing so charges them to keep a watchful eye over the parish church, to ensure its proper maintenance, to concern themselves with the insurance of church properties and to assist the incumbent generally in the temporal affairs of the parish. It is, too, the archdeacon who places a newly instituted parish priest into the legal possession of the temporalities of the benefice, and the outward, visible and audible signs of his doing so are his laying of the priest's hand upon the key of the church door and his direction to him to toll the church bell so that the parishioners may know that a new priest is in charge. All this follows the priest's institution by the Bishop and whilst this may be done anywhere, the induction must of course take place in the church itself. In the diocese of Carlisle the practice was that both ceremonies should be carried out together and within the context of an act of worship, and that I am sure lends to the occasion the solemn significance which the opening of a new chapter in the life of a parish merits. Such archidiaconal duties, discharged in different parts of the diocese, clearly bring the archdeacon into very close contact with the church's lay officers as well as with the parochial clergy, and he would be a poor archdeacon who did not see in these formal responsibilities rich opportunities for pastoral concern for clergy and laity alike.

There is a clue to another aspect of the archdeacon's work in the Ordinal within the Book of Common Prayer, where it will be seen that it is the Archdeacon who presents to the Bishop men to be admitted to the office of deacon and deacons to be ordained to the priesthood. In doing so he has to declare their fitness for the office and that in itself presupposes that he will have made appropriate enquiries about them or will have known them personally for some time. It was interesting for me that my first appearance in Carlisle Cathedral, a week or so after my Institution and Collation, was at an Ordination – historic since it was the first time that an Ordination had been broadcast and it was my privilege to preach the sermon which in that Rite comes at the beginning of the service. The day was one when the Church was becoming acutely aware of the desperate shortage of men for the ministry and I felt that the occasion demanded an address which not only set before those who were being ordained some estimate of the solemn vocation upon which they were entering, but also one which might encourage young men who might be listening to the broadcast to offer themselves for the Ministry. The address evoked a number of letters from young men and boys in different parts of the country and these I answered in detail, putting the writers into touch with those near their homes who could offer them counsel. Four years elapsed before I knew for certain that the bread cast upon the waters had returned. I received two letters from men not among those who had written at the time of the broadcast – who requested my prayers for them on the occasion of their impending Ordinations. 'Forgive this intrusion,' wrote one 'but I ask you for your prayers since it was your words broadcast from Carlisle Cathedral in 1951 which led me to decide to offer myself for the Ministry.'

Meanwhile, because I saw that part of the Ordinal as laying upon the archdeacon a special responsibility in respect of men for the ordained ministry, I put before the Bishop the idea of our establishing an annual residential conference for schoolboys, between the ages of 14 and 18, who might like to hear something about the life and work of a priest and the training necessary for it. Bishop Bloomer warmed to the idea and we inserted a paragraph in parish magazines throughout the diocese under the heading 'For Boys Only', which invited any who cared to come to send in their names through their parish clergy. The short residential conference, which attracted boys from grammar, secondary modern and public schools, became an annual event attended by 30 to 40 boys, many of whom came each year. Lectures about the Church and its Faith, the Bible, the Sacraments and the priestly vocation, with discussion groups and questions, evoked a lively response, and those who came to give the talks – parish priests, newly-ordained deacons, students from universities and theological colleges, teachers, scientists from Windscale, and others – invariably went away feeling that they had done something worthwhile. From those conferences the diocese built up a supply of ordinands and as I write I can recall many clergy serving in the church now, at home and overseas, who as schoolboys heard in these gatherings God's call: 'Who will go for us and whom shall I send?'

Since, to the great grief of Bishop Bloomer, the diocese had no Diocesan Retreat or Conference house the conferences were held at Rydal Hall, which was at that time in use as a hotel and held under lease from the le Fleming family. The best time to gather the boys together proved to be sometime between the Christmas feast and the New Year, when the hotel was closed. I used my powers of persuasion with the proprietor to open up for our benefit. This he did, reluctantly at first but readily in subsequent years. It was when settling the account for one of these conferences and hearing something about the proprietor's difficulties in getting sufficient staff to run the hotel at the height of the summer season, that I made one of those trivial off-the-cuff remarks which proved subsequently to be significant. The poor man was bewailing his lot – his problems of staffing, of stocking, of accounting, of taxation, and as I picked up my receipt I quipped: 'One day you and your wife will have had enough. When that day comes, ring me.' But despite his problems he continued to run his hotel and to open up after Christmas for our special benefit.

In 1954 came a happy surprise for me, conveyed in a letter from the Bishop, to the effect that an anonymous donor had offered to provide the necessary funds for me to go to the Anglican Congress in Minneapolis. Up to that point in my life I had never left the shores of England and although I had been telling my parishioners about the great Congress, which was to gather together clerical and lay representatives of the Anglican Communion from all over the world, it had never occurred to me that I might be one of those delegates. From one angle I was reluctant to go, for absence in August meant my being away when Ambleside Church was at its fullest, but I discovered that by going by air I could at least be in the parish on the first Sunday in August, fulfil an engagement on the Monday, and still be in Minneapolis for the start of the Congress on the Wednesday. I had, however, never been in an aircraft and it was with trepidation that I waited at Prestwick, to which a kindly parishioner had driven me, for the flight to be called. The parishioner who had been my

chauffeur handed me a present as she left the airport – a novel by Somerset
Maugham. Frankly I was too much on edge to settle to reading and when I
opened it to find on the fly leaf the ominous words: 'Short is man's life', I
decided to read no further. Within twenty minutes of take-off I was beginning
to accept the words as a prophecy when, following the customary crackling
which precedes the pilot's sepulchral tones, he began: 'Ladies and gentlemen,
I regret to inform you . . . '. The announcement ceased and was followed by
further crackling and a similar solemn summons. I was not the only one who
fastened his belt! But this time the announcement went further! 'Ladies and
gentlemen, I regret to inform you that we are unable to land . . . ' again the
crackling which not only terminated the announcement but also left us in
suspended animation. A few moments elapsed and the words were repeated
'unable to land at Gander Airport'. So what? A few moments further tension
and the truth was out. 'We are proceeding to Rejkjavic'. Thus, by accident,
did I visit Iceland and when in future years people who have travelled the
world have asked me, with an air of superiority, whether I had visited Spain
or Italy or the Netherlands or Scandinavia, or indeed anywhere else outside
the United Kingdom, and I have had to profess profound ignorance of all
these countries, I have discovered one way by which I could not fail to put
a stop to the embarrassing examination. It was merely to ask, 'Have you
ever been to Iceland?' and as the question has invariably been answered in
the negative I have generally been able to regain the initiative by speaking
all too confidently about a visit which lasted less than two hours!

The week in Minnesota was notable for the lavish hospitality of my American hosts, for the Congress itself, its importance residing in my judgement in
the fact that it happened more than in anything it might have achieved, and
for the way in which I was hurtled from place to place on the following
Sunday morning when within 150 minutes I preached at services in three
churches the last one being 35 miles away from the other two. The third
of these services was followed by an open-air congregational picnic, under
blazing sunshine and in a temperature in the low nineties, an occasion made
colourful by frocks and shirts of every hue and pattern, and made lively by
whole families of Moms and Pops and kids who had worshipped together.
Set in Hiawatha country with the sound of laughing water nearby the scene
was memorable and, true enough, as Longfellow has it:

> *Dark behind it rose the forest*
> *Rose the black and gloomy pine trees,*
> *Rose the firs with cones upon them;*
> *Bright before it beat the water,*
> *Beat the clear and sunny water.*

But what followed was not a picnic in the accepted sense of the term at
home. A series of trestle tables set in a long line in the middle of a green
meadow adjacent to the church's 'parking lot', which itself was strewn

with Cadillacs and lesser automobiles, held about fifteen huge bowls each containing quantities of food but, as I was to discover, no two containing the same – chicken legs wallowing in white sauce, meat morsels mixed with rice and laced with wine, sausages wrapped in sliced ham, corn on the cob and, off, and vegetables, ordinary and exotic, and in such variety that nothing in the seed man's catalogue was unrepresented. Grace was said, and said by all, and the host directed me as chief guest to the table arming me meanwhile with an outsize plate and a fork. I stabbed a chicken leg and a few morsels from two or three of the bowls and stepped from the table only to be arrested immediately by the host, who in an agitated whisper bade me to take something from every bowl or 'certain of my ladies will be desolated if the chief guest passes their efforts by'. I obeyed, and having done so pondered with misgivings the Hellvelynic proportions of the food on my plate. That was the day when I learnt a lesson which has served me in good stead on many similar if more modest occasions since. The chief guest must be seen to accord to every lady the courtesy of accepting her offer, be it mince pies, sausage rolls or iced cake, but he must take care not to be seen to 'lose' some subsequently in the melee of people anxious to meet him. When, some days later, on the 1,500-mile train journey from Minneapolis to Boston, Massachusetts, I pondered over the 'skedules' sent me in respect of lectures and sermons I was to give in various places in the eastern states over the next three weeks, I shuddered every time I saw any reference to a parish picnic, and never more so than when I read again a letter of the zealous rector in Delaware who was arranging four such 'so that people in the north, south, east and west areas of my parish will have opportunity to meet you', between 6 and 10 p.m.

The three weeks which I spent subsequently in Massachusetts, Connecticut, Rhode Island and Delaware, were very much working weeks with Sunday sermons, week-day lectures, talks to Rotary Clubs (one such, in Danbury, presenting me with a new hat with my name embossed in gold on its leather lining). The sermons, following the liturgical readings for the day, were the least demanding part of my programme though I did find it disconcerting to be told as I mounted the stairs to go to bed on a Saturday evening that the morning's sermon was to be broadcast. Knowing from experience with what precise timing broadcasts from Mansfield and Ambleside were arranged I saw myself stopping up all night to refashion my address until the rector assured me not to concern myself about that since, as he put it, 'they won't cut you off doctor, you can be sure of that'. The week-day lectures were given 'to order' and touched such subjects as The Church of England, its history, its government, its national influence, its parochial life, its ministry, its liturgies. On three occasions I subjected myself to a post-coffee session of questions on anything to do with the UK and I recall several such 'press conference' sessions with impromptu questions and answers on for example the Royal Family, *The Times*, 'Red China', the Houses of Parliament, the Peerage, English Soccer, our hospitals, our schools and the BBC! Nor shall I ever forget the evening when a certain rector was training six of his laymen to become lay readers.

Between them they were made to read from the lectern the Book of Ruth during which time the rector sat at the back of the church hurling abuse at them from time to time for poor diction, for 'making nonsense of the story', for slovenliness or for not adopting the right stance at the lectern. I squirmed as I listened to his rough treatment of this little band of volunteers and reflected that had they been Englishmen they would not have suffered it. But for them, if not for me, the evening ended happily. He announced that they would now read the whole book through once more and added, to my astonishment, for there had been no consultation between us as to the merits or demerits of such sessions, that that done 'the Archdeacon will get into the pulpit and preach a fifteen-minute sermon on the Book of Ruth'. He bade them 'just you listen with all your ears as he takes the story and coagulates the truths which emerge from it'. I could not resist beginning that sermon by telling those apprentice lay readers that if ever their rector asked them to preach a sermon at ten minutes' notice they should demur.

The American tour was exciting, exhilarating and exhausting and the seven-day voyage home in the Cunard Liner *S.S. Parthia*, with the Bishop of London and Mrs. Wand and the Bishop of Ripon (Dr. George Chase) as my travelling companions, provided an opportunity for relaxation for which each of us was ready.

The established pattern of my ministry in the parish and diocese was quickly resumed and although evening meetings with school managers and trustees were by that time less frequent since the status of most schools had been settled, there were many calls from parishes in the diocese to hear something about the work of the Anglican Congress and the parochial life of the Episcopal Church in the United States. Measuring the ultimate value of such vast jamborees is never easy but my recollection is that reports which I was able to give to church councils about the impact of the Anglican Communion all over the world as demonstrated by the presence of black and white, brown and yellow peoples eager to demonstrate their adherence to it, were such as to kindle a new interest in missionary enterprise. At that time it seemed to me that American episcopalians had much to teach Anglican congregation in England about the meaning of Christian stewardship and indeed of Christian fellowship. The American Episcopal parish is not a geographical area but a list of people and it seemed to me, not only that all those on it were knit together in close fellowship but that all of them recognised and discharged the obligations of stewardship which their Christian commitment imposed upon them. I venture to say that measured in terms of service and monetary support American Episcopalians (i.e. Anglicans) were at that time far more alert to the demands of Christian commitment in terms of money and service. For example, I heard at the door of an American Church something which I had never heard, and never expected to hear, at the door of an English Church. It was a newcomer to the parish introducing himself as such to the Rector – 'I'm new here Rector. Maybe if I drop round to see you this week you can tell me whether there's any bit of work I can do for the Church.'

From the Congress itself there emerged a message which was significant then and maybe even more so now in the light of the recent controversy surrounding Dr. Edward Norman's *Reith Lectures*. I see in the formal Congress message, which was sent to 'all the forty millions of our scattered brotherhood the world around', expressions of convictions, hopes and desires which both Dr. Norman and his fiercest critic, Dr. Mervyn Stockwood, could approve. I discern that in the Christian book there is no such thing as an autonomous social gospel which can persist apart from the One Gospel of our Lord and Saviour Jesus Christ, and that makes the essential task of the Church that of proclaiming that Gospel loud and clear and of bringing men and women to the knowledge and love of God. But conversely the proclamation of the one Gospel of our Lord and Saviour Jesus Christ shows it to be pregnant with personal and social implications which it is the responsibility of the Church to spell out and of individual Christians to seek to implement in their own lives and in the societies in which they live. As between Christian proclamation and Christian action it is never a question of 'either . . . or but of both . . . and'. Thus when that Anglican Congress spoke with burning sincerity about Compassion it preceded its remarks with a call to oldness in the proclamation of the One Gospel on which it based its appeal. The people in the pews today, and I dare say many of the clergy in the parishes, are seeing Dr. Stockwood in the role of Martha and Dr. Norman in the role of Mary. Nor will their judgement be disturbed by an attempt to dismiss it as simplistic. The Martha–Mary anecdote is a story of imbalance in Christian devotion. Martha was not to be impeded in her service, but she needed to be warned of what could happen if that aspect of devotion represented by Mary should be disparaged or minimised. The part which Mary chose was 'the good part' – i.e., good in the sense of essential. It was only a part, but it was that part which alone could inform, inspire and sustain the Christian action in which Martha was so happily immersed. The message from the Anglican Congress summed it up thus:

> Boldness and Compassion – boldness to say before the world whom it is we believe, what He does, what He wills; Compassion to understand the pain and sorrow of life for the greater part of mankind, and to share it. It is right to condemn the false ideology of the communists which draws its strength from the misery of mankind, but it ill becomes Christians who profess their faith in the Father Almighty to remain blind and deaf to this misery and to fail to do whatever we can to establish justice among men and make human brotherhood a reality . . . Therefore we have of necessity thought much about two words, mission and evangelism . . . two words which, we came to see, are really one.

I recall that that was the dominant note – first the Church must itself come to grips with its faith in God, must engage itself in mission and evangelism to proclaim God in Christ, must discern afresh the conception of itself as the

Body of Christ and must as such move out into the world with a heart of compassion, teaching, healing and caring.

We must ever remember that it was the Church's civilising mission which blazed the trail of the pioneer in the fields of education, healing, justice and human welfare generally. That mission is not ended, but if in the process of Christianising the secular the Church falls to the error of secularising Christianity pushing the transcendent and Living God to the periphery, muting its proclamation of the Gospel of Christ, devaluing the classical acts of Christian piety – then it will call down upon its head the rebuke of the Living God, 'Woe unto the foolish prophets that prophesy out of their own hearts.' That way spells abdication.

My departure from Mansfield and accession to an Archdeaconry did not result in a break with the Convocation of York of which I had been a member since 1945. Since, however, I appeared in 1951 in a different guise protocol demanded that I be formally introduced into an assembly which I had attended regularly for six years. The short ceremony fell to the Dean of Carlisle (Cyril Mayne) who among other complimentary remarks added that I had attained a measure of fame in that I would go down in history as the priest who preached the sermon at the first Ordination ever broadcast. I was never among those clergy who could be relied upon to intervene in every debate on every subject but I did from time to time contribute modestly to the discussions, notably on the recruitment and training of men for the ministry. Recalling my own boyhood and my longing then for some priest to say to me 'Why shouldn't you offer yourself for the ministry?' or to hear such a general call in a sermon, I pleaded that Church leaders should be more forthright in the matter of seeking out and calling young lads whose fidelity, demeanour and intellectual ability might suggest them as possible candidates for the ordained ministry. I noted that Our Lord did not wait for volunteers as the Church seemed to do; he summoned men to follow Him. The Bishop of Sodor and Man (J. R. S. Taylor) took me to task for such an impious suggestion. It was, he said, the work of the Holy Spirit alone to call men to the ministry and that must always be an inward call. That was, however, in the 1950s. Some years later the word 'recruitment' became respectable and I was reassured, the more so when Russell Barry in his *Vocation and Ministry*, published in 1958, emphasised that the inward call of the Spirit can be 'mediated or muted by external forces'. He added,

> Recruitment is not conscription, nor is it the cajolement by 'appeals' – a note which a living Church must not strike. But neither is it waiting for volunteers. It is looking for men and putting the call before them, either by direct or more indirect methods. How shall they hear without a preacher, and how shall they preach except they be sent?

However, undeterred by the Bishop of Sodor and Man's inhibition, and with the warm support of Bishop Bloomer, I pressed on with our annual schoolboys' conferences during which we tried as, Bishop Barry puts it, 'to penetrate through fog banks of ignorance and misunderstanding about Christianity itself or the nature and mission of the Church', to sound the Church's call, and to expound and explain the nature of its ordained Ministry. That call comes to many, of course, in later life but it ill befits the Church to despise the 'little Samuel'. At one of the many CACTM (now ACCM) Selection Conferences which I attended and chaired I asked each of the nineteen potential ordinands whether he had ever been a choirboy. Fifteen had been! They had spent hours taking part in Liturgies beyond their mental capacity to comprehend, in singing Psalms many of which they could not possibly understand and hymns in which symbolism and classical theology were intermingled with happy abandon – one might have thought with disastrous results to their spiritual development. But 'God moves in a mysterious way His wonders to perform', and the erstwhile choirboy, clothed in robes which conceal the mischievous imp within, becomes under the hand of God his priest, his Bishop indeed – as, for example, the 63rd of Carlisle, the 130th Bishop of London (Gerald Ellison), and I doubt not many others.

Another of my modest interventions was an attempt to rid the Convocation of the Latin Litany which preceded its deliberations in York Minster. Inevitably the gathering of Archbishop, Bishops and Clergy aroused the interest of visitors who gathered at the west end of the nave often in large numbers. What they heard was a 'mumbo jumbo' which they could not understand and which, I hazarded a guess, was not understood by half of those taking part in it. The fact was that the clergy were no longer learned in the Latin tongue and it seemed to me that the Litany recited in Cranmer's English would be both more seemly and more prayerful, and incidentally more appreciated by our visitors in the Nave of the Minster. I would myself have chosen to have had it sung in procession as in the days of yore but I suppose it would be argued that if half the clergy knew no Latin half could not sing and the end result could have been no less unseemly. However, though my plea for the abolition of the Latin Litany was supported by a few, the classicists, and those who affected to be, won the day and the extraordinary procedure, which to my knowledge baffled so many visitors and meant nothing to an ever rising percentage of clergy, persisted. However, there has since been a change of heart and mind and on the too rare occasions when the Convocation meets the opening prayers are now said in the English tongue and 'the congregation is thereby edified'! Maybe in the light of that I am permitted to say, with Sir Winston Churchill, 'I have not always been wrong'.

Convocation, like the Church Assembly of the day and the Synod of today, met more frequently than was necessary and although I was faithful in my attendance the journey from York back to the parish and diocese was always marked by an eagerness which none would have detected on the outward run. Yet such was the lust for debate that there were never lacking clergy who could bubble over with enthusiasm and talk interminably about the minutiae in such things as Canon Law which, whilst it deals with some mighty themes, offers infinite scope for those who revel in creating much ado about nothing. Those interminable debates began with the publication of the *Report of the Archbishops' Commission on Canon Law* in 1946 which taking as its basis the Canons of 1603, called for the revision of some, the deletion of others and the addition of new Canons designed either to embody recent legislation or to catch up with customs which had become acceptable. Undoubtedly it was a mighty and necessary task but that it consumed too much time over too long a period for too many people there can be no doubt. I do not question the value of the exercise itself though I suspect that many would now pose in relation to it the question which little Peterkin put to old Kaspar in Southey's *After Blenheim*, 'But what good came of it at last?' I would see that question not as cynical but as searching, for a cursory glance at the Canons could prod many a priest, convict the conscience of many a church councillor, and activate many an atrophied Anglican.

These references to the ponderous ways of Convocation must not be seen as undervaluing the administrative and conciliar side of the Church's work. These there must be and the Church deserves and demands the best. Certainly an archdeacon can scarcely escape them for it is his part and lot to ensure the proper functioning of the church councils within his archdeaconry and to keep a careful eye on the church's properties and financial affairs. Annually he delivers a Charge to the churchwardens on admitting them to office and from time to time issues Articles of Enquiry and engages in Visitations designed to enable him to give to his Bishop a picture of the state of affairs, spiritually, and materially, within that part of the diocese for which he has a special responsibility. The arrival of such Articles was not invariably welcomed by churchwardens since paper work was required but personal Visitations to church councils were happy and useful occasions.

So the triple task continued with frequent self-questioning as to whether each of my three 'masters' – parish, archdeaconry, education – was getting its fair share of my time and thought. Happily the parochial clergy respected the Bishop's request to them not to entice me away from Ambleside on a Sunday, and if on weekdays I had of necessity to be out and about the diocese for committees, for lectures to groups of teachers, and to address church councils, I was rarely away from the parish for a whole day. Correspondence was heavy but fortunately I had the help of an able secretary in the person of Joyce Pooley of Hawkshead who was good enough to continue to help me to the end of my tenure of the educational work even though meanwhile she had married.

Just before Christmas 1955 there came to me from St. James' Palace a letter, which though brief I read and re-read, such was the surprise it gave me. It read:

Reverend Sir,
I have the honour to inform you that I have received the Queen's Command to offer you the appointment of a Chaplain to Her Majesty,

and I shall be pleased to receive your acceptance of Her Majesty's gracious offer.

In your reply will you please give me your full Christian names, style and degrees.

I am, Reverend Sir,
Yours obediently,

(sd) SCARBOROUGH
Lord Chamberlain

I doubt not that my Bishop was fully aware of Her Majesty's intentions though he had not, and wisely, whispered anything to me. Nevertheless I did recall that a few weeks before, I had received from Walter Ewbank, then Chaplain of Casterton School, a Latin Ode based on a rumour which apparently had reached him, which spoke of some honour about to be conferred on me by Her Majesty. The translation of the Ode did not, however, disclose the nature of the honour nor did I discern the basis of the rumour. It would be churlish of me to deprive those who did Latin at school, much less those who pursued classical studies at University, of the opportunity of testing themselves out on this Latin Unseen:

> En crescit bona fama, Borea per oppida serpit,
> Nec celanda tibi nec cohibenda diu;
> Fertur enim merito venerabile nomen honore
> Ipsam Reginam tollere velle tuum.
> Dic, vera est fama haec? credo, nisi vera, lateret;
> At patet; est ergo digna putanda fide.
> Accipias igitur felicia verba benigne,
> Accipias numeros laetitiamque meam:
> Sit Pater auxilio tibi tempus in omne Supernus;
> Sit Regina tuo fausta ministerio.

> The news which spreads through every Northern town,
> You may not stifle nor for long disown,
> The Queen with honours due – so tells the fame –
> Seeks to enhance your Venerable name.
> What now? this tale if false had ne'er been heard,
> But since we hear, we must believe its word.
> Deign then to accept these words which wish you well,
> And these my verses which my pleasure tell:
> May God above your helper ever be,
> And the Queen be blessed in your ministry.

For this translation of the Latin Ode I am indebted to the Reverend Hugh Bates, sometime Chaplain and Tutor of St. Chad's College, Durham and one of my Examining Chaplains.

The arrival of the Lord Chamberlain's letter revealed all and I passed it across the breakfast table to my mother without comment; nor had I mentioned to her previously the dark Latin Ode. The joy which shone from her countenance as she read it multiplied a dozen times the pleasure which was mine in receiving it.

The news appeared in *The Times* on Christmas Eve and any hidden fears I might have had that Ambleside and Rydal might not be getting from me a fair share of my time were dissipated immediately as an avalanche of congratulations – telephone calls in rapid succession and an overflowing letter box – assured me of the pleasure which the appointment was giving to the parish. Nor were the parishioners slow to make it clear that they intended to bask awhile in the reflected glory. As one put it, 'After all you've been our Chaplain for nearly five years.' The subsequent visits to preach in the Chapel Royal of St. James's Palace were stimulating and enjoyable and there was not a whisper of dissent at the Vicar's absence on those Sundays – not even when one of the visits coincided with the Rushbearing Festival.

Two amusing memories touching the royal chaplaincy spring to my mind, each concerning the scarlet cassock which a Chaplain to Her Majesty wears. The proximity of Ambleside Church to the Vicarage was such that I seldom divested myself of a cassock throughout a Sunday and that had attracted no particular attention in summer or winter as I went to and from vicarage to church. I had to abandon this practice, however, on discovering that when the tourist season was at its height the sight of a scarlet-clad priest was so appealing to colour-camera-armed visitors that I could be stopped two or three times in the hundred yards from the vicarage gate to the vestry with the polite request, 'May I take a snap of you?' The scarlet cassock afforded an eagerly-grasped opportunity to Canon Charles Nurse, a very much loved and highly respected parish priest in the diocese, who subsequently became Archdeacon of Carlisle. It was his habit, and one in which the diocese delighted, to enliven the dinners at the Bishop's biennial Clergy Conferences, by reading out phoney telegrams which he alleged had just been delivered. These would be witty shafts directed at anyone from the Bishop himself to the youngest deacon. My first appearance in a scarlet cassock at one of the conferences drew from the Canon the following telegram which he announced in a dead-pan voice:

I've just received this telegram addressed to the Bishop. It reads: 'Will swap Red Dean for Red Archdeacon and pay the difference.' Geffrey Calltuar.

Needless to say the conference collapsed into uncontrollable laughter in which the scarlet-clad archdeacon joined.

It was appropriate that in 1958, when Anglican bishops from all over the world came to the United Kingdom for the Lambeth Conference, one of those who visited Ambleside was Stephen Tomusange from Uganda.

Since, as I write, that unhappy country seems at long last to be within sight of release from Amin's bondage, the circumstances of the Ambleside connection are interesting. In his address the Ugandan bishop pointed out that at the time Ambleside Church was built his country was completely heathen. No Christian missionary entered it until 1857 and the Church's missionary enterprise was marked by hundreds of martyrdoms under the fierce rule of the heathen king – grandfather of the King of Uganda at the time the Bishop was speaking. The first Bishop was murdered as soon as he set foot in the land but the Church was undeterred and a second Bishop was appointed. However, anticipating the possibility of a similar fate, Bishop Tuck left his wife at home and that home was in Ambleside. The Ugandan bishop created a deep impression, not least on the young people. As he spoke of the brave pioneer work of the Christian Church in his own country, of his grandfather who, as he said, 'really did bow down to wood and stone as you sing in your hymn', of his father's conversion to Christianity and his own commitment to Christ, Stephen Salongo Tomusange, Assistant Bishop of the Upper Nile and subsequently of West Buganda, presented a picture of a fearless and advancing Church and in doing so did much to nurture the sense of responsibility towards its maintenance which the Mother Church must bear. Following the service that morning the Bishop was surprised and delighted to find in the congregation a handful of people who could speak his own language, but that was no surprise to me for I was able to tell him that Ambleside's visitors came from all over the world and that on a summer Sunday morning in 1956 I spoke to people from thirteen different countries as they left the church.

The autumn of 1958 saw me once more deprived of the assistance of a colleague when Tony Wharton left to become Vicar of Northowram in the diocese of Wakefield. Ambleside had long since taken him and his wife Marjorie into its heart and they by their sincerity, sensitive pastoral concern and enthusiasm for their work had left their mark upon the parish. Not daring to raid the diocese of Southwell for a third colleague I turned this time to Birmingham diocese and was fortunate enough to light upon and entice to the parish Clifford and Elizabeth Jobson, who came from a parish with a population equal to that of the whole County of Westmorland, to share their many gifts with Ambleside's residents and visitors. But our close vicar-assistant curate relationship, happy though it was, was destined to be short.

Bishop Victor Turner, who for 14 years had been Bishop of Penrith, had announced his intention to retire at the end of that year and the Diocesan had in confidence expressed his hope that I might succeed him, stressing of course that the appointment was not vested in him but in Her Majesty. I had known Victor Turner for 25 years since we worked together in the Southwell diocese and I knew that there, as in the Diocese of Carlisle, his ministry had always been greatly appreciated. From my arrival in Ambleside our friendship became more intimate since his home was then nearby at Hawkshead. He was a greatly loved man who, because he understood the life and work of a parish priest, was able to bring to his episcopal work patience and understanding. On holiday in Borrowdale Bishop Barry dropped by chance into a Lakeland church where Victor Turner was instituting a new incumbent. Speaking to me of the incident he commented 'Old Victor was preaching as ever from the Bible, taking a text, expounding it and applying it. He does that splendidly. I just can't do it! But if it is true, as Richard Baxter, said that 'the world is better able to read the nature of a man's religion in a man's life than in the Bible', there too Herbert Victor Turner served well his God and his neighbour. Whilst the possibility of succeeding him as suffragan bishop appealed to me, for the eight years in which I had served in the diocese had been abundantly happy and my association with Bishop Bloomer was warm and compatible, I was far from sanguine about the possibility that I mentioned it to no one, not even my own kith and kin. But I was not to be left in suspense for long. On Christmas Eve 1958 there arrived with the Christmas cards an envelope the like of which I had not seen before. The letter within it read:

10 Downing Street
Whitehall

My dear Archdeacon,
I have great pleasure in informing you that the Queen has been graciously pleased to approve your appointment to the Suffragan Bishopric of Penrith in succession to Bishop Turner on his resignation at the end of this month.
  Yours sincerely,

(signed) HAROLD MACMILLAN

It was a particular joy to me that my younger brother and his wife and undergraduate son were with us at the time and although the public announcement of the appointment was not to be made public until New Year's Day it meant that whereas my first Christmas in Ambleside vicarage had been shadowed with family sorrow my last Christmas there was radiant with family joy. Yet within a month the curtain of sorrow was to drop again for that same brother rising from bed on Sunday morning to worship as was his wont in the little church of St. Enodoc in Cornwall was taken suddenly ill and died in a matter of hours. On Christmas morning he with his family and my mother had received the sacrament at my hands. On the night before his death he had talked with me about his intention to be present at my Consecration. The stunning news of his passing reached me at lunch time on the Sunday and it was mine to break it to my 83 year-old Mother whose fortitude in grief once more put my dejection to shame. But still 'the King's business' in the shape of conducting Evensong had to be done and since I had no colleague I had to leave the house of sorrow for the house in which I had so frequently comforted the sorrowful. In the course of the afternoon the news had spread throughout the township and the congregation were sensitive to my feelings as I commended my brother to God's keeping and asked for their prayers for myself and mine.

The patronage of the benefice of Ambleside was then in the hands of Mr. Michael le Fleming and in due course he nominated as the new vicar Kenneth Warren, at that time Vicar of St. Andrew's, Wigan. This was specially pleasing to me for although he and I had seen little of each other for a quarter of a century a friendship forged in college days had been sustained and I knew that Ambleside would pass into the care of a warm-hearted, able and dedicated priest. He could not, however, come to Ambleside before the end of September and in the circumstances the Bishop asked me to continue to look after the two parishes for the intervening months and as, by that time, I had relinquished the educational work, that period proved to be very rewarding in that with less administrative work there was more time for pastoral visiting. Furthermore I had, of necessity, to find somewhere to live.

It was a coincidence that as at Mansfield I had set in motion a scheme which was not completed until after I had left the parish, so at Ambleside a scheme of a different nature had reached its planning stage but was completed only after my departure. At Mansfield it was the beautification of the closed churchyard and its transformation into a Garden in the heart of the town; at Ambleside it was the provision of more adequate vestry accommodation so that the clergy and the choir of thirty men and boys could have rather more breathing space and at the same time have access to those facilities which our forefathers, strangely insensitive to the normal functions of nature, had unfortunately omitted. I passed the plans to my successor with a pencilled note attached bearing St. Paul's injunction 'Let all things be done decently and in order'. He saw to it that they were.

When the moment came to say 'Good bye' to Ambleside and Rydal the good folk, having already presented me with a silver pectoral cross engraved with the words *Dominus illuminatio*, and a cloth of gold cope and mitre, showered upon my mother and myself further monetary and other gifts, and handed them over with such generosity of word and deed that I felt very humbled but at the same time very sure that despite limitations, weaknesses and failures God had used me in some measure for his work. The parish priest can ask no more. So in the last *Vicar's Letter* that I addressed to parishioners I turned again to those simple duties which exercise so profound an effect upon the life of a parish and which equip God's people for their caring ministry, and wrote:

Keep the faith then! Hold fast to the things which are most surely believed among us. Remember that the simple duties of going to church, saying your prayers, receiving the Blessed Sacrament of the Altar, knowing and loving God's Word – these in the end are the decisive influences in our lives. These are the sources of spiritual and moral power. From these come fellowship and love, goodness and beauty and truth. By these we live. In the words of St. Paul 'Be perfect, be of good comfort, be of one mind, live in peace; and the God of love and peace shall be with you.' No parish priest could conceive for his people any greater joy.

10

From Parish Priest to Suffragan Bishop

St. Paul told his young convert Timothy that 'If anyone aspires to the office of a bishop, he desires a noble task,' and in so saying he might well have foreseen his young friend's future. If 'aspires' means, as its Latin origin suggests, 'to pant after', I doubt whether Timothy did any such thing though he did in fact become the first Bishop of Ephesus. I recall my personal embarrassment when thirty years ago a peer of the realm prophesied in a public speech in Nottinghamshire that I should become a bishop and how that embarrassment became more acute when his words appeared in the county press. I was thoroughly happy and fulfilled in what I was doing then and certainly did not 'pant after' the office of a bishop which in any event was, in those days, all but exclusively reserved for graduates from Oxford and Cambridge with a preference for those who had also been to one of the Public Schools. Certainly when the office of bishop came to me I recognised in it, as Paul has it, 'a noble task' to which I looked forward with eager hope, confident that I should find in it the same satisfaction and abounding joy in ministry which had been mine since the day of my ordination.

Yet as the day approached for my elevation to the episcopate I have to admit that there was a cloud, 'no bigger than a man's hand' perhaps, which appeared from time to time in an otherwise bright sky. It was the realisation that I should no longer be a parish priest. I found no difficulty towards the end of 1958 in handing over the education portfolio, more particularly as it was into the capable hands of Robert Holtby (now Dean of Chichester) who left the staff of St. Edward's School, Oxford for a residentiary canonry of Carlisle to succeed me in the office of Director of Religious Education for the diocese. But the thought that I should cease to enjoy the intimate ministry of a parish priest was another matter.

All Christians are called to serve God – there is indeed a true priesthood of the laity – but the man who answers the call of God to be a parish priest sets his feet, in my experience, onto a path which, though frequently uphill and stony, opens up ever-widening vistas of redemptive and caring ministry,

185

priestly, pastoral and prophetic, which are both alluring and exciting. None of these is denied to the bishop of course, but it is the parish priest whose glorious privilege it is to build up the local Church as the focus of Christian life within a clearly defined and workable area which the bishop entrusts to him. In doing that faithfully he cannot but establish a very intimate relationship with his parishioners. He penetrates their lives with the message he is empowered to proclaim. As the alert pastor he is concerned to protect the flock, and not least 'the lambs', against the insidious dangers which threaten them in contemporary society. As the steward of the mysteries of God he mediates to his people, and not least in public worship through the ministry of the Word and Sacraments, that divine grace which Charles Wesley described as 'the light of life eternal which darts into our souls and floods with joy the house of clay'. The parish priest thus becomes the family chaplain, the family friend, the man who is at hand to rejoice with them that rejoice and weep with them that weep, the counsellor, the guide and the reconciler. I share the conviction expressed by Bishop Russell Barry in his *Vocation and Ministry* where he writes: 'I do not believe that anyone could spend a week with a good and efficient parish priest, watching his work and counting the blessings which it brings into other people's lives and not recognise this as the most worthwhile of all jobs.' No wonder that in a recent research which sought to discover who among the country's workers, whether by hand or brain, experienced the highest degree of job satisfaction, the members of the clergy came top of the poll.

The parish priest is the key person in the parochial system, which system in its turn offers the highest hopes of ensuring the presence within a given area of the living Body of Christ, worshipping, witnessing and working. In recent years the growth of the so-called extra-parochial ministries has tended to suggest that there might be some better way of doing the Church's work than that of stationing a man of God in a parish as the priest and pastor of the people. But the specialist ministries – and some such there must be in boarding schools, hospitals, prisons, the Services and other residential situations – can never replace the parish priest in the total field of Christian enterprise.

On this a further word is relevant. In recent years there has been developed a supplementary ministry which has gone under the unfortunate title of the 'auxiliary pastoral ministry' – unfortunate because 'pastoral' is the aspect of ministry which demands more time than men already committed to secular vocations should be expected to give. By asking too much of such men, or by their eagerness to offer too much, it could be that the Will of God, far from being done, is being frustrated. (The young solicitor who had been ordained 'into the APM' – as folk are wont to say – and who boasted that he was 'never home at nights now' was surprised to meet an episcopal challenge, 'What about your wife and children? Don't they feel deprived?'). 'Pastoral' in the sense of shepherding, caring, visiting, it can scarcely be. Indeed APM could more aptly stand for 'auxiliary priestly ministry', or even 'auxiliary prophetic ministry', but since both smack of the pedantic, even though they indicate the spheres of ministry which such men can more easily offer without abdicating marital and parental responsibilities, maybe we should settle for 'non-stipendiary' or 'voluntary' Ministry. (Since writing this the Church has settled for 'Non-Stipendiary Ministry'. It seems pedantic, if not misleading, to designate those admitted to the Ministry in this way as 'Non Stipendiary Ministers'. They are priests and should be so named.) My conviction is that valuable, indeed essential, as this voluntary ministry is to the total ministry of the Word and Sacraments, those admitted to it should never be seen as other than supplementary. If at any time some misguided bishop, priest or layman, in Synod or outside, should begin to propagate the notion that such a ministry should be 'substitutiary', gradually eliminating the office of the full time parish priest, then it will be for the Church Militant to become so, in a virile demonstration against a proposal which would change the character of the Church of England, gravely impoverishing its work and influence and thus dealing a blow to the national life. Bishop Hensley Henson would say as much in stronger language. In his *Church and Parson in England* he warned, over fifty years ago, that 'If the Church should come to take a low view of its ministry and think it matters little whether its numbers are adequate, its training sufficient and its discipline sound' it would be 'heading for spiritual shipwreck'. I rejoice to see the development of a voluntary supplementary ministry and I hope that it will persist, but I long to see too a growth, and an impressive growth, in the full-time parochial ministry which hitherto has been the strength of the Church's work and witness, and to which we must look for its revival and renewal. In the field of the ordained ministry the parish priest remains the archetype.

Though for fifteen of my first twenty-five years in the Church's ministry I had held other offices alongside that of parish priest – director of religious education, rural dean, archdeacon – it was ever in the parish that my heart was set and from the parish that I derived the greatest satisfaction. Thus when the moment came to me to accept the office of a bishop in the Church of God I reflected that the richest of the gifts which I could lay before the altar was the experience which had been mine for a quarter of a century as a parish priest in industrial, urban and rural areas – shepherding the people of God, reaching out to the unbelievers and the doubters, encouraging the dispirited, teaching, caring and ministering the means of grace through ties of sacrament and prayer.

In the few days of quiet retreat which I spent before my consecration in York Minster on St. Matthias' Day 1959 I recall that elation was tempered by a sense of unworthiness. Looking back across my life at that time I could indeed thank God that he had done marvellous things with me and for me, but as I read again the solemn words of the Bishop's Charge to those about to be ordained priests, I could not but experience, as every priest must do from time to time, the pressure of the failures, the inadequacies, the weaknesses, the sins which mar the ministry. Whether he had read Richard Baxter's *The Reformed Pastor* or not, no priest on self-examination can be unaware of the reality of what he cited as the peculiar 'sins of the ministry' – pride, wordliness, neglect of ministerial duties, partisanship and conduct which belies the doctrine. That good man's warning to his brethren – 'Take heed to yourselves lest you unsay with your lives what you say with your tongues and be the greatest hinderers of your own labours' – was doubtless born of personal failure. The grace of Holy Orders does not stifle the lower nature – not for Peter who denied the Christ to whom he had sworn his allegiance, not for Paul who feared lest having preached to others he might yet himself be a castaway and not – let the laity note – for 'the vicar'. Too often we are unprofitable servants, 'as prone to sin as other men . . . more vulnerable to temptation'. Because our 'actions are more influential' our sins 'are more scandalous'. There in that lovely Bolton Abbey Church, as I prepared myself for the solemn hour of consecration, I did indeed count my blessings but as I read an edited version of Baxter's great book on the pastoral ministry it was to confession that I was driven and through it the way of renewal opened up. Inside the cover of the book before me was a quotation which sent me on my way rejoicing. It was from the pen of my former curate Thomas Wood who, writing in the February 1949 issue of *Theology*, said:

> The severity of Baxter's censures was more than matched by the warmth and fecundity of his exhortations to true pastoral renewal. The voice which, like a sword of judgement, so sternly drove his brethren to their knees in shame, became always a crutch of compassion raising them to a new vision of 'the glory of our high employment', to a nobler conception of the dignity and privilege of their office, and to that inward consecration of mind and heart without which every pastoral endeavour must remain unfruitful.

Thus strengthened I continued my journey to York recalling that on the morrow a train would set out from Windermere carrying nearly four hundred people – men and women, boys and girls – from Ambleside and Rydal to be present at the Rite of Consecration. I knew too that all the roads from Cumbria to York would be traversed by clergy and laity alike concerned to witness the solemn act and to add their prayers to mine on that great day. They were joined, as I was to learn later, by parishioners from Newark and Coddington, from Worksop and Mansfield and by college friends whom I had not seen since college days ended. Furthermore it was especially pleasing to me that I was to be consecrated by Archbishop Michael Ramsey with whom I had had no close contacts since our occasional meetings thirty years before when he was lecturer at Boston and I was senior curate of Newark. I recall our meeting in Bishopthorpe that night when I saw him as a potential Archbishop of Canterbury, capable of bringing to that high office such rich skills as a teacher of theology and as an expositor by word and example of the elements of the spiritual life, as would stand him in line with the great William Temple. (Those who recall his Enthronement Sermon – 'There went with him a band of men, whose hearts God had touched' – will remember it for what I will call its profound simplicity of appeal to all men of goodwill to go with him in his task.)

It is the privilege of the bishop-designate to invite a priest of his own choice to preach the sermon at his Consecration and I was happy to ask the erstwhile Vicar of Newark, then Provost of Blackburn Cathedral, William Kay, under whom I served the first three years of my ministry, to be there with me that day for that purpose. In his sermon he began by drawing the attention of the congregation to one who had preceded me, and indeed himself, in one of the prebendal stalls of Southwell Cathedral – the great and holy Lancelot Andrewes, who was successively Bishop of Chichester and Ely, and finally of Winchester. He set the seventeenth-century bishop before me as a pattern and example, as a bishop, he said, who did not 'try to be original, flamboyant, pompous, dramatic or even popular' . . . 'a strong, resolute and gentle character whose inner secret was the rich treasury of his devotions'. He counselled me to go to my new vocation with 'the spiritual joy which lifts the soul above fretting details, gives larger meaning to life – a life to be poured out in humble persevering prayer and service'. He concluded with a phrase which the youngest members of the vast congregation remembered as evidenced by essays they wrote in school subsequently – maybe the only part which ten-year-olds could understand. 'Go with God,' he said, 'to your Apostleship. Let holy charity your outward vesture be and lowliness your inner clothing. Go with God.' When I entered the Minster that morning *The Preces Privatae of Lancelot Andrewes* was not among my devotional aids. But it has been with me ever since and there is an old saying that if anyone prays with Bishop Andrewes for a week he will wish to pray with him to the end of his life.

Following the sermon at a Consecration the Bishop designate, up to that point robed merely in a cassock, withdraws to a Chapel and is vested in a rochet and chimere, a pectoral cross and the episcopal ring. At my consecration the choir and congregation took up the theme of the address as they sang *St. Patrick's Breastplate*. The ancient Rite, eloquent in word and ceremony, moved on and was subsequently finely described by Charles Hales, Reader in the Diocese of Carlisle, in an article contributed to *Prospect*. He described the occasion as one with

fellowship at many levels: the fellowship implicit in the symbolic laying on of hands at the centre and climax of the Rite; the fellowship of the Eucharist; the fellowship of our pride and delight in the elevation of Sydney Cyril Bulley to the episcopate: withdrawn from us though he was, we yet walked with him in spirit as he was led by two bishops to be presented to the archbishop . . . The great Rite moved majestically forward. What a superb rite it was, what a glorious setting for it, and how magnificently was it administered! Dignity, solemnity, beauty, mystery, in fluent progression; the true significance of episcopacy clearly pointed out by the Provost of Blackburn; the modulations of the Archbishop's voice; the majesty of the Royal Mandate, and singing of such chaste purity and truth as to seem out of this world. That indeed was where we felt ourselves to be; and if we had to return from the heights of spiritual exaltation to the prosaic level of our daily lives, it was surely with a renewed and revitalised consciousness of our spiritual heritage and responsibility.

Soli Deo gloria.

The words bring the occasion vividly to mind and compass its significance and splendour faultlessly, but there were two moments, one poignant, one prodigious, experienced only by me and all but overwhelming in their impact. As the great procession entered the Minster, the choir singing the Psalm 'Levavi oculos', I was suddenly confronted with the picture – dare I say, the vision? – of my dead brother whose absence I had been lamenting to my aged mother, herself present in the Minster, only hours before. It was as though he stood by to watch me pass to my consecration and to add his strong voice to that of those who were singing 'The Lord shall preserve thy going out and thy coming in from this time forth for evermore.' The vision was momentary but so real that I could scarcely resist the impulse to stretch out my hand towards him and as scarcely fight back the tears which so easily could have dropped. It was a poignant but precious experience undimmed by the years. The moment I have described as prodigious came as the hands of the Archbishop and of eleven other bishops were laid upon my head and the solemn words were spoken, 'Receive the Holy Ghost for the office and work of a bishop in the Church of God now committed unto thee by the imposition of our hands.' Here was mystery and history. Mystery in that this was the medium by which the plan of God disclosed by Christ – 'I will build my Church' – is perpetuated and pursued; history in that both ceremony and words, deliberately retained at the Reformation, links the Consecration with the most primitive times and order. The visible Church gives its assurance, authority and recognition to the priest whom it calls to the office of bishop and imparts to him an illapse of the Holy Spirit. Surrounded as I was by twelve bishops, and kneeling beneath the pressure of those hands, I sensed both the mystery of the Rite and its historic significance – an awesome experience indeed. Rising from my knees I experienced a moment of elation in which, hindsight suggests, that vast congregation of my friends would have shouted themselves hoarse, or clapped their hands sore, had they been permitted to respond to that moment by the sort of acclamation which was once part of the Rite. Such a response would have made a lasting impression not least on the minds of the school-children who subsequently wrote essays on 'My Day in York'. Inevitably these contained references to the train Journey from Windermere, to the York Museum, to the Shambles, to the splendour of the Minster, but it was the act of worship itself and significantly the laying on of the Bishops' hands – often grotesquely illustrated – which won the most frequent mention. 'The part of the day,' wrote an 11-year-old boy, 'which I liked best was the service. All the bishops present laid their hands on the archdeacon's head. The biggest thrill of all was to know that I had seen a consecration.' That after all must be counted as high testimony from a small boy who in the same literary effort relates that he enjoyed his dinner 'of meat pies, cabbage and potatoes, prunes and custard, and plenty of it'!

Since it was not possible for Ambleside to anticipate the arrival of a new vicar until the autumn I was able, with the help of retired clergy, to edge my way gradually out of the office of parish priest into the work of the suffragan bishop. During those months I found myself caught up in a process which took me back more than thirty years to my service in a house agents' office. At that time the Church Commissioners accepted no responsibility for housing suffragan bishops and I had of necessity to find a house suitably positioned and modestly priced. Finally, to my great joy and with the help of friends and a mortgage, generous in dimension and modest in interest, I became the proud owner of Fox How – a house famous in the literary, ecclesiastical and educational worlds in that it was built in 1834 by Dr. Thomas Arnold during his years as Headmaster of Rugby. When the deal was clinched the vendor, a Presbyterian, was gracious enough to say that he imagined that there was nothing that he could have done which could have afforded the spirit of Dr. Arnold greater pleasure than this passing of his old home back into Anglican hands and furthermore into the hands of a bishop who himself had been caught up in educational work for so many years of his ministry.

When I first stepped into Fox How as its lawful owner I stood within the hall recalling the great men and women from the worlds of literature, theology, education, history and philosophy, who – as American professors who called on me used to say – had trodden the boards before me. I sensed around me ghosts both eminent and kindly but reflected that there could be some whom I could not describe as kindred spirits. But they were all there – the Arnolds, Thomas and Matthew, the Wordsworths, the Brontës, Coleridge, Southey, Keble, Quillinan, Harriet Martineau, Fred Faber, Whately and others whose visits there were brought to my notice by correspondents from time to time. Not all these visited the house during the life time of Thomas Arnold; Charlotte Brontë's first visit for example was after his death in 1842. Arriving late in the evening she wrote subsequently, 'The house looked like a nest, half buried in flowers and creepers, and dark as it was I could feel that the valley and the fields around were as beautiful as imagination could dream.' The mention of a visit by John Keble may surprise some who, remembering only the antipathy which existed between the two great churchmen, might think that I am in error in including him amongst the eminent visitors. Let it be said that in fact Keble's visit was arranged before but occurred after Arnold died, and the popular notion that these two men of God were bitter enemies and remained so to the time of Arnold's premature death is mistaken. Dean Stanley puts the record straight:

These two held their opinions with a zeal and tenacity proportionate to their importance; each believed the other in error pernicious to the faith and dangerous to himself; and what they believed sincerely, each thought himself bound to state, and stated it openly, it may be with too much of warmth; and unguarded expressions were unnecessarily, I think inaccurately, reported. Such disagreements in opinion between the wise and good are incident to our imperfect state; and even the good qualities of the heart, earnestness, want of suspicion may lay us open to them; but in the case before me the affectionate interest with which each regarded the other never ceased. I had the good fortune to retain the intimate friendship and correspondence of both, and I can testify with authority that the elder spoke and wrote of the younger as an elder brother might of a younger brother whom he tenderly loved, though he disapproved of his course. While it was not in Arnold's nature to forget how much he owed to Keble; he bitterly lamented, what he laboured to avert, the suspension of their intimate intercourse; he was at all times anxious to renew it; and although where the disagreement turned on points so vital between men who held each to his own so conscientiously, this may have been too much to expect, yet it is a most gratifying thought to their common friends that they would probably have met at Fox How under Arnold's roof, but a few weeks after he was called away to that state, in which doubts and controversies of this life will receive their clear resolution.

Though I suspect that my sympathies in their controversy might have been more frequently with the author of *The Christian Year* than with the Headmaster of Rugby, at least in their respective theological standpoints, I was happy, on reading Dean Stanley's estimate for the first time, to know that the spirits about me were not at war. I hung in the hall of Fox How a small reproduction in oils of Thomas Phillips' National Gallery portrait of the man whose home it had been – even though the views he held were at one time so suspect among the clergy that the Archbishop of Canterbury refused to allow him to preach at the consecration in Lambeth Palace Chapel of his friend Edward Stanley as Bishop of Norwich. On any reckoning, however, Arnold stands among the great and I was determined to discover how it came about that this southerner – he was born in the Isle of Wight – came to know and love the Rothay Valley and to build in it the house which was now my home.

It was in the autumn of 1830, when there were grave civil and political disturbances in the country, and the dark shadow of the cholera made the lives of many the more miserable, that Arnold's letters to his friends became overcast with gloom. He was preaching vigorous sermons against the evils of the day and missed no opportunity to use the power of his pen against them. He became exasperated at efforts made by some who thought to combat those evils whilst remaining neutral towards Christianity. He started his own newspaper, the *Englishman's Register*, calling the Church to its responsibility to reform itself, to Christianise the nation and to challenge those who were seeking an answer to the nation's discontents without reference to Christianity. The paper failed but he battled on – in sermons to the boys at Rugby and elsewhere, in letters to the press, in essays and in magazine articles. It was during this period of stress that the 'thirst for a lodge in some vast wilderness' became 'almost irresistible'. A letter to a friend indicated that he had found such a retreat and his excitement can be measurement by the style of its heading:

RYDAL!!! December 23, 1831

We are actually here . . . Nowhere on earth have I seen a spot of more perfect and enjoyable beauty, with not a single object out of tune with it, look where you will.

And in the following April, writing to John Coleridge from Rugby School:

I could still rave about Rydal. It was a period of five weeks of almost awful happiness . . . Our intercourse with the Wordsworths was one of the highest spots of all . . . and my almost daily walks with him were things not to be forgotten . . . We are thinking of buying or renting a place at Grasmere or Rydal, for not only are the Wordsworths and the scenery a very great attraction but as I had the Chapel at Rydal all the time of our last visit I got acquainted with the poor people besides and I cannot tell you what a homelike feeling all of us entertain towards the valley of the Rotha.

Within a year he was able to write:

Our Westmorland house is rising from its foundations . . . It looks right into the bosom of Fairfield – a noble mountain which sends down two long arms into the valley, and keeps the clouds reposing between them . . . Behind we run up to the top of Loughrigg, and we have a mountain pasture, in a basin on the summit of the ridge . . . The Wordsworths' friendship, for so I may call it, is certainly one of the greatest delights of Fox How . . . and their kindness in arranging everything in our absence has been very great.

By 1834 the house was built and thereafter the Arnolds were always in residence during the school holidays, frequently taking with them from the school sixth-formers who were housed in farmhouses nearby. From 1834 to his death in 1842 there are in letters to his friends countless ecstatic references to Fox How and its surroundings which he described on returning from a holiday in Italy as 'in such beauty that no scene in Italy appeared in my eyes as comparable to it'.

Fox How remained in Arnold's hands until 1923 when Frances, youngest daughter of Thomas, died. To Thomas in his letters she was often referred to as 'little Fan'. When I made Fox How my home there were still many about who talked to me about 'Aunt Fan' and the great work she did for the Church and for the community. During her time the procession of the eminent to the house made famous by her father included Longfellow and President Wilson. This, then, was my home for the seven years in which I held the Bishopric of Penrith. But there was to be still another Rugby School association; the pastoral staff which I used once belonged to Bishop Claude Blagden, formerly Bishop of Peterborough, who retired to the Lake District. The Bishop had been Rector of Rugby and the Staff had been given to him by the boys of the School at the time of his consecration.

I started my new work with the enormous advantage of knowing those among whom I was to work and of knowing that they approved of my appointment. Such a deluge of letters had descended on me from the clergy and laity of the diocese that it was apparent that what Her Majesty had done, aided and abetted by the Bishop of Carlisle, was something which those among whom I was to exercise my episcopal ministry welcomed cordially. One cannot keep such letters forever but when the moment for destruction of a bundle of over three hundred came I extracted one, which for its uniqueness, brevity and charm deserved to live longer. Coming as it did from the Dean of Carlisle, Cyril Mayne, sometime Professor of Greek at Durham University, I might have anticipated its being penned in that tongue. But unlike Walter Ewbank, who on several occasions graced me with verses in Latin, the Dean said all in the vulgar tongue:

> What a seemly evolution
> For a pupil of Saint Chad,
> And the very best solution
> We could possibly have had!
> And what luck to have a Sydney
> Of the right and proper kidney
> Whom it pleased the blessed Thomas
> To promote to honour from us!
> May the Grace of God attend you
> And the flock of Christ befriend you!

And who could blame him for using the Christian name, Sydney, which although my first, had never been used since my baptism? Being himself a Cyril he was well aware that that name confronts the poet with rhyming difficulties and clearly he shrank from anything which might suggest a link between the budding bishop and a certain bushy tailed arboreal rodent. But whether in prose or in verse those letters from people with whom I had worked as parish priest, director of religious education and archdeacon sent me to the new work with a song in my heart.

In the early weeks of my tenure of the See I did in fact miss those intimate contacts with congregations, and in particular with children and young people, which the parish priest enjoys, but as the work gathered its natural momentum there were rich compensations. I found the visits to the parishes for Confirmations, the contacts with deanery chapters, church councils and parish youth groups immensely rewarding. There was, however, one activity which I had been enjoying for twenty-three years which came to an abrupt halt and which nothing replaced. It was something to which throughout my time as a parish priest I had attached immense importance or its educational and evangelistic value – namely the preparation of a sizeable monthly magazine. Over the years the writing of these, as of reports on schools, lectures to teachers and others, had consumed many night hours – hours when creative writing was undisturbed by phone or visitors. There were, of course, the invitations from local papers to write something for their columns at Christmas and in the New Year numbers, but for the most part writing was at a minimum and my years as Bishop of Penrith saw me earlier to bed – that is at a *post-meridian* rather than an *ante-meridian* hour – than had been possible in any of my days as a parish priest and director of education or subsequently as a diocesan bishop. Even so a yearning to achieve something in oil painting often trapped me in a Fox How attic until the small hours of the morning.

My predecessor in the See, Victor Turner, had in his farewell speech to the diocese, described the suffragan bishoprics as 'the happiest jobs in the Church of England' and certainly those who knew him would say that happiness was ever writ large across his face. During my years as archdeacon we frequently shared a car to our Carlisle meetings and in this way had ample opportunity to compare notes about our work. To say that we agreed on every aspect of it would be palpably absurd but we certainly agreed whole-heartedly on our estimate of our chief, Thomas Bloomer, whom we both held in high regard and affection.

I had not been in the suffragan bishopric many weeks before I realised that I was to be more than an episcopal curate to the Diocesan; I was to be an intimate colleague sharing in every aspect of the episcopal oversight of the diocese. There were to be no areas of the work reserved exclusively to the Diocesan. The Confirmations, usually rather more than a hundred a year, were to be divided so that each of us visited as many parishes as possible for that purpose. Institutions of new incumbents which, like Confirmations, afford rich opportunities for the bishop to get to know his laypeople, were to be similarly divided and I was invariably invited to take part in the Ordinations. These public occasions apart there was frequent joint consideration touching movements of the clergy, appointments to canonries, arrangements for clergy conferences and plans for the development of particular aspects of the work of the Church in the diocese. I was free to accept any invitations which came from within the diocese either directly concerned with deaneries or parishes or with other facets of community life – though we generally checked to avoid the possibility of our both being present at any 'secular' function to avoid over-weighting an occasion with episcopacy! Nor had I forgotten an off-the-cuff remark of my first vicar during my curacy days: 'If you should ever become a bishop you shouldn't imagine that you have to be present at every little dog-hanging.'

I began to experience in the episcopal work the same satisfaction and happiness which had been mine in the office of parish priest. There was now greater leisure in which to meet the clergy and their families in their own homes and to receive at Fox How any who were seeking advice or encouragement. Inasmuch as I still held the office of archdeacon there was still some paper work to be done but since this was at a minimum I was able for the first time in twenty-three years to dispense with the services of a secretary; though when a whimsical parish priest began a letter to me with the words 'Insofar as I am able to decipher your Lordship's letter . . . ' I took up typewriting in earnest and became a fairly speedy but not always accurate two-finger banger.

At the summer Diocesan Conference in 1959, shortly after my Consecration, the Bishop expressed the hope that someone might offer the diocese a sizeable house which could become a diocesan retreat and conference house, and this was a need we discussed together frequently. Indeed during my time in Ambleside a house in that township, bequeathed to a religious community, but surplus to its needs, came on to the market but efforts I made to acquire it for the Church were frustrated. Meanwhile I continued to use Rydal Hall for our annual Schoolboys' Conference and on each such occasion the secret hope which I had long cherished, that it might one day come into the hands of the Church for its work, was kindled afresh. It was never that I saw it as something merely for the Diocese of Carlisle. It was that since there was only one Lake District the Church which was fortunate to minister within it should grasp the opportunity, if it ever should arise, of getting hold of a piece of 'plant' in the heart of the Lake District which could contribute richly to its teaching and caring work. Here was a stately home, never likely to be used again by the le Fleming family. The surviving life tenant of the estate, Mr. Michael le Fleming, lived then in Rhodesia. The house itself, with its thirty acres of gardens and woodlands, its mountain stream and waterfalls, was just the sort of property set in just the sort of environment which could afford facilities for retreats, for summer schools, for house-parties, for conferences, for reading parties, for parish holidays – indeed for anything which in any way could contribute to the strengthening of man's hold upon the Christian Faith and the Christian Way. This was the hope at the back of my mind when we worked hard to save the little Church of Rydal from closure but I had then to conceal the hope in dark language. How then was the hope finally realised?

'The day has come'. Those were the four words I heard when I picked up my telephone just after lunch on a Saturday in November 1961. For a moment I thought that I was being threatened, until the caller reminded me of something I had said to him a few years before. 'One day you and your wife will be tired of running this place. When that day comes ring me and say nothing to anyone.' Within an hour I was in the Hall discussing with the proprietor terms for the purchase of the remaining sixteen years of his lease. We reached an informal agreement and in the same week I sought the confidence and material help of three wealthy and generous churchmen whom I judged likely to be sympathetic to such an enterprise. With the promises in my hand to provide two-thirds of the purchase price, I hurried to Rose Castle with the plan which was, as I anticipated it would be, very eagerly approved by the Bishop who saw in it an answer to a need of which he had long been conscious. Confidentiality was preserved until the secretary of our Diocesan Board of Finance – James Lister who served the diocese with outstanding ability and dedication for thirty years – and one or two members of the Board with knowledge and experience of buildings and values, had had opportunity to consider the proposition. The end result was that I was able to put the plan before the Diocesan Conference in 1962 and although there were a few people whose feet were colder than any on the platform, the proposal was welcomed by an overwhelming majority.

The legal wheels turned slowly but in the spring of 1963 Rydal Hall was duly opened by Bishop Bloomer who had meanwhile appointed Alan Batty, then Vicar of Cleator Moor, to serve as its first priest-warden. In his address the Bishop made it clear that we were doing something not for ourselves alone but for the whole Church, adding in his most whimsical manner, 'After all, the Diocese of Carlisle is the most beautiful diocese in the Church of England and we should not begrudge sharing its beauty with others less fortunate.' Within ten years of its opening we had been privileged to entertain sixteen thousand guests from all over the United Kingdom and from thirty-three countries outside and when, in 1970 we were able, following the death of Mr. Michael le Fleming, to purchase the freehold of the property, an appeal was launched which yielded sufficient to enable us to make considerable improvements in the house and in the grounds and to bring into use buildings on the estate which had not been available to us under the lease. When in 1968 I appointed Alan Batty to the directorship of education and moved him to a residentiary canonry at the Cathedral, his place as priest-warden was taken by David Dixon, an effervescent extrovert who had made his mark as Vicar of a West Cumberland industrial parish and who, with imagination and enthusiasm, built on the firm foundations which Alan Batty had laid. His interest in the scout movement prompted him to develop camping sites in the spacious grounds thus extending the opportunities afforded by the Hall to exercise a Christian influence over thousands of young people. In all this work Rydal Church has played an essential part and the expensive decision to restore it which the little village took so daringly in 1957 has been wholly and amply justified.

Towards the end of the 1950s the Christian Stewardship method of meeting the Church's needs began to be taken seriously in the diocese of Carlisle as elsewhere. The city itself had seen it at work in the parish of Upperby, to which parish Michael Underhill had imported it from New Zealand, to which country he subsequently returned as Dean of Christchurch Cathedral. The Diocesan Bishop asked me to chair a Christian Stewardship Committee to encourage development of the method. At the outset progress was slow for here was something new and therefore in Cumbrian eyes suspect, but gradually prejudices were broken down and when parishes saw that the Bishop, his suffragan and his archdeacons were all committed and prepared to help parishes by their presence and words, the climate changed. In 1960 we appointed Mr. J. R. Wivell as our first Diocesan Director of Stewardship and he and his successor, Mr Harry Cameron who followed in 1964, busied themselves within the parishes encouraging, advising and organising. As chairman of the diocesan committee my diary became dotted with a new type of entry: 'speak C.S. dinner at . . . ', and I must declare that I found that these occasions did far more than ensuring a meteoric rise in parochial incomes. These Christian Stewardship dinners, or suppers, which could be seen as the climax of the preparations for the campaign proper and as a prelude to a lay visitation of the homes of the parish, were also occasions of genuine *koinonia* in which fellowship of the worshipping community was expressed and strengthened and many whose interest in the Church had long been tepid was rekindled.

Such gatherings, normally attended as they were not only by the regular worshippers but by other parishioners whose attendance at church was minimal, and occasionally by civic dignitaries, afforded a valuable opportunity for Christian education and evangelism, for saying something both about the stewardship of time and talents and money, and about the meaning and relationship of such New Testament words as *agape* and *eucharist*. They were indeed occasions on which I grasped eagerly the opportunity of singing for my supper! My mention of Christian Stewardship in an earlier chapter indicates the extent of the opportunity for mission opened by such campaigns when rightly directed. See them as concerned only with the material welfare of the Church and they bring but transitory benefit; see them as concerned with its spiritual welfare, with the building up of the Kingdom of God in the parish, 'and all these things shall be added unto you'.

Another of the special areas of work in which Bishop Bloomer asked me to take a particular interest was our College at Greystoke. I say 'our' College but in fact when it started it was not strictly a diocesan enterprise; it was the brainchild of John Norman, then Rector of Greystoke, a beautiful Cumbrian village which, according to Arthur Mee, 'stands out among its simple neighbours like a gem'. Inspired doubtless by the character and history of the village with its great Collegiate Church of St. Andrew with its Priest's Room and Library, its ancient Canons' stalls with their exquisite misereres, the Rector saw it as an appropriate venue for helping men who had some sense of an inward call to the sacred ministry to attain the necessary academic qualifications which might enable them to move on to specific theological training. I recall his sounding out the idea with me at the time I was heading the education work of the diocese and I see even now the glow of delight in the eyes of a man with a vision as I gave him my assurance of support for what he had in mind. He knew, as I knew, that the diocesan bishop would see such a venture as very much in tune with hopes which he had expressed on more than one occasion. The College began in 1957, very modestly with eleven men and without any formal consultation either with the diocese or with the Central Council of the Church for Training for the Ministry, which latter body I feared might strangle the infant college with red tape.

The aim was to receive men over the age of 18 who, conscious of an inward call to the ministry and lacking the necessary academic attainments which could secure entry into one of the traditional theological colleges, were prepared to set aside their secular work and to undergo a period of testing. They were to be no charge on the Church, locally or nationally, and to that end they were to be directed to gainful employment which they would pursue on three days a week. Wages were to be pooled and from these, augmented by a generous convenanted gift from Anthony Cropper, a devout and loyal son of the Church, Greystoke residents prepared to house and feed them would be paid from the common fund. Applicants were to be interviewed by the Rector and myself and my custom was to tell them that once accepted, their academic potential would be tested by their response to tutoring for 'O' and 'A' levels, their spiritual potential by their readiness to put themselves under the discipline of a Christian collegiate life, their leadership and pastoral potential by the ease with which they could enter into the spiritual and social life of the village community, and their 'stickability' by the determination with which they bent themselves to a task and a programme which could not but be tough. We turned down many applicants in the course of the years; we turned out a few who failed our tests; we accepted the verdicts of a few who turned themselves out.

Soon after this daring venture began, manna from heaven fell upon Greystoke in the person of Bishop Eric Graham who retired from the See of Brechin to take up residence at Matterdale Vicarage. The Bishop had, in the course of his long ministry, been Principal of Cuddesdon for ten years and, good and holy man that he was, he offered immediately to help in any way he could. Success was thus assured for he brought to the enterprise wisdom and experience and became a tower of strength both to the College Council which was formed in 1962 and to all who came to us from different backgrounds, from different parts of the country and occasionally from overseas. Greystoke Pre-Theological Training College was seen as a valuable contribution by the Diocese of Carlisle to the ministerial manpower needs of the Church and before long the Church's Central Council for the Ministry recognised its work by making a modest per capita grant in respect of each student whom we accepted for testing. The College remained, however, as I had always contended that it should, a 'private enterprise', not a subject for 'nationalisation' either by CACTM or its successor ACCM, though I hasten to add that these smiled upon us. It should go on record, as we boast about the fact that there are approximately eighty priests working in the Church today, who might never have reached Ordination but for what Greystoke did for them, that in terms of hard cash none have cost the Church less. The men were taught and tested with only a minuscule charge on the Church's funds, and that was possible because the succession of Wardens – John Norman, Richard Horton, William Roan and William Bucks – did what they did for the men with no payment beyond their incumbents' stipends; the tutors, Bishop Graham and many clergy in the vicinity, together with Charles Young (sometime Headmaster of Rossall), Miss Grace Perigo (sometime Headmistress of Bury Girls' Grammar School), Francis King (sometime Housemaster at Winchester) and Mrs Mortimer (widow of Bishop Robert Mortimer who in his retirement from the See of Exeter took up residence in a village nearby) – all gave their services freely and devotedly week by week through the academic year.

Bishop Bloomer saw in the College an answer to a call which he had made twenty years before for a new approach to the recruitment of men for the ministry which would draw in some for whom the traditional methods of training made no provision. When the College Council was set up in 1962 he became Visitor and asked me to become Chairman and to keep a close eye on the entrants to and conduct of the College. From that day until I left Cumbria ten years later Greystoke was one of the names engraven on my heart. It seemed to me to merit a generous expenditure of episcopal time and thought for if the final judgement of the Church is that the choice of fit persons to serve in its Ministry is vested in the bishop, here was a piece of work which was peculiarly his even though our concern was never for the diocese of Carlisle only but for the whole Church. It was interesting that from the outset we found ourselves helping the Episcopal Church in Scotland and the Church of Ireland. During my time as Bishop of Carlisle I invited the Primate of All Ireland (The Most Reverend George Simms) to preach at the annual Greystoke College Festival and this he did expressing in the course of his address his Church's thanks for services rendered to his Province.

As I write these words I hear that the College is closing, since the supply of young men needing the sort of help which Greystoke provided is alleged to be diminishing. For those remaining, provision is being made by something called the Aston Scheme which appears to be largely a correspondence course which can in no way fill the gap the closure of Greystoke must create. Greystoke was ever small – fifteen men at the most – but the small was beautiful and richly blessed. I cannot but regard its closure as retrogressive. Despite its demise I count not a minute of the time I gave it as wasted.

Throughout my years as Bishop of Penrith I continued to take an interest in the educational affairs of the diocese and was happy to see them so admirably conducted by Robert Holtby, who succeeded me and continued to serve in the Carlisle diocese until he was appointed General Secretary of the National Society and of the Church of England Schools Council, by Alan Batty and, on his moving to the Vicarage of Penrith, by Robert Waddington whom I won from the Church in Queensland, and who himself has now succeeded Robert Holtby in the Church's top educational post. Visits to Church and County Schools and to the two Public Schools in the diocese – St. Bees and Casterton – for Open Days, Prize-givings and Speech Days, all found a place in the work programme. Casterton in particular, which counts among its old girls the Brontë sisters, invited me to be chairman of its Governing Body at a moment in its history when it was at a low ebb – in numbers and in financial resources. Supported by governors who doggedly refused to surrender in the face of seemingly intractable material problems we resolved to improve and extend the premises. It was not that there was anywhere the smallest trace of the spartan conditions which had obtained in the days of 'Jane Eyre', but rather that we were convinced that further improved premises and additional facilities would be conducive to the school's growth in numbers and that that in turn could enable it to grow in educational status and to become fiscally viable. To this end we launched an appeal for £100,000 and raised it without professional help. Over the years and under the energetic and imaginative leadership of the Headmistress, Miss Rosamund Willson, our hopes were realised and we saw the school rise in numbers from 200 to 320 which was the limit of its accommodation, and at the same time grow in educational stature. The pupil successors of the Brontë girls at Casterton through those years will remember certain highlights in its growth: the improved dormitory accommodation, the library, the covered swimming pool, the great hall (the largest in Westmorland), and the purchase of the Old Manor House, former home of the Reverend William Carus Wilson (the Mr. Brocklehurst of *Jane Eyre*). They will recall too the visits on Speech Days of eminent people from the worlds of politics, of education and religion and amongst them the Archbishop of York, Dr. Donald Coggan. They will recall how to their delight and to their and his amusement I introduced him as 'Number 2 in the ecclesiastical Top Twenty' and since then I suspect that those who received prizes at his hand have on occasion boasted that they have shaken hands with the Archbishop of Canterbury. But the highest of all the highlights was undoubtedly the descent on the school playing fields of a helicopter from which there emerged H.R.H. Princess Alexandra who arrived to open our Gymnasium/Hall thus keeping a promise she had made to me three years before that she would pay us a visit one day. Nothing could have delighted schoolgirls more than the idea of a Princess dropping from the skies and, needless to say, she won the hearts of all – the girls, the staff, academic and domestic, and the governors. The four girls in quarantine, who had resigned themselves to disappointment, in fact found themselves among the most favoured, for when I directed the attention of Her Royal Highness to the window from which they were waving she left me immediately to conduct a conversation with them. Her interest in the school and its history was not, however, the first demonstration of royal concern for what had at first been a school for clergy daughters. In 1840 Queen Adelaide paid a memorable visit and subsequently contributed generously to its development appeal. Charlotte Brontë, in *Jane Eyre*, describes the first steps of the progress of the Lowood of her story towards the Casterton of today. She mentions that 'several wealthy and benevolent individuals subscribed largely for the erection of a more convenient building in a better situation and the records show that Her Majesty was joined in this enterprise by the Archbishops of Canterbury and York, by William Ewart Gladstone and by Miss Dorothy Beale'. Determined not to leave her readers with any false impression she added that 'the school thus improved became in time a truly useful and noble institution' and she bore her testimony 'to its value and importance'.

Casterton flourishes still and when, in 1973, it celebrated the 150th anniversary of its foundation it set down its long story on a mural measuring 120 feet in length and depicting the highlights of its history within the context of the history of the times. So long as 'parental choice' is respected, so long will there be a place for such schools within the total educational prospectus of our country and more so now since the charge of social exclusiveness laid against them becomes daily less tenable. Although I am not myself a product of the public schools' system I have had innumerable opportunities in close contacts with some twenty Public and Preparatory Schools, to assess the value of the independent sector which they represent. Far from finding anything to justify the political venom which some inject into the educational debate on this subject I find much to sustain my own conviction that the particular contribution which the independent sector makes, socially, economically and educationally, is of such merit that it should continue to be open to parental choice. Indeed I would myself be happy to see a resuscitation of the 1944 Fleming Report's proposals so as to open the opportunity of making that choice to a wider circle of parents. County schools, Church schools, Grammar schools, Secondary modern schools, Secondary technical schools, Public schools, Direct Grant schools, co-educational schools, single sex schools – let them all be! Within the field of education it is not variety but uniformity of which we should ever beware.

The years of my service as suffragan bishop were years of unsullied happiness, made such by the kindly way in which the clergy of the diocese sought and accepted my ministrations, by the family nature of the diocese itself and, most of all perhaps, by the easy rapport which I enjoyed with my chief, Thomas Bloomer. Our intimate relationship was such that when, early in 1966, he confided to me his intention to retire during that year, as indeed I had anticipated, I lapsed momentarily into a mood of apprehension as to what manner of man his successor might be and whether he might hope to have an early opportunity of forming his own 'cabinet' with a younger suffragan. However, the mood was of a fleeting nature and with the aid of the Dean, Lionel du Toit, who was also in the Bishop's confidence, it was soon laughed out of court. The work proceeded and as advance programmes came to be fashioned, e.g. with Confirmations, I had to take account of the fact that those being assigned to the Diocesan for the closing months of the year would in fact fall to me though as yet the diocese could not know that.

Ultimately Bishop Bloomer announced his impending resignation, characteristically noting that whilst some people had been known to express a preference 'to die in harness' he for his part had long since concluded that whilst such an attitude 'may be all right for the old horse, it is seldom good for the harness'. The 'harness' in this case was the Church itself and the Bishop, conscious of his diminishing powers of application and doubtless of his wife's need of a greatly deserved rest from the burden and heat of the day, announced in the spring his intention to resign at the end of October 1966. This he did carrying with him the Freedom of the City of Carlisle, the gratitude of the people of Cumbria, the respect of the members of the clergy and the affection of his immediate colleagues. Within days of his departure there came to me from the Archbishop of York his Mandate which, couched in the fine language beloved of the Law, bade me in effect to 'look after the shop'. This I did, dividing my time between Fox How and Rose Castle, with the assistance of the bishop's chauffeur to whisk me around the diocese for the double portion of Confirmations.

The days were heavy and the nights were disturbed for just at that time my aged mother was taken ill, becoming bed-ridden for the first time in her life. She lingered in semi-consciousness for nine days as I watched beside her through the nights and good friends watched by day, and she died on 7 November, a fortnight short of her ninety-first birthday. Ambleside Church was filled for the funeral service conducted by its Vicar, Kenneth Warren, and once more and for the fourth time in my family, as my elder brother and I laid her mortal remains to rest, we sang Addison's great hymn,

> *Through every period of my life*
> *Thy goodness I'll pursue,*
> *And after death in distant worlds*
> *The glorious theme renew*

Fox How seemed desperately empty deprived of the physical presence of the one who had shared my home and contributed so mightily to my happiness and work for thirty years. The Christian conviction of the indestructibility of love, which is of God, itself assured us that maternal and filial love were undisturbed by death, yet the breaking of the ties of sight and touch and sound seemed somehow to wrap the house in solemn stillness and deep sorrow. I was not to know that on that very day a letter was being written which was to close that chapter of my life in another and different way. When that letter arrived by the early morning post I read it, handed it to my brother without comment and left the study; he read it, put it on my desk and went to his room. There was a poignancy about it which reduced us to silence.

An hour passed before I returned to the study, picked up the letter and read it again.

10 Downing Street
WHITEHALL

Dear Bishop,
It is my duty to recommend to the Queen the name of a successor to the See of Carlisle in the place of Bishop Thomas Bloomer.

After the most careful consideration I have decided, if you are willing that I should do so, to submit your name for the succession to this See. On hearing that this is agreeable to you, I shall be happy to recommend your name to the Queen, and I trust that you will treat this proposal as confidential until Her Majesty's approval has been obtained.

Yours sincerely,

(signed) HAROLD WILSON

Emulating Hezekiah, who received an earth-shaking letter and whose immediate reaction was to 'spread it out before the Lord', I did just that and a thousand thoughts raced through my mind. 'Heaviness may endure for the night but joy comes in the morning' was the message of the Psalmist to me just then and maybe there was a divine hand in the juxtaposition of these two momentous changes in my life. I cannot say that no hesitations passed through my mind. I was then fifty-nine and had the Prime Minister's proposed recommendation been in respect of some other diocese – save perhaps Sodor and Man – I should have felt it right to refuse, for I have never been able to believe that it could be right for a man approaching his sixties to take up so important and onerous a job as bishop of a diocese of which he knows nothing. But Carlisle was different; I had served in it for fifteen years; I knew every parish in it, and every parish priest; I had served on all its committees and was familiar with its problems, its possibilities and its potential. Hence on the day following the reception of the letter I wrote to the Prime Minister indicating my readiness to accept his recommendation. In posting my reply I reflected that a hundred and eighteen years earlier another letter from a Prime Minister had dropped through the Fox How letter-box. It was signed 'Melbourne' and it contained word of that Prime Minister's desire to submit to the young Queen Victoria the name of Thomas Arnold to succeed to the Regius Professorship of Modern History at Oxford.

Meanwhile every post was bringing me scores of letters of sympathy on the death of my mother – these from clergy and laity in the diocese and from all the parishes in Nottinghamshire on which she had stamped her warm personality and virile faith. Then came the announcement in *The Times* of my new appointment and suddenly the character of the daily post was changed so that it became a muddled and massive amalgam of expressions of sorrow and joy, of pain and pleasure, of sympathy and congratulations. Opened at random, the letters wafted me from grief to ecstasy and dropped me as suddenly again into the valley of the shadow. Here indeed was a veritable thesis on life's mutability as Wordsworth, who in that very room had talked with Arnold, might have observed:

> *From low to high doth dissolution climb*
> *And sink from high to low, along a scale*
> *Of awful notes, whose concord shall not fail;*

And concord there was as Provost William Kay, ever a writer of letters in the grand style, reminded me. Weaving the two themes together in finely-chosen words and phrases, he who had been my first mentor in the active ministry over thirty years before, stretched out the hand of a pastor of deep spiritual perception and that hand I grasped eagerly and with gratitude. But there was to be yet another blow. Within the week, and reaching me by phone in the small hours of the morning, came news that the priest who had laid to rest the mortal remains of my mother and who by the graveside had grasped my hand with the words, 'Behold, I make all things new', had himself died suddenly and without a warning illness. Ambleside Church was filled again for the funeral of its vicar, Kenneth Warren, and clergy and parishioners alike saw their new Bishop struggling to control his emotions as he spoke of one who for over thirty years had been a deeply dedicated parish priest, a firm personal friend and who but days before had been ministering to him in his own sorrow.

The Penrith chapter of my life was marked at its close as indeed it had been at its opening with personal sorrow, yet in perspective I see in it seven years of joy. The truth is that the great monosyllables of life – faith and hope and love – speak ever to man's condition; by their message sorrow is sweetened and joy is enhanced. None of us can escape the changes and chances of life, but met with reverence rather than rebellion light breaks through the darkest cloud. Well may we pray with Reinhold Niebuhr,

> God grant me –
> *The serenity to accept the things I cannot change*
> *The courage to change the things I can*
> *And the wisdom to know the difference.*

11

The Goodly Heritage

The move from the suffragan bishopric of Penrith to the See of Carlisle was unlike any other that I had made in the course of my ministry and that not merely in that it set me among the forty-three diocesan bishops who watch over the life and work of the Church of England. There was no immediate clear-cut division of duties and responsibilities. The passage from Newark to Worksop, from Worksop to Mansfield, from Mansfield to Ambleside, and from Ambleside to the suffragan bishopric, represented in each instance a decisive break with the immediate past. The passage from Penrith to Carlisle, however, at least in terms of what are now known as work-load and job-specification, was a fusion of one into the other, and more so in that there was an unfortunate delay in the appointment of a successor to myself in the bishopric of Penrith. Thus in setting down the episcopal part of my life story this fusion tends to become confusion for I have found myself already in the last chapter writing about projects which, though initiated in my time as Bishop of Penrith, did not come to fruition until my years as Bishop of Carlisle. Disentangling these two periods of my life for the purpose of biography thus presents difficulties in description which were not apparent in their progression.

What had befallen me, however, was sufficiently unusual to attract more than local interest. It was rare enough for a suffragan bishop to be appointed bishop of the diocese in which he was serving, but rarer still for one who had been an incumbent, a canon, an archdeacon and a director of education in the diocese to be so elevated. Thus among the four hundred or so letters which fell upon me when the appointment was announced in the press, and which embraced greetings from the two archbishops, bishops of the Bench as well as clerical and lay friends in Devonshire, Nottinghamshire and Cumbria, were some from people unknown to me who saw in the appointment something new in 'bishop making' which they clearly approved.

The method by which the bishops of the Church of England are appointed has long been a subject of intense controversy. In the Victorian era criticisms were frequently levelled against Prime Ministers with regard to the way they carried out this part of their duties, but these criticisms concerned their motivation in the appointments rather that the method of appointment. Peel would not promote a 'Puseyite' for example; Melbourne, whilst formally consulting the Primate was wont to go on his own Whiggish way; and Palmerton disliked and suspected what he called 'theological bishops'. True there were murmurings within the Church about specific appointments but few questioned the propriety of the system of Crown appointment. In the years following the Second World War it was just this which was being called into question so frequently. Some seeing in it Erastianism of the worst kind, would have substituted for it some system of appointment by a diocesan synod; others advocated appointment by a synod of bishops. Occasionally there have been bitter complaints that a priest's political affiliation has been a motivating factor in appointments but those who made them must surely have discounted, or have known nothing of, the immense care which the Prime Minister's Appointments Secretary – a civil servant not a 'party' man – along with his opposite number at Lambeth, exercised in their national soundings. (I have reminded many a lay critic that Mervyn Stockwood, dubbed by the popular press as 'The Red Bishop', was appointed to his See when a Tory Prime Minister occupied Number 10.) Nevertheless the belief persists among some that for the Prime Minister to have anything to do with the appointment of bishops must keep open the possibility of political bias. The TV reporter who interviewed me on my appointment could not resist the question: 'Surely the present system of state appointment of bishops must mean that the priest appointed feels some obligation towards the party in power when he is appointed?' I replied that if it were so I should find myself on the horns of a dilemma since 'I have in my file two letters in respect of my episcopal appointments and whilst both are signed "Harold", one is Macmillan and the other is Wilson'. The camera team joined the reporter in the chuckle which closed the interview. But among the faithful laity there has for long been some disquiet as, discerning an increasing ecclesiastical influence in episcopal appointments, and recognising that more and more of them were stamped 'Lambeth' rather than 'Whitehall', they suspected that other considerations were entering in which were resulting in something like a closed shop approach.

The Paul Report, published in 1964, had noted that 'a Public School background is *de rigueur* for bishops'. A few had slipped through that net provided that they had been to Oxford or Cambridge and one or other of the 'favoured' theological colleges Cuddesdon, Westcott, Wells and Ridley. In his *Anatomy of Britain* Anthony Sampson had observed that 'in 1961 three quarters of the bishops had been to Public Schools and all but three to Oxford or Cambridge'. Of the three who, quipped a prominent layman, 'must have slipped through when the Archbishop was not looking', two – the much respected Bishops of Manchester (Greer) and Carlisle (Bloomer) – were graduates of Trinity College, Dublin and one was a non-graduate who nevertheless had been to Oxford. (The position as I write shows how dramatically things have changed for there are now eight of the bishops from universities other than Oxford and Cambridge and two who are non-graduates). But what was true in 1961 was true in 1966. Thus when several of the leading laity in the diocese of Carlisle were kind enough to express the hope that I might succeed Dr. Bloomer in the See they received from me the same answer as I gave to the clergy who expressed the same wish, speaking as I told them 'unadvisedly with their lips'. It was that they should dismiss the thought and be ready to welcome a stranger into their midst. But in saying that I had not reckoned with the effect of a new piece of legislation which came into being only a month or two before my appointment.

This new legislation the Vacancy in the See Measure which, up to then, had operated only in an appointment to the Bishopric of Sodor and Man. By this Measure the Archbishop's Appointments' Secretary – at that time Mr W. Saumarez Smith – was able to meet a committee of senior members of the clergy and elected representatives of the diocese to hear their views as to the sort of priest whom they might hope to receive as their new bishop. It is within the privilege of that committee to mention a name or names of priests who might be thought by them to be suitable, recognising of course that this could not in any way arrogate or limit the Sovereign's absolute right of appointment. Precisely what transpired at the Carlisle meeting I have no means of knowing but a letter which I received from the late Sir John Hewitt, the Prime Minister's Appointments' Secretary said that he – the Prime Minister – had submitted my name to Her Majesty fully confident that my appointment would be received with satisfaction in the diocese which I had already served for over fourteen years. Hence I was able to take up the task before me with the strong impression that though appointed by 'The State' I had been chosen by 'The Church' to become 63rd in the long procession of Bishops of Carlisle which began with the consecration of the Augustinian Prior Athelwold of Nostell in 1133. Never in the idle day dreams of my youth, nor later when the kindliest of people said the most flattering things about my ministry, could I have imagined that such a high privilege could ever be mine. The journeys from Fox How to Rose Castle which I had been making from the moment of my receiving the Archbishop's mandate commanding me to 'look after the shop' assumed a new significance when I received the Prime Minister's original letter, and although 'Cyril Penrith' did not immediately become 'Cyril Carliol': I noted that the press announcement of my appointment prompted some of the clergy to address me as such immediately. I was happy to accept their error as betraying an eagerness to express their ready approval of my translation. I had yet to be elected by the Dean and Chapter and that election had then to receive the Royal Assent. Those things done the way was open for me to take my place in the long procession of Bishops of Carlisle from the twelfth century to the twentieth.

The 'Cathedra'

The rite of Enthronement, delayed for a few months, until such time as I had fulfilled my obligation to do homage to Her Majesty, was memorable for many reasons: as a massive gathering of the diocesan family, as an ecumenical assembly with all parts of the Christian Church represented and as a meeting in the House of God of 'Church and State'. But it was unique too for something which had never happened at any former Enthronement, for the service was televised and broadcast live throughout the north-west of England and the south-west of Scotland. Charles Hales, one of the Diocesan Readers and a friend from my Ambleside days, who had written so sensitively and so superbly about my Consecration in York Minster, was invited to contribute to the *Diocesan News* his impressions of the ceremony in the Cathedral. By entitling his report 'Things Seen and Unseen' he reminded the readers of the scriptural text which I used for my address that day, 2 Corinthians ch. 4, vv. 17 – end, and wrote:

> For an hour or more from three o'clock in the afternoon of April 4th those authorised and privileged to represent the diocese of Carlisle in the great Cathedral Church of the Holy and Undivided Trinity must have been chiefly conscious, among all the thoughts and images crowding their minds, of the dignified splendour of the ritual and ceremonial. For the full realisation of their significance, however, we had to await the Bishop's sermon which firmly led us out from cloistered exaltation back to the streets and to the walks of life where the spiritual must meet and contain the challenge of the temporal: the confrontation, as the Bishop more pointedly put it, of 'the temporal and the eternal in apposition not opposition'.
>
> It would have been easy, indeed pardonable, to surrender to the emotional impact of the great drama; for, like all liturgical use, this *was* a drama – being, in the Aristotelian sense, 'serious, complete and of certain magnitude with a beginning, a middle and an end; in the form of action not of narrative; in style embellished with every kind of artistic ornament'. One may say, if a moment of objective detachment be permitted, that it was the kind of high drama which the Church of England, with centuries of tradition and experience to draw on, manages with a sure touch; and the unfaltering rhythm caught up the rest of us and swept us along, willing, joyful in its majestic flow. It was, in the original sense of a much abused word, thrilling.
>
> 'Artistic ornament' there was but it was integral rather than ornamental. The setting alone would have been more than sufficient. It was no hardship to have to be seated by 2.15 p.m. Rather it was a welcome prelude to the drama: a time when the music of the organ and the architectural splendours of the Choir could be pondered and absorbed; a time for the enraptured eye to wander and not to miss such significance

as the legend over the High Altar – 'Sic Deus dilexit mundum'; a time
for the sense of history to assert itself and to bring all into focus.

The choristers of the Cathedral choir, splendidly enriched by the
Abbey Singers, made their own distinguished and worthy offering
– 'artistic ornament' of a high order, exalted and exalting. It was
gloriously enhanced from time to time in the hymns by drums, now
sounding a discreetly sonorous foundation, now startlingly dramatic (like
the Bishop's three resolute knocks on the South Door that made so
arresting a start to the main action); and by those searing trumpets,
rising to the high vault in golden radiance.

There was colour too when all were assembled. It glowed vividly in
the great east window; it lit up the pattern of sober dress with the richly
embroidered vestments of the Bishop and officiating clergy, and with
the blues and scarlets of the Officers of State.

Yet, amid all those splendours, the sense of a great Family Party
was strong. It animated the informal, relaxed gathering in the Market
Assembly Hall after the ceremony, but it had already asserted itself and
grown in the Cathedral during the Rite. It was the stronger, surely, not
only because of the scope of diocesan representation but also because of
the presence of the representatives of other Christian Communions, a
heart-warming sign of the times that gave a deeper significance to the
refrain of the closing hymn – 'One Church, One Faith, One Lord'.

It remained for the Bishop, after the Enthronement, to give his
message to the diocese. It was delivered with the authority of one
called to be 'Ruler, Teacher, Guardian, Pastor and Steward', and whilst
allowing that our heads were, very properly in those clouds to which
the Rite and Ceremony had raised us, it equally properly planted our
feet firmly on the ground: the condition of our own times with all the
problems and difficulties and challenges which must be met; and the
Bishop made it clear that, in the task to which he must address himself
he needed the vigorous support of all. It was a common task he reminded
us to which with self-abasing reverence we must all apply ourselves. But,
like St. Paul, he assured us we need 'not lose heart, because our eyes are
fixed not on the seen, but on the Unseen'.

No man could be at the centre of so impressive and deeply moving
a ceremony and act of worship without being acutely aware throughout
of the high privilege which was his and the concomitant responsibility
inseparable from it. I recall that as I moved from the Bishop's Throne –
or Cathedra – in the departing procession it occurred to me that the weight
of that responsibility was symbolised by the very weight of the pastoral staff
of the Bishop of Carlisle presented to the See in the time of Bishop Harvey
Goodwin in 1884 when the Church Congress met in the See City. Richly
ornamented with the effigies of local saints, of Carlisle's first Bishop and of
Henry I who founded the See, and engraven as it is with words reminding

the Bishop of his episcopal task – *Corrigendo, Sustenando, Vigilando, Dirigendo* – the Bishop bears with him a constant reminder both of what God can do with and through a dedicated man, with a Ninian, a Kentigern, a Herbert or a Cuthbert, and of what God sets before him as his task – to correct, to sustain, to watch over and to guide the people committed to his charge.

The 'Seal'

A cathedral is so called because it contains the Bishop's *cathedra* – throne or chair – which was ever a most important part of the episcopal insignia as the place from which he exercised his office as ruler and teacher and guardian of his people. It is probable that the first Bishop of Carlisle had his 'seat' hard by the Cathedral but subsequent Bishops had additional or sole 'seats' at Linstock, at Bewley, at Melbourne in Derbyshire (doubtless as a resting place on the frequent journeys fron Carlisle to London), at Penrith and at Horncastle in Lincolnshire. It was Walter, the fourth Bishop of the See (1225–47), who received at the King's hand the Manor of Dalston in which the Manor House had long been known as The Rose. From that date Rose became the accepted seat of the Bishop of Carlisle and as such became something of a target for attack by the King's enemies north of the Border.

Stepping for the first time as Bishop into Rose Castle I was indeed aware of its turbulent past but more so of my predecessors whose spirits were about me – soldier bishops, statesmen bishops, aristocratic bishops, scholar bishops, pastoral bishops – Johns and Roberts and Williams, Richards and Edwards and Rogers, Thomases, Henrys, Samuels and even a Marmaduke – but never a Cyril in 800 years. They were all there in spirit and a few in oil looking down upon me as I mounted the fine oak staircase which was one of the many enrichments of the Castle made by Bishop Hugh Percy during his nineteenth-century episcopate.

Rose Castle has had a long and chequered history. Set on a commanding and strategic site of great beauty, a few miles from Carlisle, and with the lakeland hills as a backcloth, it betrays its defensive origins, and in that role suffered much and often and not only at the hands of the Scots. Stormed by the Parliamentarians in 1648, it was captured by them within two hours of battle and with two Royalist casualties. Thus, for the the first and only time in history it passed out of episcopal hands and it, along with the Manors of Dalston and Linstock, part of the See's heritage, was sold by Cromwell for £4161 12s 10d to one William Heveningham, one of the regicides, who on taking possession set to work to repair some of the damage for which he and his ilk had been responsible. His sojourn was brief however, for when the bleak days of the Commonwealth had ended one 'Richardus, permissione divina, Carliolensis Episcopus' issued in 1663 his sentence of consecration of the Chapel within the Castle which he had been occupying since his own consecration in 1660. From that day through its history the

Castle suffered no further attacks for though the Chartists planned one such during Bishop Percy's Episcopate the advancing mob, doubtless on hearing of adequate arrangements made to meet them with force, contented themselves with vandalising the vicarage and church of Dalston hard by. Thus the Castle as it is today is, as to its exterior, much as Bishop Percy left it in 1856, and I doubt not that he and his predecessors from the seventeenth-century Bishop Edward Rainbow onwards, would not be displeased were they to see how well their several enrichments had been preserved. The full exciting story of the Castle and some of its more colourful occupants are graphically set out in a carefully documented volume entitled *Rose Castle* by Dr. James Wilson, a former Vicar of Dalston and Domestic Chaplain to the Bishop. But I cannot resist inserting into my own story further reference to the home in which I spent such happy years.

The 'Richardus Carliolensis episcopus' whom I have mentioned above was a predecessor for whom I could not but cherish a special affection since he was born in Mansfield and baptised in the Parish Church in which he and his family worshipped regularly. Thus our feet had trodden the same holy ground, our hands had been uplifted to receive the Holy Sacrament from the same Sanctuary; in the spirit we walked in the House of God as friends both in Mansfield Parish Church and in Rose.

Richard Sterne was appointed Bishop at the Restoration and thus faced the task of dealing with the dilapidations at the Castle. Very properly he turned his attention first to the Chapel, for whilst the usurper had made himself comfortable in the Castle, he had done nothing of course towards its restoration as a Bishop's residence. However, within four years Sterne was appointed to the Archbishopric of York – an acknowledgment doubtless of his significant contribution to the Savoy Conference which was recognised even by Richard Baxter, who might be regarded as the leader of the opposition on that occasion, who wrote that 'amongst the Bishops there was none so promising as Dr. Sterne'. No sooner had he been enthroned as Archbishop of York than Edward Rainbow, his successor at Carlisle, indicted him for having done so little to repair the Castle and having done that little so badly. For a bishop to challenge his archbishop in such a manner would offer a veritable field day for our modern media but I doubt not that the great British public would have been quick to point out the massive destruction which Richard Sterne faced as he entered his See, and the brevity of his sojourn at Rose would have been reckoned in mitigation of his seeming failure to leave the property in good repair.

Nevertheless his successor cherished the laudable ambition to restore the Castle to its pristine splendour in stature and dignity but less laudably was determined that his predecessor should foot the bills for doing so. To that end he secured the appointment of a Royal Commission to enquire into the dilapidations dispute. The litigation was protracted and sharp but ever courteous, and although the final judgement was that the Archbishop could not be held responsible for dilapidations to the Castle brought about during 'the late times of Usurpation and Rebellion', his work on the Chapel was dubbed mean in extent and poor in quality and he was in consequence ordered to pay £400 to the Bishop towards its proper repair and restoration. Since the good bishop's litigation costs far exceeded this sum his suit resulted only in his impoverishment. Nevertheless Rainbow had set his heart on rebuilding the Chapel where it had begun its life, i.e. upstairs – and that he did splendidly and to his lasting credit. It was a joy to me that during my tenure of the See a little further splendour was added in colour and in lighting in the shape of lanterns and a seventeenth-century chandelier. Rainbow's financial resources would not extend to the restoration of the ranges of buildings on the east and south sides of the quadrangle which the original castle embraced – I would say fortunately! – but the contribution which he made to the preservation of Rose as the Bishop's seat proved to be so satisfactory that for a couple of hundred years his successors had only to be concerned with alterations within and with running repairs.

In recent years there have been attempts by the Church Commissioners to drive the bishops from their ancient seats and to set them in 'desirable suburban villas' against which no one could level a charge of triumphalism or ask 'Why was this waste of the ointment made?' That the Church should be prepared to make its own contribution to conservation of ancient buildings and should strive to hand on to the future the goodly heritage it has received from the piety of past generations are apparently arguments of little weight. Hypersensitivity about the Church's 'image' on the one hand, and inflation on the other, conspire together to prompt the abandonment of the ancient episcopal residence and the sturdy Victorian vicarage, and the seller's market holds out a glittering temptation which proves too often to be irresistible. It is as though we cash in on the generosity of our forefathers to meet our increasing commitments which a more general acceptance of the principles of Christian stewardship should and could compass with ease.

During my episcopate I received a letter from Lord Silsoe, writing on behalf of the Church Commissioners, to the effect that the disposal of Rose Castle should be considered and that meanwhile it should cease to be known as a Castle. Since my observations were invited I replied in a vein which I gathered subsequently had brought light relief to a meeting of the Commissioners. Deleting the address 'Rose Castle' on my notepaper, and replacing it with 'Windynook', I noted that Cumbria was strewn with Castles in various states of ruin and repair, and severally occupied by the whole range of the animal kingdom, from rats and rabbits to entrepreneurs and earls, so that even if the name 'Rose Castle' emitted whiff of triumphalism to the Commissioners it certainly did no such thing to the Cumbrians. I added that although the Parliamentarians had indeed driven my predecessor of the seventeenth century from his house and home I could assure the Commissioners that if they arrived at the Castle with similar ill-intent they would meet with such strong Cumbrian resistance that they would undoubtedly return to the metropolis with their tails between their legs. I heard no more about the

possible disposal of Rose or of the abandonment of its ancient name, and as
ever I continued to receive from the Commissioners' officers in Millbank the
courtesy and help of which every parish priest and bishop in the land has had
experience. 'The wicked uncles of Millbank' was always a jibe which riled
me since as a parish priest, as an archdeacon and as a diocesan bishop I was
ever conscious of the magnificent service rendered by the Commissioners to
the national Church.

Rose Castle is, of course, by no means merely the private home of the
bishop, nor has it ever been. It is his 'seat', his official residence, embracing
his chapel as the focus for his work of prayer, his study for preparation for
his teaching and preaching, and his offices for the effective discharge of
his administrative responsibilities. Furthermore a bishop has to be 'given to
hospitality' and although I suspect that our predecessors, up to the early years
of this century, extended that only to the aristocracy, the evidence of this
century is wholly otherwise. In this last respect my immediate predecessor,
Thomas Bloomer, was impeded in the first half of his episcopate, since the
Castle, used as an ammunition dump during the Hitler war, was left in an
uninhabitable condition and he was housed in a small house in the city. It was
undoubtedly his persistence which encouraged the Commissioners to repair
and restore the Castle, which they did magnificently. By a modest destruction
of the unwanted and a clever rearrangement of the interior they made of it a
comfortable home and provided within it adequate office accommodation, a
useful committee room, spacious library and study facilities and bedrooms for
guests, at the same time preserving the ceremonial rooms and chapel much as
they had been through the long years of the Castle's history. Thus the Castle
became once more an essential factor in the work of the Bishop and my
predecessor made good use of it to that end. In my years there were frequent
visits of groups of men and women – 'high and low, rich and poor, one with
another' from parishes throughout the diocese, who would be received by
the Bishop or his chaplain and whose visits would conclude with an act of
worship in the chapel and not infrequently with modest refreshment.

Every major committee of the diocese held one of its meetings in the course
of the year at Rose and by this arrangement opportunity for *koinonia* for those
who contributed so richly to the work of the Church was afforded by their
being entertained to luncheon or to tea. There were adult confirmations in
the chapel, pre-ordination gatherings, valedictory retreats for retiring clergy,
entertainment of young Christians from Germany, Norway, Sweden as well
as youth groups within the diocese. Nor was the chapel merely the place
in which day by day the Offices of the Church were recited and prayers
offered for God's blessing on its work and its workers. There too the
Holy Eucharist was celebrated three times every week and residents in the
neighbouring village would on occasion join the bishop and his staff, domestic
and administrative, in its offering. The bishop's private chapel was thus made
public and all who came, clergy and laity alike, were ever welcome. There
were two occasions in the year when the walls of the Castle, impregnated as

they doubtless were with centuries of high flown talk of Church and State, echoed the merry chatter and the screams of delight of children. One such was my annual entertainment of the Cathedral choirboys during Christmas week when, following a turkey dinner, crackers and the like, they displayed their less cherubic qualities in hilarious games in which the bishop, the chaplain and the canons put up with a great deal for their enjoyment, and the Castle ghost was 'pragmatised' for their delight. The second was a Christmas party for the children of the village in which the Castle was 'the big house'. Fifty to sixty from five years old and upwards came and for four hours or so the stately staircase of solid oak was forced to accept treatment the like of which it had never suffered from the sedate steps of those who had used it for the first one hundred and fifty years of its life. It did so without a creak, but maybe it was the vast Christmas tree which rose from the great hall floor to the highest point of that staircase, or perhaps the richly coloured hand-painted Chinese wallpaper of the ceremonial drawing room, or the glass chandeliers, described by one five-year-old subsequently as 'diamonds dripping from the Bishop's ceilings', which registered most impressively in the brief intervals between eating and rollicking. Rose could never have been noisier than during those parties but with young children at play decibels spell delight and do not deny decorum.

The Staff

The diocese of Carlisle, with its 250-plus parishes and half a million people, stretches from the Scottish border a hundred miles to the south and from the Cumbrian coast eighty miles or so eastward and, as Bishop Bloomer was wont to add, 'rises a mile skyward'. My boast that it is on any reckoning the loveliest diocese in the Church of England – a concession indeed from a Devonian could not be gainsaid, for what it offers in natural grandeur in its mountains and fells and lakes and streams is in this country unique. But to see the area of the diocese only as a vast holiday resort with a surfeit of natural beauty is to take a blinkered view. Industry, heavy and light, and farming – sheep, cattle and arable – abound. Hamlets, villages, country towns, holiday resorts and industrial centres afford to the bishop the opportunity of matching the differing gifts of his clergy to the varying needs of his people. None could deny that the terrain to be covered was such that travelling was not invariably easy but I inherited from my predecessor a Cumbrian chauffeur, George Dixon, who knew every nook and cranny of the diocese and who in his fifteen years' service to three bishops of Carlisle won their lasting gratitude as well as the friendship and respect of priests and parishioners throughout the diocese. Living as he did in one of the two cottages attached to the Castle – the other housing Bob McCrone, another honest-to-goodness countryman whose green fingers matched his conscientious work in the grounds – he was ever at hand to deal with any and every crisis demanding a handyman, and as these two faithful servants were married to ladies comparably efficient and willing, domestic help was ever at hand both in and around the Castle. The Bishop's work was thus mightily supported by a loyal and dedicated house staff.

I inherited from my predecessor a 'Cabinet' – I use the term advisedly – of long-standing friends. Lionel du Toit the Dean, alleged by some, and to his amusement, to have many of the stern qualities as well as the Christian name of the Dean in the popular television comedy series *All Gas and Gaiters*, had been an outstanding parish priest before becoming Dean of Carlisle to which office he brought discipline, devotion and dedication as well as a fastidious attention to detail both in his care of the fabric and in his direction of the worship. The archdeacons – Charles Nurse, Richard Hare and Edward Pugh – in whose appointments I had been privileged to have a part, were all highly regarded throughout the diocese, as was James Lister who headed the Church House staff and whose vast knowledge of the parishes and parsonages, garnered over nearly thirty years of service, was of inestimable value to the Bishop. My Chancellor was Hugh Mais and on his appointment as a Judge of the High Court I appointed David Stinson, one of Her Majesty's Judges of County Courts and a prominent churchman in the diocese of St. Edmundsbury and Ipswich, as his successor. Happily neither was at any time caught up in the sort of ecclesiastical wrangle or clerical scandal in which the popular press delights, and apart from a few minor scuffles waged by a militant Baptist against the so-called High Church practices of an amiable parish priest, the diocese of Carlisle rarely provided for the *News of the World* and its like the sort of stories with which the appetites of their readers are titillated.

I cannot but recall that some of the vicious letters which I received from time to time from militant members of the Orange Order, angered by ecumenical gestures which I encouraged 'twixt the Anglican and Roman Churches, might have added to the work of Ian Sutcliffe, the Registrar and Legal Secretary, but written as they clearly were by men whose prejudices were deeply entrenched that they felt impelled to dip their pens in vitriol rather than ink, the missives were assigned to the waste-paper basket rather than passed to the Legal Secretary's office. I must add that Ian Sutcliffe would be the first to acknowledge the debt which he and the diocese owed to his chief clerk, Arthur Butcher, who had by then handled the legal affairs of the diocese for forty-seven years. He had become something of an ecclesiastical silicon chip holding within himself the answers to all questions, legal and quasi-legal, which the bishop or his archdeacons might pose. Arthur's office was as chock-a-block with files as the next and his desk piled high as any lawyer's with papers, ancient and modern, but everything those files embraced was also tucked away in the mind of this human computer and available to the bishop if not at the press of a button certainly at the drop of a mitre.

Thus altogether my predecessor had bequeathed to me a first-rate headquarter's staff and there were but two immediate appointments to make to complete it: a successor to myself as Bishop of Penrith and a Domestic Chaplain in succession to Walter Ewbank who had left that office for a city benefice. For the first of these I nominated to Her Majesty Reginald Foskett, Provost of St. Mary's Cathedral, Edinburgh, and until his appointment to that office a much respected parish priest in the Diocese of Southwell and Derby. He was consecrated in Carlisle Cathedral in 1967 and from then until 1970, when the ill health against which he had been fighting for a long time forced his retirement, his ministry was immensely valuable and greatly appreciated. He was succeeded by Edward Pugh who had proved himself in the office of Archdeacon and whose work I had watched for twenty years since we had been neighbours in Mansfield.

The office of Domestic Chaplain to a bishop is one of high importance. Time was when he was resident and always at the Bishop's right hand, and although a fall in the number of men offering themselves for the sacred ministry called for the sort of reassessment in deployment which suggested that a bishop could not expect to have a full-time chaplain, the position at Carlisle was such that the office could be linked with the incumbency of the tiny village of Raughtonhead hard by the Castle, and that to the satisfaction of bishop and parishioners. For my part I sought for this office a priest of many parts: a man of sensitive spirituality who would share with me in the discipline of the daily ministry of prayer for the Church, its work and its workers and in the regular offering of the Eucharist; a man whose intellectual ability was such that he could research intelligently on my behalf and examine the avalanche of papers which threaten to engulf every bishop – summarising the essential and liquidising the 'bumph'; a man who could keep his eyes and ears open that the bishop might not be unaware of any particular pastoral need among his clergy; and a man who, with all these qualities, would bring to the scene what the author of *Erewhon* described as 'a sense of humour keen enough to show a man his own absurdities as well as those of other people, but kind enough for everyone to enjoy'. I found these qualities in full measure in Burnham Hodgson whom I extracted from a country parish and who was with me throughout my tenure of the See. He and Carolyn Fisher, the secretary *par excellence*, together ensured the efficient and smooth running of the administrative aspect of the Bishop's work and brought to it the liveliness and expedition which befitted 'the King's business'. Burnham Hodgson's subsequent appointment by my successor as Archdeacon of West Cumberland was so natural a progression that it evoked no ripple of surprise either in my mind or among the clergy and laity of the diocese.

Inevitably there were other changes in the diocesan hierarchy in the course of my incumbency and these enabled me to bring in Walter Ewbank as Archdeacon of Westmorland and Furness in succession to Richard Hare who after twelve years of distinguished service in the diocese left for the suffragan See of Pontefract. Bill Hardie, whom I filched from the Wakefield diocese as a *quid pro quo* became Archdeacon of West Cumberland. Richard Bradford, who followed his twenty-four years as a parish priest in the diocese with sterling service as a residentiary canon and as Archdeacon of Carlisle, was invaluable in piercing the cackle of committees and councils to pin-point essentials.

No diocese could have been more fortunate in its lay headquarters staff – voluntary and otherwise. Eric Storey and Peter Bailey proved to be worthy successors to James Lister as secretaries, respectively, of the Diocesan Board of Finance and the Parsonages Board. And in the field of Christian Stewardship Harry Cameron succeeded Banks Wivell in the pioneer work which had established that particular aspect of mission in parishes bold enough to dare something new in Christian enterprise. Nor did the diocese lack laymen and women prepared to give of their time and talent in the service of the Church. George Inglis, John Ainley and Gurney McInnes – each distinguished in his own field of service, military, judicial and educational – brought to the chairmanship of the Board of Finance knowledge, wisdom and experience, and countless others served faithfully on boards, committees and councils. Since a bishop has to rely so much upon so many lay-people in his diocese for the proper functioning of the Church's work my story would not be complete without mentioning many such by name but there are many hundreds of others whose contributions to the functioning of the Church as an institution must never be forgotten.

On 8 November each year the Church of England remembers its 'Saints, Martyrs, Missionaries and Doctors' departed this life. Certainly within that ambit there will be many members of the clergy and of the religious orders. But any and every bishop, viewing his diocese as it were from the pinnacle, could bear witness to a vast number of lay people in the parishes who give generously, even recklessly, of their time and abilities to assist the parish priest in the cure of souls – and all this for love of God and His Church. Trained readers, churchwardens, councillors, treasurers, secretaries, organists, choristers, servers, vergers, cleaners, bellringers, Sunday School teachers, youth workers, group leaders, magazine distributors, sidesmen – none would imagine that his total responsibility for Christian service as a member of the Church is exhausted by his bit of 'church work' but each must know that what is freely given is richly blessed and each must hear the Church which in God's Name says 'please' say in God's Name too, 'Well done, good and faithful servant'. Thus I cannot forbear to pay this tribute to the thousands whose names will never be recorded but without whose voluntary service the Church's work would be gravely impeded and in some aspects brought to a halt. I find myself frequently wondering why the authors of our revised liturgy reserve to the priest the recital of those impelling words: 'We are the Body of Christ . . . '. That moment in the liturgy could surely be a thunderous reaffirmation by the whole congregation both of our unity in Christ and of each member's responsibility to recognise and discharge his own contribution to the effective mission of the Mystical Body of Christ in the world, and that through his own parish and parish church. The concept of the *laos* in the New Testament is certainly not exhausted by the 'serving of tables', as is clearly demonstrated in our modern liturgies and in the greater readiness of lay people to engage in mission and witness. But the 'serving of tables' – the administration, the money raising, the planning, the ordering of worship musically, the bellringing, etc. –

must never be despised. Even the man who did no more than lend his donkey and her foal to Our Lord has his honoured place in the Gospel story.

The *impedimenta*

The word with its military associations connotes necessary baggage which nevertheless retards progress. As a diocesan bishop I discovered much such.

The bishop's diocese is the area over which he has jurisdiction and in which his work of '*corrigeado, sustenando, vigilando* and *dirigendo*' is to be discharged. I was soon to discover what I used to think of as a conspiracy to prevent my doing it. There were invitations to lead pilgrimages to the Holy Land for the privileged who could afford that sort of thing as well as other alluring enticements to wander abroad – the latter to be hidden behind the blessed word 'Sabbatical' – all of which I eschewed whilst harbouring a secret hope that they might be repeated in retirement. But there were, too, obligatory withdrawals from the diocese. Clearly the diocesan bishop must from time to time meet and confer with his brother bishops and all must play their part in the Councils of the Church. The claims of the diocese upon his time must, however, be paramount and I confess that I came to regard the constantly recurring mandates withdrawing me from it for Synods, Convocations and Bishops' Meetings as unwelcome intrusions upon time which properly belonged to the particular task which had been assigned to me. They were *impedimenta* indeed but need they have been so heavy? Attendance at the bodies could consume all but two months of every year and never could I put my hand on my heart and say that they were invariably time well spent. The greediest consumer of time, and the one which was not invariably 'necessary', was undoubtedly the Church Assembly and its august successor the General Synod which for its frequency, prolixity and garrulity was ever a severe trial to me. But alas! Synodical Government has gone to the Church of England's head and as conducted at present is prodigal in the use of time, money and paper. The painful truth is that so long as the present palpably absurd practice of dragging 43 bishops and 500 clergy and laity to London three times a year, each armed with reports dealing with innumerable commissions, committees and councils together weighing a couple of pounds avoirdupois, so long will there be those who will ensure that time so dearly purchased is filled with tedious speeches which frequently do little more than assert the obvious about issues which could be resolved so much more speedily and happily in a much smaller body. As I sat through hour after hour and day after day of ponderous speeches about motions light and heavy, I found myself reflecting from time to time how much better employed bishops could have been in their dioceses and clergy in their parishes. Occasionally an even more disturbing thought assailed me – that in some mad moment, tormented by the spectre of an ever-lengthening string of motions before it, the Synod might decide to meet four times a year, nay five! instead of three, and that even then there would never be lacking more and more tedious effusions to fill the dreary hours. I reached the conclusion long since that for all but the incredulous, one session of the General Synod of the Church of England would be sufficient to certify the validity of Parkinson's Law.

But must it ever be so? Other provinces of the Anglican Communion manage to conduct their affairs tolerably well with annual meetings of their General Synods, as does the Church of Scotland with its General Assembly. A change along these lines by the Church of England could invest its Synod with a significance comparable with that enjoyed by the Scottish National Church and might at the same time ensure for it a really representative House of laity which at present it so manifestly lacks. Such a reform could restore to the Convocations their proper role within the Councils of the Church, for it is to them that we should be able to look for clear guidance on those great moral and social issues of the day which appear to throw the General Synod into such confusion. The Convocations for their part would be better equipped for this aspect of their work if, in our theological colleges, Moral Theology became once more the highly esteemed study which it was in the seventeenth century. Truly the problems that confront our generation are very different from those with which William Perkins, Jeremy Taylor and others grappled, but the context in which they worked is for us what it was for them – a revealed religion. The General Synod attempts too much; it must decrease. The Convocations have been devalued; they must increase. The closer association of each with its diocesan Synods could provide the necessary channel for grass-roots opinion to be considered and assessed by the Bishops and Proctors. The diocesan synods could 'stir', the Convocations could 'sift' and evaluate, sending to the annual, and I would hope, smaller General Synod only such issues and motions as in their judgement would be better served by exposition and debate within such a national but not wholly 'professional' body. I doubt not that hands of horror will be uplifted that anything so sacred as synodical government should be tampered with but clearly something has gone tragically awry. Could it be that some have begun to think of the Church as a democracy?

There was, however, one potential interference with pastoral concern which I was mercifully spared. I received no mandate to take a seat in the House of Lords and that for the simple reason that during my tenure of the See there was insufficient movement within the Bench of Bishops, either by death or retirement, to bring me into line with any resulting vacancy, since each is filled not by seniority of consecration but by seniority of appointment to a diocese. I pondered occasionally on the sort of 'I-pray-thee-have-me-excused' letter which I might have submitted to the Lord Chancellor had the fate befallen me and equally whether I should have been allowed to get away with it. This betrays no denial of the desirability of an Upper House nor of the need for the Church to be formally represented in it. It is rather an expression of a view which I have long held that there is neither need nor justification for so many of the bishops to be absenting themselves from their dioceses from time to time for attendance in the House of Lords.

But I believe too that whilst abolition of that Chamber would be a grave blow to democracy, retention in its present form is a monstrous anachronism in which the surfeit of spiritual peers is but a small factor. Few people realise that there are 1178 peers in the House of Lords. If all of them clocked into the Chamber on a single day that day would cost the taxpayers £42,308! In my judgement the first step in necessary reform would be to cease to regard the mere possession of a barony as conferring a right of admission to the Upper House. The Second Chamber does not need to be nearly twice the size of the House of Commons as at present and a membership of more modest dimensions could be built up in a rational manner which would command greater credibility. It should be a 'Ministry of all the Talents', performing a function not radically different from that being provided by the present House but benefiting from the wisdom and experience of people from many walks of life. I should want to see in it 'elder Statesmen' from the worlds of education and the arts, of medicine and law, of industry, commerce and agriculture and of journalism and broadcasting. I would hope that none of these would be chosen to represent a party line and it follows that I should not regard the House of Commons as the only or even the most appropriate 'prep school' for the second Chamber. Certainly the Church should be represented in it, and ecumenically, with the Primates and three senior bishops joined by the Cardinal Archbishop of Westminster, the Moderator of the General Assembly of the Church of Scotland and the Chairman of the Free Church Federal Council. Einstein's dictum that 'Science without Religion is blind' can be nowhere more true than in the area of political science!

For myself I was content to be spared membership of the House of Lords reflecting that it is one thing for the Bishops of London and Southwark for example, to pop into the House for an hour or so and within minutes to be back on the job, and quite another for the Bishops of Carlisle, Truro and Newcastle, for example, to do any such thing without serious inroads into time needed for the discharge of their primary responsibilities. Had my conscientious objection to membership of the House of Lords been over-ruled I should hardly have pressed it to the point of risking incarceration in the Tower for contumacy! The further *impedimenta* would have been taken aboard without serious intent an attitude which is by no means unknown to a great many members of the present House of Lords, Bishops among them, to whom the House is little more than a convenient London club. Meanwhile in a whimsical mood and with all the *impedimenta* in mind I framed a new petition for the Litany: 'From a surfeit of synods and all seductive stratagems which segregate the chief shepherd from his sheep, Good Lord deliver us'!

12

Round and About the Diocese

If it were true that the General Synod was seen by me as something of a cross to be borne – and I should affirm that notwithstanding my reluctance I attended its sessions regularly, minimising my days of absence from the diocese by travelling to and from the metropolis by night – the work in the diocese was pure joy. It was exhilarating, satisfying and rewarding. As my episcopate opened I turned first with eager expectation to the parochial clergy, known to me already of course but from thence forward a band of men who must share with me the Cure of souls and with whom therefore there must be established a very special and intimate relationship. The sustenance and deepening of that relationship was secured from the outset by regular remembrance of them and their families in prayer. Their names and needs were ever before me in the Chapel and indeed in the car since I spent so much time in it, and in this way and by frequent contact with them in person and by letter there was established a mutual confidence and, I dare say, regard. I initiated *Ad Clerum* a regular letter by means of which I could take them into my confidence about current needs and problems, and from time to time make suggestions by which our common task might be pursued more effectively. My hope was always that this would underline my conviction that I needed their co-operation to fulfil my office and that I was always available to help them in the fulfilment of theirs. Not all my hopes were realised but there was certainly sufficient response to make the letters worthwhile, and their confidential nature provided an opportunity for saying things which were 'for the family only'. It is, after all, by the active assent of the bishop, and not by any decision of a selection board, that a man is ordained, and as the final judgement of a man's fitness for the sacred ministry is his, so too is the responsibility for overseeing it, guiding it and nurturing it. I myself had been a parish priest for a quarter of a century and I knew both from personal experience as such, and from having had charge of a rural deanery in which there were thirty clergy, that the sacred office is one in which a man can find himself now on a 'Mount of Transfiguration' now in a 'Garden of Gethsemane'. There can be moments of elation and dejection, of ecstasy and depression, of achievement and failure, of fulfilment and disappointment. I knew by then that what a priest most needed from his bishop was not the constant interference with his ministry which betrays a lack of confidence commonly described as 'breathing down my neck' – but the pastoral concern which expresses itself in a lively interest in his work, which tempers criticism with understanding and counsel, which gives the timely word of praise, or encouragement, of sympathy and appreciation, and fears not to exhibit a continuing love for him and his family. That was ever my aim. By visiting the clergy in their homes and in their chapters, by accepting their invitations to be with them for special occasions of thanksgiving, for the blessing of new enterprises in Christian mission and Christian stewardship, and by a readiness to spend time in their vicarages with their families, I tried to be what I conceive the bishop has to be, first and foremost, namely the *pastor pastorurm*.

The Parish and the Parish Priest

Among the greatest of the many opportunities afforded to the bishop for enriching the relationship between himself and his people are the ceremonies concerned with the Institution of a new parish priest when invariably the whole parish turns out to be present at the act of worship into which the actual Institution is woven. The service is one which calls together all the faithful and the not-so-faithful who are nevertheless anxious to see the new man in the vicarage. My colleagues and I revised its form in such a way as to impress upon the congregation that the ministry beginning called for a new start for them as well as for the priest about to begin his work among them. In the course of the service the bishop hands to the new incumbent his Deed of Institution with the words 'Receive the Cure of souls which is both mine and thine'. The parish priest thus becomes the key man and without him in that place the bishop is impotent. Twelve months before I became a bishop Russell Barry wrote his *Vocation and Ministry*. With characteristic forthrightness he exalted the parochial system and the office of parish priest when both seemed to be imperilled by the apostles of what he called 'the stratification of society along functional and occupational lines'. He wrote:

> To scrap the parish would, in my judgement, be a fatally retrograde step, not only on grounds of sentiment and tradition but also on solid grounds of theology . . . With the parish church goes the parish priest . . . He is the key man to the whole situation. His personal leadership is indispensable. However keen and devoted the laity, nothing much will happen without the vicar. If one conviction more than another has been forced upon me in sixteen years of trying to learn how to be a bishop, it is that the parish priest is the man who matters and on whom

nearly everything depends. When there is the right man in the vicarage there is not much that the bishop need do; when there is not . . . there is little and almost nothing that he can do.

Russell Barry was given to hyperbole in making his points – never more so than in the shafts of brilliant wit which his intimates enjoyed! – but if, as one of his episcopal 'sons', I might take gentle issue with his seeming suggestion that a first-rate parish priest makes the bishop all but redundant, I would go with him all the way and certainly affirm that the incumbent who falls down on his Cure thwarts the bishop's task immeasurably. Happily in my experience, the parish priest who is a total failure is a very rare bird indeed though he is invariably the one whom the investigative journalist seizes for interview and whom he then portrays as typical of the malaise of which he seems so anxious to indict the Church. Clergy are mortals who have put their hands and hearts and minds to a high and holy task of incalculable difficulty. They are not immune from the weaknesses of the flesh and it cannot but be that here and there there will be those whose 'lamps have gone out' – the dispirited, the despairing and the disillusioned. There will too be the odd priest who, frustrated and disappointed possibly at being passed over for the appointment for which he deemed himself to be eminently qualified, becomes cynical and contentious – a burden to his Church and a heartache to his bishop. But it is the very rarity of these which gives them prominence in the eyes of a critical world. It was ever so. The Apostle Paul would scarcely have mentioned that a certain Alexander who did him 'much evil' and against whose machinations he goes out of his way to warn his son Timothy, had there been dozens more such 'Alexanders' about him. Alexander was 'news' because he was 'singular'! Looking back across my years as a bishop, and remembering that one clerical star must of necessity differ from another clerical star in glory – in dedication, in spirituality, in commitment, in initiative, drive and enterprise – I can say that I should need but one hand on which to count the clerical 'Demases' and 'Alexanders' (*vide* 2 Timothy ch. 4). The parish priests with whom I had to deal were for the most part a fine body of dedicated men – hard-working, enterprising, resilient and steadfast, men who knew themselves to be messengers, watchmen and stewards of the Lord, and who to that end strove to be found faithful. I believe that to be the overall picture of the parochial clergy of the Church of England.

But alas! their numbers have diminished alarmingly and whilst that is no cause for despair it is not a situation about which the bishops in particular can be complacent. The supply of fit persons for the ministry rests heavily upon them; they may share the task of seeking out and training, but the ultimate choice is theirs. None can know better than they how limitless are the opportunities for effective ministry open to the resident parish priest, and how seriously those opportunities are limited by the decline in the numbers in the full-time parochial ministry. When in the thirties we began to look at certain minuscule parishes where populations of a couple of hundred were being ministered to by a full-time incumbent, it was to ensure that every priest had a man-sized job that we joined the minuscule parish with its more populous neighbour. At a later stage the shortage of money and ministerial man-power began to dictate further unions until now, when we appear to have reached a situation in which we find three, four or five parishes under one incumbent.

I submit that his has gone as far as it can without changing the character of the Church of England. Bishops must resist the easy acceptance of the situation by those who predict with seeming satisfaction that the Church's annual intake of men for the full-time parochial ministry will drop to 250 in this decade. The anonymous editor of the preface in the current issue of *Crockford's Clerical Directory* seems to reflect this complacency. He is certainly right when he says 'that need not be the end of the Church', but I suggest that such a crisis of staffing unresolved could well mean the end of the Church of England as we know it. The Church which from the dawn of our history has proudly claimed and accepted responsibility for the pastoral care of the people of England cannot abandon the parochial system for the 'congregational'. That would be abdication. Its concern is now, and must ever be – the pastoral care not merely of those who seek it out and worship regularly in its parish churches, but of that greater number too who must be sought out, shepherded, cared for, reclaimed for Christ, and by God's grace brought within the fellowship of His church. An influx of non-stipendiary priests and a more lively involvement of the laity must certainly be welcomed, but whilst these can augment the ministry of the parochial clergy they cannot in the end be substitutes for it. In the urgent need for more full-time clergy no voice has been more compelling in recent years than that of Archbishop Donald Coggan. I could wish that there were more evident signs that his timely call was being heeded.

In our Diocese of Carlisle we tried, by my preserving a continuing personal interest in seeking out promising young men for the ministry through the parishes and schools as well as by the work in our pre-Theological College at Greystoke where we catered for older men from far and near, to ensure a continuing supply of parochial clergy. From the Greystoke work alone there are now eighty men serving in the ministry of the Church at home and overseas, and a great number of the lads who were wont to attend our annual enquiry conferences subsequently offered themselves. We tried too to keep abreast with stipend levels, pitiful though those levels were. I recall that at my last meeting of the Diocesan Board of Finance in 1972 I moved, to the surprise of many, that we should increase the stipend of an assistant curate to £1000 a year plus a free house or an allowance for lodgings. In those days that was regarded as revolutionary; even so it was accepted by the laity on the Board who were ever ready to improve the material lot of the clergy. Two other interests of mine on behalf of the parish clergy were the creation of a fund by which they and their families could be given an annual holiday and, further, the acquirement of small houses or bungalows in different parts of the diocese for the use of retired clergy. The latter interest evinced the quip from one parish priest that 'the Bishop's hobby is saving bungalows'.

The holiday fund was initiated by a surprise gift of generous dimensions which came to me from a winner of an 'ERNIE' prize who suggested on sending it to me that he would not be offended if I refused it as ill-gotten gains. I replied that had he invested his money in the purchase of a sow he might have had a return of two little pigs, or eight, or 'what-have-you', and might then, out of the goodness of his heart, have sent one to his bishop for his deep-freeze. I should have accepted such a gift with gratitude and alacrity. Since, however, he had invested his money in a bond rather than a sow and this had yielded a 'litter' which was beyond his immediate needs I could accept his gift happily and would use it to create a holiday fund for impecunious clergy. Such was his delight that he sent me further gifts for the same purpose from time to time. Thus annually I took the tenancy of several small houses in Wales, in Galloway and other parts of Scotland and these were used throughout the summer by clergy who could not otherwise have afforded a break. By writing and speaking about the plight of retiring clergy who had not the means of finding anywhere to live I was able to encourage gifts and bequests of small properties and these, together with provision made by the Church of England Pensions Board – provision which has increased considerably in recent years – proved to be a great help to men who having borne the burden and heat of the day were able to settle happily into a home in which they could spend the rest of their lives without undue anxiety. Fortunately these houses were in areas in which a retired priest could count on opportunities arising for a continuing Sunday ministry so long as health and strength permitted.

Confirmations

One of the frequently recurring duties of every bishop is to administer the Sacrament of Confirmation. In this I followed the practice of my immediate predecessor in resisting the idea of gathering confirmands together in great numbers in some so-called central church. This method deprives the smaller parishes of the opportunity of something in the nature of a revision lesson for the parishioners which presence at a Confirmation provides. Furthermore it prevents the confirmands themselves from bearing their witness within the congregation in which they are or should be known. Since the members of that congregation should be those who applaud the young Christians in their progress, and accept a measure of responsibility for encouraging them in it, it is clearly desirable that they should be witnesses of their Confirmation. Thus in the diocese of Carlisle my suffragan and I administered the Sacrament about 110 to 120 times a year in parishes great and small, and no parish priest was ever denied a request for a Confirmation in his own parish church. After twenty-one years as a bishop I have passed my thousandth Confirmation. I can look back with joy upon great and moving occasions in my Cathedral and my Chapel at Rose Castle, in parish churches throughout Cumbria, and in Oxfordshire, Berkshire and Wiltshire, in military establishments from Hadrian's Camp for Army Apprentices to the Royal Military Academy at Sandhurst, in school and university college chapels, in prisons and hospitals, in sick rooms and old people's homes – sometimes for a single person, sometimes for a handful, sometimes for a hundred or so.

I can say, humbly and sincerely, that constant repetition of the Rite has not in any way diminished it for me. Its sacramental character and deep significance, for the individuals concerned and for the Church as a whole, have combined to invest both the Laying on of Hands, and the opportunity to speak to young people and others at so decisive a moment in their lives, with a profound solemnity. Thus though I am fully aware of the wastage from the Church of many who have been confirmed, and grieve for it, I have no patience with the cynical layman – and less with the cynical priest – who speaks of Confirmation disparagingly as a 'church-leaving certificate'. If the grace of the Sacrament is dimmed or thwarted, the fault lies not in the sacrament itself but in us – in inadequate preparation for its reception maybe, in failure to 'follow through', in meagre pastoral care, in lack of parental support. Certainly the Sacrament of Confirmation – whether the word is taken to mean 'strengthening' or 'completing' seems to me to be academic – is the Sacrament of the Holy Spirit conferred in the laying on of hands with prayer, and bestowing upon the confirmand that same *dynamis* with which He invested the Apostles at the first Pentecost. The *dynamis* or power abides ever as a potential; the Sacrament is not merely the perfection of baptismal initiation but also the sacrament of power and fortitude for those who go out into the world with the words 'I turn to Christ' on their lips and in their minds and hearts. Let no one – bishop, priest or layman – ever say a word which can be seized upon and interpreted by a critical world as diminishing Confirmation!

Having said as much I must confess that I thought that the Rite as administered in our Church was gravely impoverished when the prayer 'Defend O Lord this thy servant N with thy heavenly grace that he may continue thine for ever . . . ', once said over every confirmand, was reduced to the ten-word prayer 'Confirm O Lord thy servant N with thy Holy Spirit'. The change was an impoverishment since the person receiving the Laying on of Hands was henceforth no sooner on his knees in front of the bishop than he was off them again returning to his pew. However, the Series 3 Confirmation Rite offers something which, if embraced understandingly, enhances the dignity of the administration and at the same time enriches its significance. I refer to the act of consignation, the anointing of the forehead of the confirmand with the sign of the Cross, a ceremony which reaches back to the third century. This simple but impressive act, added to the laying of hands with some such words as 'The seal of Christ unto eternal life' looks back, as it were, to Holy Baptism when we were born in the Spirit and subsequently signed with the Cross, and forward to the life which, led by the Spirit, must be lived for ever under the sign of the Cross.

Though most of those who present themselves for Confirmation are young people whose ages range from 10 to 18 – and I do not believe that there is any 'right' age – in recent years an increasing number of adults have been coming forward. Whilst most are happy to be confirmed alongside the young folk it was my custom to arrange at least two 'adults only' Confirmations annually, generally in the Chapel at Rose Castle for people living in the north of the diocese and in Rydal Parish Church for those in the south. Confirmations were for me great and happy occasions and both in the service itself and in the gathering of candidates, parents, godparents and friends in the parish hall afterwards, there was a rich opportunity for the whole family of God in the parish to meet together in fellowship with their bishop.

Among the Young

The schools of the diocese with which Miss Veronica Medd, who served the diocese very ably in its educational team for nearly a quarter of a century, kept in close touch, were visited by my suffragan and myself from time to time. Each of us undertook twelve such visits every year arranging with the head teachers to spend a whole morning, occasionally a whole day, with the children class by class. These visits were appreciated by the teachers and entered into with zest by the youngsters as witness the illustrated letters which frequently reached me following a school visit. St. Johns-in-the-Vale Youth centre, watched over by Geoffrey Darrall and his wife, and Rydal Hall, also afforded opportunities for the Church's work amongst young people. The grounds of the latter were strewn every summer with scouts from throughout the United Kingdom, camping under the wing of the Church and meeting for worship in the little Rydal Church which they filled to overflowing. I recall one particularly memorable visit I paid to the camps when I stumbled across two Irish troops whose boys' ages ranged from 12 to 16 – both from Northern Ireland, one from a Roman Catholic parish, one from an Anglican. They were camping side-by-side in perfect amity, intermingling to such an extent that the two scoutmasters averred that the two troops were in and out of each other's territory throughout the day, playing together and eating together with happy abandon. In the hearts and eyes of children neither creed nor colour separates one from another. I left them as they settled around their common camp fire and came away asking myself: 'Who sows the seed of hatred which creates division where once there was none?'

School speech days provided another episcopal hazard which I was happy to risk, and which I greatly enjoyed once I discovered that five minutes light-hearted bantering evoking peals of laughter could purchase ten very valuable minutes of rapt attention for speaking of the things which concern the noblest recipe for growing up. I use the word 'hazard' deliberately for I cannot forget the occasion when one such visit was followed by a report in a national paper that the Bishop of Carlisle had refused to present their prizes to certain girls at a Grammar School because he judged their miniskirts to be too short.

The picture which the report conjured up in my mind of bishops gambolling around their dioceses armed with tape-measures to check the lenth of young ladies' skirts and young gentlemen's hair was nothing if not evocative, but as the Head Boy of the school, in his thank-you speech, had referred to me as a 'swinging Bishop', doubtless because on that occasion I took as my 'text' the lyric of the current top of the pops, the charge against me might have been regarded as 'out of character'. In fact what happened was that the senior mistress, welcoming a couple of 'old girls' back to the school to receive prizes awarded to them in respect of their last year's work, deemed them to be inappropriately dressed to confront a bishop on so auspicious an occasion.

The reporter who rang me about the incident determined to preserve some part of his titillating story, posed the direct question: 'What would you have done bishop, had the girls come to the platform in their mini-skirts?' By replying that I should have given them their prizes and enjoyed the experience immensely I 'won' the girls and 'lost' the senior mistress. There are certain situations in which even a bishop is denied total victory.

Young people were being looked upon with great suspicion just then, more for their dress and the length of their hair than for their behaviour and when, following the miniskirt incident, I heard of a young lad actually being held back from Confirmation because his hair was too long, I judged that a few words about the Church's responsibility for young people and its need of them for its witness and work might not be amiss in my address at an impending Diocesan Conference. One sentence which caught the eye of the cartoonist of the *Cumberland Journal* declared that 'the Church of today needs the youth of today with all their bubbling enthusiasm, their awkward questions, their miniskirts, mod gear and discs'. I had, as it were, unwittingly thrown myself on to his drawing board.

The Written Word

Because a bishop must make himself available to all and sundry for counsel and because mine was a far-flung diocese with its two most populous centres, the city of Carlisle and the then County Borough of Barrow-in-Furness being 90 miles apart, I published each month a diary of my public engagements so that clergy and laity alike would know where in the diocese they might be able to catch up with me. Looking at those diaries now I find myself wondering how I survived their stern demands: Confirmations, Institutions, meetings, preachments, school visits, lectures, after-dinner speeches are among the public engagements some of which involved my getting home not long before midnight. Add to these the administration, the staff meetings, the sermon preparation, the interviews which consumed the hours at the Castle – and you have the recipe for the happiness and fulfilment which was mine, and which will tell the layfolk how a bishop fills his time. There was one task which was always reserved for the night hours when the telephone had ceased, the staff had left, and I sat alone in the Castle's spacious study.

That task was the preparation of the Bishop's Comments in the monthly *Diocesan News* which not only went into fifty thousand homes throughout what is now Cumbria, but was always eagerly awaited by the press and which, in some strange way, found its way to distant places overseas as was proven by letters touching its contents which reached me at different times from Australia, New Zealand, South Africa, Canada, Uganda and Nigeria. It was a piece of work which I enjoyed immensely and always regarded as worthwhile following as it did my conviction, expressed earlier in this story, of the importance of the written word in the proclamation of the Gospel and in its considered application to personal and social problems. Perusing those copies of the *Diocesan News* I recall the long night hours I spent in researching and writing those articles. Worship, Apartheid, Marxist Communism, Prayer, Religion and Science, Euthanasia, Evangelism, Secular Humanism, Christian Stewardship, Drugs, the Church's weaknesses, The Use of Leisure, Education, Strikes, Meditation, Transplant Surgery, The Cross and its Message, Life and Death, Churchgoing, – are some of the captions which hit the eye as I flip through the pages now. Writing against a deadline about subjects which demanded more than cursory treatment was never particularly easy when one was trying to examine some of the most intractable personal and social problems of the hour through Christian spectacles and to express one's thoughts in words which could be of help to the greatest number. Extracts from the articles frequently appeared in the national and local press and on occasions in such surprising places as the *Rand Daily Mail*, the Salvation Army's *Bandmaster*, the *Journal of the Inspectors of Taxes* and Mrs. Mary Whitehouse's *Viewer and Listener* which published an article of mine and attributed it to Dr. Bloomer. Such reports could not but invite correspondence, some laudatory, some otherwise, for no one who ventures to write about such things as Apartheid, Marxist Communism, or even Christian Unity can avoid getting some kicks as well as ha'pence. To receive the former graciously and to pursue your offended correspondent courteously can result in winning him over and I recall one such victory crisply expressed on a postcard which read: 'Thank you bishop very much. I'll say no more. You have converted me.' One's correspondents were not invariably so courteous or so easily converted. The anonymous letter was always consumed and consigned to a necessarily ample waste-paper basket though I remember with a naughty delight an occasion in my parish priest days when I was able to write a letter beginning 'Dear Miss P——, Thank you for your anonymous letter'. A tell-tale typewriter had given her away!

Great Occasions

It is, of course, the singular experiences which come to mind most readily as one reflects upon the past, though the special mention of them in no way demeans the continuing day-by-day work which fills a bishop's life. Among the highlights were the biennial Penrith Training Conferences when with the aid of eminent speakers from the worlds of Theology, Industry, Commerce and Politics we tried to apply the principles of our Faith to the intractable problems which beset us in the industrial and social scenes. There were the residential Clergy Schools at Blackpool and Swanwick when all of us were refreshed by being 'all together with one accord in one place' and helped by eminent theologians and experts in pastoralia. There were the great missionary gatherings held in several centres of the diocese addressed by Bishop Trevor Huddleston, all attended by huge crowds and each turning into a lively press conference in which questions rained upon the bishop from every quarter of the halls in which they were held. There were Royal visits in different parts of the diocese and, at the time of the 1968 Lambeth Conference, visits by bishops from the Anglican Communion overseas with a memorable diocesan gathering on the lawn of Rose Castle on a day so warm that even the African bishops described it as 'comfortable'. There was the 'African Day' when, in a vast marquee on the lawn at the Castle, we held a sale of goods which in the course of the previous month had been dropped into the Bishop's car on its travels around the diocese – a sale which helped us to go to the aid of the Church in Nigeria which had suffered so badly in the civil war. There was a visit of Christian students from Germany who filled the drawing room at Rose Castle and who for two hours examined and cross-examined me with hard questions. The questions (and their answers) were translated into English, swiftly and apparently faultlessly, by one of my ordinands, Richard Hill, now Vicar of Walney. I recall but one of the questions, posed by the German student with a smile and translated by my interpreter with a twinkle in his eye. It was, 'As it appears that Episcopacy is the stumbling block to reunion of the churches in your country, ought the Church of England to consider giving it up?' It was the only question for the answering of which I needed no help from my interpreter for, meagre though my knowledge of German was, it did include the word 'Nein' – and the answer was warmly applauded.

Meeting people, greeting people, talking with people, counselling people – all these are essential elements of the bishop's ministry, as indeed is the ministry of touch – the handshake, the blessing, the laying on of hands, the anointing, even the affectionate embrace of the little child. But they must be people from every stratum of society. Acceptance of an invitation to visit the Solway Colliery at Workington, to spend some time with miners underground – indeed in that instance under the sea-bed! – and to have a snack with them in their canteen, was no less important than, for example, being the guest of honour and chief speaker at the Bankers' Institute Annual Dinner. A day at the Garlands Psychiatric Hospital mingling with patients was as significant a sphere of ministry as another with Medical Officers of Health, Psychiatrists and Social Workers spelling out, at their invitation, the spiritual dimension of their work. The preachment to thirty or forty village folk in a remote country church presents an opportunity for *kerygma* to be no less esteemed than that afforded by the great congregation gathered for some special service in the Cathedral. The workers in the Atomic Energy station at Windscale or in the shipyards at Barrow were as much within the bishop's pastorate as the children in the schools and students in the Teachers' Training Colleges at Ambleside and at St. Martin's, Lancaster. (The latter institution is in fact in the diocese of Blackburn but situated where it is and being what it is – a new Anglican foundation – both dioceses helped to sustain the pastorate within it and in my years of membership of its Governing Body I saw it grow rapidly under the inspired leadership of the irrepressible Dr. Hugh Pollard its first Principal, who for his importunity got all that he needed for the extension of its buildings and the rapid growth of its student body.) All these recurring opportunities, touching as they do different aspects of the bishop's work, furnish a variety which enables him to take a fourteen-hour-day in his stride.

No reference to diaries is needed however to recall the 'once only' experiences which create a deep and lasting impression. One such was my unadvertised and unreported meeting by the side of Coniston Water with the mother and widow of Donald Campbell who on 4 January 1967 met his death there in his attempt to break his own water speed record of 260.35 m.p.h. in his turbo-jet hydroplane Bluebird. There, near the spot where the tragic accident happened, privately and in a quietness broken only by the lapping of the waters at the lake's edge, the Vicar of Coniston (John Hancock) and I conducted what must have been the shortest and simplest burial service ever given to a world-renowned sportsman. Committing his body to the waters we commended his soul to the gracious keeping of his Creator, and in the solemn silence and stillness we could not but be conscious of the presence of the Living God unutterably near.

In striking contrast I recall an occasion in St. Cuthbert's Church, Carlisle when a great assembly covered every inch of nave and aisles and gallery to hear Pastor Richard Wurmbrand tell his story of the sort of persecution suffered by Christians behind the Iron Curtain who dared to set God above 'Caesar'. So doing he revealed that despite the personal sufferings he himself had endured in imprisonment, in torture, in bestial abuse, his faith was not broken. He did not speak as a man enlisting sympathy but as a man desperately anxious both to alert Christians in the West to dangers which beset their fellows whose unhappy lot it is to live within the grim grip of Marxist Communism, and as a man urgently bespeaking our prayers for them. Wurmbrand, dismissed unfortunately even by some churchmen as a simple Bible-thumping Baptist Pastor with a mission to provoke the Communists, was telling a story different in substance but alike in intention from what the world has since heard from the lips of men of the calibre of Alexander Solzhenitsyn and Andrei Sakharov.

The people present that night, who dropped £500 into the collection, were by so doing expressing their abhorrence of a regime which denies fundamental human rights and their resolve to help those who suffer under it. 'Religious liberty' is indeed written into the Constitution of the USSR but it is a strange understanding of 'liberty' which denies to Christians the right to propagate their Faith, which allows slanderous attacks to be made in the press against Christians and their religion, denying them the right to make reply, which persecutes Jews and, contrary to the Charter of Human Rights, denies them even the opportunity of turning their backs on the country for ever. When an assembly of the size of that which gathered in St. Cuthbert's that night disperses there is normally much chatter. I could not help but notice that the great crowd left very quietly as though stunned into silence by what they had heard.

There was a very different conclusion to another memorable event in the same church. A representative of the Latvian community approached me in the autumn of 1968 to ask whether the Latvians living in Carlisle and the Borders might have the use of a church in Carlisle for an act of worship of commemoration and prayer. Their wish was to commemorate the 50th anniversary of the creation of Latvia as an independent state in 1918, to recall how by force and by fraud their country was annexed by the Soviet Union in 1940, how they and their loved ones had suffered under the Sovietization tactics which followed, how one tyranny was exchanged for another by the German occupation in 1941 to 1944 and how since then their homeland has been under the Soviet heel. A simple piety marked the representative as he spoke of their desire to meet each other in a church and to worship together in their own tongue. So they came to St. Cuthbert's – from southern Scotland and Northern England, young and old, and the young still being taught their mother tongue by parents and grandparents and many still hoping that one day Moscow's imperialistic policy would be checked and their country freed. The service was conducted by a Latvian Pastor from Manchester and although I could not follow it, I could sense the fervour in which they entered into both the prayers and the singing. Mine was the privilege of preaching to them and I wove my address around the words, 'How can we sing the Lord's song in a strange land?' They listened intently and when, following the last hymn, to their astonishment, and indeed to mine, I gave the Blessing in their own language, the Pastor told me subsequently that his people were so touched that many were at that point reduced to tears.

The service was followed by a very jolly party in the Church Hall when the young folk donned national dress and led the assembly in traditional Baltic dances – a party into which the Bishop and the Member of Parliament for Carlisle (Mr. Ronald Lewis) entered with zest. The *Church Times* reported the religious side of the occasion concluding its brief reference with the sentence, 'The Bishop of Carlisle preached the sermon and gave the Blessing in Latvian'. The insertion of one comma in that sentence might have saved me from many leg-pulls from my brother bishops! Learning the Aaronic Blessing (Numbers ch. 6, vv. 24–26), 'Dieus tas Kings Lai tevi svetee un pasarta . . . ' so as to be able to pronounce it without reference to a script and in a way which the congregation would appreciate, was a formidable exercise which occupied much silent recital in the car on the preceding days, but when a rehearsal in the vestry before the service won the approval of the Latvian pastor I went to it with confidence. Four years later, when I was about to leave Rose Castle, a small deputation of Latvians came to present me with a bound volume of the history of their country and people and with a three-branch candlestick of Latvian craftsmanship – a generous gesture from people for whom I had done so little.

Things Ecumenical

Among the singular occasions were the invitations I accepted in the interest of good inter-church relations to preach in churches of other Communions, more especially each year during January and in and around the designated week of prayer for Christian Unity. So many of these came – Congregationalist, Methodist, Presbyterian, Salvation Army and Roman Catholic – that an impish incumbent was heard to ask 'I wonder which Church pays the Bishop's stipend in January?' The exercise was a valuable one both as a demonstration that the divisions within the Christian Church though still 'unhappy' were no longer bitter, and as an opportunity to declare and declare again that the things which divide Christians from one another are infinitesimal when measured against the abyss which divides the Christian Church as a whole from the forces of anti-Christ in the world. Three such occasions spring vividly to my mind, each memorable and worthy of mention.

The Salvation Army Citadel in Carlisle was but a couple of hundred yards from the Cathedral. It was in the Cathedral on a Sunday in September 1800 that the Bishop of Carlisle, Harvey Goodwin, rounded upon the Salvation Army in his sermon as reported in the *Carlisle Patriot* of 10 September 1880. 'I cannot refrain from saying that I was deeply pained by the report of the doings of what seems to call itself the 'Salvation Army,'' he said. The Hallelujahs and the Amens interspersing the proclamation of the Gospel seemed to distress him as did the 'Laughter and pitiful joking'. He asked, 'What kind of "salvation" can come from the tactics of such an army I cannot imagine. If the newspapers are to be trusted the whole affair seemed to be the most painful burlesque of all that could be called religion . . . I see nothing in the proceedings recorded last week which seems to me consonant to the Spirit of Christ and much which St. Paul would condemn if he visited Carlisle.'

In fact St. Paul didn't. but Mrs. 'General' Booth did and within ten days. To a packed audience in the Theatre Royal she took the bishop to task for his 'unprovoked denunciations'. She outlined the purpose and methods of the Army and expressed the conviction that such a spiritually-enlightened man as the bishop might have reached different conclusions had he attended one of the Army's meetings himself. She examined the same passage of Scripture as did the bishop in his sermon (1 Corinthians ch. 14, vv. 33–34) and step-by-step sought to show him where he was wrong in attributing its warning specifically to the Salvation Army. Touching on his words about 'laughter and pitiful joking', she asked, 'If a man preferred to be called Hallelujah Bob, how was that different from being called the Lord Bishop? . . . If a man preferred to have a tune on the fiddle instead of the organ, his bad taste might be pitied but if he wished it, let him have it! Did they think that the angels were very particular what sort of instrument was used so long as the heart was in tune?'

I doubt whether the good bishop – and he was a good bishop – was chastened by all that but I am sure that he realised how incautious his remarks were. It was with all this at the back of my mind that I walked into the Salvation Army citadel on that Sunday morning and ventured in the course of my address humbly to redress my good predecessor's inauspicious remarks. 'That was nearly a hundred years ago,' I said 'and I am sure that were he here now to read the record of the Salvation Army in the pages of evangelistic enterprise and social service in this land and all over the world, he might yet refrain from shouting a Hallelujah or an Amen, but he would recall the words of his and your Lord, "Inasmuch as you have done it unto one of the least of these, you have done it unto Me".' It was a devout Salvationist who wrote me subsequently saying that they had not received what he called my 'historic apology' in a spirit of gloating for he was pretty sure that if he had lived in Bishop Goodwin's day he might have taken a similar attitude. 'They were rough days,' he added, 'and many church-going people must have been alarmed, but we are a different army now . . . we still make a lot of noise and we like to be cheerful and bright in our worship, but I believe that the heart of our Army beats strong and we can still be used as a channel for God's grace in our very needy world.' On 5 January 1972 I was present at the opening of the Salvation Army's new citadel in Carlisle.

Carlisle's proximity to the Scottish border and the consequent frequency of marriages 'twixt Scots and Sassenachs no doubt account for the liveliness of the Carlisle Kirk which, though in the heart of the city, had necessarily to be embraced within the Annan Presbytery. It was my privilege to be the preacher there on a Communion Sunday when I was struck first by the excessive courtesy offered to a bishop by a Church in which I understood episcopacy to be nothing accounted, and next by the quiet reverence with which the Kirk's simple Communion Rite was celebrated. Never in any of my own churches had I been met by a phalanx of gentlemen in frock coats and never in any non-Anglican Church had I sensed the intensity of awe which marked their approach to Holy Communion. Not long after this visit I was able to arrange a historic 'rapprochement' between the two National Churches when, on hearing that the newly-appointed Moderator of the General Assembly of the Church of Scotland intended to include the Annan Presbytery in his Visitations, I invited him to take part with me in a brief ecumenical service in the Cathedral. This we did, each extending to the other the hand of fellowship and each expressing on behalf of our respective churches our joy for the breaking down of barriers and our hope for a continuing and growing mutual respect and understanding. Though the occasion was apparently of no interest to the English press the Scottish national papers made much of it and it could well be that an invitation extended to me subsequently to be a Guest of Honour at the opening of the General Assembly in Edinburgh stemmed from that gesture. It was an invitation which I accepted eagerly if only to compare the proceedings with the General Synod. Perhaps the onlooker to a gathering of that kind, viewing the proceedings dispassionately, tends to judge it more sympathetically than the participant, but I certainly thought that as a Council of the Church it compared more than favourably with the General Synod. I suspect, however, that I was predisposed to look upon it the more benignly since I went to it from Holyrood Palace where I was entertained generously and graciously and awakened, I recall, by the sound of the pipes reminding me of the truth and power of 'amazing grace'!

None of these excursions into the ecumenical field was, however, so prodigious as that which fell to me on 18 January 1968 when by accepting an invitation from the Roman Catholic Church to preach in St. Bede's in the City in the Week of Prayer for Christian Unity, I became the first Anglican bishop to preach in a Roman Catholic Church. The events leading up to what Fr. Laurence Wells, who was the parish priest there, describes as an 'ecumenical first' are of such moment in the saga of inter-church relations that I am persuaded to set them down in full as Fr. Wells relates them. It may be recalled that up to that time Anglican pulpits had been opened to Roman Catholic priests but the compliment had not been returned. In the autumn of 1967 a 'feeler' was put out to me as to whether if such an invitation should be made I would be likely to accept. My answer was an immediate 'yes' though even as I gave it I pictured that there could be strong protests from the members of the Orange Order and other ultra-Protestants. Fr. Laurence Wells, now parish priest of St. Cuthbert's Blackpool, wrote:

It all began informally in conversations I had with Dean du Toit. About the time of the meeting of the sub-Committee of the Carlisle Council of Churches Fr. John Coventry, at that time secretary of our Bishop's Ecumenical Commission, was visiting the Diocese and I asked him, in the presence of Bishop Foley, if it was now permissible for us to invite Anglicans to preach in our churches. His answer was an emphatic 'yes' and when our sub-Committee met in October 1967 it was agreed that we should make a bid to get approval for you to preach in St. Bede's. I telephoned to our Bishop during the meeting, and he asked for a couple of days to consider the request. In that two days he got into touch with Bishop Holland of Salford, at that time chairman of our Ecumenical Commission and he agreed that we should be given permission. When Bishop Foley gave me the decision he added that he would like to come along and take part in the United Service. The November meeting of our Hierarchy followed about three weeks later and Bishop Holland reported the tentative permission given to us and the Commission's approval was given. They went further. It was at that meeting that it was decided to invite Archbishop Ramsey to preach in Westminster Cathedral and Cardinal Heenan duly wrote to invite him to do so. So Canterbury and Westminster took their lead from Carlisle and I think we have legitimate cause for a little pride. I shall never forget the service; there were more than 700 present that night. Bishop Foley said the prayers, the Baptist minister read the Lesson, and I remember the consensus of opinion afterwards that your address could not have been better suited to a great occasion. To the best of my knowledge you are right in believing that this was the first time that an Anglican Bishop had preached in a Roman Catholic Church – a truly memorable occasion.

As Bishop Foley, the Roman Catholic Bishop of Lancaster whose diocese embraced Cumbria, walked with me from the presbytery in the church grounds to the west door of the church we compared notes as to how many protesting letters we had each received when the news of the 'ecumenical break-through' had been announced in the press. I cannot remember the numbers save that his was greater than mine but if truth be told I suspect that each of us feared that our act of worship might be interrupted as was not unknown in Carlisle. In fact our fears proved to be groundless. The bishop's insistence that there should be no 'order of precedence' in our processional entry, that we should walk side-by-side and sit similarly in the sanctuary, were gestures that many of the lay folk noticed and most saw in them something more than common courtesy. Our act of worship moved forward splendidly and being 'altogether with one accord in one place' there was a lively consciousness of the Spirit's Presence. On such occasions there is always a moment of high splendour and rapture and for me on that evening it was to hear a great congregation from different parts of the One Church joining in the Te Deum and other hymns of praise known to and loved by them all. Five days later, on 23 January, Archbishop Michael Ramsey preached at a great ecumenical service in Westminster Cathedral, becoming the first Archbishop of Canterbury to do so.

Victor Hugo somewhere likens the soul to a bee which 'goes from flower to flower as a soul from star to star, and gathers honey as a soul gathers light'. I believe that all such ventures into ecumenism see souls gathering light for those who go to them with enquiring minds and eager hearts. Truly they leave the churches labelled as they entered them – Baptists, Anglicans, Roman Catholics, Presbyterians, Salvationists – having sacrificed nothing in the field of religious freedom, either of worship or assembly, but they have been with Jesus, and touching the hem of his garment they have found themselves very close to one another. In this way the unity which Christians have already in Christ is both demonstrated and nurtured and in God's good time will be manifest even to a purblind world. Thus does the Spirit work. If, however, the impatient among us think that we can beat the Holy Spirit at his own game by pushing our own views of doctrine and ecclesiastical organisation in a manner which deeply offends others who, with equal sincerity, think differently from us, we shall not only burn our own fingers but impede His work. In the quest for the Unity of Christendom there is certainly a task of enquiry and formulation which belongs to theologians but the victory lies, under God, not in their hands but in the hands of the people in the pews. A greatly revered figure in the Church of England as in his own church of Rome is that of Cardinal Mercier, Archbishop of Malines early in this century. Deeply concerned as he was with the task of formulation, he yet recognised it as secondary not primary. 'In order to be united,' he said 'it is necessary to love one another; in order to love one another it is necessary to know one another; in order to know one another it is necessary to meet one another.' Councils and commissions may talk for years about creed and ritual and polity, and since a thousand years are but as yesterday in God's sight that need not disturb us unduly. So long as we continue meeting one another in Christian action and Christian worship, thus nurturing within ourselves and demonstrating to the world a love so staggering in its impact that the unbeliever must perforce think again, he may yet say, 'see how these Christians love one another' – and be impelled himself to seek the Source of that love.

The Anglican–Methodist Débâcle

Since I have gone down in ecclesiastical history as one of the seven bishops (the other six were Bishops Moorman [Ripon], Taylor [Sheffield] Bowles [Derby], Easthaugh [Peterborough], Williams [Leicester] all of whom voted against, and Key [Truro] who abstained) who felt unable to approve the scheme for the unification of the Anglican and Methodist Churches which was first promulgated in 1967, I feel impelled to say something here about that troubled chapter in our common history which led me into a dark night of the soul. It was undoubtedly the conviction of many people, Anglican and Methodist, that the scheme would have a divisive rather than a unitive effect which led to its final rejection. The petulant protagonist may complain bitterly about it, but he must remember that there is no more sacred freedom than the freedom of religion and religious worship and people will see the slightest suspicion of any attempt to restrict that by imposition as sacrilegious. The 'Mayflower' spirit is not easily quenched. These were not fears which I shared at the outset for though I nursed in secret hesitations about the efficacy of the scheme to achieve its purpose I put my trust in a clause within it which, in my judgement, was a necessary safeguard against the possibility of riding roughshod over the consciences of any considerable number of church members.

When in 1967 the Interim Statement of the Anglican-Methodist negotiations was published I wrote a thousand-word article in our *Diocesan News* directed largely to the laity and expressing the hope that they would give it searching and careful study. It was known throughout the diocese that the Dean of Carlisle (Lionel du Toit) had had part and lot in the preparation of the Report and had spoken enthusiastically about its proposals up and down the country. I cannot pretend that I was ever so completely convinced as he appeared to be that the proposals would achieve their end. Even so, recognising that when bishops meet in synod they surrender something of their sovereignty in a desire to reach unanimity, I withheld my hesitations and in speeches in the diocese, both to Anglicans and to Methodists, I presented the scheme as one meriting support. In 1967 I wrote:

> Undoubtedly the representative commissioners responsible for the statement have been searching for a compromise which it is thought might be acceptable to both Anglicans and Methodists as not inconsistent with their past teaching and traditions. Compromise is undoubtedly one path to a Union of Churches. Whether it is the path to Unity is for all of us to judge. In the last analysis the question to which we may well have to address ourselves is not a question about words episcopacy, priest, presbyter, ministry – or the often conflicting ideas which lie behind words – it is a question about Unity. Will this document, if its proposals are implemented, bring two Churches together so that they shall be no more twain but one? That seems to me to be the bar of judgement to which this interim statement must be brought ultimately.

The article mentioned the rumblings of dissent which were already being heard in the land and the need to ensure that what we did would be something which would reconcile the whole Church of England with the whole Methodist Church and would at the same time do nothing to impede our growing relationships with the Roman Catholic and Orthodox Churches. As to the proposals before us at that moment I wrote:

> My own view is that each Church should be asked to give something like a 90 per cent acceptance of the proposals as an earnest of its intention to avoid secession on either side. If support on this scale could come from both churches, we could go forward rejoicingly and with the hope that the tiny minority of dissenters, Anglicans and Methodist, could perhaps be encouraged to think again. If, on the other hand, following all our heart-searching, all our discussion and all our prayers, it beomes evident that the statement cannot win the whole-hearted support of something like that number, we could hardly but take that as an indication that this is not the way forward or that the time is not ripe. This sets before us the measure of our task of understanding, in explanation, in persuasion and in prayer. If we give ourselves wholeheartedly to these and win

through, there is all joy. If we give ourselves wholeheartedly to these and yet fail, there is no shame.

The debate continued, in the diocese of Carlisle as elsewhere and, doubtless like other bishops, I did my share of expounding and commending the proposals for the Union though since we had in our midst one of its chief protagonists, Lionel du Toit, the burden of presentation of the scheme within the Diocese fell most heavily on him. I spoke both to Anglican and Methodist gatherings and met in each approval and opposition – Methodists who feared 'an Anglican take-over' and Anglicans who tended to regard the debate as an academic exercise as 'the bishops are determined to bull-doze the scheme through' whatever the opposition. However, before our Diocesan Conference met on 1 February 1968 I wrote:

> In our own Church there are bishops, priests and lay-people who cannot in conscience accept them. There are others who cannot in conscience reject them. For my part, I can say that I have hacked my way through doubts and difficulties to a point where I can give qualified approval. Approval it must be for me . . . but qualified because the doubts and imponderables are such, that unless the measure of acceptance of the scheme approaches 90 per cent in each Church, the danger of secession in one or the other, or both, would be such as to make improbable the attainment of the end sought. I shall therefore say 'Yes'. But I shall not claim a monopoly of Divine Guidance. I shall rejoice that others with a comparable desire for the Unity of Christendom and with equal sincerity will say 'No'. If the overwhelming voice, clerical and lay, in both Churches, is in the affirmative, we must go forward and can do so with confidence. Otherwise we must stop and think again.

Our Diocesan Conference was held in Carlisle Cathedral and despite appalling weather proved to be the best-attended for many years and in the course of the Eucharist members marked their cards in silence. Whilst majorities approved the attempt to effect a Union, only 55 per cent of the clergy and 59 per cent of the laity could accept the Service of Reconciliation, whilst just under 58 per cent of the clergy and 70 per cent of the laity were prepared to give the Convocations an all-clear for final approval to Stage I of the Scheme. It soon became apparent that the picture as Carlisle saw it was not substantially different from other dioceses. However, in a desire to be objective, I reminded the diocese in the March issue of the *Diocesan News*:

> Proctors in Convocation are not, of course, delegates carrying card votes, but representatives who must vote as conscience dictates. But conscience has to be informed, and one of the informative sources must be the general mind of those whom the proctors represent. As clergy, they may not be unmindful of Jeremy Taylor's principles concerning

conscience, and they may recall his words, 'We are not to choose the way because it looks fair, but because it leads surely'. Clearly there has to be a shift of opinion, modest on the laity side, but massive on the clergy side if, in July, the Convocations are to be able to go forward with confidence.

In the July issue of the *Diocesan News* I turned to the subject again, this time to ask two things of all Christian people in the diocese — first that each and every one would find place in his private prayers for those upon whom would rest a great responsibility on 8 July, and secondly that there should be corporate intercession:

> I would wish the parochial clergy to make special arrangements to facilitate this . . . I would suggest as appropriate, that a celebration of Holy Communion in every parish church could well be part of those arrangements. You may well ask, 'What shall we pray?' I answer, 'Do not pray that God will do what you want. Pray that God will do with His servants what He wills'. For Christians to be faced with a dilemma is nothing new, nor is there any promise anywhere that they will be preserved from difficult choices.

I then quoted William Bright's great prayer and asked that everyone should use it on behalf of the members of the Convocations on that day:

> O God, by Whom the meek are guided in judgment, and light riseth up in darkness for the godly: grant us, in all our doubts and uncertainties, the grace to ask what Thou wouldest have us to do; that the Spirit of Wisdom may save us from all false choices, and that in Thy light we may see light and in Thy straight path may not stumble.

What I asked others to do, I did myself and many times a day as the hour approached. I read and re-read the paragraph in the Commission's Report headed 'The need for a common mind: To proceed with plans for Union against substantial opposition would be intolerable'. It would be 'unthinkable that either Church will go forward unless it is conscious of overwhelming support'. That there was 'substantial opposition' was irrefutable. Nearly 6000 of the parochial clergy had declared in solemn Synod that they could not in conscience take part in the Service of Reconciliation and well over a third of the lay members of the Diocesan Conferences felt the same. In the House of Laity nearly half the members rejected the scheme. In the Methodist Church the numbers reflected the same disquiet, the voting in the Carlisle Methodist District being 801 against and 638 for. In the light of all this it seemed to me to be a matter of integrity. To dismiss all this opposition as without significance would be to turn the whole consultation into a cruel hoax. I decided that I must cast my vote against unless in the course of the debate anything transpired which might convince me otherwise. Frankly I was distressed by the insensitive tenor of the debate, by the way in which the chief protagonists of the scheme, from the two Archbishops downwards, (I doubt not but out of a burning zeal to secure its acceptance), seemed to me to be determined to do just what many had feared – to bulldoze it through against the massive opposition at the grass-roots.

A reasoned speech by the Bishop of Ripon (Dr. John Moorman), who was known to be deeply disturbed by the proposals, was somewhat contemptuously dismissed by the Archbishop of Canterbury with a reference to what was 'in the Ripon bag'. My plea that to go forward, contrary to the promise embodied in the Report that to proceed with plans for reunion against substantial opposition, would be not only a breach of integrity but in the end a grave blow to the ecumenical movement, was similarly and peremptorily dismissed. (Among the many letters which I received subsequently were some which made the point that my speech was unanswered because it was unanswerable).

But undoubtedly the speech against the motion which most shook the Synod was one coming near the close of the debate – that of Lionel du Toit who had been expected to support the cause he had so long championed. In an impressive entreaty he confessed his own inability to do something which he then saw would create a tragic division in the Church of England and he appealed for rejection of the scheme.

The end result on that day was that the Methodist Conference, meeting in Birmingham, voted in favour of going forward by 77 per cent; the Convocations' vote reached only 69 per cent, against the necessary 75 per cent. I went home with a heavy heart, not because the scheme had been defeated, but because so many, particularly among the bishops, had as it seemed to me, been ready to throw integrity to the winds in their determination to achieve a victory. Other bishops in addition to the seven had indeed told me privately that they shared my anxiety fully but when it came to voting they were apparently prepared to put 'collegiality' before 'conviction'. In the September issue of the *Diocesan News* I wrote:

Tuesday 8th July 1969 will, in my judgement, go down in the history of the Church of England and of the Methodist Church not as an inglorious day as the petulant contend, but as the day when the two Churches, saved from a decision which would have created deep division and dissension in each, were challenged to enter into a deeper ecumenical commitment on a people-to-people basis. At the end of the day many were disappointed and many were relieved. Among the latter were not only the thousands of clergy and laity who had had conscientious objections to the scheme of Union throughout the debate, but also, as my postbag revealed, a great number of enthusiasts for the scheme, from all over the country, Anglicans and Methodists alike, who had come to believe that to proceed with it against the evident substantial opposition,

would have been both dishonest and disastrous. The restraint with which
the leaders of both Churches have spoken has put into true perspective
the irresponsible and hysterical utterances of some of the clergy who
have done nothing but harm to the cause. There is no disaster. Nor are
we back to square one. There is a setback, but according to the Abbe
Courturier, perhaps the greatest of the twentieth-century Apostles of
Unity, such a set-back is a grace permitted by God.

The real truth is that we have all been given a sharp lesson – the people
at the local level and the people at the top. It is this: Church legislation,
like State legislation, can never be far in advance of public opinion.
This may often impede progress towards the unions of Churches, but
it need never impede the continuing growth of the Unity of Christians.
The latter is the only power strong enough to further the former, and
the plain truth is that it is not yet strong enough. Union imposed on
Christians who are not at one among themselves is a façade of Unity
which could deceive men for a while, but God not at all. The task
now, of Anglicans and Methodists, and indeed of all concerned with
Unity, is to carry the ecumenical movement from the Councils of the
Churches to the congregations of the Churches – from the top to the
local levels. It is there that the Unity we already have in Christ is to be
nurtured. It is from there that it will be manifested in ways meaningful
to the world. It is the growth of Unity there – at the grass roots as we
say – which alone can stimulate and sustain the desire for Union . . . If
there was any tragedy on July 8th, it was not in what happened. It was
in our failure to see that what happened was inevitable. The Church
of England is not, in this scheme, at Unity in itself. Nor indeed is the
Methodist Church. The stage when Union can be accomplished by such
a scheme is not yet. It may be near or far. None can tell. But if from this
cathartic experience we get the message, it will yet be seen that to those
who love God 'all things work together for good'. This is no time for
the disappointed to be disgruntled or for the relieved to rejoice. This is
no time for tears or for cheers. This is a time to interpret the writing on
the wall – a time to discern what the Spirit is saying to the Churches.

It will be recalled that a further attempt to push through a scheme of union
was made in 1972 but on that occasion no doubt assailed my mind. I had by
then reached the conclusion that our so-called unhappy divisions, from which
bitterness had already been expunged, would not be healed by pieces of clever
ecclesiastical engineering in which conflicting ideas and beliefs are concealed
in deliberately ambiguous phrases. They will be healed – and very slowly as
is nature's way – by the growing together of the people in the pews, whether
of the Parish Church or of what Bishop Michael Ramsey, when Bishop
of Durham, referred to in a convocation debate as 'the Chapel round the
corner'. It is these with whom we have to reckon, these whose religious
experiences differ, whose traditions are disparate, whose ways of worship

vary, whose policies are dissimilar but whose sincerity and convictions are not to be called into question. In my judgement the Church which is the most ecumenically-minded is the Church which shows itself to be the most welcoming host, anticipating from its family conformity with its own ethos yet making no such demands upon guests who come to it accepting Christ as Lord. As for the individual Christian, the noblest host is he whose arms are spread the widest and the most gracious guest is he who enters with eyes the least critical. These exalt Unity; they could even effect a Union which does not deny it. No artificial scheme of Union can ever do that since inevitably it seeks to impose itself and in doing so does no more than moves the lines of division. Growing together pew by pew as it were is a slower way to Union, but it is the surer.

So in 1972 when the General Synod of the Church once more was unable to approve the scheme before it, the black and chocolate-coloured covers of the book which was wrongly entitled *Anglican-Methodist Unity* was closed as offering no through road to the unification of the two Churches so that they might become one. Anglicans did not on that day say 'No' to Unity as some of the subsequent press headlines proclaimed. Unity with Methodists is something we already have, as we have with Roman Catholics, within the Body of Christ which is the Church. What we said 'No' to then was a scheme for the unification of our two Churches, because we had already committed ourselves to the conviction that 'it would be unthinkable that either Church will go forward unless it is conscious of overwhelming support'. To regard that as a cataclysmic disaster from which there is no recovery is impious. If there are yet differences of administration, there is but One Spirit and that One Spirit has been mightily at work, drawing the members of Christ's Church ever more closely together in Christian action, in Christian witness and even in Christian worship.

For all this a great Te Deum must rise from the whole Church of God. But having sung it we must not belie its sincerity by giving way to a petulant despair or angry impatience when hopes are deferred by the failure of our little schemes. The Christian story does not lack proof that God has a habit of turning set-backs into stepping-stones. (When Paul and Barnabas fell out with one another when planning the second missionary journey, because Barnabas wanted to take young Mark, and Paul would have none of it since he deserted them on the first, the end result was not 'no missionary journey' but two missionary journeys, one by Paul and Silas and one by Barnabas and Mark.) You can't catch the Spirit out! He will find a Way. What matters most in the ecumenical venture is not where we are at any given moment but which way we are looking. All who are touching but the hem of Christ's garment at any given moment cannot be very far from each other by whatever name they call themselves. We must lend no countenance to defeatist talk! We must press on 'looking unto Jesus, the Author and Finisher of our Faith'.

13

Changing Scenes

Given the truth of William Cowper's dictum that 'variety's the very spice of life which gives it all its flavour', the bishop's should, of all lives, be the most 'tasty'. Certainly it lacks nothing in variety. He must rub shoulders in his day-to-day work with children, with adolescents and with adults; he must establish points of contact with manual workers as with professional; he must teach and preach and lecture to the unlettered as to the learned; he must discharge his stint of administration efficiently, he must take his place on committees, councils and commissions; he must be as ready to enter into the joys and hopes of his people as into their sorrows and anxieties; he must be at home in the little country church with its simple offering of worship as in the great town church or cathedral where there is splendour in music and ceremonial. In these latter days too he must be ready, often within a single day, to move from the Book of Common Prayer to Series I, II or III, and so to take his part in any one of these as to project the impression that none other offers so fine a medium for the worship of almighty God.

Within the broad spectrum of what is called 'churchmanship' the bishop must emulate St. Paul in becoming 'everything in turn to men of every sort' which means not that he lacks a mind or preferences of his own but that he recognises that intolerance will prevent him from understanding the mind or preferences of the other man. (In practical terms this can mean that the bishop must on one Sunday allow himself to be censed by the Anglo-catholic without himself becoming incensed, and on the next Sunday steel himself from blurting out an impatient 'No' when the Evangelical replaces the time-honoured 'Let us pray' with the irritating and often mawkish rhetorical 'Shall we pray?').

No bishop can escape the changing scenes. He will find them alternately simple and complex, sorrowful and joyful, tedious and exhilarating, prosaic and imaginative, solemn and informal, exhausting and invigorating. But there is one 'constant' through all of them, in purpose over-riding, in practice under-girding – that he is, and should be seen to be, God's man about God's

245

work. If any struggling Christian Pilgrim, trying to do just that within the context of his own commitment, should think that what is difficult for him is easy for a bishop, let him dismiss the thought! Even St. Paul was fearful lest having preached to others he might find himself rejected; none knew better than St. Augustine that coming to serve the Lord he must prepare his soul to meet temptation; and the saintly Thomas à Kempis in his *Imitation of Christ* issues a warning, surely from personal experience, when he says, 'Fire tries iron and temptation tries a just man'. When Bishop Rainbow restored the Chapel at Rose Castle after Bishop's Sterne's abortive attempt, he set it immediately over what is now, and probably was then, the study-library and office. I saw a parable in that juxtaposition. In the study and the office the incidents of the changing scenes were planned and prepared; in the Chapel above the 'constant' was contemplated and nurtured. The wide variety of challenges and opportunities following swiftly one upon another might well have palled but for the contemplation of the 'constant' which drew them together and sustained them in a symphony of dedicated ministry.

But no bishop can face all this alone. He needs his inner cabinet of colleagues – his suffragan, his dean and his archdeacons. Though each was independent in his own sphere, all were concerned with me for the co-ordination and planning of the work of the diocese as a whole. I was fortunate to have about me men of spiritual and intellectual calibre, of pastoral experience and zeal, and in the course of our regular meetings, which began in the Chapel, continued in the study and ended in the dining room, we established an easy relationship in which hopes, ideas and aspirations would be freely discussed. The burden of patronage is one sphere of a bishop's work which he will be only too anxious to share with his senior colleagues and this we did, not only in respect of the filling of the livings but also in appointments to honorary canonries of which there never seemed to be enough to meet our corporate desires. Filling the benefices was not, in fact, a particularly difficult task in a diocese 'where every prospect pleases' and I was, from time to time, able to help bishops in the northern industrial dioceses to place men who needed to experience a different sort of ministry from anything they were able to offer. Private patrons were not, in my experience, the ogres they are sometimes held to be by ecclesiastical politicians and certainly in the Carlisle diocese, where the chief private patron is the Earl of Lonsdale, I was invariably invited by him to suggest a suitable priest for a vacant benefice whom he would then interview and at whose institution he would normally be present.

The introduction of Synodical Government imposed upon us the need to redraw the boundaries of our rural deaneries so as to ensure that each would be big enough to create a viable deanery synod. I had no stomach for this kind of operation but my archdeacons saw it through successfully and paved the way for me to appoint as rural deans able priests with sufficient time and experience to establish the new bodies along lines likely to enlist and sustain active clerical and lay interest. This done, Archdeacon Nurse undertook the revision of the superb map of the diocese which his father Canon Euston Nurse, sometime Rector of Windermere, had prepared and presented to the diocese in 1918. So far as the operation of the new system of Church Government was concerned in the diocese all of us did our best to secure the acceptance of its principles and the active pursuit of its intentions, though I recall that there were murmurings of dissent on the part of some who had served very faithfully on the Diocesan Conference for many years and who found themselves not needed on the smaller Diocesan Synod. Nevertheless the latter body was one of which the Church could be proud and – continuing the practice of my predecessor in moving its meetings around the diocese – knowledge of its proceedings, and the substance of its debates, found place in the many local papers which flourish in Cumbria.

Thus, through all the changing scenes the bishop was not alone, but he could sometimes be lonely, not for lack of willing advisers and helpers but from recognition of the truth that at the end of the day, synodical government or no, the intractable problem, the parochial wrangle, the priestly failure, the marriage breakdown, the threatened libel action against an incumbent for an incautious remark in a parish magazine, the heart-rending pleas of divorced people for permission to 'remarry' in a church – these landed on the bishop's desk, and their resolution was his and his alone. He must correct, he must appeal for repentance, he must direct, he must arbitrate, he must write the disappointing letter or go through the agonising interview and sometimes he must rebuke. I cannot claim to have been good at this last. Confrontation with lying or dishonesty or slander or wilful neglect of duty has never been, as they say, my scene. It was not so with erring schoolboys; it did not become so with erring clerics, or layfolk for that matter. For my part a sleepless night would precede the interview at which a rebuke might be necessary and face-to-face with a delinquent I found it terribly hard to be a stern judge. Certainly I could never have concluded such an interview, as Archbishop Garbett frequently did, with the words, 'I'm sorry for you at the Day of Judgement' not merely because I should have been afraid to seem to pre-judge the issue against the Day but also because such words could hardly have been the most appropriate to a penitent rising from his knees! I can recall, and happily now, two clerical delinquents, now beyond the grave, concerning whose behaviour laity indicted me for what they called my weak reaction in giving them the opportunity of a new start. I saw those two men redeemed to a new life in which each offered to the end of his days a ministry which was received eagerly and blessed richly. One of my accusers subsequently had the courage to admit that what he had called my weakness had 'paid off', a retraction which I felt heartening even though I should have expressed it differently. Truly the sombre scenes were happily rare, but if truth be told, so harrowing that 'the constant' was sometimes hard to discern.

Not so in the solemn scenes, such, for example, as the laying to rest of the bodies of faithful soldiers and servants of Christ. These were shot through with thanksgiving for lives marked by devotion and service. Inevitably the

bishop only rarely conducts but he is expected to be present and to speak at
the funerals of priests and lay-people who have been prominent in the life
of the Church in the diocese and such occasions, echoing the Christian hope
of eternal life, are never morbid. I can even recall a gentle titter of laughter
throughout the Church at one such when at the funeral of a warrior for
righteousness noted for her stern 'John Baptist approach' to laxity in the
moral law in society as in individuals, I referred to her as both 'upright and
downright'. But I never came away from such funerals without a twinge of
unease that the bishop appeared, and properly, at the burial of some prominent
person in the life of the Church or State but never at the laying to rest of the
body of some simple humble and devout soul, unknown outside his own
community but who within it had given a life-long example of fidelity in
Christian worship and Christian service. I expressed a hope through the *Ad
Clerum* that I might be given the opportunity of doing just this if only once
during a year and the thought was clearly appreciated by a number of the
parochial clergy. It was a naive hope of course for almost invariably I was
already committed to other engagements when the call came.

But the day did come when, en route to an evening appointment, I was
able to be present at the funeral of old Tom, who by twenty years, had
outlived the Psalmist's span of threescore years and ten. Tom was a miner
who throughout his life had remained a devout son of the Church. For 60
years he had sung in the choir and for 40 had been churchwarden, and still
in the village there were those who could recall with gratitude the hours he
had spent as a younger man helping the young people of the parish to share
his strong faith. The tiny village church was full of those who were there to
mourn, conscious that a faithful Christian was no longer with them in the
flesh, but there too to celebrate with thanksgiving for the life of this humble
man of God. 'Old Tom's dead and the bishop's coming to bury him,' they
said. At the beginning of a brief address I denied both assertions. 'Old Tom
isn't dead,' I said 'and I haven't come to bury him. Certainly we shall lay
to rest the worn body in which he lived here in this village but we shall
commend Tom himself to the gracious keeping of the Living God whom, to
your knowledge, he has served with fidelity and zeal throughout his long life.'
There was no pomp and ceremony, no funeral march no exquisite singing, on
that April afternoon in 1970 but the daffodils in the churchyard, risen from
their winter grave, and standing erect in their splendour, seemed to echo the
words we had just heard, 'Death is swallowed up in victory'. Old Tom was
not dead!

The writer of the Old Testament book of Ecclesiastes declares that 'sorrow
is better than laughter' – a value judgement with which, I doubt not, the saints
would concur, not merely for what it implies about sorrow but also that it
leaves a place for laughter, though this poor disillusioned Preacher seems only
to have experienced the 'laughter of the fool'. Among the bishop's changing
scenes there were opportunities to mingle mirth with discourse in that I was
frequently invited to speak at the annual dinners of various professional

societies or guilds and I accepted such invitations whenever possible. These gatherings provided valuable opportunities for meeting the men (and from time to time the women) who in Cumbria presided over the worlds of banking and insurance, of law and management, of farming and valuing and of various charitable concerns.

Following George Herbert's advice in *The Country Parson* that when 'men are in company instruction seasoned with pleasantness both enters sooner and roots deeper' I found the after-dinner speech an admirable medium for just such an exercise. Sandwiched as it was between a more than satisfying dinner and the subsequent wine-bibbing, the speech could embrace serious teaching provided that it was introduced with mirth and peppered with humour. I enjoyed these occasions immensely for their fun, their fellowship and for their didactic value. Among the evenings lodged firmly in my memory was an occasion when I found myself, at a Banker's Institute Dinner, speaking immediately before the Chief Cashier of the Bank of England whose name appears on our treasury notes. Disclaiming any intimacy with the Old Lady of Threadneedle Street, but having briefed myself pretty thoroughly beforehand, I spoke of him as a gentleman 'whose name is to be found everywhere – in shops and offices, in factories and farmyards, in gentlemen's wallets and ladies' handbags, in dance halls and night clubs, in banks, in casinos and even in brothels, but only very occasionally, so rarely indeed that when it occurs it is remarkable – his name is to be found on a church collection plate'. The peals of laughter which followed the quip created just the right atmosphere in which I could press home a few truths about Christian Stewardship! On another such occasion the Scots' Guards were happy to accept the proposition, received with laughter, that meagre as my knowledge of the army was, I would be prepared to concede that they bore no relation to *Dad's Army* if they for their part would accept my word that *All Gas and Gaiters* was more fictional than biographical. That was as good a lead as any into a talk on Christian philosophy of work and leisure. The letter of thanks which I received from the colonel subsequently sticks in my mind for one sentence. It noted that I had restored his confidence that 'an after-dinner speech to soldiers does not have to be bawdy to be both instructive and very amusing'.

On another occasion, and this at a Rotary function at the beginning of the New Year, I was invited to address myself to the question, 'What happened to the Good Old Days?' Inevitably in preparing this one thought of William Morris, the poet and artist, who a hundred years before had completed his masterpiece *The Earthly Paradise*, in the prologue of which he indicted the despoiling side of the Industrial Revolution and looked back to his 'good old days', to a London unspoilt. I quoted his lines:

> *Forget six counties overhung with smoke*
> *Forget the snorting steam and piston stroke,*
> *Forget the spreading of the hideous town;*
> *Think rather of the pack horse on the down,*

> *And dream of London, small and white and clean,*
> *The clear Thames bordered by its gardens green.*

Having prepared the talk I then translated it into verse in the William
Morris style. I asked, 'Would William Morris, writing now, say something
like this?

> *Forget five million cars, the roads, the speed,*
> *Forget those noxious fumes on which we feed*
> *Forget the blinking lights, the ceaseless noise,*
> *Think rather of the quiet and the poise,*
> *Of olden days; the friendly horse and coach,*
> *The tuneful horn to herald its approach.*
>
> *Forget the sputniks hurtling round in space,*
> *Forget that crazy, costly lunar race,*
> *Forget those noisy jets which steal men's rest;*
> *Think rather of our fathers' lively zest,*
> *For simple things; the home, the cottage craft,*
> *Pursued with pride, for life and not for graft.*
>
> *Forget that blaring juke box, glare box too,*
> *The lust for motion and the long bus queue,*
> *The nervous wrecks, the suicides, the crimes;*
> *Think rather of those warm and placid times*
> *When life was slower, pleasures all home-spun*
> *And families gathered round the fire as one.*

Or would Morris, I asked, tell us how fortunate we are to have rid ourselves
of the bad things in what we are now wont to call the 'Good Old Days'?
Would he indeed question whether there ever were any good old days, and
say something like this:

> *Forget the sweat of labour and the toil,*
> *The wasting candles, smelly lamps and oil,*
> *Forget those daily trips to village pump,*
> *That foul disease-infested refuse dump.*
> *Forget those curtained beds and warming pans,*
> *The old zinc bath, the bedroom water cans,*
> *Those foul earth closets, squalid back to backs,*
> *And with it all – that monstrous window tax.*
> *Think rather of the vast electric power,*
> *The h and c laid on, the bath, the shower,*
> *The fridge, the telly and the family car,*

The flushing cisterns and the cocktail bar.
Be mindful too of telephones and post,
And that commodious oven for Sunday's roast.
Remember sirs, there was no golden age
That had not dross upon its every page.

I remember that evening well, the only one in which I indulged in a hobby to meet the requests of hosts wanting to hear how I viewed 'to-day' in the light of 'yesterday'. Many of those present asked for copies of what one called 'Morris up-dated' and I made one of those vague promises which I am sure must be common among public speakers, that maybe, one day, I should have time to meet the request. By this the promise is fulfilled!

There were times when the bishop's whimsicalities spilt over into the vicarages – to a schoolboy son of the vicarage mourning the defeat of his favourite football team and to another bemoaning the demise of steam trains and their replacement by diesels. The children of Urswick Primary School, who won a prize of £5 and sent it to the bishop for his *Rydal Hall Appeal*, enclosing it in a picture card of an owl, were surprised to receive his letter of thanks written in verse as if by the owl himself. But perhaps no one was more surprised than the desperately hard-working parish priest who, discovering a tiny velvet bag in his vestry after an episcopal visit sent it to Rose Castle on the assumption that it was in some way connected with the episcopal regalia. I sent it back with this letter:

Dear George, it was most kind of you
To forward me this bag,
But though it is of purple hue,
It's still not mine, you wag!
It's true I visited your church
And in the vestry robed,
But you must do some more research
However much you've probed.

This bag is certainly not mine
Attractive though it is –
If I do other than decline
'Twould be an awful swizz!
Into your church I nothing brought
Remotely like this clout;
It's therefore certain that I ought
To carry nothing out.

It may perchance have held a pyx.
I cannot tell. Ask John!

> If he disclaims, you're in a fix –
> Dilemma's horns you're on –
> Destruction would be wrong,
> Yet day by day I feel you'll groan:
> 'To whom does it belong?'
>
> So here's episcopal advice
> About this trying quest,
> Though brief, I think it will suffice
> To calm your troubled breast.
> Just push it in the cupboard strong
> As accidental swag,
> Until the owner comes along,
> The Vicar to de-bag!

I never discovered who was the more surprised – the secretary to whom the letter was dictated or the priest who read it over breakfast on a winter morning, but both enjoyed the fun. My domestic chaplain and his family became accustomed to receiving their Christmas greetings in verse appropriate to their hobbies, and Lord and Lady Coggan have had many chuckles over His Grace's entry for 'Crockford – Series 3' which I provided for him on his retirement. Like Robert Burns, 'I rhyme for fun', but I did once receive £5 from the *Daily Mail* for some political Limericks on the Common Market which have since appeared in literary studies of the Limerick, notably in *The Limerick Makers* by Jean Harrowven (Research Publishing Company). Not all the changing scenes were in sombre colours or in solemn tones!

The Bishop of Carlisle, who has the whole of the Lake District in his diocese, cannot be unmindful of the catalogue of literary giants who derived their inspiration from its singular beauty and by their works opened up that beauty to the world. Cockermouth and Hawkshead, Rydal and Grasmere spell 'Wordsworth' the world over, and there too can we trace the footsteps of the Arnolds. Ambleside and Coniston count among their famed inhabitants John Ruskin, Fred Faber to whom we owe many great hymns, and Mrs Hemans who *inter alia* stood the boy on the burning deck! Nor was I ever driven through the narrow roads of Sawrey without reminding my chauffeur to take special care lest Beatrix Potter's Jemima Puddleduck or a Mrs. Twiggy Winkle should perchance be crossing the road! Maybe it is from the pen of Hugh Walpole who, like Samuel Taylor Coleridge and Robert Southey before him, lived in Keswick, that one of the finest pen pictures of the Lake District, in prose at least, comes. He concludes his novel *Vanessa*:

> There is no ground in the world more mysterious, no land at once so bare in its nakedness and so rich in its luxury, so warm with sun and so cold with pitiless rain, so gentle and so pastoral, so wild and lonely; with sea and lake and river there is always the sound of moving water, and its

strong people have their feet in the soil and are independent of all men. During the flight of the Eagle, two hundred years are as but a day – and the life of a man, as against all odds he pushes towards immortality, is eternal.

Maybe not all these literary titans were orthodox Christians but all, living and working amidst such natural grandeur, have by their writings led the hearts and minds of many at least to the doorway of life's spiritual dimension and some indeed into its halls. Thus when in 1970 I was invited to preach in Cockermouth Parish Church at a service celebrating the bicentenary of Wordsworth's birth in the town where he was born, and which according to De Selincourt 'enshrined for him all his child experience of a happy family life', it was not difficult to pluck from his writings some gems with which to illustrate the profound truth that 'It takes more than bread to keep a man alive' – (St. Matthew ch. 4, v. 4). In an address which attempted to expound the relationship of religion and art – that 'without art, religion is dumb and without religion art lacks the highest significance of which it is capable' – I suggested that the dedicated prophet and the dedicated artist were engaged on the same task, pursued in different ways, but still the task of enlarging the spiritual vision of mankind. I concluded the address:

All this is the measure of our Lakeland poet's contribution to the awakening of the spirit of man. It does not ascribe to him perfection in character, in judgment or in expression. Like all men his life and his work are not without their stains. It ascribes not perfection, but a vision of where perfection is to be found, a recognition that in its pursuit we must start from where we are – here in this lovely world of nature, here in this harsh world of 'getting and spending', here –

> *Not in Utopia – subterranean fields –*
> *Or some secreted island, Heaven knows where!*
> *But in the very world, which is the world*
> *Of all of us, the place where, in the end*
> *We find our happiness or not at all.*

We start here and by aspiration and grace, helped of course by what the poet in *The Excursion* calls 'the imperfect offices of praise and prayer', we press on, calling to aid all that can sustain, direct and uplift the spirit. Thus do we find the Spirit of the Universe, God Himself, revealed we believe in the Person of Our Lord and Saviour Jesus Christ, in communion with whom in our prayers, in our worship and in our daily strivings towards the moral law we share a peace and a joy which the world – ever 'too much with us' – can neither give nor take away. We are they who have not only discovered that it takes more than bread to keep a man

alive. We have discovered what it takes and we have discovered where
to find it.

The Church in Cumbria has another claim to the gratitude of the com-
monality. Long before 'conservation' became an 'in' word there was an
incumbent in Cumberland who was pressing home the truths of stewardship
in the matter of natural beauty. The National Trust, now the watchdog
of the nation's treasures, natural and material, was the brainchild of Canon
H. D. Rawnsley, Vical of Crosthwaite, Keswick from 1882 to 1917. Here
was a priest who could never go to his parish church without lifting up his
eyes to the mighty Skiddaw towering over 3000 feet above the little township
which was his parish. He was a doughty Cumbrian, deeply versed in its lore,
a lover of its flora and fauna, and a man of God who saw the Divine imprint
on the hills and the vales and the meres and the rivers. This was the man
who long before the Lake District became a National Park – the largest
in the land – saw that something must be done to prevent the despoiling
hand of unthinking man from doing irreparable harm to a scene of majesty,
grandeur and solitude without parallel in our land. Thus when the National
Trust launched Enterprise Neptune under the patronage of the Duke of
Edinburgh in 1965 and its Northern Regional Officer asked me subsequently
to give it the Church's blessing by becoming chairman of a committee drawn
together to further it in Cumbria, I recalled Rawnsley's work, and indeed his
austere widow whom in my early days in the diocese I had met frequently
on committees and in her home at Allan Bank in Grasmere. I yielded to the
Trust's persuasions.

The committee met from time to time at Rose Castle and whilst all the
members did more work than I in furthering its aims, my own contribution
was one which spread knowledge of what was needed and why it was needed
throughout the schools of the diocese. I suggested that the school-children of
Cumbria should be invited to try their hands at writing poetry extolling the
beauties of the area in which they lived and of the sea and of the coastline,
and to enter these in competition. Again I was able to enlist others to do
the time-consuming work of judging the entries, and the children had the
satisfaction of knowing that their poems would be read by well-known poets
– Miss Margaret Cropper, Mr Norman Nicholson, Mr John Betjeman (now
Sir John) and the then Poet Laureate, Mr C. Day Lewis. I was to discover
immediately that poets, like economists, disagreed as to what was good and
what was not so good, but the end result was satisfactory both in the judging
and the kindling of interest among young children in Enterprise Neptune and
indeed in the National Trust itself. For my part it was not a greatly demanding
task and I learnt much from the correspondence with the poets, not least from
Sir John Betjeman who wrote encouraging remarks on some of the children's
efforts. Among the changing scenes this was but transitory but I felt that being
involved in it I had honoured Rawnsley's memory and work and, maybe,
kindled in the minds of Cumbrian children a reverent approach to their

environment. I suspect too that Robert Southey, sometime Poet Laureate, whose body lies in Crosthwaite Churchyard, would have approved of my encouraging the children's excursion into what he called 'the arts babblative and scribblative'.

A red letter day in the diocese of Carlisle was 9 September 1972, for it was then that five trains, each carrying rather more than 500 people left from Carlisle, Barrow and West Cumberland all bound for York – not for a trip but for a Pilgrimage to the Minster which was in that year celebrating the five hundredth anniversary of the Consecration of the present Church and giving thanks too for the completion of great works of restoration which had cost two million pounds. The idea for such a pilgrimage was conceived by Alan Batty during his spell as Bishop's adviser for Education and the eduction staff, together with Ian Gennan the Diocesan Officer for Mission, who on that day became 'Minister of Transport', planned what proved to be a most memorable occasion.

The Pilgrimage as such is a religious exercise with sixteen hundred years of history behind it, for from the time that Constantine the Great, who was in fact proclaimed Emperor at York, embraced the Christian faith, pilgrimages of the faithful to places made holy by their association with the physical presence of Christ or of the first Apostles became more and more common. Our pilgrimage was indeed to a holy place for the Metropolitical Church of St. Peter at York stands on ground first hallowed by prayer and sacrament over a thousand years ago though at present it hides its oldest fabric in its crypts, the oldest of what is above ground being mid-thirteenth century work. In a message to the pilgrims I noted that we could find places with a comparably long Christian history within our own diocese but York Minster, as the metropolitical church of the Province and as a place touched by so many of the great heroes of the Christian Faith, known and unknown, could at that moment in its history be for us both an inspiration and a place for renewal of our allegiance to Our Lord and His Church.

Our massive congregation assembled in the Minster's nave, impressive in its height and width. We sang the great hymn of the deacon whom the Church of England refused to advance to the priesthood – William Williams – and we sang it to the tune which has carried its words around the world: *Guide me O thou great Redeemer* to *Cwm Rhondha*. During the singing our procession moved through the church to the nave altar where I expressed to the Primate and Metropolitan our greetings and two lay folk did the same on behalf of the laity. Dr. Coggan replied: 'God grant that you may by your pilgrimage to this Cathedral Church catch a new vision of His glory and His will, that you may be inspired to serve him more faithfully in Jesus Christ our Lord.'

The Archdeacon of Carlisle (Richard Bradford) then presented to the Dean of York (Alan Richardson) 'a small token of our esteem for the Mother Church of our Province subscribed by those of us who have made this pilgrimage today'. The Dean spoke briefly to welcome us and then by a complicated system worked out by the organisers, some toured the city as others toured the Cathedral, and this process of coming and going continued through the afternoon until 5 o'clock when once more all the pilgrims filled the Minster's nave for the closing act of worship. Sandwiched between fanfares were these acclamations which the great congregation was invited not to say but to shout! And shout they did!

V. Who is the King of Glory?
R. The Lord of Hosts, he is the King of Glory.
V. King of Kings and Lord of Lords
R. KING OF KINGS AND LORD OF LORDS
V. Risen!
R. RISEN
V. Ascended!
R. ASCENDED!
V. Glorified!
R. GLORIFIED!

There followed George Herbert's *Let all the world in every corner sing* and after my address and the offering of appropriate prayers a final hymn, in the writing of which the Diocesan Youth Officer (David Ellis) and I had collaborated, was sung to the *John Brown's Body* tune. Standing as I was in the pulpit as this was being sung and seeing this vast congregation throwing itself with a transcendent fervour into the words and music, each verse concluding with a tremendous crescendo:

> *Glory, glory Hallelujah . . .*
> *For God lives with us still*

was for me, as I am persuaded it must have been for others, a deeply moving experience which undoubtedly imprinted itself indelibly on the minds and memories of all. Our act of worship closed with a prayer which caught the theme:

> O Heavenly Father, set our hearts on fire we pray thee
> by the power of the Holy Spirit; inspire our minds with
> the vision of a world won for thee; and stir our wills to
> pray and work until thy will is done . . .

On the homeward journey when my suffragan and I, travelling in different trains, went from end to end visiting the faithful in each compartment, we were left in no doubt that they were a 'happy band of pilgrims'. They talked eagerly of their experiences, and in particular of the final act of worship and its firm affirmation of the abiding presence of the Living God among us. It had indeed been an excursion, but an excursion into holiness and our spirits were the stronger for it.

The recollection of that day prompts me to comment on the power and value of hymn singing as an aspect of worship which enables a congregation to articulate convictions and feelings which without the hymn writers' aid would remain inexpressible. Bishop Barry used to say that *Hymns Ancient and Modern* was the average layman's only source book for theology – an assertion which rightly directs attention to the potentially didactic value of hymn singing though perhaps underestimates the confusion of mind created by some hymns which mingle Bible-based orthodox theology with poetic and often exotic imagery. Even so Barry was substantially right; the common man has learnt more Christian theology from the hymn writer than from the professional theologian whose writings are normally beyond his understanding. That fact apart, hymn singing which is brisk and bright rather than torpid and cheerless can voice for a congregation something of what the fellowship of the Holy Spirit means.

In this area, as alas in others, our dear Church of England has been terribly suspicious of enthusiasm, writing it off too glibly as misguided religious emotion. In fact, of course, the very word *enthousiasmos* means 'God-insideness' and if hymn singing awakens us to an awareness of truth, emboldens us to confess it before men and encourages us to order our lives in the light of it, then let us sing and sing and sing – not just the best of the old hymns (the worst are horrendous!) but also the best of the new. The new are suspect first because they are unfamiliar, secondly because they are attempting the very difficult task of expressing an ancient Faith and an ancient Gospel in a modern vocabulary and idiom, and thirdly because they are frequently set to tunes less staid than those to which Anglicans are accustomed. The older among us tend to be conservative but I have to confess that I am finding many of the new hymns stimulating and inspiring.

It was in Workington Parish Church, during the incumbency of Arthur Attwell who came to us from the Deanery of Kimberley and is now Archdeacon of Westmorland and Furness, that I first heard Sydney Carter's *Lord of the Dance*. The Church was full with a congregation whose ages must have ranged from 4 to 80 and when at the end of the Eucharist they all joined exuberantly in singing that lively hymn, I began to examine my prejudices. Not all those who were singing it so heartily would understand its every sentiment, but proclaiming, as they were, Jesus as the Lord of the Dance of life and reciting his triumphs over the worst the world could do, they would at least be reminded that their personal commitment to Christ had set them on the winning side in the battle of life. Nor would its jolly 'Shaker' tune, despised I suspect by the professional musician, leave room for any thought that the Christian Way, demanding though it is, can be other than exciting and exhilarating. Thus, I am now quite happy to '*Tell out my Soul*', to join others to '*Go tell it on the mountains*', to '*Sing Hosanna to the King of Kings*', to pray '*Lord Jesus Christ you have come to us*', to be confronted with the searching question '*Were you there when they crucified my Lord?*' – and a great many othrs. But let no one rob me of the gems of Watt, of Addison, of Wesley of Whittier, of Faber, of Newton, of Newman, of Heber, of Herbert of Keble, and of those many saints of old, among them the Bernards of Cluny and Clairvaux! Maybe the old wine is better but there is a sparkle about the new which conduces an enthusiasm which is not to be despised since it cannot but help to build up the spiritual life of the congregation, particularly among the young people who respond more readily to the lively than to the ponderous.

Clearly a diocesan pilgrimage involving something approaching 3000 people is rare among a bishop's changing scenes, but there are others, rare too but less so, which specially rejoice his heart and excite the devotion and attendance of great numbers of people. I have in mind the Ordinations of men to the sacred ministry and the Consecration of new Churches, momentous occasions and somewhat analogous in that their common concern is separation for Divine Service – of men, of buildings.

Time was when Ordinations were all but invariably held in the Cathedrals but the practice appears to be common now, as ours was in the diocese of Carlisle, to administer the Rite in different churches so that congregations in the main centres might be able to take part in solemnities which spell out so clearly the nature and function of the ordained ministry and the indelible character of Holy Orders. Thus the Cathedral, the Abbey Church of Holm Cultram and the mother churches in Barrow-in-Furness, Penrith, Kendal, Ulverston, Cockermouth, Dalton in Furness and Workington – each in its turn was, during my episcopate, the scene of great congregations witnessing what I regard as one of the most impressive of the Church's solemn rites. I have found that layfolk seeing the ceremony for the first time, have been deeply moved both by the outward and visible signs – the laying on of hands by the bishop and the priests around him, the delivery to each one of a Bible with the august words which accompany the action – and by the stern questions that precede it calling again and again for a determination to be diligent in teaching, in ministering doctrine and sacraments, in pastoral care, in prayers public and private, in personal behaviour, in setting forward 'quietness, peace and love' and in obedience to the bishop. Many a young man must have risen from his knees elated indeed that he had at last fulfilled his heart's, desires and reached a momentous stage in his Christian commitment, yet nevertheless conscious of the awesome responsibility which he had taken upon himself. Such were my feelings at my own ordination and such were my feelings for those upon whom I laid hands. The prevailing note was, however, one of joy for the promises made were all undertaken 'the Lord being my helper', and the gift imparted was 'In the Name of the Father and of the Son and of the Holy Ghost'.

Following a happy precedent set by my predecessor in the See my custom was to invite the newly ordained and their immediate relatives to join me in some hostelry nearby for lunch so that our fellowship sealed in *eucharist* could be expressed in *agape*. Of the forty men whom it was my privilege to ordain most reached that great day in their lives along the traditional path of university and/or theological college, but among them too were older men who had seen service in other callings – a farmer, a policeman, a blacksmith, a draughtsman, a teacher, a clerk. The Living God does not reserve his calls to the sacred ministry to men of one class or of one age though the Church itself has not always been as ready and as eager to further the realisation of those calls by the provision of adequate funds to train and facilities to provide the basic education which some men have lacked. Nevertheless the pattern of the ministry today is such that the popular notion that the Church of England recruits its ministry solely from the middle classes is as unintelligent as that which describes it as 'the Conservative party at prayer'!

A bishop can surely be permitted a modicum of self satisfaction after an Ordination! By the grace of God he has been privileged to send out other messengers, watchmen and stewards of the Lord 'to teach and to premonish, to feed and provide for the Lord's family; to seek for Christ's sheep that are in the midst of this naughty world, that may be saved through Christ for ever', as the ordinal in the Book of Common Prayer expresses it so finely.

The Consecration of a new church building affords a similar satisfaction in that it sees the Church staking God's claim to a new area and expressing God's care and concern for those who come to live within it. When Dr. Cyril Garbett was Bishop of Southwark he complained to his Diocesan Conference, 'I have been a bishop for six years and have not yet consecrated a church'. That was not the petulant grumble of a bishop who thought that he had been missing out on a significant aspect of a bishop's ministry, but the basis of an appeal by an eager bishop asking for £100,000 for the provision of new churches in the vastly expanding housing estates in South London. That was in the 1920s. Carlisle's problem in this connection was never so vast as Southwark's though by the time it confronted us in the third quarter of the century it cost much more than £100,000. Our new areas were within the See city itself, in Barrow-in-Furness, in Whitehaven and in Workington. The diocese was in fact facing the need for money for the new churches at the same time as it was facing the need for money for the improvement and reconstruction of its church schools and I was very much involved in the latter process. One blunt Cumbrian expressed that somewhat pungently, devout Christian that he was, 'there's t'Archdeacon shoutin' for new money for t'schools and t'bishop shoutin' for money for t'churches'. My retort was that we were at least shouting in harmony and that results suggested that we were doing it uncommonly well satisfied him.

In the course of my incumbency of the See I had the privilege of four Consecrations: two of them in new areas in Carlisle and Barrow where the Churches of St. Elizabeth and St. Aidan were provided to meet the needs of the people re-housed from the town centres; one of them (St. Paul's Barrow) enlarging a church proving to be too small to contain all who would worship in it, and one (St. Matthew's Barrow) replacing a building which had been erected in 1878 and at that time had been described by the 58th Bishop of Carlisle (Harvey Goodwin) as 'nothing more than a twenty years' makeshift'.

Three other churches had been consecrated with the original St. Matthew's on 26 September in that year when four bishops descended on the fast-growing township – the Archbishop of York and Bishops of Carlisle, Hereford and Sodor and Man – to Consecrate the four 'Evangelist' churches on the same day and at the same time. Of the original buildings only St. Mark's survives. The solemn consecration of a Church is an occasion so rich in its ritual and ceremony that it is unfortunate that so few people ever have an opportunity of taking part in it and of drawing from it the lesson about worship as an acknowledgment of God's sovereignty which it implants so surely. The recital of the Petition for Consecration and the Bishop's subsequent demand for entrance see the main door opened from within and the congregation hears the bishop call down the Peace of God:

> Peace be to this house from God our Father,
> Peace be to this house from His Son who is our peace,
> Peace be to this house from the Holy Ghost the Comforter.

Moving towards the sanctuary he uses his pastoral staff to make the ALPHA and OMEGA sign on the ground previously strewn with sand. There is a blessing at the door with further signings of the Cross, a hallowing of the Font and of the Altar, which is then furnished with the sacred vessels. The sentence of Consecration is read by the Chancellor of the Diocese who then places the Deed of Consecration on the Altar to be signed and sealed immediately by the Bishop. All things done the Bishop turns to the congregation and declares, as I did at the Consecration of the new St. Matthew's in Barrow:

> By virtue of our Sacred office in the Church of God we do set apart for ever from all common or profane uses this House under the dedication of Saint Matthew, Apostle, Evangelist and Martyr, and do dedicate the same and whatsoever herein is consecrated by our prayers and benediction, for the ministry of God's Holy Word and Sacraments.

The Eucharist follows either immediately or, as in the case of St. Matthew's, on the following day, when it was my privilege to administer both the Dominical Sacraments of Holy Baptism and Holy Communion.

Through the years of my episcopate new shools were being built and extensions added to existing schools; I dedicated seven such the last of which, a primary school in Carlisle bearing the name of the 58th Bishop of Carlisle, Harvey Goodwin, was opened by Dr. Donald Coggan, then the Archbishop of York.

'Consecration', 'Dedication' – the terms are used loosely and without distinction and in one sense rightly so for each concerns the hallowing of people or places for worship and for service directed to Almighty God – the act of consecration different only in the sense that it is deemed to be irrevocable. But 'consecrated churches' and 'dedicated buildings' can fulfil their special purposes only so long as there are consecrated people – people, that is, who recognise that 'the first and great commandment' is spelt out supremely in the worship of God and the second 'which is like unto it' in the service of mankind.

A very different scene concerned especially with the service of mankind was the dedication in 1970 of a little building set amidst the wild moorlands above Ulpha in an area of lakeland which for the most part the trippers leave severely alone. The lakeland artist Delmar Banner and his sculptress wife Josephine de Vasconcellos who live hard by in Langdale – hard by that is, as the crow flies not as the hiker walks! – came one day upon the sort of sorry ruin for which they and friends who shared their concern had long searched. That person was Beckstones, a derelict sixteenth-century farmstead. It was Josephine who posed the question, first doubtless to herself, then to God and finally to the bishop. 'Can these bones live?' The sculptress, who has so often expressed her living faith in splendid works of religous art which even today beautify cathedrals and parish churches, suddenly saw before her, not a pathetic pile of dead stones which spelt dereliction, but a tiny hostel for boys in trouble, fashioned out of the same stones. Opening its doors, as it would, to the young who might come for fellowship, for adventure, for vision, for renewal, for re-creation, even the hills around would rejoice for the new life within them. At its heart there must be a little Chapel where perchance minds might be led from the wild beauty around to the Author of all Beauty, Goodness and Truth.

So it came to be. Teams of boys came from Approved Schools with their training instructors to breathe new life into the dead stones and gradually the derelict was restored, the dead was brought to life, the ruin became a hostel where two or three could gather together and where in their fellowship one with another, they might encounter the Lord of Life. It could indeed be another Emmaus – or an Outpost thereto. So the work must be done within the ambit of the Church's concern and must be dedicated to the glory of God and the highest welfare of His children. The dedication took place on 2 May 1970 when a considerable company gathered (many from London since what was being done was in association with the Church of England Council for Social Aid) to call down God's blessing upon the building and the venture of which it was to be centre. I have always found, as I did again on that afternoon, that there is something strangely serene about an act of worship in the open and on that day, blest as it was with sunshine, when the natural excitement of the occasion was stilled and only the mountain stream chattered on, the words of dedication assumed a majesty which matched the august grandeur around us:

In the faith of Jesus Christ we dedicate this building. May it stand ever for that which is true, noble, just and lovely. May the Spirit of the Living God illuminate the minds of those who direct its use. Here may the sinful find pardon, the lonely find friends, the wayward find purpose, and all find themselves. In the Name of the Father and of the Son and of the Holy Ghost

Only a handful of the great company could squeeze themselves into the cabin-sized chapel but there too, before the tiny Altar which came from the crypt of St. Martins-in-the-Field, and from which in the days of the First World War Dick Sheppard had ministered the Holy Sacrament, the hallowing was completed:

> May the benediction of thy Presence O Lord rest upon this place and dwell in the hearts of all who shall come here. Here may the young be strengthened in resolve and hope; here may they be inspired to walk the way of Jesus with gladness, courage and humility, to whom praise and glory evermore.

Following all of which there was much merriment during which the boys from the Approved School served teas, sorted out parked cars, joined in an impromptu episcopal sing-song and doubtless felt themselves 'walking tall' in their warm acceptance by a company of people whom they might have regarded as very distinguished! From that day to this Beckstones has persisted unassumingly but effectively in the work which it was founded to do and there is not lacking evidence to suggest that the need foreseen is being met and that many a derelict young life has been fashioned anew.

The setting for the last of my changing scenes was the great fourteenth-century hall of Durham Castle, once the home of the Bishop of Durham and now, as for a century or so, of University College. There in 1932 I had received my Bachelor's degree and three years later my Master's degree. There was no thought then that I should ever step inside that impressive place again for further academic awards, but in fact 36 years later it was there that I received at the hands of the Chancellor of the University, Mr. Malcolm Macdonald, the degree of Doctor of Divinity, *honoris causa*. The ceremony was conducted with the customary academic ritual and ceremonial and the Great Hall was splashed here and there with colourful hoods and gowns. Durham University has not been noted for profligacy in the matter of honorary degrees but on that afternoon, along with my D.D., the Chancellor conferred the degree of D.Sc. on two eminent scientists – the Viennese psychologist Dr. Conrad Lorenz and the Swedish professor of Physics, Dr. Kai Siegbahn, the degree of D.Litt on the anthropologist Dr. Lucy Mair and the degree of Master of Arts on Fr. Bernard Payne, the Librarian of Ushaw College. The public Orator Professor W. B. Fisher, whose task it was to present each of us to the Chancellor with an appropriate introduction, described me a 'a unique specimen of *episcopus ex grege Dunelmensis*, or to speak more plainly the sole existing English bishop from among our graduates'. With obvious references to things I had said and written he spoke of me as uniting in my career 'two of the best known activities of Durham: theology and education' and expressed it as appropriate that the University should honour its 'one and only occupant of a major British See'. If ever in my career I felt a little pride it was then as I reflected not only upon the truth of that statement but on the fact that I was also the first of the 'Sons of St. Chad' to have become an English diocesan bishop. Following the formal ceremony, the bishop who as a boy had no stomach for science and could never master its essence or its jargon, found himself in easy conversation with the Director of the Max-Planck Institut fur Verhaltensphysiologie and with the 'father' of a particular branch of spectroscopy known as Electron Spectroscopy for Chemical Analysis – but neither then nor now would he care to be examined in either discipline even at the most elementary level.

Earlier in my story I passed over in just a line an occasion which I am told merits expansion since it touches something which arouses people's interest not to say curiosity. I refer a the ceremony of doing homage to Her Majesty before I could pass to my Enthronement. For me the day was memorable both for the solemnities and for what followed them. The homage ceremony takes place privately in Buckingham Palace where the new bishop meets first the Clerk of the Closet. It happened that that office was held then by Bishop Roger Wilson of Chichester, an old friend of mine from Southwell days. Having donned our Convocation robes we were led by an equerry to the audience room at the door of which he announced our presence and we were ushered into the royal presence. The Queen having greeted me with a handshake sat in a chair rather more episcopal than regal. I knelt in front of her and when she had enclosed my hands within hers, I repeated the quaintly phrased Oath administered by the Home Secretary (Roy Jenkins):

I, SYDNEY CYRIL BULLEY, Master of Arts, having been elected BISHOP OF CARLISLE, and such election having been duly confirmed DO HEREBY DECLARE that Your Majesty is the Supreme Governor of this your Realm in Spiritual and Ecclesiastical things as well as in Temporal AND that no foreign prelate or potentate has any jurisdiction within this Realm AND I ACKNOWLEDGE that I hold the said Bishopric as well the Spiritualities and the Temporalities thereof only to Your Majesty and for the same Temporalities I DO MY HOMAGE presently to Your Majesty,

So Help me God . . .

Meanwhile the Clerk of the Closet stands by holding a large cushion on which is a copy of the Holy Bible. He proffers the Bible to the bishop who kisses it and thus completes the formal ceremony. To the cynical all this would be seen as no more than a clip from *Iolanthe*; to me it was a page of history invested still with great significance, albeit somewhat Erastian. The formalities over, Her Majesty engaged me in conversation for approximately ten minutes, with the Clerk and the Home Secretary joining in from time to time. With handshakes all round the Bishop and the Clerk left with a final bow.

Leaving the Palace, Roger Wilson and I repaired to the House of Lords for lunch and it was there as we waited in a small room for a vacant table that, following a gentle knock at the door, there loomed around it the head of none other than the comedian Frankie Howerd. There was an apology for the intrusion, and then an explanation that he was in search of a particular bishop with whom he was to have lunch and an enquiry as to where he might find him. When I suggested that he should try the bar the comedian assumed his customary shocked expression and began in his best T.V. style to imply that I was 'mocking Francis' by suggesting that a brother bishop was to be found in the bar. There followed a couple of minutes of pure comedy between us after which I led him to the bar where he did in fact find his quarry.

Thus at 12.25 p.m. on 8 March 1967 I was talking with Her Majesty the Queen and at 12.50 I was talking to Frankie Howerd. Did ever any man move so swiftly from the sublime to the ridiculous?

14

New Horizons

In 1963 there was published the *Paul Report*, a formidable document of 300 pages summarised in 62 principal recommendations dealing with the deployment and payment of the clergy. Following its presentation to the Church Assembly in 1964 Diocesan Conferences debated its contents and the hope was expressed that Ruri-Decanal Conferences would do the same. It fell to my lot, at the request of my chief at the time – Bishop Bloomer – to speak about it at the Carlisle Diocesan Conference, and this I did though somewhat reluctantly since there were sections of it in which he and I did not see eye-to-eye. Being the man he was, however, he encouraged me to address myself to the Report with no inhibitions and this I tried to do. Only a small part of the Report is germane to this part of my story – that dealing with the retirement of the clergy and with what the report itself calls 'an open system of promotion'.

With respect to the retirement of the clergy the anonymous editor of the preface of the 1972 edition of *Crockford's Clerical Directory* is in error when he asserts that I called for the compulsory retirement of the clergy at the age of 65. In fact on that section I reiterated views I had long held which were in fact in tune with the Report, namely that it should be made possible at the very earliest moment for parochial clergy to retire at the age of 65 and that if by then they had served for forty years in the ministry they should receive a full pension. I supported that recommendation not merely because it had been accepted by then that 65 was the normal male retirement age but because it had always seemed to me that a man ordained at the age of 23 who for over 40 years had thrown himself into a job of work demanding a selfless expenditure of physical and mental energy deserved a measure of leisure in the evening of his days. Eight years were to elapse before legislation to that end was approved and a great many priests now take advantage of it. They know they are and will ever remain priests, and they find opportunities for a continuing ministry and will continue to do so in the light of the unions of benefices now taking place.

It was on the section of the report dealing with 'promotion' – I use the Report's word – that I went beyond its recommendations. Commenting that the Church did not provide a career structure for its ordained officers it noted that the priest

> suffers from disabilities which impede few other professional men . . . he cannot canvas his abilities or experience; he cannot apply for promotion however worthy he may think himself. The Church has a 'Closed' system of promotion . . . One may perhaps bypass the conceivably endless discussion about the ethics of promotion by saying that something quite modest is under discussion – how men get moved to posts of greater challenge, greater responsibility and sometimes greater reward.

The report went on to propose all sorts of ways in which 'the inadequacy of the Church's system of promotion and preferment' might be remedied, suggesting *inter alia* a central directory of clergy, the appointment of 'town deans' and what it called 'bishops-in-little' and the replacement of 'freeholds' by 'leaseholds'. It was suggested with regard to the last mentioned recommendation that an incumbent whose freehold or leasehold expired on his 70th birthday could seek an extension of it from his bishop. (What bishop of 69 years of age would dare say 'NO' to such a request!) The report saw that what was needed was 'some more general increase of promotion possibilities', but it did not, in my judgement, grasp the nettle which is that in a ministerial structure such as that in the Church of England, which is a pyramid with a very narrow apex, people can move up only as people at the top move out. It was at that point in my speech to the conference that I said that bishops, and maybe other dignitaries, should retire at 65 quipping, I recall, that a man continued to be 65 until the day before his sixty-sixth birthday. It was no sudden or ill-considered comment. Just after I became Bishop of Penrith I had had a casual late night conversation with Archbishop Fisher in Lambeth Palace. It began with an off the cuff remark on his part to the effect that he ought to retire but that he wondered who there was to succeed him. I guess that he made the remark deliberately to draw out a comment or two from an unwary young bishop, but I recall that when I answered immediately, 'I can think of at least four worthy successors' his glances were swiftly moved to his forehead and a great roar of laughter filled the drawing room as he demanded to know the names of my four potential Archbishops of Canterbury – one of whom did in fact succeed him. It was to him, I think, that I first used the phrase that so long as those who got to the top of the pyramid, or near to top, froze on to their jobs beyond the age at which in every other profession men would retire if only *'pour encourager les autres'*, long would there be countless clergy of outstanding ability who would never be given the opportunity of exercising their gifts in the upper echelons of the Church's ministry. I got little further with him then – save that he agreed that the day would have to come when there would be an acceptable and accepted retiring age. Our hour-long debate was never renewed but I received many kindly letters from His Grace from time to time, notably on my appointment to Carlisle, on my contribution to the Anglican-Methodist debate, and on my retirement.

Reverting to the Diocesan Conference I recall that among the questions following my speech one priest raised the time-honoured comment that Archbishop Garbett had done his best work when he was past the age of 70. I replied that I could not regard it as either true or complimentary to suggest that the Archbishop was a late developer but that on his own admission he did his best work during his time at Southwark. (In this connection it is interesting to learn from Canon Charles Smyth's great biography of the archbishop that he went to York very conscious of what he called his 'old age' [67] and that in the light of it he was persuaded that he had not the qualities which the office demanded.) In a later comment in his diary he goes so far as to say that he was not happy at York. During his days at Southwark he had expressed the view that bishops should retire at 65, but approaching that age, and subsequently as year succeeded year, he lifted the desirable retiring age. On going to York at the age of 67 he told the Prioress of Whitby that 'bishops should retire at 70', but very shortly after he was expressing a conviction that he should retire at 75. On his seventieth birthday, however, he expressed the hope, in his diary, that he might be able to do another seven years work, and although on his eightieth birthday he writes of 'my rather sudden realisation of my age', he was yet resolved to put in another year by which time he thought people might not expect him to go on much longer! The truth was that the old man, tired and lonely, could not 'let go' even though years before he had seen his own projected appointment to the Bishopric of London thwarted by Arthur Foley Winnington-Ingram's determination to hold on to the See at all costs, which he did until he was 82.

Each in his turn had, from the Church's angle, made the same grave mistake. Inability to 'let go' had seriously checked what the *Paul Report* called 'promotion possibilities'. Now, of course, bishops are required to retire at 70 and it is noticeable that many are doing so much earlier. Since in the secular world one of the answers to massive unemployment must surely be earlier retirement it behoves the officers of the Church to set an example within their own sphere and as retirement does not deny them a continuing ministry they can do this with the assurance that it is in no way 'the end' either for themselves or for the Church. Cosmo Gordon Lang's fear on his impending retirement from the Primacy – 'from a somebody I shall become a nobody' – can in fact be a benediction, for what man thrust constantly into the public eye has not longed for a little privacy! Thus I stand where I did – that in their sixty-sixth year diocesan bishops should move from the apex to afford opportunities for others to make their contribution but I would concede that the Primates, who do not normally reach their high office, and should not, until well into their fifties, should see their seventieth birthday as the day when they should make way for others to enter into their goodly heritage.

When 1972 opened I needed no reminder that in the course of it I should move into my sixty-sixth year and I began to consider not whether I should retire but when. The convictions I have outlined above were still with me but I cannot pretend that I was never haunted by plausible reasons for setting them aside. Deep satisfaction with the work I was doing, a proper pride in the office I held, and the loyalty of my colleagues saw to that! I could have succumbed to the disease of 'indispensibilitis' as easily as I could have caught a cold, but only a very poor view of the overall quality of the Church's total ministerial manpower could have sustained the notion that it lacked an able, dedicated and experienced priest who could succeed me to lead the diocese in writing the next chapter in its long history. I had, moreover, been given the privilege of working for 21 years in the diocese of Carlisle, and if I may be allowed to count the four years at university as years of work, I had been working 'flat out' (if the crude expression be permitted) for nearly fifty years. If sometimes I had been tired in my work whether as parish priest, director of education, archdeacon or bishop, and for 14 years of my ministry several of these at once, I had never been tired of it.

Uppermost in my mind just then was an ambition I had nursed for many years, the realisation of which would ensure that I did not retire into a vacuum. In the course of my ministry I had twice been approached to consider demanding episcopal appointments overseas and on each occasion the home Church was persuaded that my duty was to continue the work I was doing. I accepted the judgement of my superiors but confess that in doing so I made a mental note that when the day of retirement came I would, come wind come weather, do a bit for the church overseas. I was now ready to pursue that resolve. Thus early in the year I informed Bishop Ian Shevill, secretary at that time of the Society for the Propagation of the Gospel, that by the year's end I could be at the disposal of any overseas bishop who might be able to use me for a year or so and that without charge on his diocese. I made the one maybe cowardly proviso that I could not at my age start learning Swahili or some other foreign tongue. After consultation with the Primate and after receiving through the Prime Minister (Edward Heath) Her Majesty's permission to resign the See, I announced my intention to the diocese in the spring meeting of the Diocesan Synod. I suspect that few who heard it realised the traumatic nature of the battle 'twixt the bite of conscience and the pull of heart of which that announcement was the culmination. But I slept soundly and at peace that night, and as the days and weeks passed was greatly strengthened by an avalanche of letters from clergy and laity alike all regretting my decision (I would not have had it otherwise!) but all writing kindly letters expressing gratitude and good wishes.

I took with a pinch of salt a phrase which occurred in one form or another in many letters from laity 'I did not think you were anywhere near 65! Among my letters were two or three from diocesan bishops applauding my action, one of whom said succinctly, 'You are right of course. I wish I had the courage to do it.' However, one senior clergyman, never averse to publicity, did indeed thrust a sword into my soul in a letter to the press in which he bitterly criticised my decision to retire but this letter, wounding though it was, was offset by the kindness which marked all the other letters which whilst expressing regret that I was leaving appreciated that my decision was in line with convictions I had voiced before; the phrase 'courage of your convictions' occurred in more than one letter. An evocative headline 'Bishop keeps a promise' – was it in the *Church Times*? – suggested either that the episcopate generally was not noted for doing just that or that the writer of the news item could remember other bishops who had called for earlier retirement but had forgotten their call by the time they reached the age they had cited as appropriate! In the May issue of the *Diocean News* I commented:

> The next six months will be very precious to me and I doubt not very difficult too. Only a man with a heart of stone could contemplate the breaking of a happy 21 years' association with people and places, and the relinquishing of so privileged a charge without a good deal more than a tinge of sorrow. But the Church is not here for my convenience and I must do, not what I might desire, but what I conceive to be in the best interests of the vast work which the Church is charged to do. I have long held the view that for the health of the Church bishops should not hold on to their privileged positions much longer than the age of 65. It is, of course, easier to express one's convictions than it is to implement them when they strike home; hence I have not found the decision easy, but having made it I am at ease. Furthermore I am greatly encouraged by the way in which the principle which motivated me has won the approval of so many inside and outside the diocese. But now, please, let me forget it for six months.

Forget it I did, for the months from then until the end of November had their customary toll of public engagements with visits to seventy parishes for Confirmations and institutions, to schools for pastoral visits and to others for prize-givings, and all the varied engagements which make a bishop's life so absorbing. Teaching by the written word continued too, and this touching the Archbishop of York's Call to the North, the new Liturgies, the Christian approach to leisure, the tragedy of unemployment, the danger and ruthlessness of Marxist Communism, and the power of 'amazing grace'.

But there was one aspect of all this which I could not forget during those six months and that was towards what new horizons I should walk. From April onwards I began to receive letters from diocesan bishops in different parts of the world with pleas comparable with that of the Macedonians, 'Come over and help us'. All these in response to my readiness, widely advertised by Ian Shevill, to 'do something for nothing for the overseas church'. Setting some of these aside was not difficult but having reduced the letters to six and counting each of the bishops who wrote them as among my friends, the task of deciding whom I should disappoint was incredibly difficult, so much so that my good secretary, Carolyn Fisher, for the first time in her period of service, found opportunity to call my attention to unanswered letters. Papua New Guinea, Australia, Melanesia, New Zealand were among enticing invitations offering different types of ministry – training ordinands, administering diocesan education, teaching in Christian schools, service as Chaplain, directing diocesan Mission. At length I accepted an invitation from the Bishop of Bathurst N.S.W. who had served on a committee with me at the 1968 Lambeth Conference, to be Chaplain at All Saints' College for boys in his diocese and to fill in some of the gaps which the absence of the Headmaster on sabbatical through 1973 would create. As I had just appointed Robert Waddington, who had been Headmaster of a similar College in Queensland, as Diocesan Director of Education in succession to Alan Batty, I was able to draw from him the encouragement which a 65-year-old needed to fortify him for so bold a venture.

My last ten days as Bishop of Carlisle could not have embraced more adequately the varied aspects of a bishop's work. Everything was there – committees of the Board of Finance, of Rydal Hall, of Greystoke College Council, of Pastoral Reorganisation and a meeting of the Diocesan Synod at which the diocese bade me farewell with warm wishes, kind words and a fat cheque. But most significantly for me the last days had within them the three episcopal acts which had meant more than any others to me through my years as a bishop. The period began with an Institution of two parish priests to new charges; there followed three Confirmations and, on the last evening of my episcopate, an Ordination in Holy Trinity Church Carlisle.

I can recall an incident in the Cathedral when a layman asked me, as we stood in front of the Bishop's Throne, whether I experienced moments of elation and exaltation when I ascended it on the occasions of my visits. I had to answer 'No'. 'In fact,' I added 'the reverse could be true for it is so commodious that it reduces me to size!' Pressed by him to cite moments in my life and work as a bishop which transcended others I admitted that there were such, and that I found them in the Laying on of Hands in Confirmations, in the Institution of parish priests to new parishes, and in the Ordination of men to the Sacred Ministry. These were the acts which I had always found deeply impressive and the recital of certain words within them was a constant reminder of the high privilege which a bishop enjoys, of the solemnity of his office and of the heavy responsibility inherent in it. Within each Rite there was for me the instant, grave and momentous, when words pregnant with meaning beyond the temporal and material, were said over or to the one who knelt before me. Heard as they have been by thousands of Christian pilgrims, ordained and lay, their reproduction here may serve to awaken the memories and stir up the wills of God's faithful people.

At the Confirmations in those last ten days, one in the little church of St. Cuthbert at Holm Cultram, one in the Parish Church of Penrith and one in St. John's, Workington, young confirmands knelt before me as ever, and laying my hands on the head of each one I prayed:

Defend O Lord this thy child N with thy heavenly grace that he may continue thine for ever and daily increase in thy Holy Spirit more and more until he come to thine everlasting kingdom.

Similarly at an Ordination the ordinand kneels before the bishop who lays his hands upon him and, joined in this act by other priests surrounding him, he commissions him to the Order of Priesthood:

RECEIVE the Holy Ghost for the office and work of a priest in the Church of God, now committed unto thee by the imposition of our hands. Whose sins thou dost forgive, they are forgiven; and whose sins thou dost retain they are retained. And be thou a faithful dispenser of the Word of God, and of His Holy Sacraments; In the Name of the Father and of the Son and of the Holy Ghost. Amen.

And handing the newly ordained priest a Bible the bishop continues:

TAKE thou authority to preach the Word of God, and to minister the Holy Sacraments in the congregation where thou shalt be lawfully appointed thereto.

When the priest is given a Charge of his own he again kneels before the bishop for the act of Institution. The Deed of Institution, couched in the language of law which far from concealing the solemnity of the occasion seemed to me to enhance it, is then recited as the incumbent-to-be holds the episcopal seal. At my last Institution the parish church of Warcop was filled with parishioners from the village itself and from Musgrave hard by. They witnessed the Institution of their vicar and heard the time-honoured words:

CYRIL, by Divine permission Lord Bishop of Carlisle to our Beloved in Christ Reginald Williamson, Clerk, GREETING. WE do by these presents admit you to the Vicarage and Parish Churches of Warcop with Musgrave in the County of Westmorland and our Diocese of Carlisle (now vacant by the resignation of Robin Lang Wilson Jones, Clerk, Master of Arts, the last incumbent thereof). AND we do hereby duly and canonically Institute you in and to the said Vicarage and Parish Churches and invest you with all and sundry the Rights Members and Appurtenances thereto belonging. (You having first before Us subscribed the Declarations and taken the Oaths which in this case are by Law required to be subscribed and taken). AND we do by these presents commit unto you the cure of the souls of the Parishioners of the Parish of Warcop and Musgrave aforesaid both yours and ours SAVING ALWAYS to Us and our Successors Bishops of Carlisle all Ordinary and Episcopal rights and jurisdiction and the dignity and honour of our

Cathedral Church of Carlisle. IN TESTIMONY whereof our Episcopal Seal is hereunto affixed GIVEN under our hand this twenty-first day of October in the Year of Our Lord One thousand nine hundred and seventy two in the fourteenth year of our Consecration and of our Translation the seventh.

The document, signed and sealed was then handed to the new parish priest with the awesome words:

RECEIVE the Cure of souls which is both mine and thine –

awesome because by these words there is established a mutual trust between the bishop and the priest, and that a trust which concerns nothing less than the spiritual welfare of the people of God within a given area.

'Defend O Lord this thy child with thy heavenly grace' . . . 'Receive the Holy Ghost for the office and work of a priest in the Church of God' . . . 'Receive the cure of souls which is both mine and thine' – grave utterances all of them yet affording me moments of ecstasy, for do they not get near to the very heart of the work and ministry of a bishop? It was then that I felt most acutely that Christ was confirming my heart's desire to work and speak and think for him, as Charles Wesley puts it, that I was being used to 'guard the holy fire' and imparting his gift to others, that I prayed most earnestly that he would stir up his gift in me. Those were the occasions when I felt – to use the layman's words – elated and exalted.

So on 31 October 1972, having as my last public act as Bishop of Carlisle ordained to the Sacred Ministry one Michael Comber who had already served the Church faithfully as a Church Army Evangelist, I went back to Rose Castle, I confess with a heavy heart which was not lightened by the forlorn appearance of a study already dishevelled. My successor, David Halsey Bishop of Tonbridge, was already appointed and in the October issue of the *Diocesan News* I had bespoken the prayers of the faithful for him and assured him of the welcome which would be accorded him by the laity and clergy alike. Of the latter I had commented that I had never had cause to describe my clergy as John Best, the 32nd Bishop, had described his – as 'wicked ympes of Antichrist and for ye most parte very ignorante and stubborne and past measure false and sotle'. I added moreover that I was confident that he for his part would not be able to indict his predecessor as did Henry Robinson, the 35th Bishop in the line, indict his, as having had 'a great facility in committing the charge of sowles to incompetent persons'.

I remember that last night so vividly. I signed a letter or two – and for the last time 'Cyril Carliol' – and reflected that anything from then until the new bishop took up his office would fall to be executed by the Bishop of Penrith who would be receiving from the Archbishop of York his mandate to hold the fort for the ten or a dozen weeks of the vacancy. I had no qualms about that. Edward Pugh was a friend of nearly forty years' standing; his service to the diocese as parish priest, as archdeacon of West Cumberland and as suffragan bishop had been outstanding. Wise in judgement, discerning in purpose, outgoing and warm in personality he was ever the loyal colleague whose ministry was marked by an intrinsic sincerity which ensured its grateful acceptance. I knew that in him I was bestowing upon my successor an able 'first Lieutenant' whom he would soon come to value as I had done. Confidently, then, on clearing my desk I marked a few papers 'Pass to E.P.' Then there was a further attempt, having failed in many, to stuff some goods and chattels into packing cases which had for several weeks lain empty in my study their gaping mouths mocking my inactivity. Suddenly the grandfather clock, which stood so proudly at the foot of Bishop Percy's fine oak staircase, struck midnight and though I had heard it do that very frequently since it was hard by the study, tonight was different. It was as though it added a postscript to its declaration of the fatal hour – 'Give an account of your stewardship'. I left the packing cases and went to the Chapel and kneeling there in the silence and darkness I handed in my portfolio with a *Te Deum* for what under God I had been privileged and enabled to do and a *Miserere* for failures and omissions. It was Hallowe'en – the night of the saints, not especially the giants like Peter, James and John, not so much Francis, Theresa or Our Lady, each of whom has a special commemoration day, but the little people whose names are unrecorded and whose work is forgotten by man, who wobbled through life maybe 'twixt good and evil, fidelity and perfidy, achievement and failure, but who through it all pressed on 'looking unto Jesus, the Author and Finisher' of their faith, praying ever that they might be what C. S. Lewis somewhere calls 'little Christs'. I was in good company in the Chapel that night. I awoke next morning with eyes on new horizons – Europe, East Africa, New Zealand, Australia.

Within three days I was on my travels, and not without hesitation. William Hazlitt in his essay *On Going a Journey* expressed my feelings as I set foot for the first time and alone on foreign soil of Europe. 'I should want at intervals to hear the sound of my own language', he wrote and certainly that was my experience as I looked upon sights familiar to me in art but never before experienced in 'the real'. Everywhere there were marvels 'too mighty for any single contemplation'. In Milan, in Venice, in Assisi and in Rome the craving for companionship in wonder was met, and very generously, by the Church itself – everywhere by the Roman Church and here and there by the Anglican. The art student who showed me the delights of Venice and then bade me stand patiently on the Rialto for the magic moment when the setting sun would transform the scene by heightening the colours of the Palaces on the Grand Canal, and the little Italian monk who greeted me in Assisi with a deep genuflexion and a kissing of the episcopal ring, did more than ensure that I should see all. I was wandering as 'a limb torn off from society', as again Hazlitt puts it; they re-united me and the experiences shared were by the same token heightened. The little Italian who rose from his genuflexion with a stammered apology that he knew no English belied his assertion with the words 'I call American brother priest. He show you all – si!' and returned within minutes with the American who talked of St. Francis as a brother with whom he was ever in contact. By the tomb of the saint we lifted the prayer which breathes his spirit though it comes not from his hand. Other precious experiences awaited me.

Within an hour of arriving in Rome I was invited to read the Gospel at a Roman Mass in the ecumenical centre in which I stayed which was run by Dutch Roman Catholic nuns. The Mass was said by a Spanish priest in his own tongue and only the Epistle, in Dutch, and the Gospel, in English, could be followed by the handful of Religious present. Disappointment was expressed by the Sisters following the Mass that I had not joined them in receiving the Sacrament and on my admitting that I had refrained from doing so out of a desire not to embarrass them they pleaded with me to join them again on the following evening, before leaving for the airport, to read the Epistle and the Gospel in English and to receive Communion with them, all of which I was happy to do. I had a strong suspicion that had my stay been extended by a few days I might have been invited to say Mass in that little Chapel not a mile from the Vatican! As it was on the third evening I was driven somewhat madly along the Appian Way to the airport there to board a plane for Nairobi where I experienced one of those rare moments of ecstasy which waft a man into the transcendental.

I had prayed and sought prayers for Africa and its peoples throughout my ministry. I had, as a child, put my weekly penny into the missionary box and stocked many a stall at parochial missionary sales with jigsaw puzzles and bits of artistic fretwork. I had as a parish priest encouraged missionary interest among young people as among adults and brought to my parishes representatives of the various missionary societies to teach, to interest and to appeal. Now, standing before a congregation of 400 African boys on my first Sunday in Kenya left me momentarily speechless. Here was what it had all been about: 'This is the Lord's doing and it is marvellous in our eyes.' They listened intently, they sang heartily and when about 250 of them came to the Altar to receive the Sacrament, the white Host on the black hand seemed to me to be a silent proclamation of the victory of the Christ. 'He has made the two one, and in his own body of flesh and blood has broken down the enmity which stood like a dividing wall between them' (Ephesians ch. 2, v. 14) So has He done; so can He do whether the 'dividing wall' be race or colour or class or culture if, that is, He is accepted as the Way, the Truth and the Life.

The city of Nairobi did not strike me as typically African even though white faces were very rare. The vast buildings, housing banks and offices and government departments, the very lovely cathedral, the huge shops and the busy traffic all combine to give a European flavour. It was not until I went into the city's fifty square mile game reserve that I began to feel that I really was on African soil, and not until I set out on the 350-mile journey to Mombasa that I saw something of the wilder and more primitive Kenya.

On that road motorists are not infrequently impeded by elephant claiming the road by a 'sit-in' and although we met but one who obligingly stepped aside, baboons playing at the side of the road, dead jackals, doubtless killed on their night prowls, green and blue birds flitting hither and thither, jacaranda trees with their glorious purple foliage, tall coconut trees and banana trees with their huge leaves, all made the long journey very exciting. The little settlements which we passed were primitive – mud houses, some with a type of thatch, some with corrugated iron roofs, little children running around happily in their birthday suits, older children making their way on foot to their primary schools and proudly dressed in shirt and shorts, adults going about their business carrying goods on their heads – this was the authentic Africa.

In Mombasa itself huge and gracious buildings, vast stores which could vie with ours, and gift shops galore rubbed shoulders with mud shops, their wares displayed outside in a higgledy-piggledy muddle. I was very graciously entertained in a house on Nyali Beach some ten miles from the city centre and over the next ten days experienced a humid heat which not only made me shed clothing to the very point at which decency called a halt, but saw me spending most of the day consuming iced drinks and most of the night having shower after shower. A few days on safari introduced me at close quarters to all the beasts of the earth, some timid, some fierce, some beautiful, some ugly. Baboons fought wildly on the verandah of my lodge and at night jackals and hyenas prowled around in search of food. The dawn chorus started about 4 a.m. and rose to a terrific crescendo as the sun rose. Altogether an awe-inspring and unforgettable experience.

It was at Mombasa that I met with the first hitch in my progress to Australia for the shipping line denied all knowledge of the whereabouts of the container ship in which their British agents had booked me a passage to Sydney. Thus the voyage to which I had been looking forward as offering me the longest holiday since my working life had begun nearly fifty years before was snatched from me, and since the officials in the Mombasa office seemed to be unwilling even to consider refunding the fare I had already paid in England I found myself in a foreign country literally and financially high and dry! There followed days of unpleasant litigation with bewildered but ever courteous African clerks who finally agreed to book a passage for me on a liner from Cape Town but seemed content to see me walking the 2500 miles to get there. Ultimately, with the help of a generous host I flew from Kenya to Johannesburg, there to encounter further trouble in an apparent reluctance to admit me into South Africa.

Hitherto my clerical collar – or was it my purple stock? – had seemed to render my passport redundant for nowhere had it been so much as taken out of my hand for more than one cursory glance. In Johannesburg it was examined carefully and indeed eyed with suspicion. The flow of passengers moved swiftly past whilst I was invited to stand aside and subsequently to complete a form which became the subject of something like a cross-examination. Only then did I realise that my passport still bore the legend 'Lord Bishop of Carlisle' and I began to wonder whether I was to be regarded as *persona non grata*. The minutes slipped by as discussions took place in an adjacent office and I confess that I began to recall the sort of things I had written and said about *apartheid*. Less than a year before something I had written in the *Diocesan News* had appeared in one of the South African national papers, nor was that the first time that critical comments of mine had been so reported. Way back in 1949, when the word *apartheid* had scarcely been heard in our land, I had written an article under the title *Putting the Clock Back* in which I had noted that whereas General Smuts and his United Party had moved very slowly but quite decisively towards a more enlightened racial policy, Dr. Malan was clearly resolved to move towards a rigid policy of racial segregation. Church leaders at that time had sought to meet Malan to reason with him but had been rebuffed by his secretary who had declared that no useful purpose could be served by such a meeting since those seeking it 'obviously stigmatize the existence as well as the traditional policy of the country as unjust, anti-Christian and immoral'. Indeed they did and do! Many times since then I had returned to the subject. Now, I wondered, had they a 'little list'? If so was I on it? I assured them that I was but a bird of passage but being unable to produce evidence of my berth on the liner leaving Cape Town within days they were not convinced. Ultimately, however, I persuaded them that a telephone call to the shipping line in Cape Town would assure them that – as I put it somewhat sarcastically to them – I would not be in their country long enough to do what they might regard as irreparable damage to their Constitution! Expressed thus the discussion produced the first smile. They rang Cape Town and I was immediately allowed through the barrier. I walked straight to a coffee stall to receive the answer, 'I dare not serve you sir. The stall for whites is over there.' Momentarily I felt ashamed to be white but when I observed that the toilets were similarly divided according to the colour of the skin I chuckled to myself at what seemed to be the *reductio ad absurdam* of racial segregation. Pray God that the South African Government will come to its senses before it is too late to avert a catastrophe!

It was thus with a sense of defiant triumph that I accompanied the Archbishop of Cape Town on the following Sunday morning to one of the African reserves in his diocese to join a vast congregation of Africans in the Sacraments of Confirmation and Holy Communion. There the Archbishop and I were the only whites. The experience was one which I shall not easily forget, not least because the address which I gave, interpreted by a young African ordinand, was greeted with uninhibited applause and I reflected that an English congregation would have regarded such a response as highly improper if not impious. The service itself, in the Xosa language, was memorable. Never had I heard such hearty if somewhat raucous singing – all unaccompanied and led by an old man in the front of the congregation with a face like a gnarled oak, a voice which could vie with the loudest stop on the greatest organ, and eyes which shone with transcendent joy. Not for years too had I been caught up in such elaborate ceremonial. Here was a congregation which knew the meaning of worshipping the Lord in the beauty of holiness. Words and actions alike were invested with a joyous enthusiasm which betrayed the presence of the Spirit and I sensed throughout the service the rapture which prompted their lively worship. I was grateful to the Archbishop – Robert Selby Taylor, a Cumbrian – for according such a privilege to an unexpected guest.

Within a day or two I had boarded a Greek liner bound for Sydney but I soon discovered that the voyage was not to be the quiet and restful one which I had planned from Mombasa. Here were over two thousand immigrants from England, Ireland, Holland and Germany, and within an hour of embarking I found myself back on the job planning with two Anglican priests, and in partnership with a Presbyterian minister and a Roman Catholic priest, daily morning prayers, Sunday services and celebrations of the Holy Communion. It was not long before passengers became aware of our presence and there opened up a ministry of counselling and pastoral concern, more particularly to those who were beginning to feel apprehensive about their decision to emigrate. We were then half way through the season of Advent and inevitably there came a request for a service of Nine Lessons and Carols. This had necessarily to be both ecumenical and international with lessons and carols in German, English, Dutch and, to satisfy the Greek crew in particular, one or two carols in their language sung by an international children's choir after many hours of rehearsal. It was an unforgettable experience as the carols in different languages were taken up by differing sections of the vast congregation. It was memorable too for another reason. A storm blew up as we began our praises and there came the moment when the ship rolled so violently that the children of the choir, to their great delight, were wafted from port to starboard and back, and the VIP's, sitting as it were in splendid isolation and thus deprived of the protection afforded to the general congregation by their tightly-packed seating arrangements, were thrown into an ungainly muddle with the bishop on top of the surgeon's wife and the captain on top of the bishop.

The ship docked at Fremantle and I was able to spend a few hours in what I came to regard as Australia's loveliest city, Perth, where it is evident that the planners began their work with a proper regard to conserve natural beauty. The end result is a garden city where trees abound, set around a park of a thousand acres. King's Park, partly botanical gardens, partly original bushland with the authentic scenes and scents and sounds of Australia, is a supremely beautiful retreat within minutes of the city centre. I recall it now as affording me my first experience of a country of awe-inspiring spaciousness and beauty.

My year's service at All Saints' College was not due to begin until late in January and I was thus able on the liner's arrival in Sydney to fly out to Dubbo, an authentically Australian city in New South Wales, where the local Church in the person of the rector, Neville Eley, now Archdeacon of Newcastle, N.S.W. welcomed me within an hour of my arrival at my nephew's house.

It says something for the alertness of the Church there that within a period of three hours the rector and his assistant curates in turn called to welcome me, and the Bishop of Bathurst (Kenneth Leslie) rang from his home to give me the greetings of the diocese. Accepting the rector's invitation to celebrate the Holy Communion in one of his churches on Christmas Day I chose a service timed for what I thought would be the coolest hour. It was indeed, 95 degrees fahrenheit at 7 a.m. rising to 109 degrees at midday. In their sympathy for a poor Pom clearly wilting in the oppressive heat the natives were anxious to assure me that they had not had such a very hot spell for thirty years. Subsequently at Bathurst they said the same about an earthquake which all but rolled me out of bed.

Bathurst, the oldest inland city in Australia, has within its environs Australia's oldest church, consecrated in 1825 by the first, and indeed the only Bishop of Australia. As in England so in Australia it was the Christian Church which blazed the trail of the pioneer in the field of education; the college in which I was to spend the first twelve months of my retirement had been founded in 1874, only five years after the creation of the Diocese of Bathurst. Through the hundred years of its life the Church had continued to govern it and to ensure its fidelity to its Founders' intentions. I count my year there not so much as the first of my retirement as the last of my full-time active ministry. Twenty-seven periods a week in the classrooms as well as hours in the college chapel and in the schools' recreation centres left no room for bouts of nostalgia and together provided ample opportunity for effective and rewarding ministry. The boys, some from Sydney but most from the distant bushlands where flocks of sheep are counted in thousands as are the acreages of properties, were an outgoing lot, as mischievous as English schoolboys and every bit as able in trying to 'get away with it'. The stain of original sin was no less apparent on the Australian boys than on the handful of English boys whose parents had emigrated to Australia only recently. Indeed among the most disciplined in the school were the dozen Papuan New Guinea boys whose behaviour was impeccable and whose rooms and lockers reflected in their tidiness an approach to work and play which was outstanding in application if not invariably in achievement. But to say as much is not in any way to denigrate the majority who were for the most part eager, responsive and likeable. I counted it a privilege to minister to them whether in the chapel, the classroom or in their house common rooms.

The College itself was not significantly different from an English public school save that it had in its curriculum one subject unlikely to appear on one of our timetables and indeed, at that time, offered in very few Australian schools. The young Japanese graduate with an honours degree in English whose arrival at the school coincided with mine and who taught his language throughout the school, introduced himself to me with what seemed like a *cri de coeur*, 'I want to speak English English; when I speak American English, please you stop me'. I did and the more frequently since bits of American English often fell from Australian lips – a legacy from the American troops stationed in Australia in the Second World War. More and more he relied on me to break him into our ways and I was frequently called on to untangle metaphors, to explain the meaning of unfamiliar phrases and to justify, when it was possible, inconsistent pronunciations, tasks which were often far from easy. The appearance on the staff notice board of a Chapel Service List headed TRINITY SUNDAY led me into insuperable difficulties. I can hear his plea now, 'Dr. Burrey, explain to me please Trinity Sunday.' No easy task to an English Christian let alone a Japanese Shintoist! Needless to say Japanese was not universally popular among the boys but whatever odium the subject gained for the teacher of it was more than offset by the esteem in which he was held for his instruction in judo.

There was a notable evening in which the boys, their parents and friends of the school were introduced to Japanese customs and culture by the young master including one in which I became involved, namely Chanoyu. The word means 'hot water for tea' but it stands for something far more poetic than merely boiling water. The ceremony, which originated in the fifteenth century, is an elaborate one for which I was summarily drawn from the audience to be the chief guest. It was my lot to sit cross-legged on the stage whilst the host prepared the beverage according to the ancient ritual and in that position the ceremony struck me as a rather drawn out method of achieving a simple end. In Chanoyu the tea is not brewed, or mashed as the northerners say, it is in powder form and is whipped with hot water in a ceremonial bowl. The host who prepares it is not merely 'making the tea' he is performing a rite which the partakers recognise at the outset as concerned with something more than physical thirst. The formalities, which are strictly adhered to, are intended to calm the mind and thus help to make a man more aware of his inner self. The ceremony is regarded as having a spiritual value and the utensils used for its preparations are thus treated with something approaching reverence, being wrapped in silk and stored in a box designed for the purpose.

The ceremony itself, and I take it the consumption of the resulting beverage, is intended to induce in the partakers four spiritual qualities: *Wa, Kei, Sei and Jaku. Wa* is the harmony which should persist among men and which they in turn should share with nature; *Kei* suggests respect for all creation; *Sei* is for purity of heart and *Jaku* for the tranquillity of mankind and of Nature itself. The beverage which is the end result and which, as chief guest I had to partake first among the circle of Japanese students with whom I sat, is green in colour and in my judgement repulsive in taste. Painful as it was to sit throughout the proceedings I was in no state of mind to appreciate the spiritual, aesthetic or artistic aspect of Chanoyu. Nevertheless reflection suggests that it had the potential for all those qualities not least, I imagine, when as is customary not more than five people gather for it in the quiet and seclusion of a rustic garden house.

Music, drama and the arts flourished in the school alongside the studies directed towards public examinations comparable with 'O' and 'A' levels, and alongside cricket and rugby (invariably referred to as football) – a term which properly belongs to soccer! – was played with a fervour so fanatical that it seemed they lifted it from the realm of sport to that of a holy war in which no holds were barred. Hence a satirical ballad of one such battle which I wrote under the title *Anarchists Anonymous* was deemed to be far too sacrilegious for publication in the school magazine, whereas there was admitted to that august publication an *Ode of Hate to the Mosquito* which I wrote in the course of a night when thirteen attacks on my anatomy by that vicious little creature made sleep impossible. It struck me as grossly unjust that the mosquito should have attacked the Pom chaplain so viciously when he could have satisfied his urges with far greater ease by landing anywhere on the acres of naked flesh exposed by a school of boys in shorts.

As in all schools All Saints' College had its moments of tension and high drama and was not without young gentlemen who saw rules as designed not for the common welfare but as fences which invited defiance. For anyone concerned with the pastoral care of the place and with its discipline life was never dull. My twelve months there carried me back to my days in the prep school nearly fifty years before and I left having satisfied myself that boys could still be boys and that pastoralia as it touches the care of young people, whether in Kent or New South Wales, in the seventies or the twenties, and in whatever type of school, makes the same demands on the pastor in understanding and patience. I valued the fellowship of the staff immensely and in particular of Christopher Ellis, the Second Master (now headmaster of Perth College), and of Eric Barker, the Dean of Bathurst, in whose Cathedral I preached on several occasions and of the Bishop of Bathurst, Kenneth Leslie. Vast though Australia is its very efficient air services made possible acceptance of some of the invitations from clergy in the 83,000 square miles of the Bishop's diocese. Visits to Queensland, Victoria, South Australia and Tasmania for ministry to clergy, to ordinands and to men's and women's groups, enabled me to combine work with pleasure and to sense again and again the spaciousness of the country and the infinite variety of its flora and fauna.

For the one genuine holiday break which was possible I chose to go to Heron Island off the coast of Queensland and on the Great Barrier Reef. There massive coral growths of breath-taking beauty, fashioned in spectacular shapes and in every colour of the rainbow, can be examined and photographed through glass-bottomed boats. Over a thousand species of fish make their home in the area of the reef and these, of varied and brilliant colours, can be seen flashing about in the clear water. Sea-eagles, terns and herons are among the hundreds of birds which find sanctuary in the little island and the solemn sad-eyed turtle excavates with her flappers into the warm white sand and lays her eggs, eight or nine dozen, into the resulting deep cavity. During my short stay, which was not in the high season for the tiny island, the sea was about 70 degrees fahrenheit at noon and it was possible to swim and wallow in it for hours with comfort and without fear of sharks which were kept at bay by the reef itself. Visitors were few and within minutes of my arrival I walked along the mile-long beach with its clean white sands to meet but one, who greeted me with the words, 'Ah! you're from England. Do you happen to know Kendal?' – an emigrant from the Lakes who was astonished to be confronted with someone who could tell him all about the Kendal which he had left many years before. That holiday on the forty-acre island lingers in my memory for it opened my eyes to the wonders of the deep and to the fascinating drama of life and survival demonstrated by the living coral.

The Bishop of Bathurst's invitation, strengthened as it was by the Council and staff of the College, to stay with them for a second year was one which I was tempted to accept, not only because that year would see the College celebrating its centenary but also because it might have enabled me to accept invitations to Japan and Papua New Guinea to see something of the Church's work in those countries. But as I had yet to fulfil engagements in New Zealand I had to turn my back on the great and lovely country of Australia shortly before Christmas 1973 to fly to Christchurch, New Zealand, there to preach for the Canterbury Pilgrims Day celebrations and to meet again with Michael Underhill the Dean who earlier had been an incumbent in Carlisle. Other visits to the Cathedrals of Auckland, Dunedin and Wellington and to Napier where I stayed with Archbishop Norman Lesser, who was Vicar of St. John's, Barrow in Furness for eight years immediately before the Second World War, enabled me to see enough of New Zealand to reach the conclusion that if England ever expelled me from its shores or ever began to pall, it would be to New Zealand that I should turn as my new home.

Its islands together embrace scenery which leaves one spellbound for its grandeur and for its weird and wonderful phenomena in the shape of boiling mudpools and spouting geysers. Snow-covered mountains, rivers, forests, glaciers, lakes, waterfalls and caves abound in the thousand miles of islands which make up New Zealand and I should find it difficult to believe that any other country could compass such varied and superb scenery within so modest an area. I have three particularly vivid recollections – one of natural beauty, one of animal 'magic' and one of human nobility. I found the majesty of Mount Cook in the Southern Alps and the grandeur of Milford Sound to be all but overwhelming – a silent sermon exalting the greatness of God the Creator and seeming to assert the littleness of Man. Yet as Emerson reminds us:

> *So nigh is grandeur to our dust*
> *So near is God to Man.*

In the North Island there are spectacular caves including Waitomo with its incredible Glow-worm Grotto in which hundreds of thousands of tiny glow-worms light up the cave's canopy, and glow-worm threads 'fish' for food all this in the midst of great limestone formations artistic and dramatic. In the North Island is the greatest concentration of Maoris, a people who settled in New Zealand in the fourteenth century. I met many of them and admired them immensely for their closely-knit family life, for their artistry and skills and for their good humour. Over 98 per cent of them are Christian and in Rotorua, where there is a considerable Maori population. The interior of the Anglican Church has examples of Maori art forms, but more importantly a mixed congregation of Maoris and Pakeha (i.e. white people) worshipping happily together without distinction, and frequently in services conducted in the Maori language. There are no Maori reservations in New Zealand. Brown and White live and work and play and worship side-by-side and together they have made New Zealand a land of two races but one people.

I sailed from Wellington on the *S.S. Austral Ensign* of the Farrell Line a day or so after Christmas 1973 having as my travelling companions four American couples and an Australian barrister. The Pacific lived up to its name and throughout the whole voyage there was scarcely a ripple on the water. On the evening of 18 January 1974 I received from the ship's commander, acting on behalf of King Neptune, an elaborate parchment addressed 'To all denizens of the seven seas below and on the surface' to whom it declared that

WE NEPTUNE REX, Supreme Ruler, Monarch and Potentate, do hereby proclaim that the Lord Bishop of Carlisle on board the good ship *S.S. Austral Ensign* was duly initiated into the mysteries of the Order of the Trident, having crossed the Equator and, hereby and for evermore, is a member of the brotherhood of the Nautilus.

OUR REALM: Disobey these orders under penalty of our Royal Displeasure.
     (signed) NEPTUNE, Rex

The voyage was delightful: good company, good conversation, good accommodation, good food, sunshine all the way, time for reading, time for writing, time for painting, time for meditating, and the longest holiday of my life. The passage through the 50 miles of the Panama Canal evoked excitement in a mind not easily tuned to technological marvels and I found myself reading for the first time the story of the accomplishment of this miracle of marine engineering. Once through the canal we called at Vera Cruz, the chief port of Mexico, which I remember as the dirtiest city I have ever seen and as the place where I was openly swindled by a Post Office clerk with whom, lacking any knowledge of Spanish, I was unable to argue. After sojourning for a day and night in the Gulf of Mexico we sailed up the Mississippi to New Orleans, the commercial capital of Louisiana, which reflects in some of its buildings its French past. The Cathedral Church of St. Louis was built at the close of the eighteenth century when the city was in Spanish hands. We docked at Norfolk, Virginia and after a night in a far too expensive hotel I made for Washington D.C. where it was so bitterly cold in contrast to the warm seas that despite an intention to linger there for a few days I decided to leave with all speed, but not before I welcomed the opportunity of attending Evensong, beautifully sung, in the graceful Cathedral Church of St. John.

Not until I left Heathrow did the melancholy thought that I was homeless fill me with apprehension. With all my goods and chattels in store in Cumberland I was to spend nine weary months wandering about the face of the earth with a couple of suitcases vainly attempting to find on the coast of Devon or Cornwall a modest house at a price which my savings could match. It had to be the coast for had I not for years cherished the thought of a retirement cottage by the sea so close that its scent and sound could penetrate the house? My stock answer to kindly enquiries as to where I should settle in retirement had always been that it would certainly be somewhere within sight and sound of the sea. I was to find that this proved to be fiscally impossible and as I abandoned my cottage-by-the-sea quest I could hear the salutary dictum of Thomas à Kempis, 'Man proposes but God disposes'.

Now, sitting here in Oxfordshire, as far from the sea as it is possible to be in our small island, the continuing and satisfying episcopal and priestly ministry which I am privileged to enjoy, convinces me that God's disposition was right and my proposition was wrong. Parishes great and small, colleges, boarding schools, convents and military establishments are the scenes of an active retirement ministry and I am glad to have it so. Invitations to return to Devonshire, Kent, Nottinghamshire, Cumbria and Durham have all been grasped eagerly and each in its turn has kindled memories of precious experiences. All this, balanced by some reading and writing, some gardening, some entertaining and D.I.Y. has created a recipe for retirement which is so satisfying that I can commend it to retiring clerics with confidence!

Two post-retirement experiences stand out for their singularity. For a bishop in his seventy-second year to return for the first time to the church of his boyhood and there to read the Holy Gospel standing on the spot on which, at the age of twelve, he knelt to be confirmed, and subsequently to celebrate the Holy Mysteries at the altar from which as a boy he had received his first Communion, was an experience which could not but stir deep emotions. By the courtesy of the Reverend Peter Stokes, the Rector of Wolborough, that privilege was mine in St. Leonard's Church, Newton Abbot on St. Leonard's Day 1979. That visit was significant too since some local historian had concluded that I was the first of Newton Abbot's sons to become a diocesan bishop and as such I was summoned to the Town Hall to sign the distinguished visitors' book.

The other memory, stark in contrast and painful in recollection, brings to my mind pictures which one would like to forget. It was a privilege to celebrate the Eucharist and to preach in St. George's Church in West Berlin but a heart-breaking experience to be conducted subsequently around the damnable Wall with its countless pathetic memorials to those who were mown down for no other reason than their wish to escape from tyranny. The Berlin Wall, which divides a nation and thousands of families within it, remains a silent symbol of the depravity of the godless regime which erected it. In its every metre it spells out the inhumanity of the Soviet system. Its concrete, its watch-towers, its guns, its wolf-hounds, its barbed wire, its tank traps and its mines make of West Berlin a prison in which Germans are hermetically isolated from their fellow countryman. Not until I had seen all the evidence of cruelty, injustice and bestiality could I bring myself to believe all that I had read. The danger is that the West will come to accept the Wall as a natural boundary, that we shall become so accustomed to its presence as to be indifferent to its existence. But there is hope. As I walked the dour, dull, drab streets of East Berlin I lighted upon a church where men and women were singing the Lord's song in that strange land. The Wall itself had all but reduced me to tears; the sound of the Lord's song on its far side was a veritable '*sursum corda*'. The day must come when that 'middle wall of partition' must be broken down. Pray God that it will be by means of an explosive far greater than any concocted by the mind of Man. May it come about by the explosive power of divine Love!

That seems to be as good a point as any to pass to my *confessio fidei*. I cannot say that I have never entertained any doubts about the reality of God, but I can say that when, in my adolescent years, such doubts crept into my mind or were planted there, they were never allowed to possess it. I could not then read with understanding profound theological works but I could, and did, grasp eagerly anything and everything which might help me to hold to beliefs without which, as it seemed to me, life would be without meaning and purpose. I recall pouring over the books of Studdert Kennedy and the sermons of Arthur Foley Winnington-Ingram, then Bishop of London, and finding reassurance in them. Gradually experience confirmed faith which itself rested on revealed truth. I saw too much of God in good people to deny him, and I came to see in Christ God's answer to man's question. 'What is God like?' I never believed that there could be any proofs of the existence of God, at least in the sense that the word 'proof' is normally used, and that in itself assured me that similarly there could be no disproofs. When later studies introduced me to the arguments which purport to demonstrate God's existence I found them fascinating as intellectual exercises but surplus to my personal requirements! If that sounds like the word of a conceited man it is in fact precisely the opposite. It seemed to me that those arguments were probing a mystery which had already been answered by the revelation of God in Christ. However, I confess that I have many times used those arguments to help others. Early in my ministry, lost in Birmingham on my first and only visit to that city, a kindly policeman began his direction with the words, 'You must go to the Five Ways'. He probably wondered why I smiled. Making my way, as I was, to a Christian education conference it occurred to me that I might give the same answer to the 'lost' there for the *Five Way of St. Thomas Aquinas*; his proofs of the existence of God might well appeal to and help the pedagogues. Belief in God the Creator, who created and creates and who set Man at the pinnacle of his creation making him in his own image, is where it all starts. The 'sense sublime' which Wordsworth experienced permeates the loveliness of the world and when man is in communion with God through Christ that same sense possesses him. The Bible opens with the majestic declaration, 'In the beginning God . . . ' and it matters not how many million years ago the beginning was it remains true. 'In the beginning God . . . '. St. John takes up the theme as he lifts his pen to write his Gospel and writes with like majesty 'In the beginning was the Word and the Word was with God and the Word was God . . . and the Word was made flesh'.

Joseph Mary Plunket discerned the relationship between the two declarations and wrote finely:

> *I see his blood upon the rose*
> *And in the stars the glory of his eyes,*
> *His body gleams amid eternal snows,*
> *His tears fall from the skies.*
>
> *I see his face in every flower;*
> *The thunder and the singing of the birds*
> *Are but his voice — and carven by his power*
> *Rocks are his written words.*
>
> *All pathways by his feet are worn,*
> *His strong heart stirs the ever-bleating sea,*
> *His crown of thorns is twined with every thorn,*
> *His cross is every tree.*

The loveliness of the world of nature indicts the ugliness of the havoc which Man has created. Made 'in the image of God' as he is, Man should of all God's creatures reflect God's beauty, God's goodness, God's truth in a manner surpassing all others. But he cannot do that unless he remembers that he is the creature not the Creator, that he is dependent upon God and that he must stand before God ever in reverence and awe.

I believe that Jesus shows us the perfect way to do just that for he discloses to us the mind and the purpose of God completely and finally. To hear the words of Jesus is to hear the words of God; to read the mind of Jesus is to read the mind of God; to watch the ways of Jesus — caring, comforting, befriending, forgiving, blessing, loving — is to watch the ways of God. This is what invests the moral teaching of Jesus with an authority which is unique. 'He that hath seen Me hath seen the Father'. This is the mystery of the Incarnation, of God's self-disclosure in Christ. God became Man that we might know him and so becoming gave himself to Man showing Man how through Christ he could rise to his full stature and dignity as one born in the image of God. In the life and death and resurrection of Jesus we see God in action. Thus I believe profoundly what St. John in his vision heard from the lips of the Risen Christ (Revelation ch. 1, v. 18) 'I am the first and the last . . . I was dead and am alive for evermore, and I hold the keys . . . '. Christ holds the keys to life and death, the keys to the past and the present and the future, to sin and suffering and sorrow, and to all the intractable problems which torture the minds of men. The early Christians did not escape nicknames; they were called the 'Christ-people' and 'the people of the Way'. Like most nicknames these hit the nail on the head. They were not resented and one of them, 'Christiani', was in fact adopted by the early Church as the official title of those who turned to Christ. The early Christians knew that Christ had indeed shown them the Way and had promised too that those who would follow him could be assured that the Holy Spirit would inspire and strengthen them in their pilgrimage.

The doctrine of the Holy Spirit is the doctrine that God is busily at work in his world now as ever, not just in the churches but in every field of human activity. The line which the world draws between what it calls the secular and the religious is drawn not by God's wisdom but by man's limited understanding. The Holy Spirit inspires the poet and the artist, the writer and the musician and indeed all whose concern it is to contribute to the abundant life of man and that whether they acknowledge God or not. But supremely, of course, it is through Christ's Church that the pressure of the Holy Spirit becomes most apparent. Thus it was when the disciples were 'altogether with one accord in one place', when in fact they were worshipping, that they became most conscious of the presence of the Holy Spirit among them pointing to the way they should go and giving them the courage to start their work. The picture painted in the *Acts of the Apostles* is one of great commotion – a 'sound from heaven as of a rushing mighty wind' – which was probably Peter's way of describing to Luke a spiritual experience which could not in fact be compassed in words. But normally the Holy Spirit's is the 'still small voice', as Harriet Auber expresses it in her much-loved hymn:

> And his that gentle voice we hear
> Soft as the breath of even,
> That checks each fault, and calms each fear
> And speaks of heaven.

There have of course been times in history when the Spirit has caused great commotion and as a 'mighty rushing wind' has swept over men bending their wills, uprooting their prejudices and casting down great strongholds of sin, but these have been as rare doxologies to the Spirit's quiet influence. The phenomenon of speaking with tongues was very rare in the early Church and soon suspect since it could be so easily abused, as Paul makes clear in his first letter to the Corinthians (ch. 14, vv. 20–25) in which he seems to be saying pretty bluntly, 'You're showing off! Seekers after Christ are more likely to regard you as raving mad than as possessed by the Spirit of God'. Once dedicated we can all anticipate that there will be in our lives charismatic experiences though we may be slow to discern them as such. To borrow ideas beautifully – as expressed in John Mason Neale's *Golden Sequence*, the rigid will be gently bent, the frozen will be tended warmly, the parched will be fructified, the soiled will be cleansed and 'every holy deed and thought' is a gift of the Divine Spirit – is a charismatic experience.

So I believe in the Church because it is 'the fellowship of the Holy Spirit'. God knows its weaknesses are apparent to none better than to its ministers, but its weaknesses do not deny its origin or its purpose. It is the Church of God and it is made up not of 'holier-than-thou' people, but of people who consciously accept the Risen Christ as Lord, who consciously acknowledge the potential power of God's Spirit on man and who in prayer and sacrament deliberately open their hearts and minds and wills that God may possess them and use them for his purpose. I believe too that the man who claims to be a Christian cannot regard corporate worship as an optional extra designed for Christians who happen to like that sort of thing. He must see it as an activity which for him is motivated by conviction not by convention and governed by constraint not convenience. In it God manifests himself and Man dedicates himself. Man proclaims God's glory and God endows him with his Holy Spirit enabling him to reflect something of that glory in the world. This is the rhythm of the Christian life; into church to worship with others of God's family, out to the world to serve God's purpose; into church for the ministry of Word and Sacrament, intimately related in the Church's highest act the Eucharist, out to the world for the service of God and His Kingdom.

In the world and at every turn we are confronted with the cosmic struggle between good and evil, from within ourselves by reason of our lower nature and from without. The individual Christian has his personal struggle to manifest in his own life the love and the selfless service which he sees in his Christ. The Church as the Body of Christ has its struggles in confronting its adversaries – apathy, opposition, mocking, crucifixion maybe. Standing alone the struggle is beyond our powers of endurance, standing together within the Body of Christ we place ourselves consciously and deliberately within the ambit of God's grace and never more so than in the Eucharist where our hearts are touched anew, our souls are strengthened, our eyes are opened and our wills are empowered. To be at the Lord's own Service in the Lord's own House on the Lord's own day, whether we call it the Holy Communion, the Eucharist, the Lord's Supper or the Mass, is not only to obey his command – 'Do this in remembrance of me' – but to take part in the greatest of all Christian acts whereby, sealing anew our fellowship with God by partaking of the life of Christ, we seal anew too our fellowship with other Christians. 'Though we are many we are one body, because we all share in one bread'. It is as the Body of Christ that the Church moves out into the world for the fulfilment of God's plan. The man who claims the name of Christian but holds himself aloof from the Church deprives himself of blessings immeasurable and deprives the Church of that contribution to its work and witness which only he can give.

This is the Church's faith. This is my faith. To go with the Church is to go with Christ; to go with Christ is to go with God; to go with God is Eternal Life. This is a faith which determines the quality of life here and now and a faith which carries us on beyond the last horizon there to enjoy God for ever. This is the faith which enables me to affirm with St. Paul that 'I am sure that neither death, nor life, nor angels, nor principalities, nor things present, nor things to come, nor powers, nor height, nor depth, nor anything else in all creation, will be able to separate us from the love of God in Christ Jesus our Lord'.

LAUS DEO!